# RELIGION AND THOUGHT
# OF
# SHĀH WALĪ ALLĀH DIHLAWĪ
# 1703-1762

# STUDIES
# IN THE HISTORY OF RELIGIONS

(SUPPLEMENTS TO *NUMEN*)

EDITED BY

M. HEERMA VAN VOSS • E. J. SHARPE • R. J. Z. WERBLOWSKY

XLVIII

RELIGION AND THOUGHT
OF
SHĀH WALĪ ALLĀH DIHLAWĪ
1703-1762

TUTA SUB AEGIDE PALLAS · EJB ·

LEIDEN
E. J. BRILL
1986

# RELIGION AND THOUGHT
# OF
# SHĀH WALĪ ALLĀH DIHLAWĪ
# 1703-1762

BY

J. M. S. BALJON

LEIDEN
E. J. BRILL
1986

ISBN 90 04 07684 0



PRINTED IN THE NETHERLANDS BY E. J. BRILL

## CONTENTS

Preface ........ VII
Abbreviations ........ IX

Introduction ........ 1

I. Vocational Visions ........ 15
II. Extra-Scriptural Mediums of Divine Revelation ........ 21
A) *ʿĀlam al-mithāl* (World of Prefiguration) ........ 21
B) *Ḥaẓīra al-quds* (Holy Enclosure) ........ 24
C) Angelic Categories ........ 26
D) *Tajalliyyāt* (Theophanies) ........ 31
E) *al-Tajallī al-aʿẓam* (Most Supreme Theophany) ........ 32
III. Metaphysics ........ 36
A) Concept of God ........ 36
B) Cosmology ........ 45
C) *Waḥdat al-wujūd* (Unity of Being) ........ 56
IV. Psychology ........ 64
V. Mysticism ........ 78
VI. Ethics ........ 86
VII. Life to Come ........ 97
VIII. Prophetology ........ 102
IX. People of Eminence ........ 116
A) *Ḥakīm* (Wise Man) ........ 116
B) *Walī* (Protégé of God) ........ 118
C) Caliph ........ 121
D) *Muḥaddath* (Inspired Person) ........ 126
E) *Fard* (Singular Man) ........ 127
F) *Mujaddid* (Renewer) ........ 129
G) *ʿUlamāʾ* (Scholars) ........ 130
H) Philosophers ........ 131
I) *Mutakallimūn* (Scholars in the Field of Speculative Theology) ........ 133
X. *Qurʾān* ........ 136
XI. *Ḥadīth* ........ 152
XII. *Sharīʿa* (Law) ........ 160
XIII. True and False Religion ........ 171
XIV. Religious Rites and Customs ........ 180
XV. Social and Economic Ideas ........ 192

# PREFACE

Although thoroughly alive to the major contribution Shāh Walī Allāh has made to Islamic thought, Western scholarship has not until now concerned itself very much with the study of his world of ideas. On the whole, the Subcontinent, like other peripheral areas of Muslim believers, is treated in a stepfatherly fashion by European and American Islamologists. In evidence thereof, university libraries in the West appear to be slow in acquiring editions of Shāh Walī Allāh's works. Another handicap is that the latter's mental products are not only numerous but also notorious for a terse style and ample use of technical terms mostly inadequately explained. Their perusal, the present writer must confess, was much more time-consuming than he had expected.

This work has been undertaken in order to prepare a comprehensive survey of the concepts the famous Delhi scholar and mystic developed in almost every field of Islamic knowledge. Some readers may be disappointed at the little attention paid to his political views. Their significance and bearing, however, have been largely overestimated, being chiefly based on letters of which the authenticity is open to considerable doubt. In reproducing the purport of the author's expositions proper documentation is aimed at by allowing Shāh Walī Allāh himself to speak whenever possible, and reticence is exercised with regard to intuitional but unsufficiently warranted inferences and surmises on the part of the researcher. Full quotations possess the additional advantage that at the same time some idea of Shāh Walī Allāh's way of teaching and argumentation is gained. Nowhere is the application of specific Arabic and Persian terms avoided since these have a flavour of their own. The main concession made is that the headings of the chapters are adapted to the taste of the modern reader.

I am keenly aware of my indebtedness to a large number of friends and colleagues in the Indo-Pakistan Subcontinent without whose help and cooperation I would never have succeeded in doing this research. First of all, I am deeply grateful to Dr. A. J. Halepota who spent many hours initiating me into the subtleties of Shāh Walī Allāh's thought. He proved to be a patient teacher and I immensely enjoyed his friendship. Equally, I have happy memories of the warm personal contacts with al-Ustādh Ghulām Muṣṭafā al-Qāsimī who is noted for his careful editing of Shāh Walī Allāh's writings. The third friend in Hyderabad (Sind), Prof. G. N. Jalbani, rendered fine assistance by regularly supplying me with his publications in the same field.

In India I met a similar readiness to provide me with the required materials. I am most thankful for the encouragement I received from Prof. S. A. Ali in New Delhi, Prof. K. A. Nizami in Aligarh and many other people.

Special thanks are due to Prof. R. J. Z. Werblowsky who was kind enough to accept the book as a supplement to *NUMEN*. Lastly, I would like to express gratitude to Mrs. V. Schäfer-Shute for her thorough reading of the English text and for valuable stylistic and editorial emendations.

Leiden, January 1985 J. M. S. Baljon

# ABBREVIATIONS

A. Works of Shāh Walī Allāh:

| | |
|---|---|
| *Anfās* | = *Anfās al-ʿārifīn*, Delhi 1897/8 |
| *A.Q.* | = *Alṭāf al-quds fī maʿrifa laṭāʾif al-nafs*, Gujrānwala 1964 |
| *Aṭyab al-nagham* | = *Aṭyab al-nagham fī madḥ sayyid al-ʿArab waʾl-ʿAjam*, Delhi 1890/1 |
| *B.B.* | = *al-Budūr al-bāzigha*, Bidjnawr 1935/6 |
| *F.K.* | = *al-Fawz al-kabīr fī uṣūl al-tafsīr*, Karachi 1964 |
| *Fuyūḍ* | = one of the visions recorded in the *Fuyūḍ al-Ḥaramayn* |
| *H.* | = *Hamaʿāt*. The Roman numerals refer to one of the 22 chapters |
| *Haw.* | = *Hawāmiʿ*, Delhi n.d. |
| *H.B.* | = *Ḥujjat Allāh al-bāligha*, Delhi 1954/5 |
| *Inṣāf* | = *al-Inṣāf fī bayān sabab al-ikhtilāf*, Delhi n.d. |
| *Intibāh* | = *Intibāh fī salāsil awliyāʾ Allāh*, Karachi n.d. |
| *ʿIqd* | = *ʿIqd al-jīd fī bayān aḥkām al-ijtihād waʾl-taqlīd*, Karachi 1959/60 |
| *Izāla* | = *Izālat al-khafāʾ ʿan khilāfat al-khulafāʾ*, Barelī 1869 |
| *al-Juzʾ al-laṭīf* | = *al-Juzʾ al-laṭīf fī tarjamat al-ʿabd al-daʿīf*, added in an edition of the *Saṭaʿāt*, Delhi n.d. |
| *Kalimāt-i ṭayyibāt* | = *Kalimāt-i ṭayyibāt*, Delhi 1891/2. Collection of Persian letters of Maẓhar Jān-i Janān (d. 1781), Qāḍī Thanāʾ Allāh al-Pānipatī (d. 1810) Shāh Walī Allāh (25 in all) and others |
| *Khizāna* | = a chapter of *al-Khayr al-kathīr* |
| *Lamḥa* | = one of the 60 *Lamaḥāt* (ed. Ghulām Muṣṭafā al-Qāsimī). Hydarabad, Sind, 1963 |
| *Maktūb* | = *al-Maktūb al-Madanī*, Delhi 1906 |
| *Muṣaffā* | = *al-Muṣaffā*, Delhi n.d. |
| *Musawwā* | = *al-Musawwā min aḥādīth al-Muwaṭṭaʾ*, Mecca 1932-4 |
| *Q.D.* | = *al-Qawl al-jamīl fī bayān sawāʾ al-sabīl*, Karachi n.d. |
| *Qurrat* | = *Qurrat al-ʿaynayn fī tafḍīl al-shaykhayn*, Delhi 1892/3 |
| *Saṭ.* | = one of the 46 *Saṭaʿāt* (ed. Ghulām Muṣṭafā al-Qāsimī), Hydarabad, Sind, 1964 |
| *Sharḥ al-tarājim* | = *Risāla sharḥ tarājim abwāb ṣaḥīḥ al-Bukhārī*, Hydarābād, Deccan, 1949 |
| *Tafh.* | = *Tafhīmāt-i Ilāhiyya*, Dabhel 1936 |
| *Taʾwīl* | = *Taʾwīl al-aḥādīth fī rumūz quṣaṣ al-anbiyāʾ* (ed. Ghulām Muṣṭafā al-Qāsimī), Hydarabad, Sind, 1966 |

B. Periodicals and Encyclopedia:

| | |
|---|---|
| *AION* | = Annali dell' Istituto Orientale di Napoli |
| *BOAS* | = Bulletin of the School of Oriental and African Studies |
| *EI*$^2$ | = Encyclopaedia of Islam, New Edition |
| *IC* | = Islamic Culture |
| *JRAS* | = Journal of the Royal Asiatic Society |
| *MW* | = The Muslim World |

# INTRODUCTION

Great personalities in pious Muslim circles are never born without some solemn prediction. Shāh Walī Allāh records the following that occurred to his father ʿAbd al-Raḥīm: "once he visited the mausoleum of Quṭb al-Dīn al-Bakhtiyār al-Kākī[1] (d. 1236). The latter addressed him, announced to him the birth of a son and advised him to call him Quṭb al-Dīn. When I was born, however, God caused him to forget to name me Quṭb al-Dīn. He called me Walī Allāh ('protégé of God') on account of cosmic events indicating that I would be the object of God's constant beneficence (*mutawallā*)" (*Tafh.* II, 154).

At the outset, this news of a future son threw ʿAbd al-Raḥīm into confusion, since his wife had reached the age of sterility. Then the saint notified him that he had to marry a second time. A daughter of his disciple Shaykh Muḥammad of Phalit, a small town in the district of Muẓaffarnager (western U.P.), became the bride of his choice. According to a statement[2] made by Shāh Walī Allāh's son Shāh ʿAbd al-ʿAzīz, Shāh Walī Allāh was born in his maternal grandfather's house[3] on 4 Shawwāl A.H. 1114 (= 21st February 1703).

Shāh Walī Allāh claims to be a descendant of ʿUmar, the second caliph (*Anfās*, 38) and he relates that once during a *murāqaba* (meditation ceremony) the whole long line of his ancestors right back to ʿUmar, appeared to him in a shining light (*Kalimāt-i ṭayyibāt*, 160). His lineage on the mother's side is traced to Mūsā al-Kāẓim (d. 1294), the seventh *imām* of the Ithnā ʿAshariyya. In this way, he can also be reckoned among the progeny of ʿAlī, the cousin and son-in-law of Mohammed.

When his ancestors emigrated to India in the thirteenth century[4], they settled in Rohtak, a town situated between Hansi and Delhi (*Anfās* 152). He himself refers to the previous history of his race with evident delight, saying: "I hail from a foreign country. My forebears came to India as emigrants. I am proud of my Arab origin and my knowledge of Arabic, for both of them bring a person close to 'the *sayyid* (master) of the Ancients and the Moderns', 'the most excellent of the prophets sent by God'

---

[1] Chishtī saint and spiritual successor of the famous Muʿīn al-Dīn Chishtī of Ajmer. His tomb is found in Mihrawli, south of Delhi. He was surnamed Kākī because during his meditations he fed on small cakes known as *kāks*.

[2] Mentioned in a note on p. 2 of *al-Irshād ilā muhimmāt ʿilm al-isnād*.

[3] Not in Delhi as is recorded in *EI*², II, 254. In *Tafh.* II, 152 Shāh Walī Allāh speaks of my *qarya* (small town) Phalit.

[4] Possibly forced by the onslaught of Mongolian hordes (Fazle Mahmud, 'Life of Shah Wali Allah Dehlavi', *Oriental College Magazine*, Lahore 1956, vol. XXXIII, p. 5).

and 'the pride of the whole creation'. In gratitude for this great favour I ought to conform to the habits and customs of the early Arabs and the Prophet himself as much as I can, and to abstain from the customs of the Turks (*ᶜajam*) and the habits of the Indians'' (*Tafh.* II, 245 f.).

At first, his forefathers occupied offices in the judicature of the Delhi Sultanate. Later, some of them joined the armed forces under the Mughals[5]. However, his father, Shaykh ᶜAbd al-Raḥīm (1646-1719), did not wish to have any connection with the Court and in response to an invitation from the Emperor Awrangzīb (d. 1707) he wrote: ''Mystics unanimously declare: 'how horrible it is to find a dervish on the threshold of kings'. God states: 'The fruition of this world is small' (*Qurʾān* IV, 77)'' (*Anfās* 68)[6].

Shaykh ᶜAbd al-Raḥīm lived and worked in Delhi where he founded a seminary called after him. This *madrasa Raḥīmiyya* was originally located in a building associated with the Fērōzshāhī mosque in the Kotlā Fērōzshāh (Tughluqābād) area[7]. Already at the age of fifteen, two years before the death of his father, Shāh Walī Allāh was permitted to assume the responsibility of running the *madrasa*[8]. In other words, the son trod in his father's footsteps. Yet their personalities were different and there is a clear distinction between the two. When talking of his early education, Shāh Walī Allāh makes mention of what he calls 'useful suggestions' (*fawāʾid*) for daily life which he obtained from his father: ''My father advised me to recite *Yā mughnī*[9] ('O He who satisfied, whom He will, of His servants') 1100 times every day and the Sūra al-Muzzammil 40 times. And he used to say both recitations are tried means for gaining contentment of heart and independence of one's surroundings'' (*Q.D.* 122). Furthermore, he relates that he saw miracles (*karāmāt*) performed by his father (*Q.D.* 180)[10]. Certainly, both of them were teachers, but the son was a typical scholar who produced works of major importance. The father did not write any books. Both of them were mystics, but the

---

[5] S. A. A. Rizvi, *Shāh Walī-Allāh and His Times*, Canberra 1980, 203.

[6] The son, however, was not so detached from the goods of this world and not so afraid of dependence on the Royal Palace. In 1754 Shāh Walī Allāh accepted the grant of 51 *bīghās* (one *bīghā* is equal to about five-eights of an acre) of land from the Emperor ᶜĀlamgīr II as *madad-i maᶜāsh* (revenue-free grant of land) for the *madrasa* (S. A. A. Rizvi, *Shāh ᶜAbd al-ᶜAziz*, Canberra 1982, 84).

[7] Later, after Shāh Walī Allāh's return from the Ḥijāz, the *madrasa* was shifted to the centre of Delhi, not far from the Jāmiᶜ Mosque. In the War of Independence ('Mutiny') of 1857 it was reduced to ruins. No trace of it is now visible (G. N. Jalbani, *Life of Shah Waliyullah*, Lahore 1978, 43).

[8] It seems that Shaykh ᶜAbd al-Raḥīm sought to get rid of his teaching duties at the first possible opportunity.

[9] The numerical value of the letters of this exclamation is 1100.

[10] We never hear of miracles performed by Shāh Walī Allāh!

mysticism practised by the father shows more 'magical' aspects than that of the son.

In the same way as his birth, the circumstance of Shāh Walī Allāh's evincing a nature different from his father was also announced beforehand, this time not by a communication from a buried saint but through a vision vouchsafed to his mother when he was newly weaned. First, she "saw in a dream a bird of wonderful shape which came to my father carrying a sheet of paper in its bill. On it the name Allāh was written with golden letters. Next, a second bird came to him with another sheet of paper in its bill. It said: 'In the Name of God, the Merciful, the Compassionate. If prophethood after Mohammed were possible We would make him a prophet. With Mohammed, however, prophethood has come to an end'. This was the literal text, or at least the meaning of it. The first bird had a red bill, while the remainder of its body was dust-coloured like a pigeon. The remaining part of the other bird was green like a parrot". The following comment on this dream is given by Shāh Walī Allāh himself: "According to the rule of *ḥikma* (knowledge of high spiritual truths) the correct interpretation is: The first sheet of paper[11] points to the very perfection of my father, for he was a man of *fanāʾ* (passing away from self) and immersion into God. The colour of dust indicates that it relates to someone who is not concerned with metaphysical speculations. Accordingly, a pigeon and a ringdove indeed have pleasant voices but they lack the gift of eloquence. The other sheet refers to the perfection I am endowed with and consists of the capacity to analyze the excellences of prophets. A green colour appertains to someone who can expound metaphysics eloquently like a chattering parrot" (*Tafh*. II, 154 f.). Briefly summarized: the father is a typical example of sainthood, the son a substitute of prophethood.

Under the tutelage of his father Shāh Walī Allāh by the age of ten studied the commentary of Jāmī (d. 1492) on *al-Kāriya*, dealing with Arabic syntax, written by Ibn al-Ḥājib (d. 1249). Other works he had to peruse during the next five years of study were: on the subject of *fiqh* (jurisprudence) the commentary of Ṣadr al-Sharīʿa al-Thānī (d. 1346) on *Wiqāya al-riwāya* written by the Ḥanafite Burhān al-Dīn Maḥmūd al-Maḥbūbī, and the famous handbook on Ḥanafī *fiqh* the *Hidāya*[12] of al-Marghīnānī (d. 1196) except for a few pages; on *uṣūl al-fiqh* (principles

[11] With the name of Allāh on it. "I have heard this said by my father", Shāh Walī Allāh tells us, "that the *ithbāt mujarrad* (concentration on only the "affirmative' second part of the profession: no god except Allāh) is of utmost profit for attaining rapture (*jadhb*) ... I have witnessed that a pupil of my father could utter 'Allāh' 1000 or even more times in one single breath" (*Q.D.* 81).

[12] The *Wiqāya al-riwāya* is actually a synopsis of it.

of *fiqh*) *al-Muntakhab fī uṣūl al-madhhab* of the Ḥanafite Ḥusām al-Dīn al-Akhsīkatī (d. 1247); for his training in logic he made use of the *Sharḥ Shamsiyya*, a commentary of Quṭb al-Dīn Muḥ. al-Rāzī al-Taḥtānī (d. 1364) on *al-Risāla al-shamshiyya* written by al-Kātibī (d. 1276), and he also read a portion of the commentary of al-Taḥtānī on the *Maṭāliᶜ al-anwār fiʾl-manṭiq* written by al-Urmawī (d. 1283); on the subject of *kalām* (apologetics for the sake of Muslim faith) he studied the whole commentary of al-Taftāzānī (d. 1389) on the al-Nasafī (d. 1142) *ᶜAqāʾid* with portions of the al-Khayālī (d. 1456) annotations on al-Taftāzānī's commentary, and the commentary of al-Jurjānī (d. 1371) on the al-Ījī (d. 1355) *Kitāb al-Mawāqif*; on the subject of rhetorics he perused the *Muṭawwal* (published in 1347) of al-Taftāzānī; on the subject of medicine the Ibn al-Nafīs (d. 1288) summary of the *Qānūn* of Ibn Sīnā (d. 1037). However, without doubt the chief attention in Shaykh ᶜAbd al-Raḥīm's teaching was given to mystic literature. Study was made of al-Suhrawardī (d. 1234) *ᶜAwārif al-maᶜārif*, of works of the great Persian ṣūfī poet Jāmī (d. 1492), to wit his *Naqd al-Nuṣūṣ* (a commentary on the *Nuṣūṣ* of Ibn ᶜArabī's disciple al-Qūnawī, d. 1263), his *Ashiᶜᶜat al-Lamaᶜāt* (commentary on the *Lamaᶜāt* of ᶜIrāqī, d. 1289) and his *Sharḥ-i Rubāᶜiyyāt*.

Tuition in the recitation of the Qurʾān was received from Muḥammad Fāḍil Sindhī (d. 1732), and under the supervision of Shaykh Muḥ. Afḍal Siyālkōtī[13] (d. 1733) he studied Tradition (*ḥadīth*).

When he was fourteen, his father deemed it high time that he should marry. The bride assigned to him was Fāṭima, a daugther of his maternal uncle Shaykh ᶜUbayd Allāh of Phalit and a sister of Shaykh Muḥammad ᶜĀshiq who later became his disciple and his dear companion. Born of this marriage[14] were a son, named Shaykh Muḥammad[15] (± 1730-1793/4) and a daughter, called Amat al-ᶜAzīz, the prospective bride of Muḥammad Fāʾiq, a son of Shaykh Muḥammad ᶜĀshiq.

At the age of fifteen he was initiated by his father into the Qādiriyya and Chishtiyya orders as well as into the Naqshbandiyya branch of

---

[13] A man of tolerant views. In a letter to one of his disciples he makes a plea for paying attention to Hindu religion, and at the same time he states in it that belief in transmigration of souls need not be qualified as *kufr* (unbelief) (ᶜUbayd Allāh Sindhī, *Ilhām al-Raḥmān*, ᶜAzīzābād n.d., II, 29).

[14] In 1744, being a widower, Shāh Walī Allāh married Bī Irāda, a daugther of Sayyid Ḥāmid ᶜAlī Sūnīpattī. Sons of this couple were Shāh ᶜAbd al-ᶜAzīz (1746-1824), Shāh Rafīᶜ al-Dīn (1750-1818), Shāh al-Qādir (1754-1813) and Shāh ᶜAbd al-Ghanī (1756-1812).

[15] After the death of his father he moved to Budhāna and stayed there till his death (ᶜAbd al-Ḥayy, *Nuzhat al-khawāṭir*, Hyderabad, Deccan, 1959, VII, p. 422). Actually, he was somone who "was full of ecstatic dreams and was not interested in shouldering the responsibility of running the seminary" (S. A. A. Rizvi, *Shāh ᶜAbd al-ᶜAzīz*, 75).

Khwāja Khwurd, the son of Shaykh Aḥmad Sirhindī's spiritual guide, Khwāja Baqī Biʾllāh (*Tafh.* I, 11 and 15; *Anfās* 6).

So far everything had taken place along traditional lines, and if there had been no break in the course of events, Shāh Walī Allāh would have died as just one of the many meritorious Indian scholars of Islamics. Fortunately, our hero was not satisfied with the quiet life he lived and wished to widen his intellectual and spiritual horizon.

A stay to this end in the stimulating atmosphere of the Ḥijāz seemed to him to be indicated. In those days, however, a journey to the Holy Cities was a rather risky enterprise, and his beloved nearest relatives, "upon whose hearts and eyes God had put a cover", did not approve of it. So Shāh Walī Allāh had to abscond. His people pursued him, but could not overtake him and thus returned empty handed (*Tafh.* II, 153).

According to Fazle Mahmud[16], Shāh Walī Allāh left for Ṣūrat (at that time the harbour of departure for Indian pilgrims) on the 8 Rabīʿ al-thānī, 1143 (= 21st October 1730). In his autobiography[17] Shāh Walī Allāh makes mention of a safe return to Delhi on the 14 Rajab 1145 (= 31st December 1732). His eldest son by his second marriage, Shāh ʿAbd al-ʿAzīz, states that his father stayed fourteen months in the Ḥijāz[18]. It means that a full year had to be spent on the outward and homeward journies alone. Thus, his sojourn in the Holy Cities might have been from about the end of April 1731 till the end of June 1732. Before his departure he performed the *ḥajj* for the second time, at the beginning of June 1732.

In addition to the ceremonies of the *ḥajj* and the birthday celebrations of Mohammed on the 14th September 1731 (see *Fuyūḍ*, 8th Vision) the Delhi scholar gave his time to the study of *ḥadīth*. In Mecca he attended the lectures of the Mālikite Shaykh Muḥ. Wafd Allāh on the whole of Mālik b. Anas ʾ*Muwaṭṭa*ʾ in the recension of Yaḥyā b. Yaḥyā al-Maṣhmūdī (d. 848). A second teacher from whom he received instruction in Tradition, was the Ḥanafite Shaykh Tāj al-Dīn Qalaʿī (d. 1734), a *muftī* (official expounder of Islamic law) of Mecca. And in the Medinian mosque of the Prophet he could enlarge his knowledge under the guidance of the most outstanding scholar and mystic he met in the Ḥijāz, viz. the Shāfiʿite Shaykh Abū Ṭāhir Muḥammad (d. 1733) son of Shaykh Ibrahīm al-Kūrānī (d. 1690)[19]. In the companionship of his Medinian tutor he not only studied *ḥadīth* (the whole of al-Bukhārī's *Ṣaḥīḥ* and

---

16 *Oriental College Magazine*, vol. XXXIII, p. 12.

17 *al-Juz*ʾ *al-laṭīf*, 28.

18 Communication of G. N. Jalbani in his *Life of Shah Waliyullah*, 30.

19 Both of them were esteemed by Indian and Indonesian students in the Ḥijāz and keen on bringing about syntheses between opposing points of view (cf. A. H. Johns in *EI*², V, 433 and J. Voll in *BOAS*, XXXVIII, 1 (1975), 39).

capita selecta of other collections of traditions) but also mystic writings as, for instance, the *Ḥizb al-baḥr*[20] of al-Shādhilī (d. 1258) (*Intibāh* I, 136) and the *Qūt al-qulūb* of Abū Ṭālib al-Makkī (d. 996)[21]. Further, Abū Ṭāhir quite often functioned as his *pīr* (ṣūfī director), initiating him into the Shādhiliyya order (*Intibāh* I, 134), the Shaṭṭāriyya order (*Intibāh* I, 137), the Najīb al-Dīn Buzghush branch of the Suhrawārdi order (*Intibāh* I, 100) and the Sayyid ᶜAlī Hamadānī branch of the Kubrāwiyya order (*Intibāh* I, 119).

Increased acquisition of knowledge through contact with scholars from various Muslim countries should not, however, be taken as the main result of Shāh Walī Allāh's stay in the Holy Land. Even more far-reaching was the fact that through cognizance of different legal schools and divergent religious opinions he was set to think and to question: what, of all the choices offered were, in fact, the most reliable, the most valuable? Cogitations of such a nature are reflected in visions he records from his sojourn in Mecca and Medina. In them he occasionally brought doubts with which he was afflicted before the spirit of Mohammed. Thus, once he asked the Prophet: "which school of *fiqh* do you prefer so that I may know which one I ought to follow?" (*Fuyūḍ*, 10th Vision). At times, the Delhi divine received answers which, as he frankly admits, ran counter to his own sentiments[22]. This is an interesting indication that because of disputes with foreign colleagues he was compelled to abandon ideas he had previously cherished. In short: from now onwards his creative capacities were roused and put to work. Accordingly, the chief output of his scholarly activities dates from the period after his return to India.

In consequence of the gradual awakening as a result of the receipt of the Prophet's pen on the 14th August, 1731, in Mecca[23] and the heavy responsibility placed on him in view of research work to be done, on his return to Delhi he assigned the greater part of the teaching duties to assistants, keeping for himself the supervision of the *madrasa* students. In this way he could give adequate attention to both study and writing.

On the other hand, from his own account the students had a stimulating influence on his authorship. It was, for instance, at the

[20] Later (1735) Shāh Walī Allāh himself wrote a commentary on this collection of invocations credited with protective power; they are recited in particular by seafarers. He called this commentary *Hawāmiᶜ*.

[21] "I am of the opinion", Shāh Walī Allāh says, "that this work is basic to mysticism, and all that is written on the following of the ṣūfī Path is borrowed from the *Qūt al-qulūb*" (*Intibāh* I, 130).

[22] As an example the notification of Mohammed that he should not hold ᶜAlī superior to Abū Bakr and ᶜUmar (*Fuyūḍ*, 33rd Vision).

[23] See p. 17

urgent request of his disciple Khwāja Muḥ. Amīn al-Kashmīrī (d. 1773/4) that he wrote the *Qurrat al-ʿaynayn* (see p. 2). Shaykh Muḥammad ʿĀshiq (d. 1773) continuously encouraged him to complete the *Ḥujjat Allāh al-bāligha* and in a testimonial to this adherent he declares: "in the case of many books it was he who induced me to commit them to paper and he himself who undertook the neatening of their manuscripts" (*Tafh.* I, 126). In addition, his students sometimes furnished his works with glosses. Thus Mawlāna Sharaf al-Dīn al-Dihlawī wrote comments on the *Hawāmiʿ*[24], and Muḥammad ʿĀshiq prepared an elucidation of *al-Khayr al-kathīr* under the title *Taqrīr Khayr kathīr*[25].

It is also noteworthy that, although he now spent less time on the tuition of the students, their number, compared with the time before his travel to the Ḥijāz, increased significantly. Among his students the best known in the Arab world was certainly Sayyid Murtaḍā al-Zabīdī (1732-91), author of the *Tāj al-ʿArūs* (Arabic dictionary, being an expansion of al-Fīrūzābādī's *al-Qāmūs al-Muḥīṭ*), and of *Itḥāf al-sāda al-muttaqīn* (commentary on al-Ghazālī's *Iḥyāʾ*). He was born in Bilgrām (India); at about the age of fifteen he completed his *ḥadīth* study with Shāh Walī Allāh; stayed a long time after that in Zābid (Yemen) and Cairo (where he died). Another talented disciple, who has gained great repute in India[26], was al-Qāḍī Thanā Allāh al-Pānipatī (1725/6-1810). At the age of eighteen he studied *ḥadīth* under the guidance of the Delhi scholar. He composed a Persian commentary on the 3rd, 4th, 5th and 7th *waṣiyya* (exhortation, testamentary directive given to one's children and disciples) included in *al-Maqāla al-waḍiyya fiʾl-nasīha waʾl-waṣiyya*, a Persian tract of Shāh Walī Allāh. He called his annotations *Waṣiyyat-i nāma*.

If, however, one survey the thousands of pages the Delhi divine needed for the elaboration of his ideas and sees the ease with which he explains difficult subjects, one may wonder why he still asked for incitements to write. The most likely reason to my mind is that he merely wished to make sure that people were waiting for the results of his efforts and that he was doing meaningful work.

The immense amount of writing paper Shāh Walī Allāh required for the formulation of his views is certainly not due to his verbose style. On the contrary, in general he prefers to compose compact discourses.

The two main causes which eventually led to the enormous growth of his scholarly output are:

---

[24] ʿAbd al-Ḥayy, *Nuzhat al-khawāṭir*, Hyderabad 1957, VI, 105.

[25] Maẓhar Baqā, *Uṣūl-i fiqh awr Shāh Walī Allāh*, Lahore 1973, 68.

[26] Especially because of two widely known writings: 1) *Tafsīr-i Maẓharī*, a Qurʾān commentary named after his spiritual leader Maẓhar Jānjānān (d. 1782) and 2) *Mā lā budda min-hu* (on the Ḥanafī *fiqh*). In 1750 he became a spiritual *khalīfa* (deputy) of Jānjānān.

a) a wide scope of interest: he treats almost all topics of Muslim lore, Qurʾānic learning as well as the sciences of tradition, *fiqh* as well as ethics, mysticism as well as apologetic theology (*kalām*);
b) a regular repetition of themes in the successive products of his pen; consequently, if one tries to systematize his teachings, one has to gather together complementary data from different works for one and the same subject.

When attempting to draw up a list of his works arranged in order of date, one needs considerable intuition, for there is not very much to go by. Only a few writings mention specific dates of completion. For the rest, reference made in some books to earlier works can be helpful in fixing a certain sequence of appearance. Another means affording some help is the dated licences (*ijāzāt*) permitting a disciple to teach a course he had followed under the guidance of his former instructor. If titles of works of Shāh Walī Allāh himself are stated in such a certificate, it means that in any case they were composed before the date of its issue. Lastly, now and then the contents of a book (when indicating maturity of thought or a more traditional train of ideas) may give a clue in assessing a date. So, with all reserve, the following order of their creation has been reconstructed: Works written before the stay in the Ḥijāz (1731-2) include

1. *al-Qaṣīda al-lāmiyya* (Arabic) (Lyric poem with verses ending in the letter l). A verse is cited at the end of the 11th Vision of *Fuyūḍ al-Ḥaramayn*.
2. *al-Qawl al-jamīl fī bayān sawāʾ al-sabīl* (Arabic) (A Pleasant Discussion and Explanation of the Path). Qualifications necessary for the ṣūfī guide and rules for the education of the novice are expounded in it. Further, litanies and daily offices of various brotherhoods are set forth. The booklet testifies to the strong attachment of the author to his father, whose views or advice are remembered on nearly every page. Mention is made of it in the 36th Vision of *Fuyūḍ al-Ḥaramayn*.

During his sojourn in the Holy Land he prepared an Arabic translation of the Persian tract *Radd-i Rawāfiḍ* (Refutation of the Shiʿites) written by Shaykh Aḥmad Sirhindī (d. 1624). He entitled it *al-Muqaddima al-saniyya fiʾl-intiṣār liʾl-firqa al-Sunniyya* (Splendid Introduction in Defence of the Sunnī Creed). The translation was actually made at the request of his Medinian teacher Shaykh Abū Ṭāhir. Moreover, he "added useful explanatory and critical notes here and there ... (and) has also differed in several places from the original author, and has pointed out his mistakes"[27].

[27] M. G. Zubaid Ahmad, *The Contribution of Indo-Pakistan to Arabic Literature*, Lahore 1967, 115 f.

As appears from the *ijāza* (diploma) granted to his disciple Nūr Allāh b. Muʾīn al-Dīn on the 26 Jumāda 1146 ( = 4th December 1733) in which mention is made of the *Fuyūḍ al-Ḥaramayn* (Arabic) (Graces of Mecca and Medina) (*Tafh*. I, 9 and 11), Shāh Walī Allāh will have finished this record of 46 visions he had been favoured with in the two Holy Cities soon after his return to India.

The following collections of traditions compiled by the Delhi scholar also date, in all probability, from the time immediately succeeding his stay in the Ḥijāz since they chiefly contain *ḥadīths* he obtained there from his spiritual guides:

1. *al-Durr al-thamīn fiʾl-mubashshirāt al-nabī al-amīn* (Arabic) (Precious Pearls Consisting in Joyful Annunciations from the Trustworthy Prophet). The forty traditions included in this work were communicated in dreams in which the spirit of Mohammed was witnessed. They are divided into three categories:
   a) the first thirteen were those which he himself received from the Prophet;
   b) the next seventeen he heard through the medium of his father, his paternal uncle or his Medinian teacher Abū Ṭāhir;
   c) those which he received at third hand as, for instance, in the case of visions bestowed on the father of Abū Ṭāhir.
2. *al-Nawādir min aḥādīth Sayyid al-awāʾil waʾl-awākhir* (Arabic) (prophetic Traditions Relating Comical Tales). These traditions were put together merely because of their curious character. The chain of authorities on which they are based starts with a *jinn*, al-Khiḍr (a popular figure, who plays a prominent part in story and legend) or a very old man like Abū ʿAbd Allāh al-Muʿammir, who is said to have reached the age of 400. Most of the traditions in this collection came from Abū Ṭāhir.
3. *al-Musalsalāt min ḥadīth al-nabī*[28] (Arabic) (Prophetic Traditions Related by an Uninterrupted Chain of Transmitters). They consist mostly only of an *isnād* (chain of authorities) without a subsequent *matn* (text). They were handed down to Shāh Walī Allāh by his masters in Mecca and Medina with the introductory formula: 'I love you'.
4. *Arbaʿūna ḥadīthan musalsalatan biʾl-ashrāf fī ghālib sanadiha* (Arabic) (Forty Traditions mostly with an Uninterrupted Chain of Illustrious Transmitters). Shāh Walī Allāh heard these forty prophetic tradi-

[28] The other rhyming title in the same collection is *al-Faḍl al-mubīn fiʾl-musalsal min ḥadīth al-nabī al-amīn* (Extraordinary Favour Consisting in Traditions of the Trustworthy Prophet Related by an Uninterrupted Chain of Transmitters).

tions from the lips of Abū Ṭāhir. A remarkable feature is their brevity. They have the form of aphorisms, which can guide the believer in every department of life.

*al-Irshād ilā muhimāt ʿilm al-isnād* (Arabic) (A Manual for the Requirements of the Science of *Isnād*). The reason why this treatise in all likelihood dates from the period subsequent to the return from the Holy Land is, according to G. N. Jalbani, "that every scholar of Haramain he had met had written a book on this subject. He, therefore, liked to apprise people of the importance of this science"[29]

*Sharḥ tarājim abwāb ṣaḥīḥ al-Bukhārī* (Arabic) (Elucidation of the Headings of the Chapters of al-Bukhārī's Collection of Traditions). Ghulām Muṣṭafā al-Qāsimī supposes that this treatise was written about the years 1145/46 ( = 1732/33)[30].

*Alṭāf al-quds fī maʿrifa laṭāʾif al-nafs* (Persian) (Sacred Presents Consisting in Knowledge of Psychic Forces). Analysis of a mystic's inner dimensions.

*Anfās al-ʿārifīn* (Persian) (Breathings of Advanced Ṣūfīs). Contains biographical accounts of his ancestors, father, uncle Shaykh Abū Riḍāʾ Muḥammad and teachers of the Ḥijāz perod[31].

*Ḥujjat Allāh al-bāligha* (Arabic) (Peremptory Argument of God[32]). The second part of it deals with precepts implied in the *ḥadīth*. Here the author follows the classification adopted by the traditionist Muslim with one significant deviation: the chapters 16-20 (treating marriage, divorce and the like) in the collection of Muslim have been excluded from consideration. As a substitute for these topics, expositions are given of mystical issues like *dhikrs*[33], *maqāmāt* and *aḥwāl* (i.e. stages and states associated with passage along the ṣūfī Path). It is, however, the original presentation of subjects in its *first* part to which the work owes its great renown[34]. Here the Delhi scholar develops *inter alia* for the first time his famous scheme of the four *irtifāqāt* (see pp. 193-196), which may be regarded as a rudimentary social science.

---

[29] G. N. Jalbani, *Life of Shah Waliyullah* (Lahore 1978), p. 35.

[30] *al-Raḥīm* (Urdu periodical), Hyderabad May 1966, p. 875.

[31] Usually a small autobiography, named *al-Juzʾ al-laṭīf fī tarjamat al-ʿabd al-ḍaʿīf* (Persian) (An Exquisite Epitome Consisting in a Biography of an Insignificant Person) is added to the *Anfās* as a closing chapter. This tract, however, must be of a later date, since reference is made in it to the monograph *Hamaʿāt* while in the *Hamaʿāt* the existence of the *Anfās* is affirmed.

[32] Title derived from *Qurʾān* VI, 149. On p. 20 of the first part we read: "You should bear in mind, that in God's creation there are signs pointing out to the observer that God has a 'peremptory argument' (*al-ḥujjat al-bāligha*) for charging His worshippers with laws".

[33] By J.S. Trimingham aptly defined as spiritual exercises designed to render God's presence throughout one's being (*The Sufi Orders in Islam*, Oxford 1971, 302).

[34] It is prescribed as a course of study at al-Azhar in Cairo.

*Hama<sup>c</sup>āt* (Persian) (Downpours[35]). This work was completed in the month Jumāda al-thānī of 1148 ( = October/November 1735). It offers an exposition of the historic developments in Islamic mysticism and discusses the intentions and purposes as they are pursued by members of the different brotherhoods.

*al-Intibāh fī salāsil awliyā᾿ Allāh wa asānīd wārithī Rasūl Allāh* (Persian) (Heed of the Chains of Spiritual Descent of God's Protégés as well as of the Chains of Transmitters among the Heirs of the Messenger of God). This account of ṣūfī rituals and doctrines in different orders is composed between October/November 1735 and the 4th October 1747, since mention is made of the existence of the *Hamaʿāt* while the *Intibāh* itself is referred to in the *ijāza* (diploma) granted to Shaykh ʿAbd al-Raḥmān of Thatta (Sind) on the 29 Ramaḍān 1160 ( = 4th October 1747). Because of reminiscences concerning the stay in the Ḥijāz found in this treatise, we have put it close behind the *Hamaʿāt*.

*Ta᾿wīl al-aḥādīth fī rumūz qiṣaṣ al-anbiyā* (Arabic) (An Explanation of Significative Events Referred to in the Prophetic Tales). A dissertation on the esoteric background of particular episodes pertaining to the lives of persons who are ranked as prophets by the Muslims.

*Fatḥ al-Raḥmān fī tarjamat al-Qur᾿ān* (Persian) (Aid of the Merciful in the Translation of the Qur᾿ān). This annotated Persian version of the Qur᾿ān took a long time: started before Shāh Walī Allāh left for the Ḥijāz, completed on the ʿĪd al-aḍḥā (sacrificial feast) 1150 ( = 31st March 1738) and published in 1156 ( = 1743).

*Aṭyab al-nagham fī madḥ Sayyid al-ʿArab wa᾿l-ʿAjam* (The Most Pleasant Tune Consisting in a Laudation of the Master of Arabs and Non-Arabs). An Arabic ode on Mohammed with a Persian Commentary. The ode was completed on the 24 Rabīʿ al-thānī 1156 ( = 17th June 1743).

*al-Qaṣīda al-Hamziyya fi᾿l-madā᾿iḥ al-nabawiyya* (Arabic) (Lyric Poem with verses ending in the letter *hamza* in Praise of the Prophet). Composed at the end of 1157 ( = beginning of 1745). A Persian commentary on it was finished in 1762.

*Muqaddima dar fann-i tarjama-i Qur᾿ān* (Persian) (Introduction to the Art of Translation of the Qur᾿ān). Directions for translators of the Qur᾿ān.

*Hawāmiʿ* (Persian) (Downpours). Commentary on the *Ḥizb al-baḥr* of al-Shādhilī (see note 20 on p. 6).

*Saṭaʿāt* (Persian) (Radiances). Compendium of various cosmological concepts and mystic apprehensions peculiar to and dear to the Delhi scholar.

---

[35] Symbol that—like some other titles of Shāh Walī Allāh's books such as *Saṭaʿāt* (Radiances) and *Lamaḥāt* (Flashes of Lightning)—must notify the reader that the treatise in question was produced under divine inspiration.

*al-Musawwā min aḥādīth al-Muwaṭṭaʾ* (Arabic) (Arrangement of the Traditions of the *Muwaṭṭaʾ* in a Convenient Form). For the benefit of the reader Shāh Walī Allāh rearranged traditions in the Muwaṭṭaʾ at his own discretion. In addition, inferences deduced from the *ḥadīths* of this collection by the Malikites are compared with opinions of the Ḥanafite and Shāfiʿite schools. At the instance of ʿUbayd Allāh Sindhī the work was published in Mecca (volume 1 in 1351/1932; volume 2 in 1353/1934).

*al-Khayr al-kathīr* (Arabic) (Abundant Blessing[36]). This is a highly esoteric writing, and its chapters are called *Khazāʾin al-ḥikma* (Repositories of Wisdom). Shāh Muḥammad ʿĀshiq corrected the manuscript in 1161/1748.

*al-Fawz al-kabīr fī uṣūl al-tafsīr* (Persian) (Great Fruition[37] Lying in the Principles of Qurʾānic Exegesis). Thoughtful essay on multiple Qurʾānic issues.

*Fatḥ al-khabīr bi-mā lā budd min ḥafẓ fī ʿilm al-tafsīr* (Arabic) (Aid to Knowing What One Ought to Bear in Mind in the Science of Qurʾānic Exegesis). This deals with Qurʾānic expressions that are difficult to understand and which are given an interpretation in *ḥadīths* of ʿAbd Allāh b. al-ʿAbbās. This work is often appended to *al-Fawz al-kabīr* as the first and last chapter.

*Qurrat al-ʿaynayn fī tafḍīl al-Shaykhayn* (Persian) (Delight of the Eyes because of the Superiority of the First Two Caliphs). Refutation of Shīʿī aspersions on Abū Bakr and ʿUmar.

*Ṣarf-i Mīr manẓūm* (Persian) (Mīr's Inflection in Verse). For the benefit of his little son Shāh ʿAbd al-ʿAzīz, Shāh Walī Allāh turned the Arabic grammar of Mīr al-Jurjānī, called al-Sayyid al-Sharīf (d. 1413), into Persian verse. The child was born in 1159/1746, so this versified primary on etymology must have been completed about the year 1165/1751-2.

*al-Mawāla al-waḍiyya fiʾl-naṣīḥa waʾl-waṣiyya* (Persian) (Beautiful Treatise in Friendly Admonition and Exhortation). This work contains eight precepts for his children, friends and pupils.

The only thing we can establish with certainty about the following two works, which are difficult to date, is that they were written before the 4th September 1759, as they are recorded in the *ijāza* ʿAbd al-Raḥmān of Thatta received on that date (see Introduction of *al-Musawwā*, p. LIV):

1. *al-Inṣāf fī sabab bayān al-ikhtilāf* (Arabic) (Fair Elucidation of the Causes of the Legal Differences between Various Schools of Fiqh). The actual causes, so the author argues, were differences over

[36] Title derived from *Qurʾān* II, 269. In particular, abundant blessing is gained from knowledge of the divine Names, one of the main pursuits of this study (cf. *Khizāna* 2). For everything that happens in the world of man is a reflection of the divine Names.

[37] Term found in *Qurʾān* LXXXL, 11.

various problems of the Muslim Law already existent among the Companions of the Prophet. They were due to misunderstanding of certain of his acts, to forgetfulness on the part of the reporters, or to changes which took place in the report in the course of its transmission.

2. *ʿIqd al-jīd fī bayān aḥkām al-ijtihād waʾl-taqlīd* (Arabic) (Chaplet around a Graceful Neck Constisting of an Elucidation of the Characteristics of Formulating an Independent Judgment and of Unthinking Acquiescence in Received Opinion).

*Lamaḥāt* (Arabic) (Flashes of Lightning). A mystical philosophy with speculations on Being, *aʿyān thābita* (archetypes, i.e. latent realities of things), *tajalliyyāt* (theophanies), *al-nafs al-kulliyya* (Universal Soul), classes of angels, and the like. I think Khalīl is correct in assuming that this "digest of both his metaphysical and mystical conceptions belongs to a late period, since conceptions already expressed elsewhere are merely summarized as if for the already instructed"[38].

*al-Budūr al-bāzigha* (Arabic) (Full Moons appearing on the Horizon). The choice of the title suggests that this book is to be thought of as a counterpart to the *Ḥujjat Allāh al-bāligha*, for in the Preface to the latter work Shāh Walī Allāh states that its contents are like "full moons (*budūr*) which begin to rise (*bāzigha*) on the horizon of God's 'peremptory argument' (*ḥujjat bāligha*)" (*H.B.* I, 4). The expositions in this work are directed to an unknown person, who apparently represents one of Shāh Walī Allāh's students, so it can be taken as a type of text-book which recapitulates a number of topics discussed in earlier writings. In sum, this very important work, which can be qualified as *opus magnum* with even more reason than the *Ḥujjat Allāh al-bāligha*, offers us a mature and comprehensive survey of the manifold meaningful ideas the Delhi divine has evolved on the relations between God and man.

*Tafhīmāt-i Ilāhiyya* (Divine Revelations): a miscellany of short essays in Arabic and Persian, composed at different times[39]. The greater part consists of excursus on mystical[40] and theological questions. Legal affairs are also discussed and mention is made of visions the author was granted. This work also uncovers abuses and even contains sermons held on festive occasions.

---

38 Khalīl ʿAbdel Ḥamid ʿAbdel ʿAdl, *God, the Universe and Man in Islamic Thought: the Contribution of Shah Waliullah of Delhi* (1703-62) (unpubl. thesis, University of London, Oct. 1971).

39 Thus, for instance, *ijāzas* are inserted with divergent dates as 15-10-1729 (*Tafh.* I, 11) and 4-10-1747 (*Tafh.* I, 236).

40 In the second volume of this work the editors also inserted the famous letter to Effendi Ismāʿīl b. ʿAbd Allāh, in which Shāh Walī Allāh maintains that the differences between the principles of *waḥdat al-wujūd* and *waḥdat al-shuhūd* are merely terminological.

*Izālat al-khafā' ʿan khilāfat al-khulafā'* (Persian) (Removal of the Veil of Mystery from the Caliphate of the Caliphs). Vindication of the caliphate of the first two caliphs and an exposition of the different forms of the caliphate. The book gives the impression of being unfinished and the author acknowledges that he wrote it in a hurry (*Izāla* I, 8).

*al-Muṣaffā* (Persian) (The Clarified). A sister volume to the *Musawwā*, but slightly more detailed. It was published posthumously in 1766. Shāh Walī Allāh died on the 29 Muḥarram 1176 ( = 19th August 1762) in Delhi.

CHAPTER ONE

# VOCATIONAL VISIONS

The Delhi reformer was deeply concerned about the embarrassing predicament with which his co-religionists were confronted. Not only was the political situation[1] most awkward because of a continuous stream of foreign invaders, but the vitality of people's religious life was also threatened. According to him there were three major factors to which the deterioration of the spiritual attitude of his contemporaries[2] was accountable:

a) the spread of Aristotelian logic (*burhān*), as a result of which nearly all discussions about articles of belief were permeated with sterile demonstrative argumentations;
b) the baneful influence of unduly popular ṣūfīs, on account of which the people were more impressed by exhibitory raptures, cunning mystifications and poetry of the former than by the lessons of Qurʾān and Sunna;
c) excessive individualism. Nowadays "people are growing up in an age, in which everybody follows his private views ... There is no prospect of agreement or compromise. They disagree in all sorts of jurisprudence (*fiqh*[3]). Some are Ḥanafites, others Shāfiʿites, and everybody ... censures the others" (*Tafh.* I, 82 f.).

Through a number of vocational visions the man of Delhi became convinced that he was charged with the divine task of ameliorating the conditions of his homeland by means of special endowments and capacities conferred on him for this purpose.

---

[1] It is remarkable that in this work Shāh Walī Allāh himself only very rarely hints at the critical position of the Mughal rulers in his days. There is a passing reference in *Tafh.* I, 203, stating that "one day it may happen that the Hindus will obtain full power over the whole of India". Further, he writes that in the vision of the 16th May 1732, mentioned above, he witnessed how the king of the *kāfirs* (unbelievers) seized Muslim towns, confiscated their wealth and enslaved their children (*Fuyūḍ*, 44th Vision). The small interest in political affairs apparent in his books is certainly an additional argument in support of Muḥammad Ikrām's tendency to doubt the authenticity of the entire collection of political letters allegedly assigned to the Delhi divine and edited by K. A. Nizami under the title *Shāh Walī Allāh ke siyāsī maktūbāt* (Aligarh 1950) (Muḥammad Ikrām, *Rūd-i Kawthar*, Lahore 1970, 548).

[2] *Cf.* also *H.B.* I, 4: "I felt sad at heart that I had to live in an age of ignorance, bigotry, yielding to one's inclinations and boasting of one's baneful opinions".

[3] *Cf.* also *Tafh.* I, 214 where Shāh Walī Allāh harangues: "you occupy yourselves with the sciences of this world instead of those of the hereafter. You have become absorbed in questions of juristic preference (*istiḥsān*) of former *fiqh*-scholars ..., not recognizing that regulations are fixed by God and His Messenger".

The first time he received an intimation of his heavenly mission was on his way to the Ḥijāz, i.e. in the last months of 1730. Then his Lord gave him to understand: "This is a most lofty office (*manṣab*). You will only accomplish it after having fulfilled that which We command you. In a word, you have to follow the example of the prophets in your moral conduct and spiritual life. You will guide a community from amongst the people. There should be no relationship of love between you and anyone else except the association that is tinged with God's colour. If you fulfill that, you may be provided with that[4] which you hope for" (*Tafh*. II, 121).

During his sojourn in the Ḥijāz Shāh Walī Allāh obtained various heavenly encouragements to accept his special vocation: "Then another fragrance was diffused (from the side of the Prophet), indicating: God's intention with you is that through you the discomposed state of the affairs of the blessed *umma* (community) will be united ... Take care not to have disputations with the people about minutiae (*furūᶜ*) of the Law ... Again another fragrance was diffused. I noticed in it an admonition of the Prophet ... to take upon myself the burdens of the prophets ..., and to pursue what would further the integrity of men's religious conduct and the wholesomeness of their inner life (*Fuyūḍ*, 31st Vision). In another vision granted in the Holy Land on the 16th May, 1732, the Delhi divine sees himself appointed as a 'Master of the Time' (*qāʾim al-zamān*)[5]. In this capacity he is told to give a scathing criticism of the whole political system (*fakk kulli niẓāmin*)[6], for God wanted to establish a good order and wished to employ him for the execution of His designs[7] (*Fuyūḍ*, 44th Vision). The most suggestive vocational vision, however, was certainly the one granted him on the 14th August, 1731, and handed down to us in two slightly different versions. Shāh Walī Allāh describes this telling experience as follows: "In the night of the 10th of Ṣafar, A.H. 1144, stay-

---

[4] Later when staying in the Ḥijāz he received a vision which informed him of the boons God had in store for him:
a) exemption from punishments in this world and the next;
b) a peaceful life and
c) robe of honour of the 'esoteric caliphate' (*Fuyūḍ*, 36th Vision).

[5] Title of the twelfth *imām* (Ph. K. Hitti, *History of the Arabs*, London 1960, 441).

[6] As in former times it had been the task of his colleague ᶜAbd al-'Qādir al-Jīlānī (d. 1166) to exercise criticism at the court of the caliph (*Tafh*. II, 149f.). From another vision vouchsafed to him Shāh Walī Allāh infers that he had to perform the functions of a censor, thus acting as a substitute of the Prophet (*Tafh*. II, 26).

[7] On another occasion the following divine prospects were suggested to him: "It may be that the Truth will descend upon you giving a scathing criticism of the existing order of the world, just as a thunderbolt smashes and uproots everything that comes in its way ... And it may be that owing to you the earth will become full of light; injustice and exploitation will disappear from it, so that in the end there will be no need of a *mahdī*, or his appearance will be delayed for a long period" (*Tafh*. II, 120 f.).

ing at Mecca, I saw in a dream Ḥasan and Ḥusayn descending into my house. Ḥasan carried in his hand a reed-pen, of which the point was broken[8]. He stretched out his hand to give it to me, and said: 'This is the pen of my grandfather[9], the Messenger of God'. Thereupon he (withdrew his hand, and)[10] explained: 'Let Ḥusayn mend it first, since it is no longer as good as when Ḥusayn mended it the first time'. So Ḥusayn took it, mended it and gave it to me. I was delighted with it. Then, a green and white patterned mantle was brought. It was laid in front of the two (grandchildren). Thereupon Ḥusayn lifted it with the words: 'This mantle belongs to my grandfather, the Messenger of God'. And he clothed me[11] with it. Out of respect I raised it to my head and praised God; then I awoke'' (*Fuyūḍ*, 6th Vision). In the *Tafhīmāt* (II, 248 f.) version of this vision, which is evidently of a later date, we read instead of this last sentence: ''From that day my breast was opened for writing books on religious subjects''. The conclusion that he himself had to make a practical use of the pen of the Prophet had apparently been an afterthought. In the introduction of the *Ḥujjat Allāh al-bāligha*, composed some years later, Shāh Walī Allāh refers to this incident in the following words: ''Once while I sat down after the afternoon *ṣalāt*[12] concentrating myself upon God, suddenly the *rūḥ* (spirit) of the Prophet appeared and covered me from above with something that seemed to me like a garment spread over me. At that moment it crossed my mind that it somehow alluded to giving an interpretation of religion (*dīn*). Simultaneously, I felt in my breast a light which continually expanded. After a while my Lord re-

[8] Presumably indicating that in the Muslim world production of inspired religious writings had stopped.

[9] Shāh Walī Allāh seems to assent more to W. M. Watt's view that Mohammed could probably write as much as the average merchant of Mecca (*Bell's Introduction to the Qur'ān*, Edinburgh 1970, 36) than to the traditional Muslim opinion affirming that he was entirely unlettered.

[10] The words placed in brackets are supplemented from the *Tafhīmāt* version.

[11] Though Mohammed had cut off all possibilites of the investiture of a prophet after him, his work—as we shall see in chapter IX—was to Shāh Walī Allāh's mind not yet finished and had to be completed by later generations. Apparently, by the assumption of the mantle, the insigne *par excellence* of a prophet, the task of participating in the completion of Mohammed's achievements was also appointed to the Delhi divine. Later on, i.e. probably on his journey home at the end of 1732, his appointment as deputy of the prophet was confirmed by a visionary appearance of Mohammed himself. While, after the afternoon *ṣalāt*, he delivered himself to mystical contemplation in the mosque of Cambay (Ṣūrat and Cambay were in those days ports from which Indian pilgrims sailed to the Ḥijāz) he was favoured with the following *mubashshirat* (annunciation of a joyful event): ''Then suddenly I observed the spirit (*ruḥ*) of the Prophet which appeared (to me). He clothed me with a mantle. At the same moment some subtle points of the *sharīʿa* dawned upon me'' (*Tafh*. II, 248).

[12] This is the most opportune time of the day to gain divine illumination (I. Goldziher, 'Die Bedeutung des Nachmittagsgebet im Islam', in *Archiv für Religionswissenschaft*, IX, 1906, 295 f.).

vealed to me the decree He had settled concerning me: one day I would be awakened to this lofty enterprise and I would see 'the earth illuminated by the light of its Lord' ( = *Qurʾān* XXXIX, 69). Rays of light would shine from the East to the West and Mohammed's *sharīʿa* would irradiate in that time by manifesting itself in the wide gowns of convincing proofs. Thereafter I saw in a dream Ḥasan and Ḥusayn — at that time I stayed in Mecca — and it was as if they wanted to give a pen to me, stating: 'This is the pen of our grandfather, the Messenger of God' " (*H.B.* I, 3).

The special relationship which appears to exist between the man from Delhi and the Prophet is equally clearly demonstrated by the vision in which the former is invited to give the vow of alligiance (*bayʿa*) to the latter, as happens in the ritual of a ṣūfī order. "Accordingly", so Shāh Walī Allāh tells us, "I advanced (in my sitting position) to him till our thighs were pressed together. Then the Messenger of God performed the initiation rite of the hand-clasp" (*Tafh.* II, 248). Hence he knew himself united with the *rūḥ* (spirit) of the Prophet in the same way as was the case with Uways al-Qaranī[13] (*F.K.* 141).

All these exclusive visionary experiences, as may readily be understood, strengthened Shāh Walī Allāh's self-confidence to a great extent. In his autobiography we read: "God granted me the robe of revival (*khilʿat-i fātiḥiyya*) and enabled me to give new vigour and guidance to this last age, laying a new foundation of present-day *fiqh*[14] by collecting what appears appropriate (*marḍī*) in it and explaining basic notions (*asrār*) in the traditions, considerations of expediency in the laws as well as the stimulations (*targhībāt*) and all that has been brought by the Prophet from God. This is knowledge that none before me demonstrated with better argumentation ... If anyone has his doubts about this, tell him to glance into the book *al-Qawāʿid al-kubrā*, from which it appears that Shaykh ʿIzz al-Dīn (al-Sulamī, 1181-1262), in spite of his efforts, failed to realize even a hundreth part of this learning. He inspired me with the way of mysticism (*sulūk*) as approved by Him, as it should be practised in this age[15] ... I consolidated the foundations of the creed of

---

[13] A Yemeni contemporary of Mohammed who was 'spiritually' initiated by the latter 'from a distance', i.e. without his bodily presence.

[14] *Cf.* also *Tafh.* I, 153: "One of the greatest favours I received from God is that He revealed to me the causes leading to the discrepancies among the *fiqh* scholars".

[15] *Cf.* also *Tafh.* II, 125: "God blessed me and my contemporaries by granting a path (*ṭarīqa*) which of all paths affords the closest proximity to God. It is composed of five means of approaching to God: true faith, *qurb al-nawāfil*, *qurb al-wujūd*, *qurb al-farāʾiḍ* and *qurb al-malakūt* ... And my Lord revealed to me: We appoint you as leader (*imām*) of this path and We will show you its most lofty aspects". Because of the introduction of this *ṭarīqa* all other *ṭarīqas* and methods of traversing the path (*madhāhib*) can be abolished. This will produce a beneficial effect, since the existence of various *madhhabs* in mystical practice gives rise to factionalism among the people (*Tafh.* I, 81, 85).

the ancient sunnīs by proofs and arguments and by purifying them from nonsensical doubts raised by philosophers, in such a way that no room for contest is left. Upon me were poured out:

a) exact knowledge of the four (divine) perfections, *i.e.* of originating, creating, planning and guidance (*tadallī*);
b) insight into the dispositions of the human soul ... None before me reached these two most sublime disciplines. Worldly wisdom, by which reforms for this age can be wrought, was poured on me abundantly ... I was endowed with the power of discerning between the basic teaching of religion as has been handed down by the Prophet and what has been crept in and been tampered with, as well as between what is *sunna* and what has been innovated by sects'' (*al-Juzʾ al-laṭīf*, 28).

In consequence of the outpouring of countless divine blessings, our reformer holds various high offices. He is nominated the *nāṭiq*[16] (enunciator whose function it is to proclaim the revelation in a new era) and *ḥakīm* (wise man) of his age, and the *qāʾid* (leader) and *zaʿīm* (ruler) of his generation (*Tafh.* I, 124), is favoured with the epithets of ''the righteous one'' (*zakī*) and of ''the one who is blessed with final knowledge'' (*Fuyūḍ*, 15th Vision), is charged with the functions of *mujaddid* (reformer), *waṣī*[16] (plenipotentiary of the Prophet) and *quṭb* (pivot who heads the saintly hierarchy) in order to show people the right way (*Tafh.* I, 78). In his capacity of *waṣī* he is a person to be obeyed by all the world; in his hands[17] lie the best interests of mankind (*Tafh.* II, 53 f.), being enabled to give such an authoritative interpretation of the *sharīʿa* (law) that because of it even differences of opinion about details disappear (*Tafh.* I, 83).

The great talents with which our author finds himself endowed, are — as a rule — said to be the outcome of exceptional favours with which he, surprisingly, happens to be blessed. This awareness of having much to be thankful for readily and almost imperceptibly merges into unpalatable bragging: ''what a pity'', so he exclaims, ''that Plato has not seen the Greek philosophy I have!'' (*Tafh.* II, 12). And if he were to reform the conditions of the world through mathematics and astrology he would surpass Ptolemy (*Tafh.* I, 101). If we are scandalized by such excessive claims, we should bear in mind that this is a feature Shāh Walī Allāh had in common with quite a number of mystics. Ḥakīm al-Tirmidhī (d. 932), for instance, also pretended to be a pillar of the earth[18]. ''Under the guise

---

[16] *Nāṭiq* and *waṣī* are terms with very special associations in Ismāʿīlī thought.

[17] Having become ''the pillar (*watad*) of the earth. Without him the earth will not remain a couch nor heaven a roof'' (cf. *Qurʾān* II, 22) (*Tafh.* I, 84).

[18] Hasan Qasim Murad, 'The Life and Works of Hakim al-Tirmidhī', in *Hamdard Islamicus*, Vol. II, no. 1 (1979), 69.

of humble thanks to God'', I. Goldziher writes, al-Shaʿrānī (d. 973) ''tells the strangest things about his wonderful qualities''[19]. The Persian mystic Jāmī (d. 1492) claims: ''I have found no master with whom I have read to be superior to myself''[20], etc., etc.

---

[19] *Muslim Studies* (ed. S. M. Stern), (London 1971) II, 266.
[20] E. G. Browne, *Literary History of Persia*, Cambridge 1964, 509.

## CHAPTER TWO

# EXTRA-SCRIPTURAL MEDIUMS OF DIVINE REVELATION

Any exposition of Shāh Walī Allāh's thought should start with an explanation of various abstruse technical terms which he assumes the reader to be familiar with. Most of these terms can be included under the chapter heading given above.

### A) *ʿĀlam al-mithāl* (World of Prefiguration)

The *ʿālam al-mithāl* is brought into existence by the *nafs kulliyya* (Soul of the Universe) and is an offshoot of the world of the *nufūs falakiyya* (celestial souls) (*A.Q.* 116).

The place this world occupies in the universe is typical of the manner in which it functions. Situated between the World of Incorporeity and our phenomenal world, it acts as an intermediary[1] in a variety of ways. Thus "it serves for the manifestation of both the World of Immaterial Entities (*ʿālam al-arwāḥ*) (above it) as well as the forms reflected from the material world (below it)" (*B.B.* 152). In the 'light verse' (*Qurʾān* XXIV, 35) it is symbolically represented by "the olive tree, which is neither in the East nor in the West, but is situated in the middle of the trees ... Just as the fire of a lamp continues to burn in the wick through the oil (taken from the olive tree) and the oil functions as its 'mount' (*maṭīya*), similarly the Divine Form subsists in that part of the universe which happens to be right in the middle of it, namely the *ʿālam al-mithāl* which, like the well-proportioned olive tree, is neither in the East nor in the West, i.e. it is neither incorporeal (*mujarrad*) ..., nor does it belong to the category of the bodies ..., but it is between both of them[2]. That part (of the universe) is completely fitted to the purely Incorporeal, and on that account it has become its mount and mirror" (*Saṭ.* 46). If incorporeal entities (*arwāḥ*) come down to the latter, their shapes and distinctive qualities become

---

1 *Cf.* also *Tafh.* II, 180: "There things are specified for all that will befall in the phenomenal world as regards attributes, occurrences, outward and inward perfection, etc. ..., neither in summarily indicated ways as happens in the World of Immaterial Entities, nor in an elaborate manner as happens when something is brought into existence in the phenomenal world; but it holds the middle between the two as is requisite for the world of *khayāl* (imagination)".

2 "Hence it is made of material of extreme refinement ..., i.e. it is of a quality which is immune from the stain and grossness of this worldly life" (*B.B.* 152). In order that the throne of the queen of Sheba could be easily transported through the air, God invested it with properties of the *ʿālam al-mithāl* (*Taʾwīl* 66).

perceptible (*B.B.* 27). So "in the *ʿālam al-mithāl* spiritual concepts[3] are represented by bodily forms corresponding to them in import" (*H.B.* I, 13; *Saṭ.* 6).

"The *ʿālam al-mithāl* is an intermediate space (*barzakh*) between the empiric and divine world" (*Tafh.* I, 220). "It possesses the potentiality of turning an attribute of the immaterial into an attribute of the material, and *vice versa*. If there were no such intermediate power, the effects (of the divine Names and Attributes[4]) would not intertwine with the forms as they should; the form of Zayd which is conceived in the (divine) mind as the form of Zayd would not materialize, and no material form as such could have emanated from al-Raḥmān, Who is purely "incorporeal" (*B.B.* 26).

"For the *nafs kulliyya* (i.e. the universe in the aggregate) the *ʿālam al-mithāl*[5] performs the function of *khayāl* (imagination[6]) which is connected by some sort of link with the Throne[7] (upon which the Merciful One Himself sat after the creation of the universe)" (*Tafh.* I, 193). Accordingly, "when the Merciful One decrees the existence of something, its existence is (first) determined in that (intermediate) power" (*Tafh.* I, 163).

Because of its intermediate position the *ʿālam al-mithāl* receives impulses (*dawāʿī*) from above as well as from below. Impulses from above which descend into the hearts of the *mala aʿlā*[8] are of two types:

a) universal events originating from special conjunctions of the planets which presented themselves in the *ʿālam al-mithāl* while in front of the *tajallī aʿẓam*. In consequence of this, the angels of this category see to it that such an event only occurs on the earth at the proper place and time;

---

[3] This, for instance, is the case with the abstract notion of blood-relationship, for we read in a tradition that the Prophet stated: "When God had created blood-relationship, it came forward and said: 'This is the place for him who seeks Your protection against the rupture of kinship ties' " (Bu. *Adab* 13) (*H.B.* I, 13). Arguing in the same vein al-Ghazālī (d. 1111) declares that Qurʾān, Islam, and Friday having no personal existence in this world, are personified in a higher world (al-Ghazālī, *al-Durra al-fākhira*, ed. L. Gautier, Geneve 1878, 108).

[4] *Cf.* also *Tafh.* I, 194: "The *ʿālam al-mithāl* is an extensive plane in which all the Attributes of God, mentioned in the Holy Books, assume an exemplary representation (*tamaththul*)".

[5] The *ʿālam al-mithāl* is equally the source from which the celestial spheres, men and dumb beasts derive the powers of imagination which enable them to become informed of God's decrees (*Tafh.* I, 163).

[6] "It includes all that is perceived by the mind in an ideal or material form" (R. A. Nicholson, *Studies in Islamic Mysticism*, Delhi 1976, 91).

[7] which functions as the brain of the Divine Universal Planning! "In that place all that will befall in the phenomenal world is determined" (*Tafh.* II, 180).

[8] which constitute the main part of the population of the *ʿālam al-mithāl*.

b) conditions arranged for human individuals. By the intermediary of the same angels the impulses they receive are passed on to the hearts of men. Thus, somebody is inspired with a plan to escape from ruin, or he is informed of the true state of affairs by means of a vision or a heavenly voice (*A.Q.* 160 ff.).

Likewise a stream from the opposite direction arrives at the *ʿālam al-mithāl*. Thus also 'colours'[9] "rising up from the empiric world are joined to the *ʿālam al-mithāl*, block the way of the Universal Divine Planning[10] which proceeds from the World of Divine Transcendence to the *ʿālam al-mithāl*. (Owing to this collision) they are provided with a special form[11]. This is comparable to vapours ascending from the earth that reach an intensely cold stratum of air. Being dressed with the dress of rain at that region, they pour down on the earth; and appear effective in causing grass to grow and in refreshing the air" (*Tafh.* I, 220).

In conclusion we may say that the *ʿālam al-mithāl* in essence represents a world of prefiguration, in which things and events are shaped in the same way as an architect draws the shape of a house on a piece of paper before he builds it in empiric reality[12]. Its material is of a much more refined quality than that of our world, in which everything is composed of the four coarse elements: air, water, fire and earth[13]. Accordingly, having received a body of this fine and light material Jesus could ascend to heaven (*Taʾwīl* 76). The *ʿālam al-mithāl* is directly linked with the Throne of God where all Divine Planning is set up. In consequence, God's intention as to what may serve the welfare of the earth and its inhabitants are visualized in and by the *ʿālam al-mithāl* in its function of the *khayāl* of the universe.

---

[9] As, for instance, the 'colour' of believers who struggle for the cause of God; according to the Delhi divine, this can be deduced from *Qurʾān* IX, 16 ("Or do you think that you will be left in peace, as if God knows not as yet those who have struggled..?"). Nowhere is this idea better elucidated than in the statement: 'God knew that they would fight, so He loved them' (*Lamḥa* 55).

[10] This Planning (*tadbīr*) is "required by the Universal Welfare (*maṣlaḥa*) for the establishment of good provision in the world" (*A.Q.* 163).

[11] See also *Sharḥ aṭyab al-nagham* 41: "As a result of the circular movement (of colours) between the *ʿālam al-mithāl* and the world here below, an outpouring descends from the *ʿālam al-mithāl* and appears in the world. Spontaneously wonderful colours arise from the world". And in *Tafh.* I, 163 the effect exerted on earth by the *ʿālam al-mithāl* is explained as follows: "When the universal power of the *ʿālam al-mithāl* is connected with a place on earth ..., a state (*ḥāla*) intermediate between the phenomenal world and the *ʿālam al-mithāl* arises. Consequently, an undisruptable and indisconnectable body appears in the phenomenal world. It is provided with a distinctive quality, predicament, shape and size but without any flaw or defect ... An instance of such a body is the fire of Moses (i.e. the burning bush seen by Moses) (*Qurʾān* XX, 10)". And in *Tafh.* I, 224 we are told that dreams are founded on the correlations that exist between the *ʿālam al-mithāl* and the world here below.

[12] This simile is found in *Tafh.* I, 224.

[13] See *Taʾwīl* 45 and *Tafh.* I, 164.

B) *Ḥaẓīra al-quds* (Holy Enclosure)[14]

The *ḥaẓīra al-quds* appeared for the first time when the celestial spheres (*aflāk*), together with the faculties and equipped with the knowledge necessary to them, came into existence. The Self-existent was the first notion which they conceived. Hence[15] He manifested Himself in the *ḥaẓīra al-quds*.

Thereafter, when the cosmic processes required that superior angels, and souls of wise men joined with them, be brought into existence, those angels and souls were urged by their nature to feel drawn towards the *ḥaẓīra al-quds* like iron to a magnet. Consequently, the circle of the *ḥaẓīra al-quds* became enlarged (*Lamḥa* 32). The Holy Enclosure owes its name, as Shāh Walī Allāh explains, to the fact that the spiritual concentrations (*himam*) of angels and the spirits (*arwāḥ*) of perfect people 'enclose' it (*Tafh.* I, 65). It is also the place where souls stripped of their physical veils (i.e. bodily limitations) and personal characteristics[16] unite with the *insān ilāhī* (Divine Man), i.e. the prototype of the human species (*H.B.* I, 36), on account of which they become, so to speak, one conglomeration (*Fuyūḍ*, 4th Vision). The meeting of the angels and the souls of perfect men produces a flood of light and forms a halo around the *insān ilāhī* (*H.B.* I, 16). Thus, the place bears a resemblance to rays shining from a jewel (*H.B.* I, 67)[17].

It is there that the most magnificent *tadallī* (theophany) descends and because of the lightening flash of divine majesty the souls of these perfect men become bewildered. Nevertheless, this plane in the *ʿālam al-mithāl* serves them as a 'sure footing' (*Qurʾān* X, 2) and a 'marked place' (*Qurʾān* XXXVII, 164). This *tadallī*, though being one by itself, can assume manifold appearances (*burūzāt*) adapted to the attendant circumstances (*muʿaddāt*) on earth. On one occasion it appears in the shape of general prophethood, on another in the shape of the special prophethood of our prophet Mohammed, and again on another occasion in the institute of the *ṣalāt*, etc. All these manifestations meant for the sublunary world are prepared in the *ḥaẓīra al-quds* (*Fuyūḍ*, 4th Vision). Owing to its primary function of revealing divine devices for humanity[18], the *ḥaẓīra al-quds* is

---

[14] In a tradition it is used as a designation of Paradise (see Aḥmad b. Ḥanbal, *Musnad* V, 257). In Shāh Walī Allāh's philosophy, however, it has become a technical term with a very specific meaning. The adaptation of this term for mystical expositions may again have been an idea borrowed from al-Ghazālī who uses the same expression in his esoteric essay *Mishkāt al-anwār*, Cairo ed. 1904, 29.

[15] Since the *ḥaẓīra al-quds* is one of the mental faculties (*madārik*) of the universe (*ṭabīʿa kulliyya*) (*Fuyūḍ*, 38th Vision).

[16] So that the only properties left are common to all participants of the human race.

[17] In another passage specified by our author as a hyacinth (*Saṭ.* 28).

[18] Collectively as well as individually, since the *ḥaẓīra al-quds* is equally available to a

not so much a kind of marked-out space, but rather a manifestation of the Merciful One Who Himself sat on the Throne (*Qur'ān* XX, 5) reflected against a coarse substance like gypsum (*jiṣṣ*) (*Tafh.* I, 65) in the same way as the human form is reflected in a mirror[19] (see note of Ghulām Muṣṭafā al-Qāsimī at *Lamḥa* 32). Accordingly, the most appropriate qualification of the *ḥaẓīra al-quds* is the term *ḥaḍra* (used for it in *Fuyūḍ*, 29th and 38th Vision; *H.B.* I, 36; *Tafh.* I, 65) which, in a mystic context, denotes God's presence, as well as a stage of Being in which He descends and reveals Himself[20].

In one of the visions granted to the Delhi divine during his stay in al-Ḥaramayn, the following representation of the *ḥaẓīra al-quds* is offered: "I saw a plane (*ḥaḍra*) which has the same function in the Universal Nature (*ṭabīʿa kulliyya*) as the part in the nature (*ṭabīʿa*) of a human individual which is assigned to the power of will and determination connected with the movements (of the muscles). In the imagination (*khayāl*) (of a man) a predilection may arise to produce (certain) benefits or to repulse (certain) harms and, on account of this, an accurate idea (of what is to be done) is formed and consigned to this disposition, so that a decision is made and the muscles are stirred to bring about what is pursued. In the same way a powerful soul separate from bodily material (*mutajarrad*) may form an accurate idea of what should happen and notifies that *ḥaḍra* of it as soon as an intention (*himma*) arises in the above mentioned soul to produce an occurrence in the phenomenal world. Then a decision takes shape in the mind of Universal Nature and the notion of what is to happen reaches the (*ʿālam*) *al-mithāl*[21]. Thereafter, when the moment for the realization of the occurrence in the phenomenal world has come, God causes it to happen" (*Fuyūḍ*, 38th Vision).

In conclusion, we may say that in the concept of Shāh Walī Allāh the *ḥaẓīra al-quds* appears to be a major instrument for divine revelation, particularly in view of devices considered to be beneficial for the inhabitants

---

servant of God who is uncertain how to act. An instance of this is given in the *Sūrat al-anfāl*, where the Prophet's opinion is asked concerning the spoils of war (*Qur'ān* VIII, 1). It appears that he did not really know what had been ordained about this by God and how it had to be divided. When he had been drawn to *ḥayyiz al-ḥaqq* (realm of God, i.e. the *ḥaẓīra al-quds*), however, he was told what had to be done in this affair (*Fuyūḍ*, 29th Vision).

[19] The same simile is used in elucidation of the theophany Moses was favoured with in the holy valley Ṭuwā: "Accordingly, the elements of air, etc. of that place took the form of fire in order to reveal the message of God in the same way as the form reflected in a mirror reveals the one who looks in it" (*Lamḥa* 57).

[20] See also the definition in *Tafh.* I, 248: "The *ḥaẓīra al-quds* is an expression for the *tajallī aʿẓam* in the *ʿālam al-mithāl*".

[21] Which functions for the use of the *nafs kulliyya* (i.e. the universe in the aggregate) as its *khayāl* (*Tafh.* I, 193).

of the earth, for which purpose decisions are settled there, as it also functions as the will-power of the universe.

C) *Angelic Categories*

The most essential trait of angels is their function as intermediaries, or to put it in the words of Shāh Walī Allāh: "The actual raison d'être of angels is that universal expediency (*maṣlaḥa*) requires the existence of a divine zone which synthesizes the ontological levels of the unconditioned and conditioned, of necessarily existent (being) (*wujūb*) and contingent being in such a way that a bridge (*barzakh*) is formed between the two categories". (*Tafh.* I, 192).

They are perceptible counterparts (*tamāthīl*) of divine Names[22] (*Khizāna* 3), marks of a reality in the World of divine Omnipotence and, accordingly, not composed of elemental bodies which are made up of water and clay[23]. They have characteristics which differ from the characteristics of elemental substances, so that they do not change from one phase to another like Zayd who is first a child, then a youth and ultimately an old man, possessing at first a pale complexion and a slender stature and later a dark complexion and a humped back (*B.B.* 178)[24]. Their souls, therefore, are more perfect than those of men; and the materials (*amshāj*) they are composed of are more refined than those of men[25]. Consequently, they are (in the possession of) complete revelation (*waḥy*) and complete knowledge. On that account they are even superior to prophets, if the angels who bowed down before Adam[26] are left out of consideration, (*Khizāna* 3). "While the *jinn* predominate over the souls of soothsayers and communicate information to them, the angels of higher ranks predominate over the souls of prophets, and from within their ranks information is communicated from the World of divine Omnipotence (i.e. the *tajallī aʿẓām*)" (*Saṭ.* 20).

---

[22] So "daily happenings, in substance, come about by the outpouring of actualized temporal Names (*asmāʾ ḥāditha*) from the breasts of the angels nearest to God who are responsible for the management of creation" (*Khizāna* 2) (N.B. 'Names' are in fact divine powers scattered all over the Universe!).

[23] I.e. angels of a high rank are rational beings created from celestial elements, while the element of air is the most striking characteristic of the bodies of angels of a low rank (*Khizāna* 3).

[24] Angels have a steady (*qāʾim*) form (*Lamḥa* 46).

[25] *Cf.* also *A.Q.* 160: "The angels who officiate in the *ʿālam al-mithāl* are serene souls who, under lucky stars, were blown into bodies composed of the subtle elements in a completely balanced state".

[26] See *Qurʾān*, II, 33. The angels mentioned in this connection were, according to Shāh Walī Allāh, merely made of earthly elements (*ʿunṣūriyyūn*), and not of celestial material (*falakiyyūn*). The angels of high rank, however, did not prostrate themselves (*Khizāna* 3).

Though not explicitly stated, one of the deductions the Delhi divine seems to draw from the angels' possession of complete knowledge is that they are said to be the intellectual faculties of the human species who perform for the latter the same function as the intellectual faculties in regard to an individual of that species. In consequence of this, the angels provide the common Muslim believers with a much clearer notion of God than they would have had without them: "in short, the mental form 'God' which we call a conception occurring in the mind, appears to be, in (the light of) deep thinking and revealing visions, the shadow of a divine form which is fixed in the (minds of the angels called) *mala aʿlā*" (*Saṭ.* 41). Equally, in order to gain a better understanding of the rather vague idea of God's predestined grace (*ʿināya*), it has been visualized for us by the term "the invocation (*daʿwa*) of angels" (*H.B.* I, 31).

Shāh Walī Allāh distinguishes the following classes of angels:

1. The highest category. They are in the possession of souls (*nufūs*) that are breathed into luminous bodies "about the time of very auspicious conjunctions of planets ... By luminous bodies fine elements are meant, in which the substance of air dominates which cannot be perceived by the faculty of seeing". (*Saṭ.* 43). These include:
   a) the angels nearest to God (*muqarrabūn*). "These are, in essence, the embodiment of divine planning in the world, and their shape is composed of material from the World of Prefiguration. Isrāfīl embodies the general planning of the godly Man meant for human individuals, while Mīkāʾīl embodies the detailed planning. Both of them see to it that men gain a most reasonable sustenance and a good yield from their fields. Gabriel embodies the planning aimed at the acquisition of complete knowledge about laws and divine revelation" (*B.B.* 178 f.);
   b) the bearers of the Throne (of God) who are always praying for mankind[27];
   c) the *mala aʿlā* (High Council) who constitute one of the levels of the *ʿālam al-arwāḥ* (*H.* XI). In Shāh Walī Allāh's system of belief the *mala aʿlā*[28] play a foremost part in God's rule of humanity,

[27] "The bearers of the Throne are four angels: one in the shape of a man—and that is the intercessor (*shafīʿ*) for men—; another in the shape of a bull—and that is the intercessor for domestic animals —; the third has the shape of a vulture—and that is the intercessor for birds—; and the fourth possesses the shape of a lion—and that is the intercessor for beasts of prey" (*Saṭ.* 45).

[28] The notion of the *mala aʿlā* derived from *Qurʾān* XXXVIII, 69 where it is recorded that they hold disputes. According to a report found in some traditions (al-Dārimī, *Ruʾyā* 13; Aḥmad b. Ḥanbal, *Musnad* I, 368) Mohammed was informed in a dream about the two subjects of disputation: a) the ways of expiation; b) the degrees of obtaining more perfection (by, for instance, praying at night when people are asleep) (*H.B.* I, 15).

since divine Providence proceeds on the following lines: "the *tajallī aʿẓam*, whose function in the universe is comparable to that of the heart in man, reveals in the *mala aʿlā*[29]—according to universal expediency—some rather vague indications (*ruqūm ijmālī*) relating to God's predestined grace (*ʿināya*) with respect to the order of good in the world, to which pertain imminent occurrences, praise and blame[30] with regard to deeds, sayings, beliefs and customs of men. Next, in the *mala aʿlā* these hidden indications become more explicit. Consequently, they assume a *mithālī* shape in the Holy Enclosure, that is to say the place in which, on the level of the *ʿālam al-mithāl*, the *mala aʿlā* bring matters to an issue[31]. Then these *mithālī* shapes are imprinted on the minds of human beings ... Hence, two kinds of knowledge spring from their minds: firstly, knowledge of ethical categories ...; secondly, knowledge of polemics to be used against heretics" (*Tafh.* I, 201 f.). In addition, these angels "are imbued with knowledge of the divine Names and Attributes and with an understanding of the mysteries of the *ʿālam al-jabarūt* (World of Omnipotence) (*H.B.* I, 26).

---

[29] The *mala aʿlā* circle round the *tajallī aʿẓam* (*Tafh.* I, 194). As a result of it, the divine Will which is directed to the instruction of a servant and planning of certain affairs falls as a spark from the *tajallī aʿẓam* on the *mala aʿlā*: (then) after having widened its sphere of action and having absorbed powers of the *ʿālam al-mithāl*, expansion (*basṭ*), contraction (*qabḍ*) or transformation (*iḥāla*) of the earthly processes of causality is effected to the end that a form corresponding with what had been conceived by the *mala aʿlā* appears (*Saṭ.* 37). Thus events such as the appearance of a religious community or a calamity that will occur on a fixed day have two kinds of *wujūd* (existence). The one presupposes the other. At the stage of the *mala aʿlā* they are in a *wujūd rūḥī* ('spiritual' state of existence); realized in the phenomenal world they seized on a *wujūd nāsūtī* (existence in the realm of matter) (*Lamḥa* 25).

[30] See also *H.B.* I, 15: "The *mala aʿlā* never stop praying for someone who has improved and refined himself and tries to improve other people as well ..., whereas (at the same time) they never stop cursing who is disobedient to God and tries to cause disruption."

[31] *Cf.* also *H.B.* I, 16: "Their firm consensus (*ijmāʿ*) is called 'strengthening with the Holy Spirit' (See *Qurʾān* II, 87 and 253; V, 113, where this qualification is reserved for Jesus). The Holy Spirit stands for the *tajallī aʿẓam* and being strengthened with it implies a participation in the blessings of the *tajallī aʿẓam* (*Lamḥa* 58). Sometimes a consensus is reached in the Holy Enclosure about the furnishing of a device to save mankind from calamities in this world and the next, by equipping the most pure person in God's creation at that time with knowledge concerning improvement and guidance of the people". In short, "God has created the *mala aʿlā* with this end in view so that they should function in the *shakhṣ-i kabīr* ('Great Person'), i.e. the species of man, as the nerve centre functions in a *shakhṣ-i ṣaghīr* ('Small Person'), i.e. an individual of that species. Just as his nervous system regulates his body, so the *mala aʿlā* regulate (the affairs of) the human species and its individuals" (*Saṭ.* 41).

"Imprinted on the minds of human beings", i.e. of those among them who strive after perfection (*kāmil*)[32] and possess of possibilities for the fullest expansion of their personalities. The ultimate objective of man's individual efforts is the polishing of his mind (*nafs*) "to make it like a *minaṣṣa* (throne upon which a bride is raised when displayed to the bridegroom) for the manifestation of the decisions (*aḥkām*) of the *mala aʿlā*" (*H.B.* I, 51). These are the minds of which the *mala aʿlā* avail themselves for their ends, and which appear to belong to prophets, authors of a new doctrine (*madhhab*), fighters of injustice. In this way "a (new) *milla* (institutionalized religion), or doctrine, or caliphate is organized ... Reformer (*mujaddid*) after reformer then revives religious sciences" (*A.Q.* 165). These extraordinary talented persons are not, however, merely useful instruments at the service of the *mala aʿlā*; on the contrary, they themselves may enter into the ranks of the latter[33] as soon after death as "the coarse garments are thrown from their bodies. For it is not as common people think, that a perfect man who dies is lost to the world. On the contrary, he (who beforehand was composed of a substratum and accidental qualities) now becomes a pure substance and still increases in perfection" (*Fuyūḍ*, 11th Vision). Having joined the *mala aʿlā* "They become the 'stomach' for the bounteousness of God, the 'ears' for hearing many prayers of the inhabitants of the earth, and the 'tongues' for many a suitable inpiration (*ilhām*)" (*Lamḥa* 43).

2. Auxiliary angels classed with the *mala sāfil* (Low Council). "They consist of souls lesser in rank (than those of *mala aʿlā*), breathed into gaseous bodies[34] about the time of fairly auspicious conjunctions of the planets ... This group (of angels) is like a cross between minerals and animals[35], as they have no specific form: one member is like a globe, a second like a turnip, a third like a triangle, the fourth like

[32] *Cf.* also *A.Q.* 116; "According to us, the perfect man represents a distinct species among the various kinds of men, just as man represents a distinct species within his own (animal) genus. Just as man is superior to the animals because of his *raʾy kullī* (broad outlook) and the systematic refinement of his five faculties, so too the perfect man is superior to other men because of the appearance of the universal soul in his particular selfhood (*anāniyya*) making the latter an instrument of its will ... In short, the perfect man is he nearest of all individual souls to the universal soul".

[33] A similar view is advanced by Naṣīr al-Dīn Ṭūṣī (1201-74) in the *Akhlāq-i Naṣīrī*, in which it is stated that by yearning for the attainment of perfection, man attains proximity to the *mala aʿlā* (see *The Nasirean Ethics*, tr. G. M. Wickens, London 1964, 47).

[34] Because of which they move on the wind, just as a man moves on his feet.

[35] I.e. shapelessness they have in common with minerals and the possession of a *rūḥ* with animals.

a quadrangle, and so on''. (*Saṭ*. 43). ''Parallel to this abode (*ḥaḍra*) (of the *mala aʿlā*) there is another site (*ḥaṣīra*) on a lower level. It is the point to which the meditative concentrations of the *mala sāfil* turn. It is the centre of their affairs and the place where they receive their inspirations ... There by drawing near imperceptibly God is marked by affection for His worshippers, complying with some their desires, and so on'' (*Fuyūḍ*, 25th Vision). ''You should know that the course of behaviour (*sunna*) of God (with reference to mankind) is this, that when in the Unseen World an important matter has been predestined and a concept of it has been imprinted on (the minds of) the *mala aʿlā*, the *mala sāfil* are informed of the affair'' (*Izāla* I, 34). ''Characteristic of to the latter is that the sole occupation they are charged with is looking out for what may filter down (of orders given by the *mala aʿlā*) from above ... (Thus) they come to action in the same way as birds and quadrupeds if urged by their instincts ... Then they act on the heart of men and animals''[36] (*H.B.* I, 16). Their acting is mechanical, i.e. they are ''not acquainted with the principle of universal expediency'' (*H.* XVIII), and ''they do not know for what reason these impulses are put into their hearts'' (*Tafh.* I, 89). However, there is also a traffic stream in the opposite direction, from below upwards[37]. Then the initiative comes from man. This happens, for instance, when man is desirous of acquiring the perfection (*kamāl*) of the *mala sāfil*. To this end he should punctiously to observe cultic purity, stay in old mosques where saintly people used to perform their *ṣalāts*, recite the Qurʾān frequently and apply himself regularly to the *dhikr*-ritual, invocating Allāh's 99 most Beautiful Names or His 40 Best-known Names in a repetitive rythm (*Fuyūḍ*, 5th Vision). And if in this way he succeeds in obtaining abilities of the *mala sāfil*, he may have the command of the faculties

---

[36] And on the elements, as we may conclude from another passage in Shāh Walī Allāh's works, in which it is stated that these angels operate in the universe by *ilhām* (inspiration) as well as by *iḥāla* (effecting changes in elements) (*H.* XVIII).

[37] In fact, owing to a continuous stream of descending and ascending powers, things happen as they do: ''As soon as the command (''Be!'') descends and the gate of divine planning (*tadbīr*) is opened, imminent events of major importance spout like a fountain upon the *mala aʿlā* and *mala sāfil* and from there produce their effects on the mineral, vegetable and animal kingdoms of concrete being (*mawālīd*) and, in particular, on human individuals. In the course of that, a powerful stream also arises from the lowest spot (on earth), attains the *ḥaẓīra al-quds* and produces its effects there. Next, another powerful stream descends from the *ḥaẓīra al-quds* and produces effects on the three kingdoms and, in particular, on human individuals''. The powerful stream that reaches the heart of the *ḥaẓīra al-quds* is set in motion by determined persons with a definite object of pursuit. Those effects of the lower world on the *ḥaẓīra al-quds* may result in the appearance of angels and *jinns* (*H.* XXI).

of *kashf* (intuitive knowledge) and of *ishrāf* (thoughtreading) (*H.* XVIII).

3. Angels who represent protective prototypes (*muthul*) of earthly species. "At times", so we read in *Lamḥa*, 43 "cosmic processes unite to cause a deluge to destroy the individuals of a species as a whole. Then the 'prototypes' start to plead (before their Lord) ... for the preservation of their 'images' (*sc.* individual shapes) on earth. And it is for this reason that Noah was ordered to take on board 'a pair from every species' (*Qur*ʾ*ān* XI, 40) and the Prophet rescinded his order to kill the dogs, declaring: "after all they are just as much a community (*umma*)" (Mālik b. Anas, *Isti*ʾ*dhān* 14).
4. The guardian angels (*ḥafaẓa*). "These are created in order to ward off the machinations of the Devil and to repel his dirty tricks. They strive for the good of men" (*B.B.* 179).

D) *Tajalliyyāt*[38] ('radiances' emanating from the fire by which God reveals Himself)

According the Shāh Walī Allāh, *tajalliyyāt* can be discerned by three means, viz:

1. the mental image (*ṣūra* ʿ*ilmiyya*), which is imprinted upon the conceptive faculties and is a representation of the conception itself ... When a mystic concentrates upon the image he has of his Lord, an image corresponding to his belief is represented. Then that image becomes a means of revealing his Lord, and an instrument to gain him self-knowledge ...
2. the spiritual concentration (*himma*) of certain angels or people of a superior quality. When the latter endeavour by their *himma* to become an image of God, that image will be a theophany (*tajallī*) ...
3. a minute particle (*daqīqa*) that stands in opposite correlation to the Divine Essence ... and is a likeness and representation of It (*Lamḥa* 52). In a parallel passage this *daqīqa* is indicated as a *raqīqa* (subtle contact point). When a worshipper immerses himself completely in this point, he attains the theophany which is called *tajallī dhātī*[39] through self-annihilation (*Tafh.* I, 66).

---

[38] The term is derived from *Qur*ʾ*ān* VII, 139: "And when his (Moses') Lord manifested Himself (*tajallā*) on the Mount (Sinai)" (*Saṭ.* 36). The reason why God revealed Himself in this way to Moses is that "bearing his fervid nature in mind, God endowed him with a theophany of fire" (*Ta*ʾ*wīl* 50).

[39] This is a disclosure of the Ultimate Reality, neither as in a mirror nor as a phenomenon, but just as It is" (*Tafh.* I, 262).

Our author divides the *tajalliyyāt* into three categories, namely:

1. the *tajalliyyāt wujūdiyya*. Their essence (*ḥaqīqa*) is the manifestation of Being (*wujūd*), in respect of external substantiation, in forms belonging to the World of Divine Omnipotence as well as to the World of Contingency. Every manifestation is provided with special properties and distinct operations;
2. the *tajalliyyāt shuhūdiyya*. Their essence is that when the mystic concentrates himself energetically on God and Ultimate Reality is disclosed to him in different forms and predicaments, every form and predicament of the Reality revealed to him is called a *tajallī*. This occurs in proportion to his knowledge of God;
3. the *tajalliyyāt kamāliyya*. Their essence is that when someone who passes away from self into God has loosened himself from the demands of nature and has devoutly fixed his eyes on the World of Omnipotence, his soul will be coloured with the colour of the World of Omnipotence (*Tafh.* I, 261).

In a more detailed explanation of this third category of *tajalliyyāt* the Delhi divine sets out: Full happiness is allotted to a worshipper if God appears to him in the following manner: firstly, His *tajallī* operates on his *nasama* (lower self) so that it becomes cleansed of wickedness. Next, when the *tajallī* is directed to the *nafs nāṭiqa* (rational soul) the *himma* of the worshipper receives enlightenment. Then in all his doings his attention is focused on God and no longer on his own self. However, as soon as the *tajallī* is concentrated on his *ʿayn thābita* (archetypal individuality) his actions (*āthār*), perfections and stages on the Ṣūfī Path are coloured by the colour of God (*Tafh.* II, 55).

E) *al-Tajallī al-aʿẓam*[40] (Most Supreme Theophany)

We note the following statements about this concept in the works of Shāh Walī Allāh: The descent of the *tajallī aʿẓam*, "which manifested Itself in the heart of the *nafas Raḥmāni* (i.e. the universe in the aggregate) before the determination of time and appearance of the transitory world, was meant to attract the human souls to God as iron is attracted to a magnet" (*Maktūb*, 8). "It is a summary (*barnāmaj*) of the realities of the Self-existent, and therefore also a summary of the divine *tajalliyyāt* and a talisman[41] of the wisdom of the Merciful God" (*Haw.* 5); "the primordial source of every kind of *tajallī* appearing in the phenomenal world ...,

[40] In the early writing *Fuyūḍ al-Ḥaramayn* it is still called *al-tadallī al-ʿaẓīm* (Supreme Descent).

[41] I.e. a charm which can effect "une transformation de l'être humain en sorte que la vision de celui-ci s'ouvre à la connaissance de la réalité essentielle primitivement occultée" (J. L. Michon, *Le soufi Marocain Aḥmad Ibn ʿAjiba et son miʿrāj*, Paris 1973, 99).

a form that bears a likeness to God (*al-ḥaqq*) (*Saṭ*. 38), the shadow (*ẓill*) of the divine Essence (*Tafh*. I, 64) and an exemplary representation (*timthāl*) of It in the Universe'' (*Tafh*. I, 191). ''In the opinion of Ibn ʿArabī the name of this reality is *al-ḥaqīqa al-muḥammadiyya*[42]'' (*Haw*. 7). ''The very existence of this *tajallī* shows that the divine Essence has a Will that brings about changes and continuous processes of renovation in the Universe (*irāda mutajaddida*) ... Or to explain more precisely (by a metaphor): the sun and its light are inseparable from each other. The light is coupled to the sun. The effects of the light, however, are temporary (and consequently changing). Thus at midday (and not, for example, at dawn) the light makes a stone hot and causes ice to melt'' (*Saṭ*. 11). ''The *tajallī aʿẓam* is the heart (*qalb*) of the Universe and the mainstay of its affairs'' (*Lamḥa* 58). Since in ṣūfī parlance the heart functions as the seat of religious apprehension, various kinds of knowledge appear to pour out from the *tajallī aʿẓam* such as, for instance, knowledge about the apologetics (*Tafh*. I, 202). The *tajallī aʿẓam* has a special relationship with the human soul: there is nothing closer to it than the *tajallī aʿẓam*. On that account it is the instrument most suited to the refinement of the soul. ''Hence all the *sharīʿas* (introduced by the prophets) give a lucid exposition of mental concentration (*tawajjuh*) on the *tajallī aʿẓam*'' (*A.Q.* 134). ''The *tajallī aʿẓam* (as It manifests Itself in the Universe) can be assigned many Attributes and be named by many Names. Three of them, however, are basic, to wit:

1. Allāh; this Name refers to symptoms of personality and individuality to be found in this *tajallī*;
2. *qādir*; this Name refers to the power (*qahr*) operating on all the contingencies which are substantiated in the *nafas Rahmānī* ('Breath of the Merciful', i.e. the ever-spreading and self-unfolding existence which gives rise to contingent beings);
3. *ʿālim*; this Name refers to the presence of realities in the world emerging on the level of the (divine) Mind (*ʿaql*)'' (*Haw*. 3).

The *tajallī aʿẓam* has its own history, its specific periods (*adwār*), developments (*aṭwār*) (*Lamḥa* 50) and different phases (*shuʾūn*). As God says: 'Every day He is in a (new) mode of being (*shaʾn*)' (*Qurʾān* LV, 29)'' (*Tafh*. I, 116). In this connection, Shāh Walī Allāh tells us the following story: ''At the time when the planning for the world had to be arranged, the heavens and earth with all that was in them were (still) dark like an obscure night. Divine Wisdom then required that this 'defect' should be removed and that this chaotic state should be changed into a good

---

[42] I.e. ''the Reality of Mohammed which is the active Principle in all divine and esoteric knowledge'' (A. E. Affifi, *The Mystical Philosophy of Ibnul Arabi*, Lahore n.d., 70).

order[43]. Therefore, in the *ʿālam al-mithāl* a *tajallī*, by which the reality of the Self-existent could be revealed, became manifest ... For (in the matter of the reality of God) man's conceptive faculty is in need of a source and a place of refuge. And this can only be the prototype of the *tajalliyyāt*'' (*Haw*. 2 and 5). Other details of this first appearance of the *tajallī aʿẓam* are found in *Tafh*. I, 191 f. and 209 where we read: ''That which in the beginning was manifested by the *tajallī aʿẓam* did not possess any qualification (*qayd*) or epithet (*waṣf*) by which it could be identified or distinguished from that which was not equal to it ... When the celestial spheres had been created, ... the first subtle substance (*laṭīfa*) in their souls was a dominant white light. In view of the fact that the *tajallī aʿẓam* (in this first period) was expressed by this dominant white light, its name was Yazdān ... Someone, to whom dominant lights like this one were disclosed, was only acquainted with the necessitation (*ījāb*) and realisation (*kawn*) of things and making assertions about reality (*taḥqīq*). Accordingly, he did not yet discern good and bad ... Man made (at that time) a *qibla* (direction of prayer) for his direction to the Yazdān of light, fire and the sun, because of their resemblance to It. Perfect souls who lived in this first period had a continuous link with the *tajallī aʿẓam* until their *ḥajar al-bahts*[44] passed into it''.

Next came the phase which Shāh Walī Allāh names Lāhūt. It was at the time of our leader Abraham that God manifested Himself in this manner. He forbade spiritual affiliations with the stars through Abraham. He abolished the science of talismans, magic pearls (*kharazāt*), and such-like ... (In this period) the prophets continuously obtained a direct contact with God for the benefit of the *milla* along with this *tajallī* which arose from the breasts of the angels. On them were poured out knowledge of practical wisdom, of legislation, of polemics, of remembering the favours of God and His days, of trials of faith (*fitan*), and so on (*Tafh*. I, 193).

---

[43] Cf. also *Fuyūḍ*, 4th Vision: in view of the good order which had to be established by the *tadallī ʿaẓīm* operating from the *ʿālam al-mithāl* It appeared in our empiric world through many manifestations (*burūzāt*), adapted to attendant circumstances in the form of human institutes, customs and ideas rooted in people's minds.

[44] Prof. A. Schimmel kindly drew my attention to a passage in chapter 17 of Ibn ʿArabī's *al-Tadbīrāt al-ilāhiyya fī iṣlāḥ al-mamlaka al-insāniyya* in which the *ḥajar al-baht* ('gem of stupefaction') is elucidated as follows: It represents a vital center in the heart of man in the same way as the pupil in the eye. As soon as the heart is polished by spiritual exercises, this center becomes visible. Then because of the reflection of light waves transmitted by a *tajallī* (divine radiation), light spreads from this gem and pervades all recesses of the physical body. Because of that, glaring rays of light radiating from this gem 'stupify' and dazzle the mind and other faculties of the mystic (see H. S. Nyberg, *Kleinere Schriften des Ibn al-ʿArabī*, Leiden 1919, 216 f.).

"After that[45] again another universal phase came upon God". This time it appeared in the shape of the *ʿālam al-mithāl* ... An important difference, however, between this externalization (*barza*) (of the *tajallī aʿẓam*) and the former two (i.e. of Yazdān and Lāhūt) is that in the first two cases the Self-existent manifested Himself directly, whereas this last externalization was like something that appears in a mirror[46] (*Tafh*. I, 193). As soon as the *ʿālam al-mithāl*, in which *khayāl* (retentive imagination) is the dominant faculty, had been fully expanded, "the revelatory process (*waḥy*) stopped; by consequence, the mental condition of people in general degraded: they only understood the externals of the Law. Then knowledge descended prepared for man's reason, and was no longer destined for his *ḥajar al-baht*[47]. So people began to discuss matters of grammar, syntax and Arabic poetry, and produced studies on *ḥadīth*, *tafsīr*, *fiqh* and *kalām*" (*Tafh*. I, 199).

---

[45] I.e. "When the mission of the Prophet had been realized, a major part of the *ʿālam al-mithāl* appeared and the *barza* of the Lāhūt fell into the background (*Tafh*. I, 198 f.).

[46] See *Saṭ*. 46, where is explained that the *ʿālam al-mithāl* functions as a mirror for the pure Incorporeal.

[47] If the *ḥajar al-baht* is no longer active in man, it implies that he has to put up with second-hand knowledge , deduced from information received by *waḥy*.

# CHAPTER THREE

# METAPHYSICS

## A) *Concept of God*

In principle, theology is outside the range of human possibilities and beyond man's rational capacities: "God is too lofty for analogies to be made of Him with what is thinkable or sensible" (*H.B.* I, 63). Accordingly, "it is not in the habit of prophets[1] to encourage people to speculate on God's Essence (*dhāt*) and Attributes (*ṣifāt*) ... The Holy Prophet only urged them to mediate on the blessings and mighty power of God" (*H.B.* I, 86).

Although the Essence of God actually surpasses human comprehension (*idrāk*), it is nevertheless possible to obtain some cognition (*ʿirfān*) of God's Names through one's *dhawq* (intuitive anticipation), as Shāh Walī Allāh can confirm from personal experience. Then, by means of a manifestation of the divine Essence, which *idrāk* does not come into, an insight is gained into this mystery. "This is a completely bewildering experience", so the Delhi divine testifies (*Khizāna*). The exceptional benefit of being enabled to obtain acquaintance of every divine Name is usually granted to *ʿārifs* (ṣūfī gnostics) (*Tafh.* I, 15).

If the apprehension of the divine Names, which are in contradistinction to the Attributes *mujarrad* (separate from bodily material), unfortunately appears to be a privilege of a few knowledgeable persons[2], knowledge of the divine Attributes, being notifications (*ikhbārāt*[3]) concerning God's transcendence, holiness, glory and majesty in a language comprehensible to the common man, lies within the compass of our ordinary reason (*ʿaql*) (*Tafh.* I, 48). "God gave the *ʿaql* some scope for using its own discretion in order to enable it to understand His Attributes" (*A.Q.* 64 f.). It is just as well too, because acquaintance with God's Attributes is certainly required "in order that people may work towards

---

[1] What is more, "the Holy Prophet forbade us to speculate on God's Essence, saying: 'do not speculate on the Creator' ... In this prohibition discussions on the Attributes are included, i.e. trying to explain the very nature of God's Attributes, the way He is characterized by them, such as whether His hearing and seeing are different from or identical to His knowledge, whether His speech is mental (*nafsī*) or otherwise, and so on" (*Taʾwīl*, 92 f.).

[2] Similarly, it is on the soul (*rūḥ*) of a favoured *ʿārif* (gnostic)—and not of somebody else—that blessings of the divine Names descend (*Fuyūḍ*, 37th Vision).

[3] *Cf.* R. Landau, *The Philosophy of Ibn ʿArabī*, London 1959, 30: "A Divine Attribute ... is a Divine Name manifested in the external world".

their own perfection (*kamāl*) as best they can'' (*H.B.* I, 63). Attributes that evoke an image of divine Lordship (*rubūbiyya*) are especially useful for the correction of human souls (*F.K.* 13). The particular utility of Attributes which describe certain aspects of God's Essence (as, for instance, living, self-subsistent, knowing) lies in their being indicative of God's planning (*tadbīr*) and the way in which the 'best order of the world' (*niẓām al-khayr*) is guarded (*Lamḥa* 49).

For an analysis of divine Attributes the following restrictive points should be taken into consideration:

a) the Attributes of God should be viewed in the light of their final development (i.e. as being realized in the empiric world where they fulfil needs according to the moment), and not as they subsist in their 'source' (*mabdaʾ*) (i.e. in respect of the Essence of God);

b) terms should be chosen for those Attributes indicating the way in which a king makes the city-state subservient, since God has rendered the whole of creation submissive;

c) use might be made of anthropomorphisms (*tashbīhāt*), but on condition that they are not taken in their literal sense; they should merely bear the meaning they have in common parlance like, for instance, holding out one's hand (towards someone) which means (in idiomatic language) 'liberality'; and on condition that these anthropomorphisms offer not the least occasion for the idea that animal slurs are cast on God's Essence ... Hence one can say (of God) that He sees and hears, but not that He tastes and touches[4];

d) for Attributes one should make what use one can of comprehensive terms as, for instance, 'All-provider', 'Fashioner of all existing things' (*H.B.* I, 63);

e) one should never term God the Universal (*kullī*): the Eternal has no parts or whole. ''The ascription of wholeness to Him is a pleonasm. The whole is included in His Oneness ... He has separated Himself from the universal that is imperfectly formed and awaiting (His grace for its survival), and from the particular that is restricted and limited. The Universal and Particular are, in fact, categories used by reason and products of our perception'' (*B.B.* 101 f.);

f) one should reject the use of human attributes as confirmation of similar divine Attributes that might give occasion to false doctrines like ascribing to God a son, weeping, impatience, etc. (*F.K.* 13).

The Delhi divine had to discharge a double responsibility: functioning as an enlightener of the general public and initiating a spiritual élite into the mysteries of the Unseen World. Obviously, for each group a different

[4] Because the latter two verbs have sexual connotations in Arabic.

approach to theological subjects was required. "If common people are allowed to speculate freely on God, they will go astray and lead others astray" (*H.B.* I, 64). So in the *Ḥujjat Allāh al-bāligha* Shāh Walī Allāh preserves reticence with regard to the Names and Attributes of God. In his esoteric work *al-Khayr al-kathīr*, however, he takes the liberty of dwelling at length on the Names of God after having strongly dissuaded those who are not naturally gifted with a bright intellect from reading the book.

The most fundamental aspect of the divine Names, so we are told, is the circular course they take: they depart from God's Essence, appear in the creation, and finally return to their starting-point. Shāh Walī Allāh, therefore, distinguishes between 'Starting Names' (*asmāʾ badʾiyya*) and 'Returning Names' (*asmāʾ ʿawdiyya*)[5]. Both categories of Names manifest themselves on different ontological levels (*marātib*). The lower Starting Names descend, the more they become 'unfolded', i.e. appear as particular configurations of the Names on the preceding level[6], whereas the higher Returning Names rise, the more they 'condense' the configurations of the Names at a previous stage. The Starting Names are found on the following six levels:

1. the level of *Huwa* (He). It points out that He is He, i.e. irrespective of any kind of relation[7]. The only Name applicable to this stage is Allāh[8];
2. the level of Oneness (*waḥdat*)[9]. It concerns the Names *al-ḥayy* (the Living), *al-qayyum* (the Self-subsistent), *al-ḥaqq* (the Real) and *al-nūr* (the Light). They define the level of the divine Essence and are a configuration (*hayʾa*) of it;
3. the level of Unity (*aḥadiyya*)[10]. To this belong the Names *al-majīd* (the Glorious), *al-ʿaẓīm* (the Magnificent), *al-ʿalī* (the High), *al-kabīr* (the

[5] "In as far as God encompasses the universe from the point of view of its coming (into existence) as well as from the point of view of its passing nature" (*Khizāna* 2).

[6] In consequence of which they "become like a polished mirror for the realities above them" (*Khizạna* 2).

[7] *Cf.* R. A. Nicholson, *Studies in Islamic Mysticism*, Delhi 1976, 96: "*Huwiyya* indicates the absence (*ghaybūbiyya*) of the attributes of the Essence (from manifestation and perception)".

[8] *Cf.* H. S. Nyberg, *Kleinere Schriften des Ibn al-ʿArabī*, Leiden 1919, 57: "dieser (i.e. the Name Allāh) ist mit dem Benannten identisch ... Alle übrigen Namen dagegen weisen auf das Wesen hin *nebst* einer hinzudenkenden zum Wesen hinzutretenden Idee (*maʿnā*)".

[9] The qualification of these levels with terms as *waḥdat*, *aḥadiyya*, *wāḥidiyya* and *ḥubb* are clarifying additions given by Shāh Walī Allāh's grandson Ismāʿīl Shahīd in *ʿAbaqāt*, Karachi 1960, 70. "*Waḥdat*", so the latter explains, "is an equivalent of *taqarrur* (divine self-identification) and *ʿilm ḥuḍūrī* (obtaining consciousness of His Self)".

[10] Ismāʿīl Shahīd sets forth that this is actually the level of the *shuʾūn*, while the Names of the following level refer to the hidden aspect of being (*wujūd bāṭin*) (*ʿAbaqāt* 66).

Great) and *al-jalīl* (the Majestic). They establish to some extent God's grandeur (*kibriyāʾ*) which is His cloak[11];

4. the level of relative Unity i.e. Unity-in-diversity (*wāḥidiyya*). To it refer the Names *al-ghanī* (the Independent) *al-wāsiʿ* (the Omnipresent), *al-qawī* (the Strong), *dhuʾl-ṭawl* (the All-sufficient) and *al-mubārak* (the Beneficent). They unfold various features of God's grandeur;
5. the level of the Names of divine Love (*ḥubb*). This implies the Names *al-raḥmān* (the Benefactor), *al-raḥīm* (the Compassionate), *al-barr* (the Most Good), and *al-qādir* (the Omnipotent);
6. the level of Names referring to the ever-renewing divine Will. To this level belong the particular Names al-*bārī* (the Creator), *al-rāziq* (the Sustainer), *al-musawwir* (the Bestower of forms), *al-hādī* (the Guide), *al-ghaffār* (the Indulgent), *al-qābiḍ* (the Restrainer), *al-bāsiṭ* (The Dispenser), *al-khāfiḍ* (the Abaser of the proud), *al-rāfiʿ* (the Exalter of the believer), *al-mubdi'* (the Inventor), *al-muʿīd* (the Resuscitator) *al-muḥyī* (the Creator of life) and *al-mumīt* (the Creator of death).

Three strata (*ṭabaqāt*) are apportioned to the Returning Names, to wit:

1. To be reckoned to the first stratum are the Names *al-ʿālim* (the Knowing), *al-sāmiʿ* (the Hearing), *al-khābir* (the Sagacious), *al-baṣīr* (the Seer) and *al-shahīd* (the Witness). These Names are in fact so distant from God Himself that in the perspective of these Names He looks upon the world as being separate from Himself;
2. to the second stratum belong the Names *al-malik* (the King), *al-dāʾim* (the Everlasting), *al-mutaʿālī* (the Exalted), *al-ṣabūr* (the Very Patient), *al-shakūr* (the Rewarder), *al-ḥalīm* (the Forbearing), *al-rashīd* (the Leader), *al-ḥamīd* (the Praiseworthy), *al-bāqī* (the Eternal), *al-wāḥid* (the One) and *al-wārith* (the Inheritor). All that had been incongruous in the preceding stratum is now made free from impurity;
3. the Names of the third stratum are *al-quddūs* (the Holy), *al-salām* (the Giver of peace), *al-ṣamad* (the Impenetrable) and *al-subbūḥ* (the All-perfect). After this stratum there is only the Essence of God, into which these Names are ultimately absorbed.

In rounding off his exposition on the Starting and Returning Names Shāh Walī Allāh summons the reader "to behave in a humble and beseeching way towards the Returning Names. They have a right to this, for the world is on the verge of passing away" (*Khizāna* 2)

Later on, as we can gather from a passage in the *Tafhīmāt-i ilāhiyya*, the Delhi autor had to apologize for having overstepped the bounds by

[11] According to a statement ascribed to Mohammed (see Muslim, *al-Birr waʾl-Ṣila* 136).

advancing the theories given above concerning all sorts of distinctions that one may make between the divine Names (*Tafh.* I, 49). So it is no great surprise to find in this later work a more traditional view of God's nature. Now he speaks of five categories of divine potencies, again proceeding from a lower to increasingly higher levels. They are:

1. the *iḍāfiyyāt*[12]. They produce effects and actions and are of all five categories the closest to created beings;
2. the *ṣifāt thubūtiyya*[13]. These have no special relation with the phenomenal world. To them belong the Attributes of life, hearing, sight and so on;
3. the *shuʾūnāt* ('potential' Attributes) which are folded up in the (divine) knowledge. Before Attributes are actualized they are *shuʾūn* (*in posse*). Hence they form the basis of the two categories mentioned above;
4. the 'privative' (*salbī*)[14] Attributes. They are 'twin brothers' (*ṣinw*) and 'uterine brothers' (*shaqīq*) of the *shuʾunāt* but one step nearer to the *mafhūmāt*, i.e. the level of mental images that is contrasted with the level of external realities;
5. the Attribute of divine self-objectification (*taḥaqquq*). This is the mother of all Attributes and the centre which unites all levels that reflect the divine revelatory radiances (*tajalliyyāt*) (*Tafh.* II, 40 f.).

In the controversy about the primacy of 'substances' or 'adjectives' for the characterization of God's Essence, Shāh Walī Allāh appears more disposed to accept the Muʿtazilite point of view[15] than the notions prevalent among the Ashʿarites[16]. In a discussion of this delicate affair he states that to his mind the standpoint of the *ḥukamāʾ rabbāniyyūn* ('theosophists') is the most plausible, since they maintain that the Knowing precedes knowledge and the Hearer the power of hearing. "What fits best with their view is to say that in one respect the Name (*ism*) is iden-

---

[12] *Cf. B.B.* 105: They are called *ifāḍa* (outflowing manifestations), since they refer to traces of divine Names operating in the phenomenal world ... Hence one speaks of the Fashioner, the Provider of daily provision, the Feeder, and so on.

[13] 'Latent' Attributes; since they are from all eternity implied in God's Essence, they are said to be in a state of latency.

[14] I.e. Attributes denied to the Godhead, and by which His transcendency is accentuated. Thus He is defined as having no beginning, no end and no similarity to anything created.

[15] (According to the Muʿtazilites the) "atributes may be expressed by adjectives but not by finite verbs ... for the verb demands an object and suggests the existence of something besides God" (A.S. Tritton, *Muslim Theology*, London 1947, 84 f.).

[16] *Cf.* M. Allard, *Le Problème des Attributs divins*, Beyrouth 1965, 197 f.: "On pourrait résumer ainsi l'argumentation (dans al-Ashʿarī's *Risāla kataba bihā ilā ahl al-thaghr bi-bāb al-abwāb*): ... les participes ne sont pas les premiers; les substantifs leurs sont logiquement antérieurs puisque c'est d'eux qu'ils sont dérivés ... Dieu doit être décrit comme doué de vie, de savoir, de pouvoir, etc."

tical with the 'object named' (*musammā*), and in another respect the *ism* is neither identical with nor different from the *musammā*''[17] (*Khizāna* 1).

Although the Delhi scholar holds the idea that God's being in the possession of knowledge, wisdom etc. is of secondary value, he nevertheless thinks it relevant to discuss 'substance-Attributes' separately.

The 'substance-Attributes' to which Shāh Walī Allāh turns his attention are:

a) the divine Knowledge (*ʿilm*). ''God's *ʿilm*'', so he argues, ''is not like our knowledge. By means of our sensory perceptions we examine a thing in respect of its non-essential properties (*ʿawāriḍ*). Thus we find it under the aspect by which we look at it. By means of sacred knowledge, however, the Self-existent examines a thing in respect of its intrinsic constituents and origin of its existence. In short, His knowledge comprises all that can be known, the universals as well as the particulars'' (*B.B.* 102).

''God knows Himself by *al-ʿilm al-ḥuḍūrī* (i.e. gaining consciousness of His Self). Included in that self-knowledge is Knowledge of all His Attributes and all things created by Him ... And that is because the Attributes of the Self-existent are like the necessary concomitants (*lawāzim*) of quiddity (*māhiyya*) and the things created by Him are like the necessary concomitants of existence (*wujūd*)'' (*Tafh.* II, 43; *Khizāna* 9).

So it is possible to distinguish two aspects in divine Knowledge, *t.w.*:

1. one of a general (*ijmālī*) character. This has to do with an inner urge (*iqtiḍāʾ*) towards self-objectification (*taḥaqquq*) and self-identification (*taqarrur*);
2. one that is concerned with details (*tafṣīlī*). This has to do with location in being (*ījād*) and the unfolding into modes of being (*shuʾūn*). And when the Self-existent assumes certain *shuʾūn*, these *shuʾūn* are differentiated into different contingent beings. In this way, Knowledge is gained concerning contingent beings (*mumkināt*) which are found in the phenomenal world (*Tafh.* II, 50 f. and *Fuyūḍ*, 45th Vision).

b) The divine will (*irāda*). ''The divine Will arose from God's desire to effect unity in the world-order (*niẓām*) which emanated before the Will itself. And that is because there ought to be coherence between

[17] *Cf.* T. Izutsu, *The Key Philosophical Concepts in Sufism and Taoism*, Tokyo 1966, 92 f.: ''The reason why (according to the theosophist Ibn ʿArabī) they are one and the same thing is that all the Divine Names, in so far as they invariably refer to the Absolute, are nothing but the 'object named' (i.e. the Essence of the Absolute) itself ... These Names (however) ... can also be considered by themselves, independent of the Essence to which they refer ... Considered in this way, each Name has its own 'reality' (*ḥaqīqa*) by which it is distinguished from the rest of the Names. In this respect, a Name is different from the 'object named'.''

successive modes of existence (*ḥāla*). If unity of the world-order is pursued, then such a coherent sequence of modes of existence must terminate in a Will that is an actualized outflow (*ifāḍa*). Thus the world-order will certainly have its point of union in this Will'' (*Khizāna* 2).

A specific feature of this Will is its constant production of new manifestations (*tajaddud*). Daily events rely on it. Accordingly, there is a continuous outflow of *al-asmāʾ al-ḥāditha*[18] from the breasts of the archangels who are responsible for the management of creation. In a tradition reported by Abū Hurayra we read: ''When a matter is decided by God in heaven, the angels flap their wings in submission to His word. The sound produced by their flapping resembles the sound produced by a chain (pulled) over smooth stones. When fright is removed from their breasts, they say (to each other): 'What (on earth) has your Lord said?' The reply is given to them: '(He has spoken) the truth. He is the Lofty, the Great One''' (Bu. *Tawḥīd* 32). ''By this tradition is meant'', so Shāh Walī Allāh explains, ''that in the same way as prophets ask for knowledge from the source of the revealed law (*sharʿ*), the archangels ask for (detailed) decrees (*qaḍāʾ*) from the source of predestination (*qadar*)'' (*Khizāna* 2).

Although an educationist by nature, the Delhi divine has no desire to reduce the significance of predestination: ''Predestination is a truth imprinted on everybody, on people of the East as well as of the West, whatever their religion or creed, since it forms part of their ordinary knowledge ... There are people who dare contradict predestination and are of the opinion that (in that way) the requital of good and evil for man is tantamount to injustice. For our part, we maintain that man's deeds and the requital resulting from them are all included in God's predestination'' (*B.B.* 111 f.). But this faith in God's absolute predetermining power does not produce a depressive effect on the believer, for it implies that thus ''man becomes alive to the universal planning (*tadbīr*) by which the universe is kept going'' (*H.B.* I, 65). The prophetic saying: ''In His hand is the balance which may go down or rise'' (Bu. *Tafsīr sūrat al-Hūd*, ch. II) ''points at a divine planning which is based on choosing what is most expedient. If contrary processes are at work in something that is

---

[18] I.e. 'temporal' Names by which a proper course of events is brought about. Names are powers embodying Attributes in action (*cf.* A. E. Affifi, *The Mystical Philosophy of Muhyid Din Ibnul Arabi*, 33: ''He, i.e. Ibn ʿArabī, regards the divine Names as line of force''). They appear as radiances (*tajalliyyāt*) of the divine Essence on the evolutionary stage of the *aʿyān thābita*, i.e. the ontological models after which the phenomenal objects are produced in the empirical dimension of time and space (T. Izutsu, *The Concept and Reality of Existence*, Tokyo 1971, 52).

about to occur, then God takes decisive action in order to carry through an equitable adjustment (*ʿadl*)" (*H.B.* I, 167). Yet, Shāh Walī Allāh certainly allows some flexibility in the application of this dogma by his distinction of two kinds of predetermination (*taqdīr*):

1. an irreversible one (*mubram*); and
2. one left in suspense (*muʿallaq*).

The first one refers to the predisposition (*istiʿdād*) of the universe as a whole. Its predeterminate course brooks no delay.

The second one refers to the predisposition of the human individual. Accordingly, for him free prayer (*duʿāʾ*) and prudence (*tadbīr*) are of use. As to the latter possibility: for every embryo the age it will reach is preordained, provided spurs from outside figure in it. Such spurs include pious goodness and behaving with consideration; they lengthen one's life (*Khizāna* 3). In respect of the *duʿāʾ*, Shāh Walī Allāh points to a possible efficacy: "sometimes it is disclosed to a mystic (*ʿārif*) that there is an enforceable decree (*qaḍāʾ*) attached to something (indicating) that it will happen in such a manner and that the predetermination (*qadar*) of it is irreversible. Then this mystic puts up a fervent *duʿāʾ*[19] to God, and persists in praying until the moment that the decree will be changed and something different happens in accordance with the craving (*himma*) (of the mystic). In my opinion this may occur in two ways:

1. there are higher causes due to which something must necessarily take place ... Subsequently, it will be disclosed to a mystic that in its very form and shape the decree is a fixed necessity (*iqtiḍāʾ*) and through the peep-hole of this necessity he will notice that it springs from God's irreversible predetermination. However, he does not see it so clearly: only to the best of his knowledge it seems to be part of God's irreversible predetermination. Then, suddenly, his craving becomes one of the determinants of the descending decree. In consequence of the collision of this craving with the other determinants, divine Wisdom restrains the effect of one determinant and expands the effect of another ....
2. In the World of Prefiguration, God creates a predetermined occurrence from elements of a spiritual nature before. He creates it (in the phenomenal world) from physical elements.

[19] *Cf. Tafh.* II, 108: "The *duʿāʾ* is one of the causes of coming-to-be and disintegration (*kawn wa l-fasad*). A subtle point in this connection is that the *duʿāʾ* is merely of use to what is not yet fixed by an irrevocable divine decree. So ... the *duʿāʾ* of Abraham on behalf of his father and the *duʿāʾ* of Noah on behalf of his son were not answered, since the disbelief of the two (for whom intercession was made) was already predestined".

Next He sends this prefigured shape down to the earth[20] where it is to be united with its concrete form ... Then the *duʿāʾ* (of a mystic) tries to amend the form of what is about to happen. In this way, a shape created in the World of Prefiguration may be blotted out ... Such a blotting out is what called 'the checking of a decree' in the statement of the Prophet: 'Only by a *duʿāʾ* may a decree be checked' (Tirmidhī, *Qadar* 6)'' (*Fuyūḍ*, 38th Vision).

c) the divine Speech (*kalām*). It is the basis of the revealed law (*sharʿ*) and the origin of prophetic revelation (*waḥy*) (*Khizāna* 2). *Waḥy* creates an idea or an understanding of an idea in man when he concentrates his mind upon the Unseen World (*B.B.* 108). The Speech of God is ''one of the planes (*ḥaḍarāt*) of the (divine) Will, if viewed as an outpouring (*ifāḍa*) into the region of (divine) consciousness (*ʿilm*). In the outpouring of Speech a sacred form is given to every actuality (*fiʿliyya*) ... (Further,) God speaks only by means of the outpour of meaningful concepts (*ṣuwar ʿunwāniyya*) which sound in the ears of the hearers like real speech and audible letters. This is also what is meant by Shaykh Abuʾl-Ḥasan al-Ashʿarī when he says that the Speech of God is a 'mental Speech' (*kalām nafsī*) (i.e. speech without words)''[21] (*Khizāna* 2).

A noteworthy quality inherent in divine Names is their capacity to produce an accordant effect on human individuals. This happens in the process styled as *taḥaqquq bi-asmāʾi ʾllāhi* (self-realization by means of God's Names): ''By *taḥaqquq* is to be understood'', so Shāh Walī Allāh sets forth, ''that the worshipper passes away from himself and gains permanent subsistence with God ... Subsequently, Names of God enter into him; Thus powers of those Names are manifested in his soul (*nafs*) and the universe is submitted to him in accordance with those powers'' (*Tafh.* I, 230).

There are different sorts of *taḥaqquq*. ''These include:

a) *taḥaqquq* by being acted upon and by receiving an effect, as e.g. (happens with Names like) *al-mughnī* (the Enricher from whom creatures derive their perfection), *al-muʿṭī* (He who gives), *al-munʿim* (the Benefactor) ... Then a ṣūfī gnostic (*ʿārif*) often turns the face of the

[20] I.e. the destiny (*bakht*) of human souls is fixed in accordance with the actual form the universe had on the day of their coming into existence (*A.Q.* 161). ''At the time the Universal Soul happens to become (individuated as) a human soul (*nafs nāṭiqa*)—and that is mostly the case when the *rūḥ* is blown into the embryo—, the form of the cosmos (*shakhṣ akbar*) is concealed in that *nafs nāṭiqa* ... If in that hour in the phenomenal world the sun or Venus happen to be at its height, a point opposite to that sun or that Venus is given in a humal soul'' (*Saṭ.* 18).

[21] And not *kalām lafẓī* (pronounced speech).

mirror of his heart towards these Names by reciting them or by concentrating on their realities as they are substantiated[22] in the World of Prefiguration ... Accordingly, it is implied by divine wisdom that at that time God makes earthly processes (*asbāb*) subservient so that he then becomes somebody who is provided with material or spiritual possessions ...

b) *taḥaqquq* by assimilation[23], as for instance (happens with Names like) *al-ʿazīz* (the Powerful), *al-ʿaẓīm* (the Inaccessible) ... Then a ṣūfī gnostic often recites such Names or concentrates on their realities as they are substantiated in the World of Prefiguration ..., so that on account of that a connecting link (*raqīqa*), deposited in him in an opposite correlation to this (particular) Name, is eventually activated'' (*Tafh.* I, 232).

From actual experience Shāh Walī Allāh knew of this second kind of *taḥaqquq*: ''as one of the favours of God to me once a *taḥaqquq* occurred to me with the Name *al-ḥayy* (the Living), that is to say that I witnessed its reality substantiated in the *ḥaẓīra al-quds* ... Consequently, first I settled down in the forces of the celestial spheres and chose from them the force ascribed to the planet Venus[24]. Thereupon Venus came down to me while it took that force as companion. Subsequently Venus added a bit to the duration of the age as foreordained to me in the womb of my mother'' (*Tafh.* I, 233).

## B. *Cosmology*

Relating the twenty-seventh Vision, with which he was favoured during his stay in al-Ḥaramayn, Shāh Walī Allāh records: While I was waiting for an explanation of the tradition in which the Messenger of God was asked (by Abū Razīn ʿUqaylī): Where was our Lord before He created the creation? and replied: He was in the dark mist (*ʿamāʾ*)[25], the following mystery was disclosed to me: A glaring light spread over the whole area of the remote world of *ʿamāʾ*, i.e. the realm of primary matter (*hayūlā*). This light[26], he explains, is the first manifestation and *locum tenens* of the divine Essence, and the jet d'eau of the powers of the Self-existent. It is anterior to time and has a firm grip on not-being (*ʿadam*), in which continuously renewing issues of the divine Will (*al-irādāt al-*

[22] In the shape of luminous bodies (*cf.* *H.*X.).
[23] By means of a fine link (*raqīqa*) which establishes a connection between God's favourite and a divine Name of cosmic force.
[24] Surnamed *al-Saʿd al-aṣghar* (the small lucky star).
[25] See Tirmidhī, *Tafsīr al-Qurʾān*, sūra 11, 1.
[26] I.e. the *tajallī aʿẓam*.

*mutajaddida*) (required by the changing conditions of time[27]), are manifested[28]. When afterwards I kept reflecting on this, I suddenly realized that for the divine Essence it is necessary[29] to reveal the potentialities (*istiʿdādāt*) it envelops. Subsequently, at that place on the ontological level of the Self-existent (*wujūb*) the potentialities of the divine Essence appeared in a mental (*ʿaqlī*)[30] shape. Through this appearance, three kinds of entities were formed at that level:

a) the latent realities (*aʿyān*) of the things contingent (*mumkināt*);

b) the modes of being (*shuʾūn*) the Self-existent reveals in every genre of existence (*nashʾa*);

c) the epiphanic forms (*barzāt*) of the (universal) *tadallī*[31] of the Self-existent.

More details of *al-ʿamāʾ* are supplied in another passage of Shāh Walī Allāh's writings. There he sets forth: "*ʿAmāʾ* is the disposition (*ṭabīʿa*) existent in primary matter, i.e. the capacity to assume all incorporeal and corporeal forms. It subsists in al-Raḥmūt[32] (realm of al-Raḥmān) ... It is like a mirror for the Raḥmūt in which the latter shows Its beauty. By virtue of this quality it is called 'primary matter'; but in view of its being substained by al-Raḥmūt it is named 'body'[33] (*jism*); and in respect of its being the origin of (all) phenomena (*āthār*) it is called Universal Nature (*ṭabīʿa kulliyya*)" (*Tafh.* I, 158).

"When within the *ṭabīʿa kulliyya* the elements and celestial spheres came into existence, ... the individual pecularities, requirements and

---

[27] "Specific of time is the change from one state of being (*ḥāl*) into another, either through cyclic movement or by change of qualities and the like" (*Tafh.* I, 159), whereas "a thing is in eternity (*azal*) when it is not undergoing change" (*Tafh.* I, 112).

[28] For "existing in act (*al-wāqiʿ*) is the emergence of *ʿadam* from its 'purity' (*ṣarāfa*, i.e. potentiality)" (*Tafh.* II, 38).

[29] *Cf.* also *Tafh.* II, 226: "The reason why things are put into a state of latent existence (*thubūt*) before they come into actual existence (*wujūd khārijī*) is to be traced to an inner necessity (*iqtiḍāʾ*) of the divine Essence to (emanate) a universe in the realm of the (divine) mind (*ʿaql*)".

[30] *ʿAql* is actually the stage at which God becomes conscious of Himself and in which for example His potentialities may come to His mind.

[31] I.e. the Logos (see *Haw.* 3).

[32] "al-Raḥmūt is the foundation of the actualization (*wujūd*) of the phenomenal world (*nāsūt*). Through the combination of al-Raḥmūt and *al-nāsūt* are generated:

a) the celestial spheres and elements: next

b) that which forms a plane tangent to the World of Spiritual Entities, i.e. the *malakūt*;

c) that which forms a plane tangent to the bodily world, i.e. the three kingdoms of nature (*mawālīd*)" (*Tafh.* I, 157).

"al-Raḥmūt is in the first instance connected with the Throne (on which al-Raḥmān dwells), and through the Throne it is connected with the remaining parts of the *ʿamāʾ* ... From the Throne matters descend related to revelation (*waḥy*), creation and so on" (*Tafh.* I, 160).

[33] Inasmuch as 'body' is a product of the incorporeal, in casu al-Raḥmūt.

powers of the *ṭabīʿa kulliyya* were imparted to those elements and celestial spheres. When thereafter the minerals, plants, animals and man came into existence, the nature of the elements and celestial spheres was transferred into them. In consequence of this, the former (minerals, plants, animals and man[34]) function merely as mirrors in order to reflect the individual peculiarities and movements of the celestial spheres[35] as well as the nature of the elements'' (*Fuyūḍ*, 11th Vision; *Taʾwīl* 104 f.).

In addition to individual characteristics of celestial spheres (*aflāk*), earthly events and psychic experiences can mirror peculiarities of planets (*sayyārāt*). Thus, for instance, ''inspirations (*ilhāmāt*) from above descending upon perfect people may take with them (the influence emanating from) a special planet. In the Gospels a story is told with the following substance: once there were sellers of doves in the temple. This enraged God. He made the soul of Jesus an instrument for the transmission of His wrath. With a lot of trouble Jesus succeeded in obtaining an colt, which he mounted. The disciples accompanied him as a body-guard. In this way they reached the temple. He rebuked the dove-sellers severely. And the fear of God fell upon them. They stopped their activities, and some of them took to flight. This was one of the most important events announced by former prophets: by talking of a rider on an ass[36] they had hinted at this manifestation of Jesus. When this occurred there was the planet Jupiter standing in the sign of the Pisces hidden in the physical constitution (*mizāj*) of Jesus'' (*Haw.* 36). And if parts of Saturn become operative, the ties of an advanced mystic (*ʿārif*) with this world and the next are severed while the colour of the 'Love of the divine Essence' spreads over him. When he is connected with parts of the sun, his capacity to subject and rule increases. He becomes a *tadallī* (means to faciliate people's spiritual evolution) of God on behalf of His creation, and an elixir for someone who seeks a cure as soon as contact is established with the cosmic reality that correlates with Saturn standing in conjunction with Jupiter (*Fuyūḍ*, 26th Vision).

Minerals, plants, animals and man as such are actually material forms characterized by specific effects. Thus, the mineral form is in its structure peculiar to the four earthly elements and in its essence to the celestial

---

[34] Owing to this course of affairs man possesses in his inmost heart knowledge of his Lord, for initially the Ultimate Reality has been disclosed to the *ṭabīʿa kulliyya* and its parts.

[35] ''Research of the spheres has established that they are made of the (four) elements, ... and that they are in the possession of a spirit (*rūḥ*) and of knowledge'' (*Khizāna* 3). ''They possess knowledge about the *jabarūt* and *lāhūt*'' (*Tafh.* I, 180). Besides, they possess lofty *nufūs* (souls). ''When Raḥmān decrees something, its shape is printed upon those souls''. (*Tafh.* I, 167).

[36] See Zechariah IX, 9.

spheres; the vegetable form is peculiar to all that which grows from water and earth and to what is produced by itself and by its own kind; the animal form possesses the faculties of sensation, movement, will and acting on a decision of the heart; the human form is marked by the use of speech, having the potential to evolve socially and economically, doing most excellent works, and coming to resemble fully the Origin of all existence. The most noble form, however, is the *nafs nāṭiqa* (rational soul) constituting personal identity: by it Zayd is Zayd and ʿAmr ʿAmr (*B.B.* 16)[37].

Apart from the tradition of Abū Razīn ʿUqaylī's interview of the Prophet, the Koranic imagery of al-Raḥmān Himself sitting upon the Throne (*Qurʾān* X, 3) is used by the Delhi divine in elucidation of what is to be understood by cosmogony. al-Raḥmān (the Merciful One) is God's most significant Name, the 'seal' of the Names, and encompasses all realities which arise from non-being (*al-ʿadam al-baḥt*) (*B.B.* 13). "It is the channel through which, by means of eternal theophanies, the divine Essence proceeds to endow the universe with stability and actualization from eternity to all eternity" (*Tafh.* I, 51). So divine Providence (*ʿināya*) and planning descend from al-Raḥmān (*B.B.*, 25). It is to be designated as *al-ṣādir al-awwal*, the first outpouring entity. In reality, it is the result of *subūgh*, a being overfilled with the divine Essence which, like an overflowing[38] fountain, 'vomits' foam (*Tafh.* II, 39). By the *falāsifa* (i.e. the Peripatetics) it is called *al-ʿaql al-faʿʿāl* (Active Intelligence) (*Tafh.* I, 46). Yet Shāh Walī Allāh deems the assertion that the existence of the universe rests upon the *ʿaql faʿʿāl* a not very felicitous way of putting it. In general, he is not in favour of assuming the existence of intelligences as being a kind of creative and regulating powers that govern the universe, as is affirmed by the same philosophers. "To be frank", so he declares, "there is no need of an intermediary, consisting of intelligent substances in which the forms of things would be stamped. Such substances are merely hypothetic matters, existing only in the mind of the person who has invented them" (*Fuyūḍ*, 45th Vision). The Delhi

---

[37] It is obvious that Shāh Walī Allāh's cosmological theories show many points of similarity to the well-known teachings of the *Ikhwān al-ṣafāʾ* about evolutionary developments in the universe which elicited from Fr. Dieterici the statement: "auch die Araber trieben Darwinismus" (*Die Abhandlungen der Ichwān esSafā in Auswahl*, Leipzig 1883, XIII). Still there are some differences. Thus, according to the latter, the final issue of the evolutional process is not the human individual but the class of angels (*Rasāʾil*, Bombay 1305/1887, II, 119).

[38] Elsewhere Shāh Walī Allāh explains in this connection why he prefers to use similes of streaming water or spreading light: "The relationship of the universe to its Maker (*bāriʾ*) is not like that of a building to its architect, who constructs something of cement and then takes his hands off it ... No, it is to be compared to (the relation of) the sun (to the earth) which illumines the earth with its light without ceasing (*Lamḥa* 21).

scholar also rejects the view of the 'common man' who is under the erroneous belief that the world subsists on its own and is established as an isolated item. On the contrary, the world is to be regarded as an exemplary representation (*timthāl*) projected from the side of the Self-existent and an illustration of His perfection (*Khizāna* 1). God created it like He is Himself, i.e. purely good[39]. Thus it enables Him to display His beauty (*Tafh.* I, 158). Hence, when the Creator fell in love with Himself, the creation appeared[40]; the object of love was His own beauty (*Tafh.* I, 10 f.).

al-Raḥmān sat Himself upon the Throne which is upon the waters. The Throne contains all the forms (*Tafh.* I, 46). Water is the source of matter, inasmuch as a typical trait of its capability is to take on any form (*Khizāna* 3). The first thing al-Raḥmān decreed by means of the Throne[41] in respect of water was the creation of the elements and the celestial spheres (*aflāk*). Thus the spheres can now function as corporeal forms (*aṣnām*) of an agens (*fāʿil*) and the elements as corporeal forms of a recipient (*qābil*) (*Tafh.* I, 46). Subsequently, matter (*mādda*) which is fit for a mineral form cohered from the elements and condensed[42]. With matter in this receptive condition a mineral form flowed over it from al-Raḥmān. Accordingly, due to its material constitution, an inorganic nature (*mizāj*) arose. In the course of time the mineral form became receptive in its turn[43]. In this receptive state, it turned to al-Raḥmān

39 At the same time it is equally justifiable to hold that the world is different from God. Then this otherness (*ghayriyya*) refers to the finiteness of the world and its being determined in its essence (*Khizāna* 1).

40 Ismāʿīl Shahīd points out that love of the Almighty functions as a medium between *wujūd bāṭin* and *wujūd ẓāhir* (*ʿAbaqāt* 64 f.).

41 Being the source of universal planning (*tadbīr*).

42 For a more detailed description of this initial stage of evolution see *H.B.* I, 33: "When the elements (*sc.* water, earth, fire and air) are (still) small and mix in various large or small amounts, they become compounds, either of two elements like steam, vapour, smoke, mud, whirling dust, live coals, a scorching wind, a flame; or of three elements like loam, watermoss; or of four elements. These compounds possess characteristics acquired from the components they are composed of. They are named 'that which is generated by the atmosphere' (*kāʾināt al-jaww*). Thus, first the mineral form appears".

43 I.e. "in the minerals which are of the most superior quality and the nearest to substances separate from bodily material (*mujarradāt*)" (*A.Q.* 114). The same view is held by the Ikhwān al-ṣafāʾ who claim that "the first stage of the plants is connected with the last stage of the mineral substances, and the last stage of the former is connected with the first stage of the animals" (*Rasāʾil* II, 119). It is also the opinion of Ibn Khaldūn. See *Muqaddima* I, 173: "The last stage of minerals is connected with the first stage of plants, such as herbs and seedless plants" (tr. F. Rosenthal). "It was", so Shāh Walī Allāh records from personal experience, "as if I saw that the form of a mango tree—the prototype of a tree, possessing the most perfect structure of all trees—, when it humbled itself to God and made petition (for a further evolution), was split so that it was prepared for the effusion of the form of a wild animal as for instance a wild ox" (*Tafh.* II, 200).

holding out its hand like a beggar[44]. Thereupon, given that the receptive condition is inherent, being acquired and based on that form, the more complex vegetable form flowed over it from al-Raḥmān. Thus, due to its material constitution, life of the lowest type emerged. After that, according to the same procedure, al-Raḥmān poured down the animal and human forms upon condition of the availability of pre-existing forms[45]. A fully developed type of life became the result of the outpouring of the animal form, while resemblance to the Origin was the fortunate issue of the flow of the human form from al-Raḥmān (*B.B.* 18 f.).

The sequence followed in this evolutionary process, is that of increasing specialization: the human form, for instance, is actually a particularization of the animal form (*Lamḥa* 22). In the reverse process of disintegration, however, the more rudimentary a form, the sooner it becomes extinct. Accordingly, the vegetative form disintegrates as soon as the body decays. Then the animal form still exists and the latter only disintegrates until man on his journey returns to the stage of the Archetype of Man (*B.B.* 21).

After having gained its full expansion, the evolutionary process itself, has not yet attained its final point. In contrast to the Western theory of evolution, Shāh Walī Allāh maintains that the universe with everything it contains passes through a cycle: everything emanated from al-Raḥmān and is ultimately absorbed again into al-Raḥmān. In reference to this conception of the universe he relates the legend of the phoenix: "I have come to know that in the most remote parts of India there is a bird with a long neck ..., called *qaqnūs*. It ... continually changes from one state into another till it becomes very young. At that time love stirs up from within its heart, and it begins to sing. Then it so is moved by the song that it is filled with ecstacy, and is itself at last consumed by fire ... Then the spring rain falls upon its ashes and lo! another bird arises. This process goes on *ad infinitum*" (*Lamḥa* 17). Well then, in exactly the same way there is a continuous succession of *dawrāt*, cycles of worlds which alter-

---

[44] "and extending fervent supplications to Him (for a further evolution)" (*Tafh.* I, 122). This is also the view of Ibn ʿArabī of whom the following statement is quoted by al-Sharānī in his *al-Yawāqīt waʾl-jawāhir*, Cairo 1306/1889, p. 56: "God did not bring the world into existence being Himself in need of it, but because the things in their state of contingent not-yet-being (*al-ʿadam al-imkānī*) begged for existence ... And when because of their basic need of God they begged God for their existence, God accepted their prayer". In the 45th Vision Shāh Walī Allāh received in al-Ḥaramayn, he is taught that the various *nashʾāt* (evolutionary stages) do not automatically evolve out of each other. It is rather, owing to the driving force of integral (*basīṭ*) divine Love that, for instance, the *nashʾa* of man emerges after the *nashʾa* of animals. Again a point of view shared by Ibn ʿArabī (*cf.* T. Izutsu, *The Key Philosophical Concepts*, 130).

[45] For every higher grade of evolution needs to include, besides its own characteristics within itself, the characteristics of the preceding one(s).

nately arise and decline. Hence, as soon as the appearance of the most refined form, i.e. the human individual, has been effected, a process of decay sets in: "all existing things fade away, so that only the Throne and the water remain. Next, the wind of annihilation (*ʿadam*) begins to whip these two also, on account of which they too become non-existent ... Thus the realm of being becomes waste and empty. Then, after a period of complete emptiness, al-Raḥmān makes a fresh start and displays His activity of outpouring (*jūd*)[46]. Consequently, He recreates heaven and earth as they had been before[47]. The calculation of such a cycle (*dawra*) is not given to man, and not even to a heavenly agent" (*Tafh*. I, 46 f.).

A crucial question for the Delhi scholar is the issue whether the universe emanated from God all at once or in a gradual process. In principle, he deems the first assumption preferable by far: "one should not think that the Ultimate Being is actually necessary as the termination of a chain of emanations of contingent being, such that if an emanation were to emanate from Ultimate Being and another emanation were to emanate from that emanation, then the first emanation would become an intermediate link between the last emanation and the Ultimate Being. It is not like that! Rather, when a contingent being dons the dress of its existence or emanates, or whatever it may be, its existence is directly derived from the Ultimate Being without any intermediate link" (*B.B.* 10). And in another passage Shāh Walī Allāh plainly states: everything that could possibly emanate from the divine Essence emanated all at once[48] (*dafʿatan wāḥidatan*). This simultaneous emanation, however, has come about in a state of latent transcendental determination (*thubūtī*)[49] and not in a state of conceptual being (*mawjūd*), in the same way as in a seed of a tree the tree itself is latently determined before it is actually found in

---

[46] For this meaning of *jūd* see L. Gardet's definition of it: "le flux émené nécessairement de la libéralité de l'Etre premier" (*La Pensée religieuse d'Avicenne*, Paris 1951, 53). "The working of the *jūd* of God's Essence", so Shāh Walī Allāh himself explains, "can be compared with a torrential stream which flows on the earth's surface unto the moment that it strikes a dam. Then the water pervades the cracks in the dam ... and the pores of the earth and the air. In this way the water produces a very extensive effect" (*Taʾwīl* 80 f.).

[47] Though the notion of cyclical time is not unknown in Islam, it is more likely that in this case Shāh Walī Allāh is influenced by Indian thought with its primordial rhythm of "creation-destruction-creation" *ad infinitum* (M. Eliade in *Eranos Yearbooks*, New York 1957, vol. 3, p. 179), since he does not speak of cycles of manifestation alternating with cycles of concealment as propounded by Ismāʿīlī cosmologists.

[48] I.e. without omitting anything, without the need to alter or to change afterwards (see P. E. Walker, 'Ismaili Vocabulary of Creation', *Studia Islamica* XL, 82). For the same Shāh Walī Allāh makes use of a Qurʾānic expression. And in *Khizāna* 1, we read: "The first emanation (*al-ṣādir al-awwal*) 'leaves nothing behind, small or great but it has numbered it' (*Qurʾān* XVIII, 49)".

[49] Fixed in and by the divine Mind (*ʿaql*).

the world outside. The difference between *thubūt* and *wujūd*, so he argues, can also be apprehended by analogy with somebody who silently counts in his head: once he has the concept of 'one', he potentially has the concept of any number[50]; this grows out of the nature of numbers before they reach the state of conceptual being[51] (*mawjūd*) (*Tafh.* I, 107 f.). He cannot, even if he would like to do so, make an even number into an uneven; or if he would like to change the serial order[52], it is just as impossible for him (*Maktūb*, 15).

Similarly, the universe passes through three ontological levels. Necessitated by God, it is first at the level of the divine Mind, i.e. the stage of *thubūt* (transcendental determination). Next, it enters an intermediate level, called *al-nafs al-kulliyya*, i.e. the stage of *wujūd*[53] (*Tafh.* I, 192). Arriving at this level, it can neither be described as properly 'eternal' because it has left the divine Mind, nor can it be regarded as 'created' because it has not yet acquired existence in fact. Consequently, at this stage of development it has to be qualified as 'eternal in time' and 'transient' (as it is to be particularized) (*Tafh.* I, 165). After that, the universe descends into the realm of matter (*nāsūt*) and becomes manifested in bodily forms (*Tafh.* I, 159).

Among the various designations Shāh Walī Allāh uses for the universe, the most characteristic one is certainly *al-shakhṣ al-akbar* (the Most Large Person). The idea that the universe is to be regarded as an enlarged version of man is far from original. At most the term itself[54] could be called original. Muslim philosophers and mystics prefer to qualify the universe as *al-insān al-kabīr* (the Large Man). The witnessed and verifiable

---

[50] A view that may be derived from Ibn ʿArabī's thought: "According to Ibn ʿArabī, "one" is not a number at all; it is the principle and 'birth-place' of all numbers from "two" onwards, but it is not itself a number" (T. Izutsu, *The Key Philosophical Concepts in Sufism and Taoism*, Tokyo 1966, 190).

[51] I.e. becomes conceivable for the human mind. Cf. also *Maktūb*, 14: "The intrinsic determinant of (for instance) a sword's ... being what it is (*maʿnā*) is the connection of a non-existent (*maʿdūm*) with *wujūd* (conceptual being) so that it becomes conceivable and denotable".

[52] In connection with the prophetic tradition: "God's veil is a light. If He withdraws it, the splendour of His countenance would consume His creation as far as His sight reaches" (Mu., *Imān* 294), the Delhi scholar discusses the serial order of successive emanations starting from *al-wujūd al-munbasiṭ* (ever-spreading being), the origin of all other beings: "According to me the first of the veils is *wujūd* that spreads over the realities of the cosmos (*mawjūdāt*), and that is a light. Next comes the water, in which He formed the creation. Then the bearers of the Throne and the souls (*nufūs*) of the celestial spheres ... Then the *mala aʿlā* and *ḥaẓīra al-quds*. And in addition also the elements and forms which anteceded humanity. These are the basic veils" (*Tafh.* I, 64).

[53] I.e. the stage of *wujūd* that is spreading (*munbasiṭ*) over the structural forms of the cosmos (*Maktūb*, 16).

[54] It might be that our author chose the unusual term of 'person' in order to be 'justified' to attribute multiple personal traits to the universe.

realities, so the Delhi scholar explains, are actually 'one Person' (*shakhṣ*), emanating from one Principle, having one system which sustains the Person just as the system of growth and nutrition sustains a single plant (*B.B.* 12). The *ʿālam al-mithāl* functions as the intellectual centre (*khayāl*) of this 'Most Large Person'; the *ḥaẓīra al-quds* serves as the faculty by which It is enabled to participate in the knowledge of Its Lord (*Fuyūḍ*, 4th Vision); on Its mind falls the *tajallī aʿẓam* (i.e. reflections of Its creator) so that divine notions enter Its brain; the *nafs kulliyya*[55], the animating principle of the sensible world, stands for Its *rūḥ* (vital principle) while the celestial spheres, elements and three kingdoms of nature represents the organs of Its body (*cf.* note 3 of Ghulām Muṣṭafā al-Qāsimī at *Saṭ.* 1 and the note on pp. 41 f. of *Aṭyab al-nagham*). In addition to this, It also possesses a *nasama* which flows in the organs of Its body, i.e. the elements and the spheres (*Tafh.* I, 46). This *nasama* has of three faculties:

1. an intellectual one (*ʿilmiyya*) which attends to the issue of planning (*tadbīr*);
2. a physiological one (*ṭabʿiyya*): there is no body which can dispense with heat or cold;
3. a stimulative one (*qalbiyya*) that impels the other two faculties to action (*Tafh.* I, 53).

Characteristic of the 'one Person' is that It is always changing in Its state of being (*aḥwāl*), while It is in a continuous motion. That is due to the fact that the forms individualize the (universal) Physical Form (*al-ṣūra al-jismiyya*)[56] (i.e. the former, being mere accidental temporary modalities, occasion a continuous change and motion) (*Lamḥa* 16).

Whatever is found in this 'one Person' has the capacity (*ḥukm*) to afford phenomenal existence (*wujūd*) to the latent realities (*aʿyān*) of things (*Lamḥa* 11). For that reason the *shakhṣ akbar* consists of the following two component parts:

1. a receptive one styled as 'Breath of the Merciful' (*nafas Raḥmānī*), i.e. the substratum (*mawḍūʿ*) and place of abode (*maḥall*)[57];
2. an active one qualified as 'universal Soul' (*nafs kulliyya*)[58], i.e. the

---

[55] *Cf.* also *A.Q.* 27: "It regulates all that the universe comprises. Everything, from the empyrean to the earth, is within its grasp".

[56] "It is the source of effects shared by all physical entities" (*B.B.* 15).

[57] The same more poetically expressed: "*Nafas Raḥmānī* est la substance dans laquelle s'épanouissent les formes de l'être matériel et de l'être spirituel" (H. Corbin, *L'imagination créatrice dans le soufisme d'Ibn ʿArabī*, Paris 1958, 220).

[58] Later on the Delhi scholar apparently prefers to identify the *nafs kulliyya* with a kind of First Principle, adducing *Qurʾān* VI, 98 ("It is He Who produced you from one *nafs*") as a testimony (*Tafh.* I, 226). "The first entity", so he argues at that time, "which emanates through origination (*ibdāʿ*) from the divine Essence (*awwal al-awāʾil*) is the *nafs kulliyya*. It possesses two attributes, to wit:

a) a capacity of actualization—on that account the Throne appeared—;

determiner (*muḥaṣṣil*) and the one taking an abode (*ḥāll*) (*Saṭ*. 2). Or to put it more explicitly way: when the *nafs kulliyya* descends into the *nafas Raḥmānī*, it operates as a hidden formative power that endows things with their specific and individual traits (*Tafh*. I, 119). In the flow of the *nafs kulliyya* things receive their cosmic, elemental, vegetative, animal and human forms as equipment (*isti*ᶜ*dād*)[59]. Thus this *nafs* supplies matter with subsistence (*qayyūmiyya*) (*Lamḥa* 22).

The 'Most Large Person' may exhibit remarkable human features, but Its likeness with the Divine is even more striking. Does not a tradition beloved by the ṣūfīs mention that man is created in the image of al-Raḥmān (Bu. *Isti*ʾ*dhan* 1)? So Shāh Walī Allāh thinks himself justified to advance the daring statement: "with God the universe has a cohesion (*ittiṣāl*) of a rather esoteric (*wijdānī*) nature so that in a state of rapture one may judge that the universe be identical with God"[60] (*Tafh*. II, 42).

The third method Shāh Walī Allāh pursues in expounding cosmological processes is the classification in the categories of *ibdā*ᶜ, *khalq*, *tadbīr* and *tadallī*. As in the case of the evolutionary process of elemental, vegetative, animal and human forms, these four phases are direct continuations of each other; each of them builds on the previous one: "*Ibdā*ᶜ has *khalq* as complement, while *tadbīr* is the completion of *khalq*" (*Lamḥa* 35).

"*Ibdā*ᶜ (process of origination) is the emanation (*ifāḍa*) of a thing from the pure (*baḥt*, i.e. transcendental) not-yet-being (ᶜ*adam*) into (transcendental)[61] actuality (*taḥaqquq*) ... Ultimately, *ibdā*ᶜ rests on the (divine) necessity (*luzūm*)[62] (of expressing Himself) and on constraint

---

b) a capacity of potentiality, through of which water, the primary matter of the spheres and elements, appeared. By means of the Throne the forms of the spheres and elements appeared in the water" (*Tafh*. I, 109 f.).

[59] *Cf*. also *Ta*ʾ*wīl* 80: "When God created the *nafs kulliyya*, He created it with a longing for various states of being (*aḥwāl*): to become at one time a man, at another a horse, again at another time a stone, *etc*.".

[60] *Cf*. also *H*. XIII: "When a mystic (*sālik*) observes the universe (*nafs kulliyya*) in a state of ecstasy, he discerns the unity (extant in the phenomena). And when he watches the divine Essence (*dhāt*) in a state of ecstasy, the universe disappears from sight altogether. When, however, in this state he gives one glance at both of them, he will find them two separate entities".

[61] Transcendental, for *taḥaqquq* is an issue of *wujūd* that is still *a se* (*fī nafsihī*), and not *wujūd ab alio* (*bi ghayrihi*) which is a derivation (*intizā*ᶜ) from the *wujūd* which is *a se* (*Tafh*. II, 50).

[62] L. Gardet, when discussing similar ideas of the *falāsifa*, says: "nécessaire, non de soi, mais dans l'ordre de l'existence. Activement prise en Dieu, la création est un flux émanateur, *fayḍ*, un 'jaillissement', *inbijās*" (*Dieu et la destinée de l'homme*, Paris 1967, 35). For the thought of the Delhi divine it is significant that not until the order (*niẓām*) of things has already been emanated is divine volition (*irāda*) of any importance. And even then its function is rather limited: "The (divine) volition arose from God's desire to effect unity in the order which was emanated before" (*Khizāna* 2).

(*ḍarūra*)'' (*Lamḥa* 34). The first thing called into existence by *ibdāᶜ* is the *ḥaqīqa Muḥammadiyya* (Reality of Mohammed), from which all other *ḥaqāʾiq* are ramified (*Fuyūḍ*, 45th Vision); it is the stretched cord by which the whole Universe is firmly tied (*Fuyūḍ*, 16th Vision). Other *mabdaᶜāt* are the Pen (*qalam*), the Tablet[63] (*lawḥ*), the Throne and the primordial water (*Tafh*. I, 55). All of them are to be considered as holy, pure entities (*anniyyāt*)[64].

*Khalq* (creating), the final issue of *ibdāᶜ* (*Taʾwīl* 63), ''denotes a free disposal over matter and form so that many forms materialize'' (*Lamḥa* 35). As a result the celestial spheres, elements and all species endowed with their characteristics and effects came into being (*Lamḥa* 34). Forms, however, are phenomena defiled by the limitations[65] of time, place and condition (*B.B.* 17 f.). Consequently, *khalq* consists of a gushing forth (*inbijās*) of impure[66] entities (*anniyyāt*) that belong to the transient world (*Khizāna* 1).

Next, as a sequel to *khalq* there is the divine creational activity of *tadbīr* (planning). It works effective changes in the world so that what happens in it is in conformity with universal expediency. Accordingly, for instance, God causes rain to come down from a cloud to produce vegetables for men and cattle (*H.B.* I, 12).

*Tadallī* ('drawing near' after being high; said of Gabriel when he approached Mohammed: *Qurʾān* LIII, 8) the complement to divine creativity is God's coming to the rescue when universe or mankind have run into trouble. It results in disclosure of knowledge, right guidance and perfection of souls[67], and presupposes the establishment of patterns by which people's welfare is insured (*Lamḥa* 34). *Tadallī* is based on matters accepted unreservedly (*musallamāt*) and easily verifiable (*mashhūrāt*). Hence the Messenger of God was not an angel, the Holy Book not written in a language foreign to the Arabs, and the Kaᶜba not built of light (*Fuyūḍ*, 4th Vision).

---

[63] The Pen is a typification of (divine) operative (*fiᶜlī*) knowledge and the Tablet a typification of (divine) receptive (*infiᶜālī*) knowledge (*Khizāna* 3).

[64] *Cf*, also *H*. XIII where it is stated that *ibdāᶜ* is tantamount to the divine Essence's producing effects (*taʾthīr*) on the *nafs kulliyya* which is free from all impurities.

[65] Time and space are typical marks of transcience. They are created by the will of God and will cease to be with the end of the world. Still, ''by His brilliant wisdom God had tied them together, through of which the world has obtained stability'' (*Khizāna* 3). In other words, Shāh Walī Allāh develops the concept of a space-time continuum through which the universe is preserved from chaos.

[66] *Khalq* is in fact an inferior activity which is not properly applicable to the divine Essence (*Tafh*. I, 47).

[67] See also *Fuyūḍ*, 3rd Vision: ''*Tadallī* is actually a means of facilitating men's spiritual evolution''.

The *tadallī* itself is of many periods (*adwār*) and phases (*aṭwār*). In the beginning of our history events were determined by the powers of celestial spheres and elements only. The inaugurator of this epoch is said to have been Hermes Trismegistos, the Greek name applied to the Egyptian god Thot. To him are ascribed works on astrology, medicine, alchemy and magic. It is in this age that knowledge of the movements of the stars and of their pecularities welled up in the heart of Idrīs. In this era the *milla* of the *majūs*, the 'fire-worshippers', came into existence, and the sciences pursued were astrology, medical art, and black magic (*siḥr*). Thus some time elapsed.

Then, angels started gradually to appear. By the time that they had become numerous and their knowledge and their will-power had developed harmoniously, the laws of astrology became more and more inoperative. From now on the 'restraint' and 'letting loose' of causal processes were the business of the *mala aʿlā*. Accordingly, Abraham. the inaugurator and exponent of this second epoch, awakened to the insight that it would be better to divert from the stars and to concentrate henceforward upon the *mala aʿlā*. In the course of time men fell into the tight grip of the angels, and they became devoted to God by *ṣalāt*, ritual purity, belief in the angels, heavenly books and messengers of God. The Kaʿba came to function as a substitute of a former temple of the sun and the moon. In this age the *milla* of the *ḥanīfs* (followers of the original monotheistic religion) was established.

Due to the steady adherence of the will-power of succeeding prophets to the angels, the influence and moment of the *ʿālam al-mithāl* where the *mala aʿlā* reside, increased continuously. When at last Mohammed appeared on earth, the sky, heaven, and earth were completely filled with the *mithālī* form of the *tadallī*. Consequently, if at present somebody wishes to acquire *ʿilm*, *maʿrifa*, or a divine perfection, this *mithālī* form, i.e. the spiritual shape of Mohammed[68], is for him the most appropriate source (*Lamḥa* 50; *Tafh*. I, 66 ff.).

### C. *Waḥdat al-wujūd* (Unity of Being)

If one finds it difficult to analyze and reconstruct Shāh Walī Allāh's ontological ideas, it is indeed comforting to discover that the Delhi divine himself appears to have difficulty in defining *wujūd* (being). The nature of *wujūd*, so he notes, has no contrary (*ḍidd*[69]), and since we know things

[68] Obviously a hint at the opportunity offered to Shāh Walī Allāh and other divines to make inquiries of the Prophet if he appeared in visions.

[69] Here reference is made to Universal Beings which, unlike particulars, cannot be individuated through an opposite.

only by their opposite, it is difficult to know exactly what *wujūd* is (*Lamḥa* 9).

On the other hand, Shāh Walī Allāh repeatedly declares that *wujūd* is a matter (*amr*), a quality (*ṣifa*) that can be conceptualized (*intizāʿī*). Thus "*wujūd* becomes conceivable by what is in front of it, (i.e.) if the realities which are the source of many different effects (*āthār*) are surveyed in a comprehensive way ... Such an observation forms in the mind a concept (*ṣūra*) of that which is called *wujūd*" (*Lamḥa* 2). In short, *wujūd* is an entity (*maʿnā*) confirmable in the quiddities (*māhiyyāt*, in the opinion of Shāh Walī Allāh the equivalent of particular beings) (*Lamḥa* 8[70]).

In the controversial matter of whether existence (*wujūd*) and essence (*māhiyya*) are identical or distinct, the Delhi scholar notes a fundamental difference in this respect between God and the contingents (*mumkināt*). "The *wujūd* of the Self-existent", so he states, "is identical with His Essence (*dhāt*), in the sense that His Essence is *wujūd*, and *wujūd* is *māhiyya*" (*Tafh*. I, 168[71]). On the level of conceptual analysis, however, *wujūd* in contingent beings is distinct from *māhiyya*, so that "in our minds we can conceive of the quiddity of something and at the same time doubt its actual existence, and we can think of *wujūd* independently of *māhiyya*" (*Lamḥa* 8).

The *māhiyyāt* (quiddities), he maintains, are actually embedded (*maḥfūf*) in two categories of *wujūd*:

1. integral *wujūd* which spreads (*munbasiṭ*)[72] over the structural forms of the things existent (*mawjūdāt*) in the external world[73], and precedes

---

[70] Ibn Sīnā shares this view. Cf. P. Morewedge in *JOAS* XCII (1972), 432: "(For Ibn Sīnā) existence is embedded in the notion of actual entities which are instances of essences".

[71] I.e. "Dieu n'est pas définissable" (L. Gardet, *La pensée religieuse d'Avicenne*, Paris 1951, 57). According to Shāh Walī Allāh, the same applies to the *ṣādir awwal* (First Emanation) which is an *ʿunwān* (accordant qualification) of the Self-existent; Its *māhiyya* is also identical with Its *wujūd* (*Tafh*. II, 29).

[72] In the following (i.e. *Maktūb* 12f.) Shāh Walī Allāh offers an exposition of *wujūd munbasiṭ* with some more details. There we read: "This is something which subsists by itself and lends support to other existents. It is, however, indeterminate in itself without particular recognizable effects. On lower levels, however, this *wujūd* has specifications (*tanazzulāt*) which are conceivable as well as observable. Accordingly, these *tanazzulāt* become determinable by special recognizable effects.

The first level of its self-unfolding (*tanazzul*) (i.e. as *wujūd* that is non-conditioned, *lā bi-sharṭ al-shayʾ*, above the distinction between 'existence' and 'non-existence') is the *tajallī bi-nafsihi* (self-revelation). As such it is in a state of having become a universal *shaʾn* (mode of being) (of the divine Essence). The next *tanazzul* of it (i.e. as *wujūd* that is negatively conditioned, *bi-sharṭ la shayʾ*) renders that universal state explicit in cognitive forms (sc. as *aʿyān thābita*), not yet in concrete shapes. Lastly, there its *tanazzul* (as *wujūd* that is determinate, *bi-sharṭ al-shayʾ*) in shapes actually existent *in concreto*".

[73] "The relationship of *al-wujūd al-munbasiṭ* to existing objects (*ashyāʾ*) is similar to the relationship of writing with ink to written letters" (*Lamḥa* 7). (The same simile issued by

the particular beings (i.e. the *māhiyyāt*). Particular beings are, in fact, devolutions and particularizations of integral *wujūd* as such[74]. They are the outcome of a link—of which the existence is known but the essence unknown—between the ever-spreading *wujūd* and the quiddities, which are the modes of being (*shuʾūn*) and cognitive forms (*ṣūra ʿilmiyya*, i.e. the *aʿyān thābita*) of this ever spreading *wujūd*;

2. *wujūd* which is 'derived' (*muntazaʿ*) from a comprehensive examination of the particular beings (*Maktūb*, 11 f.). For, "in front of it there is something which can be ascertained empirically (*fiʾl-wāqiʿi*)" (*Khizāna* 1). In other words, being of this kind is not an invention of one's fancy (*wahm*) (*Lamḥa* 9), and not without actuality; rather it is a reality since it is derived from many realities (*B.B.* 10; *Lamḥa* 2).

According to Shāh Walī Allāh, the term *wujūd* can be taken in two senses:

1. *wujūd* that is *a se* (*fī nafsihi*). It is the outcome of *taḥaqquq* (divine self-objectivation), *taqarrur* (divine self-determination) and being a 'thing' (*shay*)[75].
2. *wujūd* that is *ab alio* (*bi-ghayrihi*). This is *wujūd* 'by way of a trope only' (*bi-ṭarīq al-majāz*), i.e. seeming. At first sight one may think that *māhiyyāt* endowed with both substance and accidents are embodiments of *wujūd* that is *a se*. But on further consideration it appears that contingent being has no share in *wujūd* that is *a se*. It is, in fact, nonexistent by itself and of no account (*bāṭil*)[76]. Only by an *ʿilla* (effective cause)—and that is location in being (*ījād*)—can it become a phenomenon (*Tafh.* II, 50).

Further, in *wujūd* different levels (*marātib*) can be distinguished possessing, so to speak, various degrees of light quantum, in the same manner as the intensity of sunlight differs from that of moonlight[77]. The highest proportion of *wujūd* is found in the powers of *Lāhūt* (the world of divine

---

Ḥaydar Āmulī, d. after 1385. See Ḥaydar Āmulī, *Jāmiʿ al-Asrār wa-Manbaʿ al-Anwār*, ed. H. Corbin and O. Yahya, Téhéran/Paris 1969, 107). Other terms, used by Shāh Walī Allāh for the same, are Raḥmān, *nafas Raḥmānī*, *ṣādir awwal* and *nafs kulliyya*.

[74] *Cf.* Also *H.* XIII: Integral *wujūd* manifests itself in *māhiyyāt* which to this end serve as moulds (*qawālib*).

[75] *Cf.* T. Izutsu, *The Key Philosophical Concepts in Sufism and Taoism* (Tokyo 1966), 113: "by the very first manifestation of its own Mercy, the absolutely Unknown-Unknowable turns into a 'thing' (*shayʾ*). And to say that the Absolute obtains 'thingness', i.e. establishes as a 'thing', is to say that the process of self-objectivation has already begun to take place within the Absolute itself. This is the appearance of self-consciousness on the part of the Absolute".

[76] *Cf.* also *Khizāna* 2: "in short, everything except God is unauthentic (*zūr*) and of no account (*bāṭil*)".

[77] Mullā Ṣadrā (d. 1641) shares this view. See S. H. Nasr, 'Ṣadr al-dīn Shīrāzī (Mullā Ṣadrā)' in *A History of Muslim Philosophy*, ed. M. M. Sharif, 1966, II, 943: "Being ... is a single reality but with gradations and degrees of intensity".

Essence). Next comes the level of *al-wujūd al-ʿaqlī*[78] (mental being), i.e. the stage at which God becomes conscious of Himself. Then follows the level of the *wujūd munbasiṭ*, i.e. the First Emanation. Linked with it is the level of the spheres and elements. Then we have the level of the three kingdoms of nature (*mawālīd*) whose relation to the spheres and elements is like the relation between boils, swellings, fever and headache and a human being (*Lamḥa* 24).

The most comprehensive notion of being in Shāh Walī Allāh's thought, however, is what he designates as *al-wujūd al-aqṣā* (Ultimate Being) which 'encompasses the units of being from above and from below and enfolds them from every side, offering no possibility of escape from Its encompassment'' (*B.B.* 10). This definition of Ultimate Being suggests, to say the least, that our author is not insusceptible to the attractiveness of the concept of *waḥdat al-wujūd* which is an idea that goes back to Ibn ʿArabī. When the Delhi scholar himself is asked to define *tawḥīd wujūdī* (unification of being), i.e. *tawḥīd* as believed in by the advocates of *waḥdat al-wujūd*, he says: ''In the world outside and in actuality[79] there is nothing save one single Reality which is Being in the sense of *taḥaqquq* (divine self-objectivation) and *taqarrur* (divine self-determination), and not in the sense of an attribute proceeding from an agent (*maṣdarī*). All things existing subsist by It as accidents of it. These things existing are to Being as waves to the sea ... The essence of their existence is their encompassment by the reality of Being'' (*Tafh.* I, 186 f.).

At the very outset of his divinely appointed mission, however, Shāh Walī Allāh still seems to be somewhat reserved towards the aspirations of the *waḥdat al-wujūd* adherents, as we may gather from the first vision vouchsafed him during his stay in Ḥaramayn. In this vision he is invited to act as an arbitrator between two rivalling parties, to wit people who practise *dhikr* and *yād-dāsht*[80] and advocates of *waḥdat al-wujūd*. In his verdict he accuses both parties of one-sidedness and incompleteness. The major shortcoming of the latter is their deficiency in the praise and love of God and their insufficient awareness of God's transcendence. Consequently, their souls do not become refined and they do not attain to their potential perfection (*Fuyūḍ*, 1st Vision).

---

[78] This stage is also indicated by the mystic philosophers as *bāṭin al-wujūd* (hidden part of being) in contrast to the next stage of the *wujūd munbasiṭ* that is characterized in this case as *ẓāhir al-wujūd* (manifest part of being). The *bāṭin al-wujūd* is the very beauty of God, and He produced the *ẓāhir al-wujūd* as a mirror by which the beauty of His face could be revealed in its full glory (Ismāʿīl Shahīd, *ʿAbaqāt*, Karachi 1960, 54 and 57).

[79] *Cf*, also *Khizāna* 2: ''Every actuality (*fiʿliyya*) has its source of manifestation in the Self-existent''.

[80] Characterized by Shāh Walī Allāh himself as the endeavour to have the World of Omnipotence reflected in one's mind (*wahm*) (*Fuyūḍ* 8th Vision).

But later, when the Delhi divine is asked for a second time to pronounce an opinion on a controversy involving the ontological ideas of Ibn ʿArabī, he appears to have come very close to the latter's view. This is no subject for surprise, because since the days of his sojourn in Ḥaramayn he had increasingly adopted in his own expositions the vocabulary of the mystic philosopher whom he held in high esteem[81].

It was a letter from an acquaintance, named Effendī Ismāʿīl ibn ʿAbd Allāh al-Rūmī al-Madanī[82], which induced Shāh Walī Allāh to reconsider his position with regard to the doctrine of *waḥdat al-wujūd* and to compose a monograph on it[83]. The question put to Shāh Walī Allāh in the letter was whether it would be possible to bring about a reconciliation between the concept of *waḥdat al-wujūd* entertained by Ibn ʿArabī and his followers and the doctrine of *waḥdat al-shuhūd* (unity-in-experience)[84] held by Aḥmad al-Sirhindī (1564-1624).

First of all, so the Delhi divine argues, one should recognize that *waḥdat al-wujūd* and *waḥdat al-shuhūd* are terms referring to two different matters, i.e.:

1. discussions about mystic experiences. One might say that this ṣūfī has attained the stage (*maqām*) of *waḥdat al-wujūd* and another one the stage of *waḥdat al-shuhūd*. In the first case one is immersed in the all-encompassing Reality, in which the world is absorbed, in such a manner that all ethical values, on which knowledge of good and evil is based and of which revelation and reason offer an explicit explanation, may be hidden from one's observation. Mystics sometimes remain at this stage till God rescues them from it. *Waḥdat al-shuhūd* implies that lover and Beloved are joined together but their individuality is preserved[85]. Thus one comes to realize that, viewed from one angle objects form a unit and seen from another angle a multiplicity of distinct matters. This stage is higher and more perfect than the former;
2. ontological questions. Here metaphysicians reflect on the relation between the transient (*ḥadīth*) and the eternal (*qadīm*). According to

---

[81] *Cf. Tafh.* II, 33 and *Khizāna* 4: "Ibn ʿArabī's range of (spiritual) knowledge (*ʿilm*) is more vast than that of any of God's protégés (*walī*)".

[82] Nothing more is known of him than his name. Was it, perhaps, a Turkish connection from the days Shāh Walī Allāh stayed in Medina?

[83] Known under different titles: *al-maktūb al-Madanī*; *Risāla fī taḥqīq waḥdat al-wujūd*.

[84] Arising "from the mystic's devotional concentration on God wherein everything but God goes out of his consciousness" (Fazlur Rahman, *Selected Letters of Shaikh Aḥmad Sirhindī*, Karachi 1968, 44).

[85] *Cf.* Aḥmad Sirhindī, *Maktūbāt* II, letter 99: "*Fanāʾ* and *baqāʾ* are 'experiential' (*shuhūdī*), not ontological (*wujūdī*), for the servant is not annihilated and not unified with God: the servant remains a servant and God God".

one group of them it is like this: The world consists of accidents which have their point of meeting in one and the same substance, in the same way as waxen models of a man, a horse and an ass possess wax as common substance. The nature of wax remains the same under all conditions. Although the models would have no existence at all if wax were not added to them, they are named after the form they assume. According to another group of metaphysicians the whole point is, that the world consists of a series of reflections from divine Names and Attributes reflected in mirrors of antipodal nonentities, like power being the antipodal entity of weakness. Thus when the light of divine Power is reflected in the mirror of weakness, the latter becomes contingent power. The same applies to the other Attributes. This is also the situation with *wujūd*. The theory of the first group is called *waḥdat al-wujūd* and that of the second *waḥdat al-shuhūd*" (*Maktūb* 5 ff.).

In Shāh Walī Allāh's opinion, a reconciliation between both theories is quite possible. For this purpose, however, three points ought to be taken into consideration:

a) one should realize that presumed disagreements between the ontological views of Sirhindī and Ibn ʿArabī are, in essence, a question of terminology[86]; they do not touch the very root of the matter. "It is a mistake to surmise that Ibn ʿArabī and his followers, or even the philosophers, would not endorse the teaching of *waḥdat al-shuhūd* as explained above. That is because, when all tropes and metaphors which impede proper understanding are cleared away, the sum of this teaching is that the contingent realities are insignificant and deficient[87], and that the Reality of the Self-existent is most perfect and significant, so that the conclusion is obvious that the contingent realities are non-entities and that the different forms of the things existing are (as is taught by Ibn ʿArabī c.s.) manifested in the Reality of the Self-existent[88] (*Maktūb* 7);

---

[86] Curiously enough Sirhindī himself declares that the controversy between the *ʿulamāʾ* and the advocates of *waḥdat al-wujūd* is reducible to a different choice of words (*lafẓ*) (*Maktūbāt*, II, letter 44).

[87] *Cf.* Sirhindī, *Maktūbāt* III, letter 58: "(The reality of the world) is like a rotating flame produced when one end of a stick of wood is put into a fire and catches fire. The other end of the stick is held tightly and quickly moved round in a circle. Then a circle of fire appears. Now, if such an appearance could somehow be perpetuated and made to exist by itself, then the *wujūd* of the world is like such a circle."

[88] It is noteworthy that present-day Western scholars are inclined to agree with the Delhi scholar and also like to minimize the discrepancies between Ibn ʿArabī's thought and Sirhindī's own interpretation of *waḥdat al-shuhūd* (see H. Landolt in *Der Islam*, 50, 19, 1, S. 61 and Y. Friedmann, *Shaykh Aḥmad Sirhindī*, Montreal 1971, 62-68), whereas Shāh Walī Allāh's compatriots generally maintain that he is in the wrong and that it is impossible to reconcile the ontological views of both mystics (see B. A. Faruqi, *Ḥaḍrat-i Mujaddid kā naẓarī-i tawḥīd*, Lahore 1967, passim).

b) it is absolutely necessary that Ibn ᶜArabī's views are properly interpreted. Unfortunately, in the course of time confusion and misunderstanding of what is implied by *waḥdat al-wujūd* arose on account of incorrect conclusions and erroneous explanations of Ibn ᶜArabī's teachings. Not only Sirhindī but also faithful followers of the Shaykh al-akbar are guilty of such misconstructions. Among the latter Ṣadr al-Dīn al-Qūnawī (d. 1263) and ᶜAbd al-Raḥmān Jāmī (d. 1492) are particularly to be blamed. From the *waḥdat al-wujūd* concept they drew the mistaken inference that *al-wujūd al-munbasiṭ* is identical with the Self-existent[89]. In this way they fail to differentiate between the One who manifests Himself (*ẓāhir*) and that which is manifested (*maẓhar*) (*Khizāna* 2).

As for the occasional divergences from Ibn ᶜArabī's views which Shāh Walī Allāh notices in Sirhindī's dissertations, he first of all reproaches his harbinger[90] for citing at times Ibn ᶜArabī incorrectly in his *Maktūbāt* (*Tafh.* II, 34). Further, Shāh Walī Allāh prefers to use Ibn ᶜArabī's technical terms of Ibn ᶜArabī instead of those coined by Sirhindī, as he regards it of little use to study technical terms (*iṣṭilāḥ*) devised by the latter (*Tafh.* I, 169). It is certainly significant that as soon as Sirhindī avows to differ from Ibn ᶜArabī, the Delhi scholar immediately shows partiality for the latter: "there are statements of the Shaykh al-mujaddid (i.e. Sirhindī) in which he says he has found assertions of Ibn ᶜArabī and his followers which he considers to run counter to his own intuition". When declaring this, so he concludes, Sirhindī commits a 'lapse in thought' (*falta ᶜilmiyya*) due to his *ijtihād* (use of individual reasoning). Yet, so he adds in extenuation, it is ex-

[89] In *Maktūb* 19ff. Shāh Walī Allāh discusses this point in more detail, stating: In his commentary on ᶜIrāqī's *Lamaᶜāt*, known as *Ashiᶜᶜāt-i lamaᶜāt*, Jāmī wrongly claims that the difference between the divine Essence and the First Emanation ( = *wujūd munbasiṭ*) is fictitious (*iᶜtibārī*). If this contention of his were correct, it would imply *inter alia*, so Shāh Walī Allāh infers, that equally contingent realities would be merely *iᶜtibārāt*, i.e. entities that exist subjectively in the mind having no corresponding objective reality. If this were true, there would be no difference between the individual items and their species except a mentally posited (*iᶜtibārī*) difference which disappears as soon as man's mental activity (*iᶜtibār*) ceases working. This is a false reasoning. The diversity of contingent realities is a fact: fire *is* different from water and man from a horse despite ever-spreading *wujūd*'s including them all. When the ṣūfīs hold that the universe is identical with the divine (*al-ḥaqq*), they merely want to indicate that the universe in its totality obtains its identity in the unfolding *wujūd*, and that this *wujūd* subsists by the Primal Reality (God). By no means do they want to deny the diversity of contingent realities.

[90] I.e. an *irhāṣ* (lit. "laying the foundation"). In the same manner as Shuᶜayb was hailed an *irhāṣ* of Moses and Zachariah an *irhāṣ* of Jesus (*Tafh.* II, 72), Sirhindī happened to be an *irhāṣ* of Shāh Walī Allāh. First, the light of prophethood gleamed faintly over the former; after that, lights of the Invisible World effulged over the latter (*Tafh.* II, 68).

cusable: "scholars may commit lapses[91], but this does not need to detract from their prestige"[92] (*Maktūb* 28);

c) contradictory theories about the relation between God and the universe can also be reconciled, if one recognizes that its authors are like the blind men of the parable. By touching and tasting various parts of a tree they tried to discover its nature. One of them gets hold of a leaf, another of a branch, again another of a flower, and a fourth one, the trunk. Reporting on their findings, one says: "The tree consists of smooth parts"; another says: "No, it is something like as stick"; in the opinion of a third it is soft and delicate, but to the fourth it appears to be extremely rough and solid. In the end an arbiter tells them: "All your statements as such were correct, but they were wrong in their limitation" (*Maktūb* 4 f.). Similarly, disagreement among the mystic philosophers has arisen about the reality of *wujūd*. Some maintain that it can be transformed into an abstract mental concept (*amr intizāʿī*) and that the *māhiyyāt* (essences) are marked by it. Other people claim that the Creator created the *māhiyyāt* and caused them to emanate from Himself; and that after their emanation in the minds of those who observe the conditions of the *māhiyyāt* an image is fixed which is called *wujūd*[93]. Well then, so our author decides, both views are right in themselves; on the other hand, each of them gives merely a limited insight into *wujūd* as a whole. In other words, they are true to a certain extent (*Maktūb* 11)[94].

---

[91] The Delhi divine levels other criticism (relating to Sirhindī's interpretation of mystic philosophers' thought) at his explanation (*sharḥ*) of two quatrains of Khwāja Bāqī bi-ʾllāh (d. 1603), observing that it obscures more than it clarifies (*Kashf al-ghayn fī sharḥ al-rubāʿiyyatayn* 2).

[92] For the reputation enjoyed by mystics (*ʿārifūn*) like Sirhindī is actually based on their revelatory experiences (*kashf*) (*Maktūb* 5), and not on their scholarly observations!

[93] "By common consent, the most notable representative of (this) ... position (of quiddity that is 'fundamentally real', *aṣīl*, and 'existence' that is *iʿtibārī*) is Yaḥyā Suhrawardī (d. 1191)" (T. Izutsu, *The Concept and Reality of Existence*, Tokyo 1971, 100).

[94] *Cf.* also *Tafh.* I, 19: "Every reality has its particular aspects (*khawāṣṣ*) and modes of recognizance. For every particular aspect there is a peculiar phraseology (*lisān*) for its interpretation. Now a mystic will restrict himself to the reality of man's individual traits, then he will concentrate on general aspects of manhood ... On one occasion he will give consideration to the being (*wujūd*) of the material world, on another occasion to the being of the spiritual world, and then again to the being of the World of Omnipotence. Every time he makes use of a phraseology (that fits the relative reality); and it is not necessary that by all these phraseologies the same things are said ... So the statements of the mystic may differ while in essence there is no contradiction".

# CHAPTER FOUR

# PSYCHOLOGY

Psychology has, as a rule, attracted hardly any attention from traditional Muslim scholarship. Yet, one exception has to be made. Throughout all ages Muslims endowed with mystical leanings have continually felt a particular need to acquire insight into human nature[1]. This stands to reason, for the development of mystic experience is a process which passes through successive levels of mental and psychic perceptions. Thus the Delhi divine states that through knowledge of one's innate predispositions (*isti<sup>c</sup>dādāt*) the mystic can find the most appropriate path for attaining full development (*H.* XVIII). "The more that is known of *laṭīfas* (psychic centres of a subtle substance), the better a soul can be refined; and whoever is ablest in discerning their various pecularities is also the ablest when people ask him for guidance" (*A.Q.* 14 f.).

Incumbent on gaining some idea of the structure of *laṭīfas*—a central notion in Shāh Walī Allāh's psycho-mystical dissertations—is a preliminary study of the essence of the *rūḥ* (spirit) (*A.Q.* 22). If properly analyzed this appears to be composed of three constituents:

1. a fine pneuma (*nasama*) produced from the four humours (*akhlāṭ*) (*B.B.* 33)[2]. "It streams in the flesh and bones like fire in charcoal or rose-water in a rose" (*A.Q.* 24). It conveys potencies of perception, nourishment and growth, through which the senses, movements of the body and digestion are activated[3]. This process takes the following course: a part of the *nasama* ascends to the brain, and is there divided into ten portions. Five of them are for the 'external' senses,

[1] Accordingly, ṣūfī scholars like the Ikhwān al-ṣafā' assigned the *ʿilm al-nafsāniyyāt* ('science of the souls') a place in their encyclopaedia.

[2] Or, according to an earlier exposition: "from vapours of the elements" (*A.Q.* 24). It should be borne in mind that in Islamic medicine humours are called 'daughters' of the elements' (M. Ullmann, *Islamic Medicine*, Edinburgh 1978, 58). A third version of its arising: "engendered in the heart from blood that has been refined" (*Tafh.* I, 247) agrees with the account of al-Ghazālī who states that it is a subtle substance coming forth from a ventricle of the physical heart (*Iḥyā' ʿulūm al-dīn*, Cairo n.d. III, 2). Again, this is a concept borrowed from the Greeks (*Islamic Medicine*, 69). The specific contribution of the Delhi scholar to this topic consists of the choice of the term *nasama* and the elaborate application of it.

[3] Or, as is set out in more detail in *Tafh.* I, 34: "The *nasama* has two abilities at its disposal: a practical one and an intellectual one. As for the practical one, it pursues food, drink, clothes, women, revenge on people who committed outrage upon its possessor and credit for his offspring. As for the intellectual one, it tries to obtain proficiency, sensitivity, fantasy, perceptivity and control of breath".

i.e. the faculties of sight, hearing, smell, taste and touch. The other five are for the 'internal' senses, i.e. the faculty of the *sensus communis* (*ḥiss mushtarik*) which coordinates the percepts of the individual 'external' senses, the faculty of retentive imagination (*khayāl*) which reproduces the objects of sensory perception, the estimate faculty (*wahm*) which perceives the insensible forms connected with the impression of sensible objects, the faculty of retaining concepts (*maᶜānī*) and the talent of knowing how to combine and dispose freely of the concepts and objects of sensory perception. Another part of the *nasama* flows down to the liver, and from there it is distributed over the organs and potencies which pervade the body for stimulating procreation and growth, for providing nutrition and shaping. Then there is a part which simply remains in the heart. For these distributive activities Shāh Walī Allāh uses the metaphor of a city-state: here the liver functions as the chief administrator who is responsible for the receipts and expenditure; the brain accomplishes the task of a pundit, who advises the king (*imām*); and the heart is the *imām* himself who rules autocratically and perseveres in his resolve'' (*B.B.* 33 f.).

The earthly body of man is the 'riding-animal' (*maṭiyya*), i.e. substratum of the *nasama*, and the *nasama* in turn can function as the substratum of the divine *rūḥ*, which has its domicile in higher worlds. In this way the *nasama* may serve as a connecting link (*barzakh*)[4] between the divine *rūḥ* and the earthly body to disclose latent dispositions of the human body ''in the manner of a fierce sun which bleaches articles of dress and tans the bleacher'' (*H.B.* I, 18f.)[5]

The *nasama*, as we have seen, *inter alia* seeks to acquire food, drink and sexual pleasures[6]. In this capacity it represents man's lower self[7], ''being inclined to the earth''. On the other hand, it possesses also a side which is directed in an opposite direction, ''feeling a tendency to what is holy'' (*H.B.* I, 19). The latter aspiration can be furthered with the assistance of the *nafs nāṭiqa* (rational soul), i.e. the second constituent of the *rūḥ*;

2. the *nafs nāṭiqa*. While elucidating the hidden meaning of Mohammed's *miᶜrāj* (midnight journey to the seven heavens), Shāh Walī Allāh states that ''the root idea of his riding on the (flying steed)

---

[4] Intermediaries are always required for the divine world to operate upon the sublunary world.

[5] For the useful purposes *nasama* still has to fulfil in man's afterlife see p. 00.

[6] *Cf.* also *Tafh.* I, 247: ''it can be taken to dark, lustful and ferocious practices''.

[7] Accordingly, the legislative activity of God's messengers bears on the perfection of the *nasama* (*Tafh.* II, 146).

Burāq was *nafs nāṭiqa*'s having taken its seat on the *nasama*, i.e. the animal perfection (*kamāl*). Thus the riding on the Burāq was a symbol for the triumph and dominance of the properties of his *nafs nāṭiqa* over his animal nature'' (*H.B.* II, 206). In another work the Delhi divine declares the *nafs nāṭiqa* to be the connecting link between the *ʿayn thābita*[8] (archetypal[9] individuality)—which is a purely holy entity—and the *nasama*—which belongs to the objects of this tainted world (*Tafh.* I, 43).

In origin, the *nafs nāṭiqa* is an ebullition from the *nafs kulliyya*[10], the 'World Soul' which ''acts as the *rūḥ* (spirit) of the Macrocosmos'' (*Aṭyab al-nagham*, 41f.). Whenever the breath of life is blown into an embryo, there is the moment in which a *nafs nāṭiqa* arises as a bubble on the ocean of the *nafs kulliyya*. This is a cosmic event, and in that very hour a human individual is structured in accordance with the position of the sun or the planets (*A.Q.* 27 and 113; *Saṭ.* 29). Thus the *nafs nāṭiqa* represents the kernel of a person's personality, ''That by which Zayd is Zayd and ʿAmr ʿAmr'' (*B.B.* 16). In addition, it orders men's lives, and from it special qualities, like the faculty of pursuing general welfare (*raʾy kullī*), arise (*A.Q.* 26). Its focus of attention (*qibla*) is the *tajallī aʿẓam* (*Tafh.* I, 141) which resides at the heart of the *nafs kulliyya* (*A.Q.* 117). A peculiarity of the *nafs nāṭiqa* is that it is able to have revelations of angels and visions of the *ḥaẓīra al-quds* through the intermediary of the celestial spirit, i.e. the third constituent of the *rūḥ* (*A.Q.* 34);

3. *rūḥ samawī* (celestial spirit). This is ''a bubble on the surface of the *ʿālam al-mithāl*'' (*A.Q.* 117), and ''a form (*ṣūra*) present in the *ḥaẓīra al-quds*, which is actually an expression for the divine radiance (*tajallī*) in the *ʿālam al-mithāl*''. This form is given to every human being. Consequently, all individuals—men of letters as well as illiterate people—are naturally drawn towards the *ḥaẓīra al-quds*: ''His happiness is in inclining to and gaining affinity with the *ḥaẓīra al-quds*; his misery is in turning away from it and in clinging to the earth'' (*Tafh.* I, 248). ''In fact, the whole basis of retribution (in the next

[8] ''The *ʿayn* (*thābita*) resembles a jet d'eau. Just as water at the time it proceeds from it is not particularized by an individual form, so in the *wujūd* (being) which proceeds from the *ʿayn* (*thābita*) things do not distinguish themselves. However, as soon as a hexagonal or quadrangular apparatus is put upon the jet, water is made six-sided or four-sided. Equally the *ʿayn* (*thābita*) assumes the form of the *nafs* (*nāṭiqa*) when in the process of individuation the *nafs* (*nāṭiqa*) 'touches' the *wujūd* (that proceeds from the *ʿayn thābita*) (*Tafh.* II, 107).

[9] *Cf. Khizāna* 4: ''By the statement of the Prophet: 'The *arwāḥ* (souls) were created 2000 years before the bodies' the *aʿyān al-thābita* are meant''.

[10] Hence it is the ''fundamental reality of the *nafs nāṭiqa*'' (*A.Q.* 27 f.).

world) lies in the attraction which his part of the *rūḥ* feels towards the *ḥaẓīra al-quds*" (*A.Q.* 31).

Turning back to the question raised in the beginning concerning the make-up of *laṭīfas*, Shāh Walī Allāh states at the end: "it is in the combinations between the *nasama* and these two subtle constituents (the rational soul and the celestial spirit) that the five *laṭīfas*[11] (perceptible to man's intellect) are generated ... The concupiscent soul, the heart and the intellect all have their stand firmly fixed in the *nasama*, but from the *nafs nāṭiqa* and *rūḥ samawī* they receive (refreshing) outpourings ..., just as the body receives refreshment from the liver by means of mesaraic veins[12]" (*A.Q.* 34 f.).

Beyond the five perceptible *laṭīfas* there exist five so-called concealed[13] *laṭīfas*, named *khafī* (hidden), *nūr al-quds* (sacred light), *ḥajar al-baht* (gem of stupefaction[14]), *akhfāʾ* (most hidden), and *anāniyya kubrā* (full-fledged ego). Whatever proceeds from these concealed *laṭīfas* cannot be perceived by the intellect or *wijdān* (a natural a-priori reason). For this purpose there is another extremely refined and sensitive organ, which in the idiom of the ṣūfīs is called '*dhawq*' (intuitive anticipation) (*A.Q.* 132).

In *al-Qawl al-jamīl*, an early writing on mysticism in which our author does not yet develop his own ideas, mention is made of *laṭīfas* in connection with *ashghāl* (meditation technics), observed by Shaykh Aḥmad Sirhindī (1564-1624): 'It should be borne in mind that — as appears from statements of the Shaykh and his followers — God created in man six *laṭīfas* as single entities designating modes (*jihāt*) and aspects (*iʿtibārāt*) of the *nafs nāṭiqa*; thus, one aspect of it is called '*qalb*', a second '*rūḥ*' etc."[15] — Then we are told that once his father, ʿAbd al-Raḥīm, in explanation of them, "drew a circle and said: 'This is the *qalb*'. Thereupon he drew in this circle another one and said: 'This is the *rūḥ*'. And he car-

---

[11] *To wit*: the concupiscent soul, heart, intellect, spirit and 'inmost being' (*sirr*).

[12] A notion ultimately based on ancient Greek anatomy. The function attributed to these veins was to transport chyle from the stomach and intestines to the liver in order that the liver could make blood and humours out of it.

[13] I.e. concealed in the *ʿālam al-mithāl* (*Tafh.* I, 182). Presumably some of their names are derived from a *ḥadīth qudsī* quoted in *Intibāh* I, 79: "In the body of the sons of Adam there is a small chunk of meat; in it is the *qalb*; in the *qalb* the *fuʾād* (mind); in the *fuʾād* the *sirr*; in the *sirr* the *khafī*; in the *khafī* the *akhfaʾ*; and in the *akhfāʾ* the *anā*".

[14] Its common meaning is: "Eagle-stone which is valued for its magic properties" (see *Dictionnaire* par R. Blachère, M. Chouémi et C. Denizeau). By our divine it is used as a technical term for "the center which is the *namūna* (model, i.e. telescope) for (the reception of light waves transmitted by) the *tajallī aʿẓam*" (*Sat.* 29). It is situated in the highest parts of the *ʿayn thābita*. "From it (divine) knowledge filters down upon the *ʿaql* and *qalb*" (*Aṭyab al-nagham*, Delhi 1308/1890, 40).

[15] The four remaining unrecorded *laṭīfas* are the *sirr*, *khafī*, *akhfāʾ* and *anā*. In this case the series begins with the *qalb* and ends with the *anā*. In other representations the first *laṭīfa* is said to be the *nafs* (concupiscent soul) and the last the *akhfāʾ*.

ried on with it till he finished a sixth circle, on which he said: 'This is the *anāʾ* (ego)'' (*Q.D.* 105). Six concentric circles, the outermost for the *laṭīfa* of the *qalb*, the innermost for the *laṭīfa* of the true self. This provides a symbolism for the journey of a mystic who, starting from the *qalb* and passing along ever more inward *laṭīfas*, progresses to his true self, and in consequence realizes self-identification with God. For, ''he who learns to know his inner self by *ʿilm ḥuḍūrī*[16] (immediate knowledge not acquired through the canals of ratiocinations), has by this knowledge learnt to know his Lord'' (*Khizāna* 9).

''Deeper and deeper'' is in religious language an alternative expression for ''higher and higher'', so we also meet a conception of *laṭīfas* according to which they are credited with finer qualities the higher they are placed in the human body. Then the *laṭīfa* of the *nafs* is considered to house under the umbilicus, a proper locality for sensuality being the junction of stomach and temper (*mizāj*). The *qalb* lies two fingers under the lẹft side of the breast and the *rūḥ* two fingers under the right side of it. The *sirr* is situated a little higher in the middle of the chest; the *khafī* is to be found in between the eye-brows, and the *akhfāʾ* in the *dura mater*[17].

Of equally increasing grandiosity and bliss are the mystic states experienced when the seeker of God ascends along these *laṭīfas*. At the stage of the *qalb* there is merely *dhikr* (remembrance of God). Reaching the *rūḥ* a 'joie spirituelle' (*ḥuḍūr*) is tasted. At the level of *sirr*, *mukāshafa* (unveiling) is granted, on account of which the ṣūfī sees the realities of the *ʿālam al-mithāl* with his physical eyes. At the height of the *laṭīfa*, called *khafī*, one enjoys *mushāhada* (contemplative witnessing) and recognizes that his *dhāt* (essence) is related to God's *dhāt*. Arrived at the zenith the *akhfāʾ*, one will receive information from the *tajallī aʿẓam*, the source of all divine manifestations (*Khizāna* 9).

The meditation techniques (*shughl*), applied by the followers of Aḥmad Sirhindī when they wish to avail themselves of those *laṭīfas*, are centred upon the so-called *nafī* (negation) and *ithbāt* (affirmation), i.e. the two parts which form the well-known formula *lā ilāhᵃ illa ʾllāhu* (there is no

---

[16] This knowledge is only obtainable through *fanāʾ* (passing away from self) (*Tafh.* II, 213) and is established, settled, and exists by the overflow (*ifāḍa*) of the Self-existent. Hence *ʿilm ḥudūrī* leads of itself to perception of the Self-existent and His Attributes, whereas its antipole, i.e. *ʿilm ḥuṣūlī* ('acquired knowledge') may only by means of reasoning (*istidlāl*) endeavour to reach this inaccessible place. Then the latter has to remain content with protraying in man's mind a form of the Ultimate Reality which, however, is not identical to the Ultimate Reality as such. So *ʿilm ḥuṣūlī* is in fact sham knowledge (*jahl*) (*Khizāna* 9). *ʿIlm ḥudūrī*, on the other hand is concerned with metaphysical (*mujarrad*) and transcendental (*munazzah*) data which stem from the innermost of the *nafs nāṭiqa* (*Tafh.* II, 96).

[17] Mulk Ḥasan ʿAlī, *Taʿlīmāt-i mujaddidiyya* (1965), 193 ff.

divinity save Allāh). "Sitting with the face turned to Mecca the ṣūfī holds his breath, and after having fixed the tongue to the palata he 'pulls' the world *lā* to the *laṭīfa* of the *nafs* (seated under the navel). Before proceeding to the *laṭīfa* of the *akhfā*ʾ he pauses a little while at the *laṭīfas* termed *sirr* and *khafī*. And after having 'pulled' the word *ilāh*ᵃ to the highest *laṭīfa* he turns the attention to the *laṭīfa* of the *rūḥ*. Finally, he 'forces' (the sound) *illa ʾllāhu* upon the *laṭīfa* of the *qalb*. By this *shughl* a kind of heat and purity is produced in the *laṭīfas*. If this *shughl* comes to full expansion, a revolving flame appears before the seeker of God. Through this *shughl* the veil on luminousness will be lifted in front of him"[18].

Before discussing the way in which Shāh Walī Allāh has elaborated this system, it might be better first to point out some striking similarities between these *laṭīfas* and the so-called *cakras*[19], a corresponding notion met in Hindu Tantrism and Yoga practice. "Nach den Vorstellungen der Tantras lassen sich ja im Körper zwischen Scheitel und Sexualorgan untereinander sechs lotusförmig vorgestellte Kreise oder Zentren (*Cakra*) besonderer "mystischer" Bedeutung underscheiden", of which the chief function is the "Dynamisierung und Sublimierung von in uns anwesenden Potenzen"[20]. They are located in the same, or approximately the same, places in the human bodies as the *laṭīfas*. The *maṇipūra-cakra* lies at the level of the umblicus; the *anāhata-cakra* is found in the region of the heart and the *vishuddha-cakra* in the region of the throat ; the *ājnā-cakra* is situated in between the eyebrows; at the top of the cranium the *saharāra-cakra* is located[21].

Another correspondence is that in the case of the *cakras* the excellence of the experiences enjoyed increases to the measure of their respective height. At the level of the heart there is only "le premier éveil de l'âme", but "tout en haut de la tête, le yogin réalise l'Absolu"[22]. The yoga technique which appears particularly appropriate for the preparation of these mystic states, is the *prāṇāyāma*, the regulation of breath; and this also forms part of the *shughl*, described above[23].

---

[18] *id*. 197.

[19] A Sanscrit term which indicates round objects like a wheel, a discus, a circle. The last meaning is interesting in view of the circles ʿAbd al-Raḥīm drew in explanation of the *laṭīfas*.

[20] J. Gonda, *Die Religionen Indiens* (Stuttgart, 1963), II, 38.

[21] M. Eliade, *Le Yoga* (Paris, 1960), 244 f.

[22] J. Herbert, *Spiritualité Hindoue* (Paris, 1947), 398.

[23] Rendering account of his contacts with *ʿulamā*ʾ outside India during his exile, ʿUbayd Allāh Sindhī (1872-1944), the well-known propagandist of Shāh Walī Allāh's ideas, tells us that the latter's research work in the field of Qurʾān, *ḥadīth* and *fiqh* had their approval; but they found it hard, if not impossible, to endorse his mystic teachings since they give forth a smell of Iranianism and Indianism. In their opinion no links can be made between Islam and those realms of thought (ʿUbayd Allāh Sindhī, *Shāh Walī Allāh awr un kā falsafa*, Lahore, 1949, 232 f.).

In treating the subject of *laṭīfas* Shāh Walī Allāh takes his own course. To begin with, he classes what are considered the three basic components of every human individual (i.e. the *nafs shawiyya*, *qalb* and *ʿaql*) in the category of perceptible *laṭīfas*. The *nafs shahwiyya* (concupiscent soul) has its residence in the liver. This potency is required for the preservation of the body and to its activities belong eating, drinking, sleep and cohabition. It is the *kūwa* (aperture) through which Satan whispers suggestions tempting to evil, impurity and fierceness. The *qalb* is a psychic center, which has its support in a fir-cone shaped lump of flesh lying two fingers under the left-side of the breast. It is the origin of the emotions and it has the capacity of making decisions. Angels use it as the *kūwa* for their inspirations. The *ʿaql* resides in the brain. It covers the area lying between the concrete and the abstract. If for example it observes individual human beings, it is able to mould the concept of a universal human form. Recollecting things of the past and planning for things of the future are part of its functions (*Tafh.* I, 171; *H.* XIX; *A.Q.* 143 f., 34 f. and 39). One of its distinguishing marks is "sure knowledge (*yaqīn*) in respect of matters closely related to traditional doctrines like faith in the unseen and belief in the omnipotence of God" (*H.B.* II, 90).

By means of the mesaraic veins these three *laṭīfas* are provided with a system of intercommunication. By virtue of this possibility of interaction, each of them may share in the special properties of the other, or may make its influence felt on the others: "If both the heart and the intellect are governed by the *nafs*, then a great many vices will result ... But if the heart and the *nafs* obey the intellect, then praiseworthy qualities will arise" (*A.Q.* 42 f. and 77). Quite often such interpenetration is indispensable in giving full scope to man's potentialities: "If there were no cognition of the displeasing or pleasing effect of vilifying or winning words, no anger or love would be roused; if there were no receptivity of the heart, no religious belief would develop" (*H.B.* II, 88).

Further, through a process of refinement, these three *laṭīfas* can regain their original constitution. The changes worked in this way, are described by our author as follows: "Still in the grip of the turbulent instinctive disposition of human nature (*ṭabīʿa*), the intellect has to consider to be true the things which come to it in a fashion adapted to the *ṭabīʿa*. After its refinement[24], however, it obtains such a certain belief in what is presented by the Law that it is as if it were a matter of empirical observation ... Still rooted in the *ṭabīʿa* the heart has to love benefactors and patrons, to hate odious enemies, to fear what is harmful and to hope for what is useful. After its refinement, however, it loves God, fears His

[24] Mainly achieved by continuous devotion to the Beloved (*A.Q.* 85).

punishment and hopes for His reward. Still in the grip of the turbulent *ṭabīʿa*, the *nafs* revels in lusts and seeking ease. After its refinement, however, repentance, self-abnegation and religious strictness are its characteristics'' (*H.B.* II, 91)[25].

Another characteristic feature of these three perceptible *laṭīfas* are the respective *maqāmāt* and *aḥwāl* they engender. As a rule, Western scholars of Islam, are accustomed to discuss *maqāmāt* and *aḥwāl* in the context of the Ṣūfī Path; *maqāmāt* representing Its stages and *aḥwāl* being the 'states' which come over a mystic during his journey. In the expositions of Shāh Walī Allāh, however, these two concepts figure primarily as psychic and ethical notions, though at times provided with a mystic flavour. They are said to be fruits of *iḥsān*, defined by H. Ritter as 'aufrichtige Gottesverehrung' (*H.B.* II, 88). When qualities of an angelic nature have become firmly established habits (*malakāt*), of which the actions follow a recurrent pattern, they are to be termed *maqāmāt*[26]. And if these actions appear like bolts of lightning, as is the case with visions, voices from heaven, they are called *aḥwāl* (traits which occur sporadically) (*H.B.* II, 91).

A fundamental element of the *maqāmāt* and *aḥwāl* pertaining to the *ʿaql* is sure knowledge (*yaqīn*) in respect of matters concerning the Muslim creed as, for instance, the articles of Predestination and Resurrection. The *maqāmāt* resulting from *yaqīn* include:

a) *shukr* (gratitude): coming to realize all the material and spiritual benefits one owes to one's Creator;
b) *tawakkul* (trust in God): which implies not worrying about making a living[27];
c) *hayba* (*sensus tremendi*, i.e. to stand in awe of God): comes from the contemplation of God's revenge and awfulness;
d) *ḥusn al-ẓann* (*sensus fascinosi*, i.e. to think well of God): proceeds from the acknowledgement of God's benefits and favours;
e) *tafrīd* (isolation from the world in order to focus all attention on God): is enfolding oneself in the recollection of God (*dhikr*) to such extent

---

[25] In *A.Q.* 83 f. the effect of the refinement of the *nafs* is said to be *samāḥa* (magnaminity), while the effects mentioned as resulting from the refinement of the heart are *ṣidq* (sincerity), *adab* (good breeding) and *wajd* (emotionality). Fruits of the refinement of the intellect are a conviction concerning the *tajallī aʿẓam*, mystical revelation (*kashf*), perspicacity (*firāsa*) into what is about to happen, and a correct interpretation of Qurʾān and traditions.

[26] This agrees with the view of Abū Naṣr al-Sarrāj (d. 988) who maintains that they are permanent conditions of the soul, equivalent to moral habits (*cf.* *Kitāb al-lumaʿ*, ed. by R. A. Nicholson, London 1963, 41-53).

[27] However, absence of any concern about earning one's livelihood is in contravention of the *sharʿ* (revealed law) (*Q.D.* 27).

that it is as if one sees God with one's own eyes. Then gloomy imaginings of one's soul disappear;
f) *ikhlāṣ* (to make God the exclusive object of faith);
g) *tawḥīd* (the state of awareness of the Oneness of God);
h) the position of a *ṣiddīq* or *muḥaddath* (*H.B.* II, 92 f.).

To the *aḥwāl* connected with the *ʿaql* belong:
a) the *tajallī* ('radiance') of God's Essence, God's Attributes and *ḥukm* (mandates) of God's Essence. That refers to the hereafter and its occurrences. Hence, on certain occasions one may obtain a mental representation of Paradise and Hell;
b) reliable clairvoyance (*firāsa*) and inner speech (*khāṭir*) which appear to correspond with reality;
c) wholesome vision;
d) sweet experience of confidential talk with God (*munājāt*);
e) self-examination (*muḥāsaba*); and
f) consciousness of one's own insignificance opposite God's majesty (*H.B.* II, 94 f.).

*Maqāmāt* pertaining to the *qalb* are:
a) concentration of one's thoughts (*jamʿ*) on the hereafter and consideration of things of this worldly life as despicable;
b) exclusive love (of God);
c) God's calling a worshipper's attention to infringement of good manners by blame, and assent once he again turns to the righteous path;
d) becoming a *shahīd* (martyr) or a *ḥawārī* (one who is freed and cleared of every vice) (*H.B.* II, 95-8).

*Aḥwāl* specific of the *qalb* are:
a) *sukr* (intoxication), i.e. that in the *ʿaql* and then in the *qalb* the light of faith begins to shine so strongly that the affairs of this world lose all significance;
b) *ghalaba* ('overcoming'). There are two types of *ghalaba*:
   1. the *ghalaba dāʿiyya* (being overcome by an inner urge). An instance of this is ʿUmar's opposition to the treaty of Ḥudaybiyya (in March 628) because of undue zeal;
   2. the *ghalaba dāʿiyya ilāhiyya* (being overcome by a divine urge). A case of this is the divine urge which Abū Bakr received in his heart to restrain the Prophet from continuous prayer, as is recorded in the story of the battle of Badr (March 624): Then he seized Mohammed by the arm and said: "Stop" (sc. your constant entreaty will annoy your Lord, for surely God will fulfil His promise to you);
c) the preference of obedience to God above obedience to anything else;

d) the *ghalaba al-khawf* (being overcome by the fear of God) (*H.B.* II, 98 f.).

Among the *maqāmāt* of the *nafs* that becomes overpowered by the light of faith Shāh Walī Allāh reckons:

a) *tawba* (repentance). Its two major effects are:
   1. *ḥayāʾ* (shame): the squirming of the *nafs* at the appearance of God's majesty;
   2. *waraʿ* (abstemiousness): turns the *nafs* away from confusion;

b) *zuhd* (renunciation): the awareness of the disgracefulness of being occupied with what exceeds man's daily wants. God has given *zuhd* as a means for perfection of the *nafs*, but He has not introduced it as a statutory obligation (*H.B.* II, 99 ff.).

*Aḥwāl* distinctive of the *nafs* are:

a) *ghayba* ('invisibility'). This means that for the *nafs* all carnal appetites disappear;

b) *maḥq* ('annihilation'). This indicates that on account of an inclination of the *nafs* toward the *ʿaql*, and the *ʿaql* being filled with the light of God, one can go without food and drink for an unusually long period (*H.B.* II, 102).

The two remaining perceptible *laṭīfas*, after the three just mentioned, are the *sirr* which lies above the *ʿaql*, and the *rūḥ* which lies above the *qalb*. Their higher position enables them to watch their lower placed partners closely. Both of them are sublimed configurations of *ʿaql* and *qalb*[28]. If the two reach their original residence and ascend towards their zenith, they witness the *tajallī aʿẓam*. The most sublime state (*ḥāla*) reserved for the *rūḥ* is indicated as *hubūṭ* ('descent'); it is comparable to the state of the nightingale, which, when in the presence of a rose, is overcome with emotion. Visions are a product specific of the *sirr*; the state characteristic of this *laṭīfa* is 'intimacy' (*uns*) (*A.Q.* 36, 75 and 104); a trait peculiar to it is that of discerning one single divine design (*tadbīr*) in the cosmos (*Tafh.* I, 20).

For the *sālik*, the traveller on the path leading to the divine *dhāt* (Essence), the *laṭīfas* serve as a kind of landmark on the upward path. At every *laṭīfa* which he reaches, he experiences the influence of the properties (*aḥkām*) peculiar to it. If, for instance the *laṭīfas* of *rūḥ* and *sirr* gain mastery over him, he enjoys spiritual delights, obtained from intimacy

---

[28] *Cf. A.Q.* 75: "What we mean by *rūḥ* is actually the *qalb*, of which the resemblance with the celestial spirit and the rational soul becomes conspicuous as soon as it has shaken off its base qualities ... What we intend to convey by *sirr* is actually that the *ʿaql* when it has shaken off its clinging to the earth, is governed by the principles of the sublime world (i.e. the world above the *mala aʿlā* and *ḥaẓīra al-quds*) and attains the apprehension of the *tajallī aʿẓam*".

of the *rūḥ* and knowledge of the *sirr*, on account of which he turns away from all material pleasures (*Tafh.* I, 231). For the ascent from the one *laṭīfa* to the other he ought to use the common methods of spiritual training. If, for example, he wishes to shift from the *qalb*-region to the height of the *sirr*, he has to observe the prescribed rules for cleansing. Meditation exercises are good for passing from the *ʿaql* up to the *sirr* (*Tafh.* I, 136).

As to the way upwards, three levels are to be distinguished: the *wujūd ẓulmānī* (gloomy existence: the lower world), the *wujūd rūḥānī* (spiritual existence) and the *wujūd ilāhī* (divine existence). If one succeeds in passing the five perceptible *laṭīfas*, the stage of *wujūd rūḥānī* is attained. Now for a further continuation of the journey the *sālik* has to resort to the concealed *laṭīfas*. Only through them can the *wujūd ilāhī* be reached. This, however, is an undertaking which must be reserved for an élite, and it is certainly too dangerous for a common man. The latter should confine himself to the cultivation of perceptible *laṭīfas* (*Tafh.* I, 181; *A.Q.* 135 f.).

In elucidation of capacities inherent in the concealed *laṭīfas*, the Delhi divine sets forth: peculiar to the *khafī* is the discovery that one and the same reality streams in all existing things (*mawjūdāt*). A characteristic quality of the *laṭīfa*, termed *nūr al-quds* ('the holy light') is its ability to become acquainted with the disputes of the *mala aʿlā* and the decisions descending from them. A specific property of the *ḥajar al-baht* is its inexplicable evanescence into the *tajallī aʿẓam* in consequence of which man becomes one of God's instruments (*Tafh.* I, 181 f.). If the *akhfāʾ* becomes the prevailing element in a mystic, he will receive information from the *tajallī aʿẓam* as well as from the *nafs kulliyya*. Yet he is favoured with an even more exalted state if the concealed *laṭīfa*, called *anāniyya kubrā*, holds it sway. Then he sees the whole universe in himself. No longer do divine knowledge and revelations filter down from above, but now he finds them in his inner self (*A.Q.* 124 ff.). When he has reached this stage (*maqām*) of *al-tawḥīd al-dhātī* (Oneness in the Essence), he possesses all divine Attributes except self-existence and eternity. In fact, he remains an *ʿabd* (servant) as before. Nevertheless, he is freed from the erroneous impression that *ʿabd* and *rabb* (Lord) are two different realities (*Tafh.* I, 169 f.).

Another interesting quality which our scholar ascribes to the *laṭīfas* is the aptitude to function as reflectors of the several categories of God's Attributes. The more delicately a *laṭīfa* is structured, the more sublime is the nature of the divine Attributes reflected on it. Upon the *qalb* falls the reflection of the *iḍāfiyyāt*, the Attributes lowest in rank. The *thubūtiyyāt*, the Attributes properly speaking such as life, hearing, sight, however, are mirrored upon the *rūḥ*. The *shuʾūnāt* which are, according to the explanation of Shāh Walī Allāh himself, the germ forms of the *iḍāfiyyāt* and *thubūtiyyāt* (*Khizāna* 5), project their lustre upon the *sirr*. It is the *khafī* which receives the reflection of the *salbiyyāt*, the 'privative' Attributes which accentuate divine transcendency, and lastly upon the *akhfā*ʾ the 'mother' of all Attributes, i.e. the Attribute of divine self-objectivation, is reflected (*Tafh*. II, 41)[29].

Besides the recorded varied figuring of the *laṭīfas* in the mystic's quest of his very identity, a final aspect worthy of mention is the function they perform in Shāh Walī Allāh's classifications of history.

In the so-called historic religions the hour of birth, the era of the founder's appearance, is taken for the most crucial event in the history of mankind. This is the *pleroma tou chronou*, the fulness of times. A somewhat illogical issue of this belief is that by the adherents of these religions, the prenatal period in general is evaluated much more highly than the postnatal ages. The Christians, for example, will without hesitation acknowledge a Moses or Isaiah as conveyers and exponents of authentic divine revelation; but the office with which they wish to credit an Augustine or Luther is that of 'father of the church' at the most, and into the process of revelation as such the latter will never enter. In orthodox Islam the same is true: The advent of Mohammed is viewed as the terminative point in an extended revelatory period, in which former prophets also officiated as agencies of God. The events *after* the blessed times of the Messenger of God are, however, of a considerably lesser religious significance, This is implicative of the well-known doctrine of Mohammed's being the seal of prophets. Shāh Walī Allāh's exposition of the five *taghayyurāt*, deteriorations, is in complete agreement with traditional views, as can be pointed out in the history subsequent to the death of the Prophet. The first *taghayyur* is the transfer of power to Abū Bakr; the second the death of ʿUmar who was the bolt on the door of *fitna* (civil war); the third, the murder of ʿUthmān, was the worst, since it turned out to be the dividing line between the age of order that preceded it and the age of chaos and anarchy that followed. The fourth *taghayyur* is the establishment of the ʿAbbāsid caliphate in Irāq. And the fifth the end of Arab dominion and the arrival of the sway of non-Arabs, of Turks,

---

[29] *Cf.* also *Tafh*. I, 104. Here the Delhi scholar mentions that besides the Naqshbandīs the Chishtīs assume that the refinement of increasingly concealed *laṭīfas* may afford an upward movement into increasingly higher worlds: "They say 'God conferred on so-and-so the rank of *malakūt* (World of Sovereignty)' when he had achieved the refinement of the *rūḥ* which consists of (obtaining) the state of delight (*surūr*) and intimacy (*uns*) and of being assembled with the souls of, for instance, the prophets; and they say: 'God granted so-and-so lofty knowledge of the *jabarūt* (World of Omnipotence)' when he had achieved the refinement of the *khafī* which consists of recognizing God in creation and the creation in God: and they say: 'God conferred on so-and-so the rank of *lāhūt* (World of the divine Essence)' when he had achieved the refinement of the *akhfā*ʾ".

whose rule is like that of the *majūs* but with the difference, that the former still observe the *ṣalāt* and confess the *shahāda* with their tongues. "I myself", so the Delhi divine complains, "being born in the final stages of this (fifth) deterioration do not know what, after this, God has in mind (for the future)" (*Izāla* I, 148 ff.). This theory of the five *taghayyurāt* is set out in a work in which the Sunni standpoint is expounded over against the Shiᶜa principles.

However, in another book of his which contains various teaching of an esoteric nature, the Delhi scholar discloses that in this personal conception the mission of Mohammed is no final event of "Heilsgeschichte", but merely a phase followed by periods of further developments of God's designs. The days in which he himself lives he experiences as the most advanced evolution of divine Revelation. The argumentation for the existence of progressive phases in God's revelations to humanity is based on a demonstration of a coming into operation of perceptible and concealed *laṭīfas* in a sequence of increasing subtleness and quality. "The human form", so Shāh Walī Allāh holds, "is founded on the completion of the *laṭīfas* of *qalb*, *ᶜaql* and *nafs*. Accordingly, the human race, with Adam as the first man, came into existence ... In the following epoch the *ᶜaql* and *qalb* of man were charged with getting to know the truth of God ... For the provision of livelihood (being an activity of the *nafs*) people were allowed to ride animals ... to eat their meat, to drink their milk and to use their wool for clothing ... Our prophet, Mohammed, marked the end of this epoch and, at the same time, he became the inaugurator of a new period[30] which was an expansion of the foregoing one. In that (new) era the gracious eyes (of God) turned to the *rūḥ* and *sirr*. Hence in that time the beloved, the perfect and the favoured was that man, in whom both of these *laṭīfas* were alert ... Next, at the time of Ibn ᶜArabī the gracious eyes (of God) turned to the *laṭīfa*, called *khafī* ... The spiritual leaders of that age were inspired with knowledge of divine Unity (*tawḥīd*) and concerning the world's vanishing into one Reality (the theory of *waḥdat al-wujūd*) ... Finally, in our days the gracious eyes (of God) turned to the *laṭīfas*, named *ḥajar al-baht* and *anāniyya kubrā*" (*Tafh.* I, 123 f.).

Consequently many prerogatives, like a full command of all facets of mysticism and an all-encompassing knowledge of the *sharīᶜa* and of all that pertains to prophecy, had been bestowed on Shāh Walī Allāh,

---

[30] In our age another Muslim Indian thinker Sir Muḥammad Iqbāl has reiterated and reformulated the same idea, arguing: "... the Prophet of Islam seems to stand between the ancient and the modern world ... In him life discovers other sources of knowledge ... The birth of Islam ... is the birth of inductive intellect" (*The Reconstruction of Religious Thought in Islam*, Lahore, 1954, 126).

himself being a chosen one of this last epoch[31], since both of these *laṭīfas* operated on him. Of this period it was said that "up to the West rays of light were shining, and 'the earth was irradiated by the light of its Lord' (*Qur'ān* XXXIX, 69)" (*Tafh.* I, 199).

---

[31] *Cf.* also *Tafh.* I, 120: "My Lord conveyed to me that after me there would be found no one having attained nearness to God but I would have had a hand in his moral education and spiritual training, until the moment that Jesus comes down (from heaven)".

CHAPTER FIVE

# MYSTICISM

### *Significance*

Although on almost every page of his writings the strain of mysticism in the Delhi divine stands out clearly, he nevertheless emphasizes strongly that sufism as such is not soul-saving, and that conformity with the Holy Scriptures is a *conditio sine qua non* for its validity: "Not one of us is someone who fights shy of scholars, i.e. of ṣūfīs familiar with Qurʾān and *sunna*, or of those firmly rooted in knowledge who are also familiar with mysticism ... Ṣūfīs without knowledge of Qurʾān and *sunna*, and scholars who are not interested in mysticism, are brigands and robbers of the *dīn* (religion)" (*Tafh*. II, 202).

*History of mysticism*. After close examination of his writings it turns out that Shāh Walī Allāh discovered seven distinct periods in the development of Muslim mystic practice and thought, *to wit*:

1. "during the initial period of Mohammed's[1] *umma* (i.e. the era of the Companions and Successors) the faculty of the limbs and organs was dominant; that is to say the heart faculty was totally engrossed in the activation of the energies of limbs and organs. What was discussed by the people of this community pertained to issues concerning the outward form of the Law" (*A.Q.* 111). "To their mind *iḥsān* (spiritual perfection) meant the performance of *ṣalāt*, fasting, *dhikr*, Qurʾān-reading, *ḥajj*, *ṣadaqa* and *jihād*. None of them was accustomed to hang the head upon the bosom in a contemplative mood ... *Kashf*[2], miracles, intoxication (*sukr*) and raptures were seldom found in them; and if they were seen, it was by chance, not on purpose" (*H.* II);
2. "After the era of the Companions and Successors, there appeared certain people who opted for over-meticulousness and extreme rigidity ... The utmost effort should be made to tame the fury of both the carnal and the aggressive self. Therefore they renounced sexual intercourse, delicious food and fine clothing ... This is the mysticism of the ordinary men: knowing to measure when performing their *ex-*

[1] The Prophet himself brought to a close the era of prophethood and was the inaugurator of the era of sainthood (*Tafh*. I, 76).

[2] 'Revelation' that is observed while awake by the faculty of *khayāl*, which can visualize objects which are not present.

*ercitia spiritualia*[3] ... The ṣūfī, who first took this line of action and laid down the rules for it, was Ḥārith Muḥāsibī (d. 857)'' (*A.Q.* 71). In that epoch ''connection with ṣūfī masters was established by spiritual conversations (*ṣuḥba*), teaching and keeping to the rules required for the refinement of the soul, not as yet by the institutes of the *khirqa* (the assumption of a patched cloak) and *bayʿa* (making the vow of allegiance) (*Intibāh* I, 2 f.);

3. ''In the time of the ṣūfī leader al-Junayd (d. 910), or shortly before it, mysticism began to reveal different aspects. Now people's principal goal was to be attached to God with heart and soul ... Accordingly, they experienced states of theophany (*tajallī*) and of being veiled (*istitār*), of intimacy (*uns*) and estrangement (*waḥshat*) ... In this period *tawajjuh*—a term which indicates that a soul concentrates on the Ultimate Reality to such extent that it is coloured by the colour of God—did not yet fully exist. People were certainly overwhelmed by the lights of obedience and worship of God, but still the spiritual state of *tawajjuh* appeared only occasionally like flashes of lighting'' (*H.* II). ''al-Junayd, the 'Lord of the Sect' was the first person to loose himself from the extremely rigid practices and who, by adopting a middle course, was able to place every spiritual exercise where it rightly belonged ... In short, the refinement of the five *laṭīfas* is fundamental for traversing the ṣūfī Path by the method of al-Junayd'' (*A.Q.* 72 f.). In this era the customs of the *khirqa* and *bayʿa* were introduced (*Intibāh* I, 3). Consequently, ''this epoch became the epoch of the *ṭarīqa* (religious brotherhood)'' (*Tafh.* I, 77).
4. In the generation of Shaykh Abū Saʿīd b. Abiʾl-Khayr (d. 1049) and Shaykh Abuʾl-Ḥasan Kharaqānī (d. 1033) another new form was given to mysticism. Through *jadhb* (attraction by God) the spiritual state (*nisba*[4]) of *tawajjuh* was attained, on account of which it was discovered that there is only one Essence, upon which all things depend. They were absorbed in that Essence and they were coloured by It; thus they no longer needed to be occupied with *awrād* (phrase-patterned devotions), *waẓāʾif* (daily offices) and strenuous *exercitia spiritualia* (*H.* II).
5. In the age of al-Shaykh al-akbar Muḥī al-Dīn b. ʿArabī, or shortly before it, the intellectual power of mystics expended and, passing

[3] In view of people who in their zeal in performing most harsh practices ''allow a noble member of their body like the hand and foot to shrivel or render a human potency like sexual lust inoperative by cutting off the penis'', Shāh Walī Allāh observes that ''such people do not know what worship is, and they are not aware that altering God's creation is a sin with which the Merciful is not pleased'' (*B.B.* 119 f.).

[4] *Cf.* *Q.D.* 108: ''It indicates a habitude (*hayʾa*) that presupposes affiliation and connectedness with God''.

beyond the stage of psychic emotions, they engaged heart and soul in search of the highest realities in order to find out the devolutions (*tanazzulāt*[5]) of the Self-existent, the circumstances at the beginning of this process, and so on (*H*. II).

6. Thereafter a perverse sect appeared in Islam. These people[6] thought that God would be identical with the world and the world would be identical with God, and that no Account or Punishment will occur there. According to us, man realizes by nature that God is Unique, approving and disapproving, forgiving and punishing (*Tafh*. I, 206).
7. Hinting at himself in veiled terms, the Delhi divine discloses: "After many ages once again another terminator and inaugurator (of a mystic period) was born. He analysed and classified the various stages of man's development to perfection, putting all of them in their proper places ... He also sifted out the types of knowledge which have been divulged by the divine will for the good of the whole world and of which the seal of prophets is the source ..., and he hopes, God willing, that by his hand new life will spring up" (*Tafh*. I, 77 f.)[7].

*The mystic venture*. In the *Hamaᶜāt*, a type of handbook for the practice of a ṣūfī, Shāh Walī Allāh prescribes that a *sālik* (wayfarer on the Path) should perform 50 *rakᶜas* in a 24-hour period: 17 for the obligatory *ṣalāts*, 12 for the *rawātib* (*ṣalāts* which are recommended and are part of the so-called *sunna rātiba*, 'established norm'), 11 for the *ṣalāts* repeated during the night, 2 for the *ṣalāt* pertaining to the sunrise, 4 for the forenoon-*ṣalāt*, and 4 for the *ṣalāt* at the sun's decline. The fasts he ought to observe are those of the ᶜArafa, the ᶜĀshūrāᵓ, the three days of every month mentioned in the traditions (= the 13th, 14th and 15th of every lunar month, the three 'white', i.e. moonlit, days) and the (first) six days of the month Shawwāl. As for the *ṣadaqa* (voluntary offering), he should feed a poor man every day from his own resources, and, besides the *ṣadaqa* at the end of Ramaḍān, he should clothe a poor person once a year. As regards his comportment in daily life, he should not distinguish himself from his own companions and family. If he belongs to the class of *ᶜulamāᵓ*, he should behave as one of them; if he belongs to the guild of artisans, he should

---

[5] Comprising the stages of *wāḥidiyya*, *ᶜālam al-arwāḥ*, *ᶜālam al-mithāl*, *ᶜālam al-ajsām* and *insān kāmil*.

[6] As, for instance, Ṣadr al-Dīn al-Qūnawī and ᶜAbd al-Raḥmān Jāmī (see *Khizāna* 2).

[7] *Cf*. also *Maktūb* 3: "one of the assignments of divine mercy for the present age is that all rational, traditional and esoteric knowledge are united in my mind in a harmonious way so that contrarities have been removed and every doctrine and theory are put in their proper context".

act as one of them, and if he belongs to the military people, he should follow their conduct[8] (*H.* V).

The mystic journey (*sulūk*) itself can be properly compared with the combustion process of ice: melting all the while it becomes water and then becomes water-vapour (*Saṭ.* 34). "Mystics", so our author expounds, "are transformed from state (*ṣifa*) to state. It happens like this: Below the ice a fire is kindled so that it melts and becomes water. After that, the heating continues till the coolness of the water disappears and it becomes tepid, hot and gets the effects of fire, i.e. of cooking, giving pain and causing blisters in the body of man. Yet, in spite of all these changes the water remains water, though through them the similarity between water and fire increases. In the same way the 'annihilation' (*fanāʾ*) and 'subsistence' (*baqāʾ*) of the mystics is not a discarding of the human form, but rather a withdrawing from qualities of an animal nature and an approaching nearer to human qualities of an angelic nature. After that, they rise to the rank of the *jabarūt*" (*Saṭ.* 40). Thus they reach the spot in the *ḥaẓīra al-quds* which is reserved for them. Finally, they rise to the realm of the *lāhūt* (*Saṭ.* 34).

The essence (*ḥaqīqa*) of the mystic journey, as Shāh Walī Allāh sets forth, "is that the *ḥukm* (rule) of one *laṭīfa* gains mastery over the other. Hence, there are two *fanā*'s:

1. the *fanāʾ* of the *wujūd ẓulmānī* (man's gloomy existence in this world) by which the rule of the *laṭīfas* of *qalb* and *ʿaql* gains mastery over the *nafs shahwiyya* (concupiscent soul), the *nafs sabuʿiyya* (ferocious soul) and the *nafs ammāra* (evil-prompting soul), which are attached to customs and usages. Accordingly, the mystic traveller is no longer governed by carnal lusts and customs ... Next, the *laṭīfas* of *rūḥ* and *sirr* gain mastery over him, on account of which he is overpowered by spiritual delight, obtained from intimacy of the *rūḥ* and knowledge of the *sirr*. Consequently, he turns away from all (material) delights ...
2. the *fanāʾ* of the *wujūd rūḥānī* (spiritual existence) by which either the rule of the *anāniyya kubrā* (full-fledged ego)[9], which is dispersed over

[8] Presumably a reference to the *khalwat dar anjuman* (solitude within the crowd), a principle dear to the Naqshbandī order. In elucidation of it our author observes *inter alia*: distinguishing oneself by the dress of a dervish gives other people the impression of hypocrisy and show (*Q.D.* 92).

[9] "In the Universe (*al-shakhṣ al-akbar*)", the Delhi divine explains, "three egos can be distinguished: 1) the full-fledged ego (*al-anāniyya al-kubrā*), i.e. the Universal Soul's self-knowledge; 2) the central ego (*al-anāniyya al-wusṭā*), i.e. the self-knowledge of the heart of the Universal Soul. In our terminology it is called *al-tajalli al-aʿẓam* ...; 3) the minor ego (*al-anāniyya l-ṣughrā*) which consists of self-knowledge on the part of souls possessing volition, i.e. angels, men, animals, and *jinn*" (*Tafh.* I, 104).

all existing things, gains mastery over the mystic wayfarer—when his own *anāniyya ṣughrā* (minor ego) fades away—; or the rule of the *ḥadjar al-baht*, which by diving into the *tajallī aʿẓam* returns to the origin from whence it gushed forth, gains mastery over him'' (*Tafh.* I, 230 f.).

If, however, the mystic journey is described *in detail*, the following stages the wayfarer has to pass can be noted:

1. the preparatory period of *ṭahāra* (purification). ''The method to be followed for this is that the *sālik* chooses a place of seclusion, eats and drinks in moderation, performs the *ghusl* (major ritual ablution) repeatedly ... and stays close to the contemplation of the light which is spread in the atmosphere (*jaww*). In a few days the light of *ṭahāra* will shine ... A distinguishing characteristic of the appearance of the light of *ṭahāra* is the enjoyment of ease, peace of mind and a friendly environment[10] (*Tafh.* I, 221 f.);
2. the performance of *dhikr*. ''In the opinion of the majority of mystics the (two) most preferable (patterns of) *dhikr* are the *dhikr* of 'negation and affirmation'[11] (stating: 'no divinity save Allāh') and the *dhikr* of the 'Name of God' (whereby the word Allāh is ejaculated continuously) ... In order to bring his spirit into a state of utmost tension, the wayfarer should dwell on thoughts of death, read edifying stories, and listen to admonitory words or pleasant melodies. Next, he should perform two *rakʿas* ..., and should say: 'No divinity save Allāh' with the tongue; (and it should be done in the way that) at the start 'no' is said from below (i.e. the navel) and 'divinity' in the brain[12] (as if it came from the pia mater, the delicate inner vascular membrane that invests the brain), (thereupon) driving 'save Allāh' forcefully into the heart ... The negation not only contemplates affection but God, but also any existence but God ... It is indubitable that if someone of a wholesome and affectionate nature performs *dhikr* in the directed manner for one or two hours, he will acquire complete tranquillity of mind, and will be troubled no more by disturbing thoughts, and he will be filled with a true yearning (*shawq*)'' (*H.* VI).

In respect of the highly debated question whether the Central Asian

[10] Whereas ''properties in contravention of the state of purity (*ṭahāra*) are engendered by using obscene language, criticising righteous ancestors ..., looking at the copulation of animals, associating with beautiful women or beardless youths ..., being afflicted with blood-diseases and cutaneous affection as purulent pustules, tetter, scabies, and itch'' (*H.* IX).

[11] ''It (this *dhikr*) contains many esoteric senses: 1) the removal of plain *shirk* (idolatory); 2) the removal of hidden *shirk*; 3) the lifting of veils from the knowledge of God'' (*H.B.* II, 72).

[12] I.e. he should make 'no' ascend from the navel to the brain; when it has arrived at the brain, he should say 'divinity'.

shaykhs of the Naqshbandī brotherhood (the so-called Khwājagān) only practised silent *dhikr* or also accepted the vocal method, Shāh Walī Allāh declares: "Some followers of the Naqshbandī order assert that the Khwājagān forbade the vocal *dhikr*. The real facts of this case are that the Naqshbandī leaders practised the vocal as well as the silent *dhikr*, the vocal *dhikr* even more frequently ... When, however, they perceived that by the Ḥanafī school the vocal *dhikr* was regarded 'reprehensible' (*makrūh*), they gave preference to the silent *dhikr*" (*H.* VI);

3. the *murāqaba* (spiritual communion with the divine Attributes). "After having attained the state of *shawq* (yearning) and having experienced its effect on his heart, the wayfarer should reduce social intercourse, keep aloof from worldly affairs and give up pleasures and the like, so that this state becomes full reality for him and devoid of any fantasy. Then he enters upon the stage of *murāqaba*.
   In the general opinion the essence of *murāqaba* is that the wayfarer's mind is completely concentrated on the divine Attributes[13] ... (so that eventually) he himself and everything else, from right and left, from above and below, from inside and out is encompassed by the Almighty, ... and he sees the splendour of God's light shining from all sides" (*H.* VII).
   After that, two courses are available to the wayfarer:
4. the course of *sulūk* and the course of *jadhb*. *Sulūk* refers to the cultivation of ethical qualities like humility, purity and passionate love (of God) (*ʿishq*). In contrast to the course of *jadhb*, it is corroborated by the *sharīʿa* (*H.* IX). The route of *jadhb*[14], the other choice the mystic traveller can make, refers to "the tearing of the veils (of the specifications) of being in order to reach the Ultimate Reality. It penetrates towards the very Beginning (*awwal*) in a retrograde motion by the way of one's ego (then: the *nafs kulliyya*, i.e. universal ego, the divine Names, and finally comes out of the *dhāt*, Essence of God). The course of *jadhb* consists of three parts:
   a) the *tawḥīd afʿālī* (Oneness in Action). It is the discovery that the universe in all its movements and in all its actions[15]—as though it were a marionette—depends on the direction and activity of One Person (sc. God);
   b) the *tawḥid ṣifātī* (Oneness in the Qualities) that appears after the

---

[13] (To this end) "some masters (of the Naqshbandī order) advise him to visualize a totally empty space or a vast light" (*Q.D.* 82).

[14] The gate of the *jadhb* has been opened by ʿAlī. "For that reason the chains of descent in the brotherhoods go back to him" (*H.* XI).

[15] Causing, for instance, death and life, poverty and wealth, disease and recovery.

*tawḥīd afʿālī*. This refers to the recognition that there is a unity (archetype) (contained) in the various forms of the phenomena as, for instance, the idea of universal man enclosed in the multiple human individuals;

c) the *tawḥīd dhātī* (Oneness in the Essence)[16]. When the wayfarer contemplates his own ego and dwells further upon it, he will through his ego reach the root of being. Subsequently, the state of *tawḥīd dhātī* descends upon him like a thunderbolt (*H.* IX). Of the curious experiences one has with this state the following report is made: "When the mystic reaches the *hayūlā* (primary matter) of everything and the origin of all, he himself becomes the origin of all that exists ... (and) receives the power to create ... This manner of creating means that he is able manifest himself in whatever shape he chooses ... Consequently, an advanced mystic (*ʿārif*) is able to become earth, water, air of fire, and to assume the shape of ... a mute animal, a plant ..., an angel, heavenly body or a star ... (And having attained that state) he possesses all divine attributes except self-existence and eternity" (*Tafh.* I, 169 f.).

*Characterization and evaluation of ṭarīqas*. In Shāh Walī Allāh's writings we encounter many detailed expositions of *ashghāl* (meditation technics) of ṣūfī orders prevalent in 18th century India, but there is no point in reproducing his description of those practices, since they are already extensively and ably explained in recent works of Western scholars[17]. Our attention will be restricted to the summary view expressed by our author at the end of an excursus on ṣūfī rituals, for they present some interesting instances of acute observation.

In the summing-up of his treatment of the *ashghāl* of various brotherhoods he states in his *al-Qawl al-jamīl*: "The goal of all *ṭarīqas* is the bringing about of a habitude (*hayʾa*) in the *nafs nāṭiqa* which they name *nisba* ('relationship') since it establishes a relation and connection with God ... Its most distinguishing feature is its being a state (*ḥāla*) in the *nafs nāṭiqa* that engenders affinity with the angels and a longing for the World of Omnipotence". (*Q.D.* 108). In the *Hawāmiʿ* the specialities of the different ṣūfī leaders are enumerated: "the fundamental *nisba* of Ghawth al-Aʿẓam[18] was the *nisba* of Uwaysī-hood[19] ...; the fundamental *nisba* of

---

[16] I.e. becoming conscious of one's oneness with God.

[17] As, for instance, by J. Spencer Trimingham in his *The Sufi Orders in Islam* (Oxford 1971).

[18] Honorary title of ʿAbd al-Qādir al-Jīlānī (d. 1166) who gave his name to the order of the Qādiriyya, "and is present in his *ṭarīqa* as a *rūḥ*" (*Tafh.* I, 85).

[19] By this *nisba* information is supplied about God's rule of the Universe and spiritual bonds are formed with the souls of ṣūfī masters and even with the soul (*rūḥ*) of the Prophet (*H.* XI).

Khwāja Bahāʾ al-Dīn Naqshband (d. 1389) was the *nisba* of *yād-dāsht*[20] (concentration on the reality of God which is stripped of sounds, words, ecstatic emotions and so on) ...; the *nisba* of the early masters of the Chishtīs was the *nisba* of *nūr* (light), *ṭahāra* (purity)[21] and *sakīna* (divine presence) permeated with elements of the *nisba* of *ʿishq* (ardent love), while the *nisba* of the Chishtī master of the intermediate period was the *nisba* of *ʿishq* permeated with elements of the *nisba* of *nūr* and *sakīna*, and ... the *nisba* of the later Chishtī masters became the *nisba* of *ʿishq* permeated with portions of the *nisba* of *tawḥīd* (consciousness of one's oneness with God). The *nisba* of the Suhrawardī order is that of the light of purity and the light of divine presence permeated with elements of the *nisba* of *yād-dāsht*". (*H*. XVI).

As for Shāh Walī Allāh's personal liking, at least before 1732 he seems to have had an unmistakable preference for the Mujaddidiyya-Naqshbandiyya order. For in a treatise written in that year we read: "in India the most illustrious and pure and the least heretical *ṭarīqa* is surely the Mujaddidiyya-Naqshbandiyya order. It has two branches, one starting with Maʿṣūm (d. 1688), the third son of Aḥmad Sirhindī, and the other with Shaykh Ādam Banūrī (d. 1643). With both branches[22] I have a firm tie" (Introduction of the *Risāla Muqaddima saniyya fiʾl-intiṣār liʾl-firqa al-Sunniyya*, Khuda Bakhsh Library, Arab. Ms. 3660). But later, in reply to a question put by his disciple Muḥammad Amīn about the preferability of the respective Indian *ṭarīqas* he makes a more differentiated pronouncement. He advances then the opinion that the particular excellence of the Naqshbandiyya[23] order lies in its performance of *murāqaba*. The best method of obtaining inner light, however, is offered by the followers of ʿAbd al-Qādir al-Jīlānī. For a proper application of the preaching of the ancients to conditions of the present, the Chistīs[24] are the right people. Suhrawardīs are to be preferred for their admirable adherence to the Qurʾān and *sunna* (*Kalimāt-i ṭayyibāt*, 160).

---

[20] *Cf.* Shāh Walī Allāh's personal advice (*waṣiyya*): "in order to obtain *yād-dāsht* one should study the treatises of the Naqshbandiyya" (*Tafh*. II, 242).

[21] By this *nisba* "a broad road is opened for the mystic traveller leading to the reality, intimacy and joy of angels" (*H*. IX).

[22] In the first chapter of the *Ḥamaʿāt* they are given the distinctive appellatives: Aḥmadiyya and Ādamiyya.

[23] Another special merit of this order is that, while later mystics are not inclined to pay attention to the injunctions of the *sharīʿa*, the Masters of the Naqshbandiyya maintain that one ought to keep the scope afforded by the *sunna* (*A.Q.* 87). Further, " the Naqshbandīs are the strongest in keeping the bestial soul in subjection and mortifying it by *yād-dāsht*. It is like this because Shaykh Bahāʾ al-Dīn himself was appointed as a moral reformer in central Asia where the people had a most vigorous bestial nature" (*Tafh*. I, 85).

[24] Accordingly, "the Chishtīs enjoy much popularity ... In India this brotherhood had the largest following" (*Tafh*. I, 86).

CHAPTER SIX

# ETHICS

In order to provide a solid foundation for any exposition on moral philosophy, one needs first of all to determine the criteria to be applied to the moral category of 'good'. In Islam the crucial dilemma is this: Is a thing good because God has designated it as such or has He designated it as such because it is good? Shāh Walī Allāh apparently prefers to avoid making a choice on this issue. Rather, he likes to suggest that both assumptions hold good. Ultimately it is no doubt dependent upon God's decision whether something is to be regarded as good (*ḥasan*) or vile (*qabīḥ*) (*Tafh.* I, 146). It is wrong, however, to think that God is like a master who is fond of giving senseless orders with the sole purpose of testing his servant's obedience. On the contrary, reason can in most cases discern the considerations of expediency contained in the divine commands and prohibitions (*H.B.* I, 4 f.).

Still, the designs of God's management extend beyond the sense deducible from most of His prescriptions. The very principle on which God created mankind is that the human individual should come up to the authenticity (*ṣiḥḥa*) specific to man (*H.B.* I, 51). Consequently, good is all that is in consonance with human nature, and vice is as repugnant to the agent as the braying of an ass (*Khizāna* 8). Man's felicity consists in giving full scope to the properties which are part of his nature (*H.B.* I, 36). "All that leads to a correct evaluation of one's self, self-confidence and dignity, is righteous and appropriate" (*B.B.* 52). Sin is in essence a deviation from true humanity (*Taʾwīl* 18). When something yields what it should not yield, or does not produce what it ought to produce, we have to do with evil (*sharr*) (*H.B.* I, 12). Therefore, according to our author, is smearing the eyelids with *kuḥl*[1] a permissible beauty treatment, because it accentuates the properties allotted to the human species; but depilation or shaving the beard is reprehensible, for in that way changes in God's creation are effected (*H.B.* I, 107 and 182). If somebody raises the objection: "Why is man under the obligation to perform the *ṣalāt* and to obey the Prophet, and why is he prohibited from adultery and thieving?", he is to be given the answer:

"These things are prescribed and forbidden him in precisely the same way as the herbivore is ordered to eat grass and is forbidden to eat meat,

[1] Antimony reduced to fine powder and used for blacking the eyelids.

and beasts of prey are compelled to eat meat and are denied the eating of grass" (*H.B.* I, 24).

Man's original nature (*fiṭra*) possesses three kinds of excellences:

1. *ʿiffa* (abstinence from what is unlawful), i.e. not becoming immersed in sensual delights, either by one's nature or by one's practice. God regards believers who achieve this quality as godfearing and pious people;
2. *tafarrus* (being endowed with acumen). By virtue of this endowment the mind can quickly deduce knowledge from Qurʾān verses, and can corroborate intuitively the reality of the Self-existent, the mission of prophets, and the truth of the Resurrection;
3. *sakīna* (assurance owing to a light descending from God). To its effects belong persistence in the duties of worship, firmness (*ṣabr*) in adversities, indignation at the enemies of God, and a stable psychic state (*Tafh.* I, 34 f. and II, 112).

Biologically, man belongs to the class of animals. Since his happiness depends on a full development of the potencies inherent in him, it is logical that the animal potency should not become divested of its own nature, should not belie its temperament and should not adopt a course of conduct contrary to its true character (*A.Q.* 51).

In man this potency is created in two ways:

1. as that of a violent and stubborn beast, like a lively stallion;
2. as that of a weak and tender quadruped, like a gelded animal (*H.B.* I, 26).

If these two types strive for an amelioration of their inner life, the former will resort to harsh disciplines and strenuous fasts and vigils, while the latter will apply himself to *dhikrs* only (*H.* XVIII).

Equally, the angelic potency in man is created in two ways:

1. like the *mala aʿlā*, of whose most conspicuous characteristic is their being imbued with knowledge of God's Names and Attributes, and the subleties of the World of Omnipotence;
2. like the *mala sāfil*, whose characteristic it is to be stirred up as will-less beings by impulses percolating upon them from above (*H.B.*, I, 26).

The former are able to interpret divine language, the latter to read the hidden thoughts of others (*ishrāf*) (*H.* XVIII).

As for the interrelation of the angelic and the animal potency, again two possibilities are given:

1. a state of tension (*tajādhub*) because of mutual attraction and repulsion;
2. a joining together in mutual convergence (*iṣṭilāḥ*). This can be effected if the angelic potency renounces its own higher goals and gets down to the level related to qualities as, for instance, generosity of

the soul, proper sexual behaviour, fixing the attention on the hereafter and not dwelling upon the present fleeting life, whereas the animal potency, for its part, tries to rise above its own ends and to aim its efforts at what is not far from the interests of the general community (*H.B.* I, 26). People in whom this symmetry between both potencies is found are, as a rule, well-mannered. Rarely do they become excited. They conform faithfully to the injunctions, but when trying to reach a higher degree of perfection they travel at the speed of a little ant (*H.* XVIII).

Among men in whom the angelic and animal potency are on strained terms, four groups are prominent:

1. When a superior angelic potency (of the type of the *mala aᶜlā*) and a powerful animal potency are in a state of tension the most eminent characters appear in the form of prophets, zealous devotees, and heroes of war;
2. if an angelic potency of a lower rank and a powerful animal potency are in a state of tension within a person, he stands more in need of practising austerities than other people. With these, however, no performance of any extraordinary acts like miracles (*karāmāt*) will ever be noticed;
3. a tension between a superior angelic potency and a weak animal potency produces individuals who withdraw from the world in order to please God;
4. people who withdraw from the world for the sake of the hereafter[2], however, develop from a tension between an angelic potency of a lower rank and a weak animal potency (*H.B.* I, 27 and *H.* XVIII).

Then, the Delhi divine also makes use of terms chiefly derived from Qurʾān to categorize believers according to the standard of ethical and religious values.

Here again he distinguishes four groups:

1. the *mufahhamūn*[3] (those who are informed by the *mala aᶜlā*). This is the highest class. They are the type of integrated personalities (*ahl iṣṭilāḥ*), equipped with a well-balanced and harmonious disposition. From the side of the *mala aᶜlā* they receive divine information and exalted experiences. Although after Mohammed prophethood was closed in principle, some elements of it continue to exist in the institution of *mufahham*-hood. Consequently, for the appearance of a *mufahham*

[2] Deeds performed to earn Paradise are valued much less by mystics—if not rejected with disdain—than acts testifying to one's love for God (A. Schimmel, *Mystical Dimensions of Islam*, North Carolina Press 1975, 39).

[3] Actually an epithet conferred upon their *imām* by the Twelver Shīᶜa (cf. *EI*² III, 1167).

similar conditions of a renewal of religion, guidance of people and so on are required as in the case of the mission of a prophet. So the *mufahhamūn* "have become lights, embodiments and representatives of prophethood" (*H.* XIX and *H.B.* I, 84);

2. the *sābiqūn* (those who excel in good works), *inter alia* mentioned in *Qur<sup></sup>ʾān* XXXV, 32. They are either people whose *laṭīfas* of *rūḥ* and *sirr* have gained mastery over their *qalb, ʿaql* and *nafs*, or individuals who refine their *qalb* and *ʿaql* with the aid of the revealed law (*sharʿ*). The integrity of their attitude (*mizāj*) implies that their animal nature is not too weak and their angelic nature of not too low a level (*Tafh.* I, 188 f.).

Among them can be counted

a) the *mufarridūn* (persons who retire to lead a solitary religious life). "A distinctive trait of theirs is that their bearing appears to be confined to the commemoration (*dhikr*) of God, always accompanied with a sound mental attitude and a proper self-control, while this commemoration takes possession of their whole bodies and powers" (*B.B.* 159);

b) the *ṣiddīqūn* (zealous persevering believers). "A distinctive trait of theirs is that their deeds appear to be in entire conformity with their words. In addition they always display sound judgment, prudence and firmness of character" (*B.B.* 158);

c) the *shuhadāʾ* (martyrs). "A distinctive trait of theirs is that the strength and energy spent in the cause of God and against the enemies of God are taken as understood among them and not taken as something enforced upon them. Their hearts are, so to say, replete with lending help and support to the faith" (*B.B.* 158);

d) the *rāsikhūn fiʾl-ʿilm* (persons who are firmly rooted in knowledge). "A distinctive trait of theirs is that their knowledge seems to have descended from God directly into their very hearts, and seems to emerge as fire struck with a flint although blended with their sound nature and perfect self-control" (*B.B.* 158 f.);

e) the *ʿibād* (true worshippers). An excellent example of this group is Abū Dharr, a favourite companion of the Prophet: "already in the pre-Islamic period he used to pray to Allāh in a way approved by God. When thereupon he became a Muslim, the teaching of worship in the right manner and the teaching of the repudiation of polytheism appealed strongly to him right away" (*B.B.* 159);

f) the *zuhhād* (ascetics). They are the people whose carnal faculty is highly purified (*A.Q.* 67). "In their eyes the world is a nonentity and (worldly-minded) men are, according to them, like the dung of camels" (*B.B.* 160);

g) persons who have the capacity of functioning as a successors of the prophets (*H.B.* I 116). Such a successor (*khalīfa*) "is driven to spread the religion of God and to relieve God's creatures of inquities" (*B.B.* 160);

h) people with a fine character (*aṣḥāb al-khulq al-ḥasan*). "These are the persons who perfect magnanimity (*samāḥa*) by generosity, humility, forgiveness towards those who do them an injustice, endurance in the face of odd situations" (*B.B.* 159);

i) those who bear a resemblance to angels (*mutashābihūn biʾl-malāʾika*). "These are the people who always observe the rule of purity, never cease praying, speak little and sleep only for a short while (since the greater part of the night is reserved for praying) ... Thus they begin to see angels and to converse with them face to face (*B.B.* 160).

3. The *aṣḥāb al-yamīn* (Companions on the Right-hand Side), *inter alia* recorded in *Qurʾān* LVI, 27. Their *qalb* and *ʿaql* are only partly reformed since their angelic nature is of a very low level and their animal nature very weak (*Tafh.* I, 189).
Among the Companions of the Right-hand Side, to whom the majority of believers belong, can be reckoned:

a) those who bear a resemblance to those who excel in good works. They apply themselves assiduously to reaching their original status (of those who excel), but their disposition is (too) weak (to succeed). They are not self-reliant. Consequently, their perfection lies in acquiring habits" (*B.B.* 160);

b) those who are imitators of zealous persevering believers. "They are concerned about nothing but sitting down in the latter's presence and listening to their speech" (*B.B.* 161);

c) those who are imitators of martyrs, of people detesting heretics and refuting Muʿtazilites and the like;

d) imitators of people who are firmly rooted in knowledge. "Those do their utmost to write down knowledge concerning the religious laws and to absorb knowledge coming from the Prophet, but to understand them they do not go back to the primary sources of those laws ... They are not disposed towards such research" (*B.B.* 161);

e) imitators of people who retire to lead a solitary religious life. "Their tongues have become supple by the commemoration of

God, whether they understand the inner meaning of it or not. Their knowledge of God is second-hand'' (*B.B.* 161);

f) imitators of people with a fine character. ''These are of moderate virtuousness'' (*B.B.* 162);

g) imitators of true worshippers. ''These are in the habit of performing many acts of supererogation'' (*B.B.* 162);

h) imitators of the ascetics. ''At a certain moment in a vacant place they may think of God and His punishments so that tears flow from their eyes. Thereafter, however, they become occupied with their family, property and means of subsistence so that they forget (God and His punishments) almost totally'' (*B.B.* 162);

i) imitators of those who bear a resemblance to angels. ''These are in the habit of taking extraordinary pains in cleansing their bodies, in observing purification and in disciplining themselves'' (*B.B.* 162). ''In short: there exist many kinds of *aṣḥāb al-yamīn*. All of them can succeed in eliminating the crookedness of their souls and are capable of acquiring some sort of salvation'' (*H.* XX).

4. The *aṣḥāb al-aʿrāf* (Companions of Limbo, i.e. the boundary between Paradise and Hell). Mention is made of them in *Qurʾān* VII, 47[4]. There exist two kinds:

a) people who are sound in body and mind but have not received the message of Islam at all (*H.B.* I, 116 f.) ''as, for instance, inhabitants of high and inaccessible mountains. They do not attribute associates to their Lord, nor do they deny Him or believe in Him ... (being) merely interested in things by which profit is gained'' (*B.B.* 163). ''When they die, they return to the state of unconsciousness—and they do not suffer punishment or reap reward'' (*H.B.* I, 117);

b) ''persons of limited intelligence like small children, lunatics, insane people, silly fools, farmers and slaves. They are ... hardly able to know and worship their Lord, resembling water which, because of its liquid quality, cannot adopt any characteristic shape ... As much faith as the Prophet considered to be sufficient for a negro slave girl who pointed to the sky when he asked her: ''Where is God?'' is sufficient for them'' (*B.B.* 164).

As we have noticed above, recognition of the interdependence between man's angelic and animal nature is imperative if we wish to get a clear

---

[4] According to Muslim exegetes, this Qurʾānic verse refers to people whose good and bad deeds are equal in number and who must remain the last to enter Paradise (J. I. Smith and Y. Y. Haddad, *The Islamic Understanding of Death and Resurrection*, New York, 1981, 91 and 218).

perception of the constitution of the various moral categories in which mankind is divided. Also, and that may sound the more paradoxical, animal appetites appear to be essential constituents of virtues specific to man, since the latter have as a substratum, out of which they grow and develop, the instincts which the human being has in common with the *abnā al-jins*, i.e., his fellow animals. Man's seven characteristics of excellence are, in fact, the result of the influence of three special capacities on the substratum of animal instincts. These three,—as it were—extra qualities, which are lacking in animals, are named *al-raʾy al-kullī* (motivation to act for the general good), *ẓarāfa* ("culture", i.e. everything appealing to soul and eye), and *takammul* (inner urge towards self-perfection). On account of these three incentives the *homo sapiens* is enabled to refine his environment and his own self. Valour (*shajāʿa*) originates in the transformation of anger sublimated in the pursuit of the general good (*B.B.* 28 ff.). One of the universal purposes it can serve is the *jihād*.

*ʿIffa* (temperance), to take another of these seven virtues, is the outcome of *al-raʿy al-khullī*'s refining influence on the urges of our sex instinct. *ʿIffa* in Shāh Walī Allāh's idiom certainly does not convey the connotation of chastity or continence. *ʿAfīf*, so the Indian ethicist argues, is the man of a strong sexual need and a passionate love of women[5], not the man of a weak sexual need and with little liking for women in general, infatuated as he might be with one individual woman in particular; whereas it is exactly the natural and seemly attitude for a woman to possess a conforming sense of attachment to one man only: "Hence, there is a universal agreement that it is honourable for a man to possess several wives, but that it is immoral for a woman to have several husbands at the same time. This is the only correct *ʿiffa*" (*B.B.* 41 f.). In other words by the term *ʿiffa*, Shāh Walī Allāh means something like displaying a proper, i.e. natural, sexual behaviour. When the lower impulses of arrogance and conceit are polished by *al-raʾy al-kullī*, its result is the virtue of *samāḥa* (magnanimity). "A magnanimous person", so it is stated, "is dignified, enduring, controlled, confident of the future, self-reliant, energetic, undeterred, undaunted, generous, forgiving, not acquisitive, unassuming and gentle" (*B.B.* 43).

If, however, the passions of arrogance and conceit are refined by *ẓarāfa*, culture, the outcome is consistency in conduct (*al-samt al-ṣāliḥ*). It is the virtue which "consists in a stable firmness of the heart in exercising

---

[5] If, however, passionate love of women induces men regularly to repudiate their wives and continuously to contract new marriages, they do not differ factually from whoremongers (*H.B.* II, 138)

control over external behaviour and thought, so that (on the one hand) no sudden delusive thought or momentary impulse, which might divert man from his habitual proceedings, arises and (on the other hand) no inconsistency in external conduct is displayed'' (*B.B.* 47). Another object of sublimation is the organ of animals and men producing sounds. If *ẓarāfa* penetrates into a strong voice, articulate and coherent speech can be effected. When *al-raʾy al-kullī* and the urge of self-perfection penetrate it, the result of it is mastery of language (*faṣāḥa*) which enables man to communicate the most profound mysteries (*B.B.* 30). Thus the tongue acts as a mirror of the mind. This function, however, is not a monopoly of the tongue. Man's limbs (*jawāriḥ*) are capable of the same, so that the external behaviour correctly reflects what is in his mind (*qalb*). If such has become a habit of a person, he possesses the sixth virtue, designated by our author as *diyāna*. This is surely a private interpretation of the term, for usually *diyāna* denotes qualities such as piety and fidelity. In the terminology of Shāh Walī Allāh *diyāna* stands for the capacity to properly co-ordinate man's cognitive faculties with his external behaviour so that his bodily gestures give an adequate expression of his state of mind (*B.B.* 46 f.). The seventh ability which marks the superiority of human potentialities over the animal disposition as such, is *ḥikma* (wisdom). ''It is attained when the pursuit of the general good and the inner drive toward self-perfection dominate man's excursions into all the different fields of knowledge ... It stimulates the mind to gain an over-all estimation of knowledge which it receives from intuition, ratiocination or divine light, as designed for mankind, and is called *sharᶜ* (revealed law) ... Wisdom should not be understood to consist of subtle speculations—a speciality of philosophers and their imitators—nor of issues involving deep intuition ...—a speciality of ṣūfīs and their like. Wisdom is rather that which guides people of a sound disposition in their workaday life and which concerns practical knowledge'' (*B.B.* 30, 38 and 40).

The human being, however, is not merely a refined animal being of a higher evolutionary stage; he also occupies a middle position between animals and angels. While angels can only be righteous and 'knowing' (i.e. acquainted with the Law) and animals do not have any notion of justice and knowledge of the Law, man as intermediate has been entrusted with *taklīf*, with being accountable. Consequently, he has perfection *in posse*, not *in esse* (*H.B.* I, 19 f.).
To that end God has committed an angelic and an animal power to each individual's charge.

In view of this disposition, the human individual has available to him two ways of improving his moral standard:

a) eradication of his bestial nature, the method approved by Neo-Platonists and by mystics striving after trances (the *majdhūbūn*)[6];
b) correction of one's bestial nature. In this case the bestial is 'wrapped up', while its substance is still kept intact. For this second way the model guides, *imāms*, are the abovementioned *mufahhamūn*, the highest class of men, who are charged to maintain and renew the *dīn*, favoured as they are by the light of prophethood (*H.B.* I, 52 f.).

The latter approach, consisting in the reform of man's bestial nature, is undoubtedly to be preferred. It is easier: the eradication of that nature requires the practice of rigorous austerities, an exertion beyond the capacity of the majority of people. It is of more avail to society: by following in the footsteps of the *mufahham* prophetic ends of general welfare are pursued, whereas the adoption of the first method results in sainthood, which is clearly of very limited utility to economic and social life.

If the second course is adopted, the most commendable line of conduct is to focus one's attention on the four cardinal virtues, being the best 'fabric' in which to 'wrap' bestial nature. "These four virtues are precisely the ones which all the prophets have exhorted the people to assimilate. There can be no question here of any abrogation (*naskh*) and no room is left for any change" (*A.Q.* 52).

The four basic moral excellences, advanced by the Indian scholar, are purity (*ṭahāra, naẓāfa*), humility (*ikhbāt, khudūᶜ*), sublimation of the mind (*samāḥat al-nafs*), and rectitude (*ᶜadāla*)[7]. Purity affects the most remote depths of the soul, sanctifies it and links it up with angels, so that an affinity with them is created. Thus, purity prepares the soul for gaining moral perfection (*H.B.* I, 54 and 174). By *dhikr* and recitation of the Qurʾān the second fundamental virtue, humility, is nourished. "When a man devotes all his efforts to realizing God's presence throughout his being, ... he experiences the same feeling of awe as do people in the presence of kings ... and gets into the same state of mind as the *mala aᶜlā* when standing in front of the bewildering Majesty of their Creator" (*H.B.* I, 54). Through humility he may obtain a glance at the World of Omnipotence (*jabarūt*) (*H.B.* II, 67). Thus, humility prepares the soul for the acquisition of perfection in knowledge, i.e. the capacity to absorb divine knowledge. Endurance and firm resolve are essential to the gain-

---

[6] Neo-Platonism taught an asceticism which was identified with the purification necessary to rise to ecstasy.

[7] The four cardinal virtues as enumerated by al-Ghazālī, Ibn Miskawayh, Ibn ᶜArabī and Ibn Sīnā are: *ḥikma, shajāᶜa, ᶜiffa* and *ᶜadl*. The first three of these so-called Platonic moral excellences function on the lower level of *al-akhlāq al-fāḍila* in Shāh Walī Allāh's ethics, i.e. they are part of the additional qualities which animals lack, and are not qualified to serve as attributes to elevate man to the angelic sphere.

ing of the third virtue, *samāḥat al-nafs*, by which man attains complete independence from the impulses of the self[8] (*A.Q.* 93). If *samāḥa* refers to promptings of restlessness and impatience, it is called *ṣabr* (voluntary resignation); if relating to lust for revenge, it is termed 'forgiveness'; if it regards impulses of greediness, it is named 'munificence' (*sakhāwa*) and 'contentment' (*qanāʿa*) (*H.B.* II, 68). The fourth cardinal virtue, *ʿadāla* is primarily concerned with man's socio-political conduct. It is, to use Shāh Walī Allāh's own words, "the property to establish in an easy way a righteous, healthy order in family and civic life"[9]. Like *samāḥat al-nafs*, *ʿadāla* is a comprehensive attribute, including a series of praiseworthy and useful sub-qualities. For, if *ʿadāla* is connected with man's personal behaviour, his ways of sitting, standing, sleeping, speaking, and dress, it expresses *adab* (urbanity); if it has to do with care of property, it is called *kifāya* (good care); if it pertains to economic dealings, it is termed *ḥurriya* (honesty); if it refers to public issues, it expresses statesmanship (*siyāsa*); and if it bears on sociability, it is named 'civility' (*ḥusn al-muḥāḍara*) or 'solidarity' (*ḥusn al-muʿāshara*) (*H.B.* II, 68 f.). In conclusion, our author remarks that there may seem to be some incongruity between *samāḥat al-nafs* and *ʿadāla*, or, as we should say, between personal ethics and social ethics, but he warns against putting up a sharp division between them. The prophets used to point out that both virtues are to all intents and purposes complementary: *samāḥat al-nafs* rests on *ʿadāla*, and *ʿadāla* is made complete only by *samāḥat al-nafs* (*H.B.* II, 84).

For the cultivation of the four primary virtues, Islam supplies the appropriate means. *Ṣalāt*, connected with the purity of cult, offers room for the expression of humility and purity. The institute of *zakāt* is eminently suited to the development of *samāḥat al-nafs* and *ʿadāla* (*H.B.* I, 164).

"The quality (*ḥāla*) which is composed of those four cardinal virtues is called *fiṭra* (properly developed disposition)" (*H.B.* I, 55). There are, however, three perilous impediments (*ḥijāb*) that may prevent man from reaching such a disposition, to wit:

1. the physio-biological impulses of man (*ṭabīʿa*). They are occasioned by hankerings of the body after things like food, drink, sexual intercourse, and so on. The lower self (*nafs*) submits to the orders of the body, harbours a secret love for those hankerings and fails to heed the original nature of man (*B.B.* 113 f.);

[8] *Cf.* also *H.* XVII: "If this property has become rooted in man, all mean habits, which constituted a constant treat to his soul during his life, will be wiped out at one stroke in the hour of his death ... Most probably one's being exempt from the punishments of the grave depends on (the availability of) this property".

[9] "Through it the approval, favour, mercy and blessings of the *mala aʿlā* are gained" (*A.Q.* 53).

2. customs. These are an impediment if man's concern is to imitate the speech, style of dress, character, and social behaviour of the intelligentsia. In that case he will lend his ear to what he hears from his entourage instead of paying attention to information coming from the World of Omnipotence (*B.B.* 193)[10];
3. misconceptions about God (*jahl biʾllāh*). "Their substance is that man may have a mistaken concept of God because of his inability to think abstractly, whih is due to his having no proper talent for intellectual intuition and speculative thought" (*B.B.* 114). The worst fallacies into which he can then fall are:
   a) to believe that God is in the possession of human attributes;
   b) to imaging that human creatures can possess divine Attributes. In the first case we have to do with anthropomorphism (*tashbīh*), in the second with giving companions to God (*ishrāk*) (*H.B.* I, 57).

---

[10] Yet, one should not be too critical of customs. They may also render momentous support to the believer. A proper conveyance of the principles of belief in the Unity of God throughout the ages is extremely difficult, for it concerns an article of faith that can only be understood by intuition (*wijdān*); only very few people have a full grasp of it. If there were no customs, belief in the Unity of God would be renounced. Moreover, those who are fully occupied with their work and lack inner peace would not concern themselves with the message of God if there were no customs.
Nobody, therefore, should give up customs, unless he is endowed with reason and is well versed in making logical inferences on account of which his mind can dispense with the need for customs (*B.B.* 195 f.).

CHAPTER SEVEN

# THE LIFE TO COME

In the level of existence (*nashʾa*) qualified as 'the Return' (*maʿād*) Shāh Walī Allāh distinguishes four stages:
1. the intermediary stage (*barzakh*),
2. the Grand Resurrection (*al-qiyāma al-kubrā*),
3. the Day of Judgment (*yawm al-dīn*) and
4. Paradise and Hell (*Khizāna* 9).

"When a man dies, his *nafs* (*nāṭiqa*) clings closely to the imperceptible body[1] (of his *nasama*, psychic constitution). In this state he can only perceive with the help of inner senses such as the *ḥiss mushtarik* (*sensus communis*)[2], *wahm* (power of abstraction) and *idrāk* (logical comprehension)" (*Khizāna* 4). In the intermediary stage, the *nafs nāṭiqa* is still in need of a residu of *nasama* (being in the possession of nerve-centres that can absorb painful or pleasant sensations), so that man can be punished or be pleased[3] (*Tafh*. I, 166 f.). The trial to which man is subjected in the grave is different from the account to be rendered to God at the Day of Judgment: "in the grave, people are examined according to their singularities (*akhlāq*) and habits (*malakāt*), whereas during the Last Judgment they will be questioned about their actions and religious convictions" (*Khizāna* 9). Deeds which deserve requiting in the grave are fastened to the 'exterior' (*ẓāhir*) of the *nasama*, while deeds to be requited at the Resurrection are fastened to the 'interior' (*bāṭin*) of the *nasama* (*Tafh*. I, 234). In Hell only

[1] No longer having his earthly body at his disposal as a 'riding-animal', man at his death becomes "like a rider whose horse is taken away" (*Saṭ*. 25). The soul is no more agitated by external factors like hunger, thirst or anger, so it can reflect colours of the Holy World (*ʿālam al-quds*)" (*H.B.* I, 31). "At that time the angelic nature expands, while the animal nature becomes weaker" (*H.B.* I, 34).

[2] This faculty enables to hear without an ear, to see without an eye, and so on, and is a particular characteristic of the *nasama*. In afterlife it produces ethereal (*mithālī*) shapes which are of the same kind as those in which *jinns* and angels appear (on earth) (*Fuyūḍ*, 2nd Vision).

[3] For, when sojourning in the grave "two angels will come to him, one named Munkir and the other Nākir. They will question him on his religion and on Mohammed. If he is a firm believer, he will reply: 'My religion is Islam and Mohammed is the servant and messenger of God'. A door will then be opened for him towards Paradise, and a space will be made there for him as wide as the eye can see. A voice will say to him: 'Sleep the sleep of a bride', but if he happens to be an unbeliever or a hypocrite, he will reply (to the questions put to him): 'Alas, alas, I do not know'. At that moment his grave will be made so narrow that his ribs will be pressed together, and he will be struck with hammers of fire" (*B.B.* 150).

deep-rooted vices originating from the heart will be punished, and not adventitious (*ṭāriʾ*) bad habits[4] developed, for instance, under social pressure, such as making a show of one's works to men in order to be praised by them (*riyāʾ*), being out for a good reputation (*sumʿa*), and so on (*Tafh.* II, 61).

"In the intermediary stage two kinds of requital are realized:

1. the experience of delight or pain there is gained from good or evil habitudes ... Such an experience can be 'without a veil', as an ill person experiences sudden sensation; or 'behind a veil'[5], as a sleeping person sees his rage in the form of a wild beast, his bilious temperament in the form of fires and flames;
2. inspirations effected by angels who are appointed at that place to confer favours or to torment. Thus these angels appear to him as solacers or desolators" (*Tafh.* I, 252 f.).

As a consequence, most people of Mohammed's *umma* (community) who, as a rule, possess only slight animal characteristics and a weak angelic nature endure punishment for the greater part in the grave, so that they will be assembled on the Day of Judgment as 'light-weighted ones'. Those who are in the possession of a vehement animal nature — as is mostly the case with people of preceding *ummas* — will incur more punishment at the Resurrection than in the grave; or rather, they may not even be punished at all in the grave, but only at the Resurrection (*Tafh.* I, 234).

When, in this manner, some time has passed in the grave, the *nasama* becomes increasingly weaker in its structure and qualities, whereas the human *nafs nāṭiqa* begins to awake from a deep sleep[6]. From now on the latter[7] has to take upon itself the full responsibility for the deeds man committed during his earthly existence. At the same time atmospheric phenomena[8] occurs as a natural consequence of the decomposition of all spherical bodies (*B.B.* 140 and 152). Since during his stay in the grave man gets rid not only of typical features of his character but also of his

---

[4] On this score our author disagrees with al-Ghazālī who states in the *Iḥyāʾ* and the *Kimīyā* that bad habits (*akhlāq*) will also be punished in Hell.

[5] Because he belongs to the people of a slumbering psychic disposition (*B.B.* 148 f.).

[6] The World of the Grave, so Shāh Walī Allāh sets forth, can rightly be compared with a dream-world where — such in contrast to earthly experiences — dreams are never interrupted by an awakening (*B.B.* 148, *H.B.* I, 34). On the Day of Resurrection man will be transferred from his state of dreaming into a sphere of existence where the objects witnessed are an objective reality, "and not of a subjective character like a dream" (*B.B.* 153).

[7] Having attained its full development (*subūgh*) (*Khizāna* 4).

[8] These are catastrophic events at the end of the world preceding and announcing the Day of Judgment. According to Shāh Walī Allāh they "will happen three or four centuries from today" (*Tafh.* I, 162).

body, at the time of his resurrection from the dead he appears to have at his disposal a mental power and a bodily shape, that are specific to the human form. On the Day of Judgment nobody will be blind, deaf-and-dumb or suffer in similar fashion. He who happened to have had all kinds of delusions before will now possess a pure mind, able to grasp adequate knowledge of God (*Tafh.* I, 253).

Still, one should not think that the 'Gathering' (*ḥashr*) of the bodies and the return of the souls (*arwāḥ*) to them on the Day of Resurrection will be "a life that starts again from the beginning. No, it is simply a completion of a former genre of existence, in the same way as indigestion is the consequence of overeating. Were it otherwise, people on that Day would be different from those who led an earthly life and could not be punished for what they had done" (*H.B.* I, 37).

The reason why the dead may acquire a perfect shape at the Resurrection is that the *arwāḥ* are supposed to put on a bodily garment composed partly of corporeal elements and partly of constituents of the *ʿālam al-mithāl* (*H.B.* I, 19)[9]. In such an environment — i.e. owing to a permeation of components of a *mithālī* nature —, "conceptual matters (*maʿānī*) can take on a corresponding bodily form, as happened to David, to whom angels appeared representing two disputants in a lawsuit on whom he had to pronounce judgment; subsequently he understood that it was a typification of his violation of Uriah's wife (*Qurʾān* XXXVIII, 21-24) ... Most occurrences of the 'Gathering' will be of this kind ... There the souls (*nufūs*) all alike will witness (conceptual) objects that have assumed a visible form; accordingly, the guidance promulgated through the mission of the Prophet will be represented by a basin (*ḥawḍ*)[10], and the deeds for which the souls are held liable will be represented by weights[11], and so on" (*H.B.* I, 37).

On the Day of Resurrection "the World of Prefiguration (*ʿālam al-mithāl*) will be disclosed to man ... If we wish to describe in common parlance the scenes which most of the people in this World will witness, we can say (in the words of the messenger of God; see Mu., *Īmān* 299): On that Day, God will gather the people. And they will see Him without having doubts about seeing Him. And He will say: 'Let everybody follow

[9] As a consequence, an other-worldly body is more perfect and talented than this world's body: in this world there are predications (*aḥkām*) which only pertain to the body and other which merely regard the soul; in the hereafter, however, all predications are applicable just as well to the body as to the soul. There one might say: "My body understands" like one says 'My mind understands" (*Khizāna* 3).

[10] *Cf.* also *Khizāna* 9: "There the basin will be the materialization of the Prophet's guidance, since there is a strong resemblance between knowledge and water".

[11] *Cf.* also *Khizāna* 9 where it is stated that the balance (*mīzān*) stands for the divine attribute of the faculty of discrimination by which good and bad actions are discerned.

the thing he worshipped'. He who worshipped the moon will then follow the moon; he who worshipped idols (*ṭawāghīt*) will then follow idols. Subsequently, he and the other idolators will fall into Hell. This community (of Muslims) alone will be left while there are still hypocrites amongst them. God will come to them in a shape different from the one they know. Then He will say: 'In am your Lord, so follow this shape'. The believers will cry out (as the frightened Mary did when Gabriel suddenly appeared before her): 'We seek refuge from you with God' (*Qurʾān* XIX, 18). They will remain standing till their Lord comes to them in a shape they know. Thereupon He will lead them to Paradise." (*B.B.* 152 f.).

In another passage Shāh Walī Allāh gives the following more detailed account of this *visio beatifica*: "On the Day of Resurrection God will be seen by the believers in two ways:

1. He will reveal Himself in a manner which will be even more convincing than what reason deems credible. It will be as if it is a beatific vision with man's physical eye; there is, however, no question of a being opposite, a geographical place, a colour or a perceptible form (*shakl*)[12]. This is the kind of vision taught by the Muʿtazilites and other people. This view as such is correct; but the mistake they make is to consider this interpretation of the *visio beatifica* the only thing possible (sc. leaving no room for other explanations);
2. He will assume various shapes for them[13] (*Tafh.* I, 145), each of which will be adjusted to someone's private belief ..., as is the case with somebody who sees everything as red, when he holds a red glass before his eyes, and sees everything as green, when he holds a green one before his eyes, while the thing observed is in both cases one and the same object (*Lamḥa* 53).

In Paradise "bliss consists of two degrees:

1. Physical indulgences in the form of food, drink and sexual intercourse. All this is imprinted upon the World of Prefiguration, due to the fact that It functions as a mirror for the Corporeal World.
2. Being attracted to higher regions" (*B.B.* 154). Then two possibilities are open to the blessed one:
   a) to ascend by means of his *ḥajar al-baht*, Thus the latter will reach its home, *tajallī aʿẓam*;

[12] *Cf.* also *B.B.* 154: "The only veil remaining between the inhabitants (of Paradise) and their Lord is the cloak of divine Grandeur".

[13] I.e. "not God will be transformed from one shape into another on the Day of Resurrection, but men will see Him in different shapes" (*Taʾwīl* 103).

b) to ascend by means of his *nafs nāṭiqa*. Thus the latter will attain its region of origin, the *nafs kulliyya*. Finally, it may become a virtual image (*shaʾn*) of the Divine Being (*Tafh*. I, 128)[14].

---

[14] In *Tafh*. I, 227 this cycle of human existence is depicted as follows: the very beginning of human life is when a tiny piece (*nuqṭa*) of God's love becomes an individual *nafs nāṭiqa* and it is transported to the world here below. After its earthly life it experiences a second birth and becomes a jewel for the rays of God's World of Omnipotence. The *nafs nāṭiqa* becomes a mere appendage like a sixth finger of a man's hand. Finally, the *nafs nāṭiqa* is annihilated, the jewel hidden and the rays vanish. At that moment God terminates the journey. The cycle (*dawra*) has come to an end. The tiny piece of God's love has returned to its beginning, and relaxes from the hardships of the journey.
In *Saṭ*. 24 we read that for every individual who comes into the world here below there is a cyclical process to go through. In the beginning he is an incorporeal *ʿaql* (intellect). When the appointed time has come, he descends into the world of the senses along the same stairs as he will ascend as soon as he as completed the duration of his earthly life. Then he will reach the same point as he started from, and he will again become the same separate *ʿaql* he originally was.

## CHAPTER EIGHT

# PROPHETOLOGY

Man, the Koran teaches, was created as a *homo religiosis* (*Qurʾān* XXX, 30). A *dahrī*, a materialist, so Shāh Walī Allāh infers, is someone who rejects the knowledge of God granted him by birth (*H.B.* I, 79). In other words, Islam has, in principle, no need of a founder of religion or of a religious guide.

However, and that is also underlined by our author, man is neither an angel nor a beast. An angel cannot do anything but act righteously, and a beast is bound to follow his instincts without any commitment to ethical rules of conduct. Man is a combination of angel and beast. He possesses angelic leanings and animal passions (*H.B.* I, 26). History shows that from time to time people deviate from true humanity. Then wrath is roused against them in the *mala aʿlā*. Nevertheless, agents are sent to warn them in order to give them the chance to mend their ways. "For, God has several tongues at His disposal and many modes of expressing His solicitude. Pouring His wrath upon a people in one tongue does not preclude the possibility of His showing solicitude for them in another tongue!" (*Taʾwīl* 18)[1].

There are several kinds of prophets[2], but they have one pecularity in common: God did not create a *majāzī* (earthy) but a *jawwī* (ethereal) form for their spirit (*rūḥ*) and body in contradistinction to non-prophets whose acts and innate dispositions are 'coarse' (*wathīq*), proceeding as they do from their *majāzī* form. Part of this prerogative is that they gain a *tajallī dhātī* (manifestation of God's Essence) through a 'sloughing off'[3] (*insilākh*)

---

[1] *Cf.* also *Tafh.* I, 179: "The divine Manager does not leave the affairs of mankind to take their own course. On the contrary, He is full of eternal grace to men and wants to establish a good order. For that reason He has sent prophets".

[2] Or in the imaginative style of our author: "Prophets are sons of one man by different mothers: the father they have in common is the divine education preparing them for prophethood; the different mothers are their innate and acquired dispositions" (*Taʾwīl* 56).

[3] The prophets slough off their humanity and thus move toward the angelic stage (*Cf.* Ibn Khaldūn, *The Muqaddimah*, tr. F. Rosenthal, London 1958, I, 199). Moreover, apart from being distinct in character, prophets also differ in quality and success. In general the following two major classes can be distinguished:

1. The great ones. These are they who voice the language of the epoch (*dawra*) and the cosmic conjunctions (*qirānāt*). Triumph and victory are inseparable from them.
2. Those who preach in order to force proof on the people and act in accordance with God's wont (*sunna*) when assigning and announcing a disaster before it actually happens. These might be killed and find no credence with the people (*Tafh.* I, 102).

A major difference between Mohammed and the other prophets is that the *tadallī ʿazīm*

of this loosely attached ethereal form. Accordingly, when they concentrate their being upon God, this form of them fades away (*Tafh.* II, 15). Other properties with which every prophet is equipped are:

1. affinity (*tashabbuh*) of his *ḥajar al-baht*[4] with the *tajallī aʿẓam*;
2. affinity of his faculty for retentive imagination (*khayāl*) with the *mala aʿlā* due to which he gains knowledge from the *mala aʿlā*;
3. affinity of his practical abilities with the *mala aʿlā* through which he gains immunity from sins, purity, piety and righteousness;
4. civism of his rational soul (*nafs nāṭiqa*); his *nafs nāṭiqa* will have the special attribute that when its shadow falls on our phenomenal world, mankind is favoured with the blessings of both moral training and well-ordered polity;
5. the capacity to keep his three faculties in balance, that is to say that his concupiscent faculty, in the case of being profuse and abundant, is subdued by his leonine faculty; that his leonine faculty, in the case of fierce violence and 'boiling', is subdued by his rational faculty; and that his rational faculty, in the case of stiffness and drowsiness, is subdued by the *mala aʿlā*;
6. enjoying good fortune through victory over his enemies, winning the affection of beloved people, and continuance of his *milla* (religious community) and reign for a long period (*Qurrat* 328; *Tafh.* I, 240).
7. the seven virtues are fully developed in him. In addition to this, he dedicates himself to a world higher than this world, for in his very nature he is attuned to the World of Prefiguration, and his personage resembles the (ideal) human form because of the universal plan the (divine) Giver has in mind, as seen in His gifts;
8. all his knowledge is a gift bestowed by God, and not the outcome of any brainwork or reflection pertaining to the cultivated habits of a human being. All his knowledge is practical knowledge, not suited to abstract thought[5];

---

(God's mighty preservation) remained with him after his death in contrast to the other prophets who were cut off from it as soon as, at the end of their life, their mission had been accomplished or terminated. That is because at the Resurrection he will be a witness against all people as well as an intercessor for the sinners amongst them (*Fuyūḍ*, 10th Vision).

[4] It is the point of contact and link by which man gets into touch with the *tajallī aʿẓam* (*Saṭ.* 29).

[5] The prophets were *ummīs*, i.e. men whose hearts were not spoilt by outward intellectual achievement and learning (for this definition see A. Schimmel, *Dimensions* 218). *Ummī*-hood of prophets implies that "they did not classify the primeval and eternal Names of God ... They considered them as belonging to one and the same level ... Reference is made to them in God's Word: 'Say, all things are from God' (*Qurʾān* IV, 78). And they considered the renewing Names (*asmāʾ mutajaddida*) which come after them

9. he is endowed with a disposition that preserves from disobedience to the Law which has come down from the Creator;
10. he performs miracles, and this may happen in many ways: firstly, being distinguished from other people because of an inherent perfection gained by his contact (with the Unseen World), wonderful acts may appear from his body and psychic disposition which do not appear from others. Hence, he possesses the gift of reading hidden thoughts in others, finds his prayers answered, receives reliable announcements of glad tidings, has the capacity to do hard work as, for instance, walking long distances or being strenously active, is able to produce effective charms, to keep complete control of the situation and to apply the technique of inductive divination (*firāsa*). Secondly, if in the Unseen World it is deemed necessary that the prophet make a successful appearance so that his prestige is enhanced and his position strengthened, then he will gain victory over his enemies, and subdue them. Their hearts will be seized with fear and they will no longer be capable of any harm by artful machinations. Thirdly, after contact with the (divine) Sources, his mind is broadened; its knowledge and aspirations are now reckoned among the means of identifying the divine pre-determining Decree. Fourthly, if atmospheric occurrences take place through celestial processes of causality, the Source of the human species may consider them to be a remedy for the corruption by which human society is afflicted. Subsequently, the Chief Planner (of the universe: God) turns these atmospheric occurrences into a punitive miracle of the prophet (*B.B.* 175 f.). A striking instance of this is the Qurʾānic story of Ṣāliḥ and the she-camel. "In the *malakūt* (World of Sovereignty)", Shāh Walī Allāh explains, "every wickedness takes the shape of an animal, since wickedness possesses a natural affinity with animals ... At the request of Ṣāliḥ the wickedness of the people appeared in the shape of a she-camel. When they had killed it, the wickedness (like a soul which is no longer confined to a body) spread on all sides. A hurricane arose", accompanied by earthquakes. In this way, the punitive wonder was adapted to the environment of the Thamūdites, since they lived in a region of mountains and caves (*Taʾwīl* 21 f.).

---

and have to do with location in being and guidance as belonging to a different level. Reference is made to the latter in God's Word: 'Whatever good visits you if from God; whatever evil visits you is from yourself' (*Qurʾān* IV, 79) ... The prophets kept aloof from making any mention of *aʿyān* or *nufūs nāṭiqa*, and they only began to explain the properties of the *nasama*" (*Tafh.* II, 155). The same holds true of their knowledge of esoterics. Mohammed and the other prophets gave no indications concerning speculative mysticism (*ʿilm-i ḥaqāʾiq*). They merely offered information about the practice of sufism (*ʿilm-i sulūk*) and the refinement of the soul (*A.Q.* 22).

According to common Muslim creed, prophets need to dispose of miracles (*muʿjizāt*) in order to prove their identity and to silence opponents. But Shāh Walī Allāh disagrees with orthodoxy in the postulate of their being a *conditio sine qua non*, and declares against it: "this is not a fixed rule. It is necessary, however, for there to be something similar to which people can give credence. That may be a rational argumentation (*burhān*), a (heavenly) book or a mode of conduct (*samt*) distinct from that of other people" (*Khizāna* 5). Besides, various so-called 'miracles' that are thought to be occurrences infringing upon the customary course of things, turn out to be normal phenomena when observed[6] more closely.

To give an example. Many Muslim scholars imagine that the words ("the moon is split" in *Qurʾān* LIV, 1) refer to a miracle God performed for Mohammed. But according to our author, it is not necessary to assume that the moon actually split in two. In corroboration of this, the view of Ibn al-Mājashūn[7], a Mālikite jurisprudent, is cited, stating: "This phenomenon was occasioned by a cohesion of small particles of water into, so to speak, one plane. Behind it there was a mountain or a dense cloud. Together these produced the effect of a mirror. When the moon was reflected in it, people observed two moons in the sky. Since a part of the reflected and a part of the real moon were concealed, two halves were seen in the sky" (*Taʾwīl* 103 f.)[8].

Shāh Walī Allāh exercises more caution in regard to orthodox critics than in the case of his elucidation of the moon's splitting when he deals with the story of Mohammed's *miʿrāj* (the ascent to heaven): "the journey by night to the Further Mosque, and then to the Lote-tree of the boundary and so on took place in a bodily way while the Prophet was

---

[6] *Cf. Taʾwīl* 8 f.: "You should know that when God in His rule of the world displays a breach in the course of nature, He nevertheless does this within the framework of the customary sequence of natural events, however unstable this may be. On this account breaches in the course of nature still have slight natural causes. It is as if these natural causes are always there whenever God's decree is executed". In *Khizāna* 4 we read: "A breach in the laws of nature is impossible. It can only be a 'breach' from the point of view of the normal observations made through our ordinary perceptive faculty".

[7] The same Ibn al-Mādjashūn is quoted when the Delhi divine sets forth that, under extra-ordinary conditions, people may acquire subjective impressions to which no objective reality must be attached: "If, as is declared by Ibn al-Mādjashūn, all traditions make mention of a change of location of God when He is seen at the time of the Resurrection, it comes to this: that God will make alterations in the organs of sight of His creatures so that they will see Him descending ... Yet, in His majesty He will remain the same as ever and will stay motionless where He was" (*H.B.* I, 14).

[8] This hypothesis is qualified by the present day scholar Muḥammad Zāhid al-Kawtharī (d. 1952) as one of the eccentricities of the Indian divine, and rejected on the ground that the practice of the enchantment of the eye is unworthy of a prophet (*Ḥusn al-taqāḍī*, Cairo 1948, 97).

awake. This occurred however in a zone lying between (*barzakh*) the World of Prefiguration and the world below ... (There) spiritual entities (*ma*ʿ*ānī*) assume a bodily shape''[9]. (*H.B.* II, 206)[10].

Another device to present preternatural events in a more of less plausible way is the resort to psychologic and almost Freudian interpretations of wonderful prophetic tales. Thus we find the following version of the creation of Eve: ''Sensual tendencies were also alive in Adam. So he began to hanker after a female of his kind, and in his excited state he imagined the form of a female. Accordingly, out of his imaginative vision, woman came into existence'' (*Ta*ʾ*wīl* 13).

In the career of Mohammed[11], the archetype and completion of prophethood, Shāh Walī Allāh discerns the following stages:

a) A preparatory one. At first, before his actual prophecy, three suns were shining. I.e. three qualities which are also met in a *ḥakīm*, namely *ḥikma* (wisdom), ʿ*iṣma* (immunity from sin) and *quṭb bāṭinī*[12] (potential leadership) developed within him. (*Tafh.* II, 13). Thus, he became fit for Gabriel to descend to him with revelations.

b) Now three stars in the shape of *waḥy*, *ḥifẓ* and *quṭb irshādī* arose in opposition to the three suns earlier present. *Waḥy* (revelation) is, so to speak, sublimated *ḥikma*; its concrete effect was eloquent and admonishing preaching. *Ḥifẓ* (protection), i.e. ʿ*iṣma* on a higher level, gave rise to juridical qualities for the settlement of quarrels. In *quṭb irshādī* (effective leadership) the abilities contained in the *quṭb bāṭinī* found full scope. It offered worldly dominion as a concrete effect. Consequently when these stars began to shine for the Prophet along with the three suns he was commanded to proclaim the message of God to both men and *jinns*.

---

[9] Accordingly, ''the rivers which rise at the foot of the Lote-tree of the boundary stand for the divine mercy that streams from the world of Sovereignty (*malakūt*) to the world here below'' (*H.B.* II, 207).

[10] ''It is obvious'', so Sayyid Aḥmad Khān (d. 1898) concludes from this passage, ''that Shāh Walī Allāh was not sure that the *mi*ʿ*rāj* did take place in a bodily way, though he does not say so plainly. He speaks of a *mi*ʿ*rāj* with a *barzakhī* body, from which it follows that this did not occur with an ordinary body. Thus his view agrees with those who claim that it was not performed in the body''. (Sayyid Aḥmad Khān, *Tafsīr al-Qur*ʾ*ān*, Aligarh Institute Press 1895, VI, 66).

[11] I.e. when the third stage (*nash*ʾ*a*) of Mohammed's evolution was entered upon and he had started his earthly existence. Initially, in the first stage he existed as the so-called *ḥaqīqa muḥammadiyya* (Reality of Mohammed), representing the first thing created by God. From this all other realities derive. Accordingly, his Reality is the connecting link between God and the remaining realities. The second stage is named *al-rūḥ al-muḥammadiyya* (Spirit of Mohammed). Thus all prophets derive their knowledge from the *rūḥ* of Mohammed which functions as the intermediate link between them and God (*Fuyūḍ*, 45th Vision).

[12] According to our author, it is a synonym of *wajāha* (distinction). It implies dignity, serenity of mind and the ability to show what true religion really is. Because of it one receives various divine favours as, for instance, answer to prayer (*Tafh.* II, 20).

c) But when his attachment to the higher world continued to increase and his noble character was progressively polished[13], the three stars turned into shining full moons. At that time it was said to him: "Utter openly that with which you are charged" (*Qurʾān* XV, 94). Thus he was ordered to oppose and argue with the unbelievers in Mecca.
d) Next, these full moons became, on account of his strong attachment to the angels, 'inward' suns. Then he was told: "Leave is given to those who have been wronged" (an inaccurate citation of *Qurʾān* XXII, 39); and he was commanded to emigrate to Medina. From that moment he belonged to the Messengers possessed of constancy (*ʿazm*).
e) In the last phase of Mohammed's prophetic evolution "There did not remain any spot on earth but Divine Light had entered therein in a most brilliant form" (*Khizāna* 6). So he fulfilled a double mission; a limited one on behalf of the sons of Ismael, and a universal one for the whole world[14] (*H.B.* I, 84).

In Shāh Walī Allāh's prophetology the usual discussion whether prophecy is a natural gift or merely a divine favour is evaded[15], and whether

---

[13] Shāh Walī Allāh, however, is too faithful to the traditions to assign any kind of impeccability to Mohammed. Commenting on the prophetic saying: "There is at times some sort of cloud upon my heart; on a day like that I seek forgiveness from God a hundred times" (Mu. *al-Dhikr wa ʾl-duʿāʾ* 36), he declares: "The cloud points out that the Prophet was enjoined to adopt the same kind of soul as that of an average believer ... so that he might offer a clear example for the believers when laying down rules for them" (*H.B.* II, 76). There are three categories of people who desired to be illuminated by the light of Mohammed's prophethood and had a share in some of the above-mentioned properties, namely:
1. The inheritors of wisdom, immunity from sin and distinction. This category includes the members of his family and his servants. Here two subdivisions can be made:
   a) those who inherited these qualities on account of their innate purity, magnanimity and ethereal shape. Amongst them are ʿAlī, his children, Fāṭima, Ḥamza, and his children;
   b) those who inherited them on account of sharing both the sweet and the bitter experiences of life with the Prophet. They are his wives and servants.
2. The inheritors of divine protection (*ḥifẓ*), instruction (*talqīn*) and leadership. They are the most prominent Companions, for instance, the four rightly guided caliphs.
3. Those who were specific objects of God's Providence, and inherited godliness and spiritual knowledge. These are the Companions who devoted themselves to spiritual perfection (*iḥsān*), for instance Anas b. Mālik and Abū Hurayra (*Khizāna* 7 and *Tafh.* II, 14).

[14] Accordingly, "In consideration of the completion of this universal mission the Prophet obtained laws in addition to the Torah such as, for instance, those pertaining to poll-tax (*jizya*), land-tax (*kharāj*), expeditions against the infidels and measures of precaution against falsifications of the Holy Writ (*taḥrīf*)" (*H.B.* I, 123).

[15] Our author simply states: "Prophethood ... is neither a natural disposition (*jibillī*), nor a quality that may be acquired through strenuous efforts" (*Izāla* I, 51). It is actually, something midway insofar as prophets have an innate receptivity (*istiʿdād*) of it (*Tafh.* I, 178).

it can be acquired by human effort or whether it depends entirely upon heavenly interference[16]. The reason is that, on the whole, the interest of our theologian is not focussed on subtle distinctions between the domains of God's activities and those of man. In his system of thought all attention is drawn to the *interrelation* of cosmic, divine, terrestrial and human powers and effects. In the universe anything and everything is mutually correlated, a premiss emerging from the concept of *waḥdat al-wujūd*. As for the appointment of a prophet, two complementary conditions ought to prevail:

1. The presence of a man with some extraordinary properties. For the receipt of *waḥy* he needs to possess special intellectual gifts such as, for instance, a close spiritual affinity with the *mala aʿlā*; and for the sake of the preservation of his excellent practical abilities (*quwwat-i ʿāmila*) he must be immune from error (*Izāla* I, 51). Such a personality becomes an instrument that God wants to have for Himself alone. Hence He declared to Moses: "I have brought you up for My own sake" (*Qurʾān* XX, 41) (*H.B.* I, 24).
2. On earth there must be a situation that presses urgently for the mission of a prophet. Only when both conditions are met, "will God decide from above the seven heavens to reform the people and to rectify the crooked by putting into the heart of the most wholesome and most righteous of men the impulse to preach correct knowledge to his people so as to rouse them to actions of moral improvement" (*Izāla* I, 51). An occasion calling for the appearance of a prophet is an absolute necessity. Thus, had there not been the perverseness of the Ninevites, Jonah would not have become a prophet (*Khizāna* 5).

There have been three crucial moments in history when the sending of a prophet was particularly required. Thus Shāh Walī Allāh distinguishes three periods of *jāhiliyya*, heathendom, instead of two as is done in current Muslim theology. Besides the periods between Adam and Noah, and between Jesus and Mohammed, he marks out a third *jāhiliyya* of the epoch after the public appearance of Hūd and Ṣāliḥ. At that time we see the emergence of *millas* with worshippers of stars and naturalists. It is Abraham who succeeds in dispelling this darkness of religious decay by his fight against astrology (*B.B.* 188 f.).

These actions of reform, it should be noted, had a still wider significance than being merely a refutation of false belief. They occasioned simultaneously a turn in the history of religious thinking. For righteous believers in the period after Adam also used to assume the existence of particular potencies in heavenly bodies which determined the

---

[16] *Cf.* F. Rahman, *Prophecy in Islam* (London 1958), *passim*.

course of events on earth. Idrīs is to be looked upon as the first astrologer (*Taʾwīl* 17). From the time of Abraham, however, believers began to recognize that apart from cosmic powers it was particularly the angelic forces which had had a regulative function in the history of the world. In this new age knowledge trickled from them upon the minds of the leaders of humanity, and from now on *sharīʿas* descended for the guidance of mankind (*Taʾwīl* 28). "The *tajallī aʿẓam*, being the jet d'eau of the powers of the Self-existent", so our author sets forth in another writing, "has various *shaʾns*, as God states: 'Every day He is in a (new) mode of being (*shaʾn*)'[17] (*Qurʾān* LV, 29). Hence the prophets, as interpreters of eternal language, announced the *shaʾn* which had arisen in their age and on account of which they had been sent. ... It is because of this that the views of prophets differ with respect to laws[18], the mystic path, the hereafter, and so on. In this way, one may understand why the statements of Jesus about spiritual delights to be enjoyed in the hereafter differ from ... the statements of Mohammed which make mention of bodily delights in the hereafter that will be derived from food and drink, sweet ladies and pure garments.

For the *shaʾn* of which Jesus was the interpreter went by the *ḥajar al-baht* and the organs of spiritual communication, called *sirr* and *rūḥ*, whereas the *shaʾn* of which Mohammed was the interpreter was adjusted to less refined organs of spiritual communications (as the *nafs*, *ʿaql* and *qalb*)" (*Tafh.* I, 116). Similarly, the type of prophetic miracles was adapted to the spirit of the age. People in the time of Moses were fond of magic. Consequently, God provided Moses with the miracle of the staff and white hand. People in the time of Mohammed were renowned for poetry and rhetorics. Accordingly, God sent down the miracle of the Qurʾān (*Tafh.* I, 81 f.).

To my mind, this is a very important view of Shāh Walī Allāh. In the West an often repeated objection to Islam is that this faith would not know of a God who is continuously acting in the history of men, and that

---

[17] *Cf. H.B.* I, 80: "By *shaʾn* I mean that commensurate with divine wisdom the Universe has periods (*adwār*) and phases (*aṭwār*). Whenever a new period arrives, "God makes known in every heaven what is to be its task" (*Qurʾān* XLI, 1), instructs the *mala aʿlā* what is proper, passes relevant enactments (for men) and tells (them) what will serve the public interest".

[18] In his annotated Persian translation of the Qurʾān, called *Fatḥ al-Raḥmān*, Shāh Walī Allāh comments on the divine words: "the matters on which you are at variance" (*Qurʾān* XXII, 69): "in this Qurʾānic verse an allusion is made to the fact that the *sharīʿas* differ because of the difference of eras. Nevertheless, this variance of their legislations does not prevent the prophets from unanimity with respect to the essence (*aṣl*) of their creed (*dīn*)". "All of them", as we read in *H.B.* I, 86 f., "are agreed that no associates should be attributed to God in one's worship and seeking help, ... that He as predestined all events before He creates them, ... that Resurrection, Paradise and Hell are 'real', etc.".

the idea of a constant divine concern for mankind would be alien to the teachings of the Qurʾān[19]. Well, then, the Delhi divine argues, Abraham acted not only as a preacher and reformer but also as an instrument of God's progressive revelation. This notion is still more explicitly developed in Shāh Walī Allāh's exposition of the sciences which he finds explained in the Qurʾān. The third science consisting of the remembrance of God's favours to men, demonstrated *inter alia* in His creation of heaven and earth is, according to him, a knowledge with which Abraham was especially endowed. The fourth science pertains to the recalling to mind of 'the Day of the Lord', i.e. of events Allāh caused to happen in order to reward the obedient and to punish the sinner. That kind of instruction became the privilege of Moses. The fifth science relates to the reminder of death and what follows upon it[20], the eschatology. Insight into that knowledge was revealed to the seal of prophets, Mohammed (*H.B.* I, 55).

The prophets provide further benefit that is not bound to their actual presence by means of their life stories, to the extent that these tales denote significant 'basic ideas' (*uṣūl*). To demonstrate this point our author composed his *Taʾwīl al-aḥādīth*. The title was derived from *Qurʾān* XII, 6 where Jacob says to Joseph: "And God will teach you the elucidation of tales" (*F.K.* 46). And when the same Joseph states: "Thou (o God) art my *walī* (guardian) in this world and the next" (*Qurʾān* XII, 101), he implicitly—so Shāh Walī Allāh concludes—regards himself a *walī Allāh* (a favourite of God). And that gives the Muslim Indian mystic cause to discover a close affinity between himself and Joseph, and to express the hope that he might became an 'expansion' (*sharḥ*) of that godly man (*Khizāna* 5). In other words, we are given to understand that just as Joseph in his capacity of *walī Allāh* had been taught the explanations of events prefigured in dreams, the Delhi scholar—being an expansion and namesake—has been endowed with equal talents enabling him to disclose the deeper meanings of the prophetic stories.

Let us consider a few examples. When Abraham looked at the stars, the moon and the sun, their setting showed him that it was not they who created him[21]. Here the root idea is God's jealousy. The story itself is

---

[19] *Cf.*, for instance, L. Gardet in *EI*² I, 406: "(In the Qurʾān) there is, strictly speaking, no progressive revelation of Allāh".

[20] Elsewhere our author explicitly declares that in the beginning of the cycle of history (*dawra*), i.e. at the time that the powers of the spheres were the origin of most events, mankind could not yet dispose of knowledge about e.g. a resurrection after death. In those days people's knowledge was restricted to astrology, and the like (*Tafh.* I, 66 and 68).

[21] Reared in a pagan milieu, Abraham arrived at monotheistic belief through personal observation of the orbit of the heavenly bodies (*Qurʾān* VI, 75-79).

merely the outward form (*Ta*ʾ*wīl* 4 and 7). The Qurʾān tells us that at a given moment God commanded the angels to prostrate themselves before Adam. The underlying idea of the myth, it is argued in this treatise, is to explain that by the prayers and pleadings in favour of the sons of Adam the angels are actually worshipping God. Hence Adam and his sons are a *qibla* for their worship (*Ta*ʾ*wīl* 13). Shāh Walī Allāh comments on *Qur*ʾ*ān* II, 54[22] as follows: "This event was essentially a Mercy for the righteous Israelites (since by it they were purged from inpious fellow citizens), and a way to rehabilitation for the insolent Israelites, for which at that time they were prepared (by rousing penitance in their hearts when at the point of death) ... So long as they continued to exist in this life, they would never come to a sound faith, their inferior nature forming a stumbling-block. Hence the best thing for them was that they should be killed in a state of obedience, in order that during the interval between death and resurrection their souls could make still greater progress" (*Ta*ʾ*wīl* 48 f.).

"You should know", so we read in the Introduction to the *Ta*ʾ*wīl al-aḥādīth*, "that whenever God from the Primal Level (where He resides) brings down knowledge upon mankind via the tongue of a human being, it is not communicated by tropes and allusions ... but put in terms of everyday occurrences. This happens in the same manner as when knowledge of what is about to happen is infused in a person's senses. He then receives a dream made up of voluntary or compulsory actions and of inanimate or animate bodies somehow indicating what is about to happen ... (After all) all things that happen in the world are virtually dreams[23]; they are made up of root ideas and of outward shapes (*ashbāḥ*). One of the root ideas implies that God wants His worshippers to live prudently by means of inspirations, transformations (effected in the properties of elements, as for example in the fire which produced a cool effect as soon as Abraham had been thrown into it by his opponents) and contrivances ... Accordingly, He selects from the course of events the one which at that very moment furthers the object of pursuit in the best way ... The event which then appears represents the 'outward shape' and the dream as such, while God's prudent management represents the root idea and the purport of the dream" (*Ta*ʾ*wīl* 3 ff.).

The prophets then appear to be valuable for the illustration of mystic experiences. To the mind of Shāh Walī Allāh they can function as proper

[22] Where Moses is saying: "O my people, you have done harm to yourselves by taking the calf (for a god). Therefore, turn to your Creator (in repentance) and slay one another".

[23] Inference from the prophetic saying: "men are asleep, and when they die, they awake".

prototypes in an ascending progression of stages on the road a mystic travels to reach ecstasy. The way itself is marked by seven *dawāʾir*, regions[24] which have to be traversed one after the other (*Tafh.* II, 62 f.).

The first of them is the *dāʾira* of *īmān* (faith). This is the province where Adam resides as the exemplary model (*imām*). Faith implies obedience to God with heart and body. This was an occupation specific to Adam who aimed at the correction of his lower soul (*nasama*) for which he had to fight with the Devil (*Tafh.* II, 71). The *nasama* as such often tries to draw man's rational soul (*al-nafs al-nāṭiqa*) to lower impulses. Consequently, if the *nafs nāṭiqa* wants to come into closer contact with its origin, the *nafs kulliyya* (universal soul), it must loosen its fetters with the *nasama*. Now that is exactly the activity, in which the mystic traveller is engaged in the second *dāʾira*, called *sharḥ al-ṣadr* (*Tafh.* II, 64). Here he has to reduce the influence of the *nasama* and to strengthen the power of the *nafs nāṭiqa*[25]. By doing this he follows the exâmple of Idrīs, who is the prophet belonging to this *dāʾira*[26]. In the third phase, named *qurb al-nawāfil*[27], the *nafs nāṭiqa* is prepared for the receipt of theophanies. The exemplary model in this territory is the prophet Noah. The fourth *dāʾira*, designated as *qurb al-wujūd*, is marked off by *ḥikma*, which is insight into creation and so on[28]. This is the speciality of Abraham and Joseph. Then follows the region of the *qurb al-farāʾiḍ*, on account of which theophanies can reach man's *ʿayn thābita*[29]. The *imām* in this domain is Moses. The sixth *dāʾira* is characterized by *qurb al-malakūt* (proximity brought by association with the world of angels). The foundations of this way of approaching God is the *ḥadīth qudsī*: "if God loves a servant, He tells Gabriel. Then Gabriel

---

[24] These regions parallel the seven celestial spheres, and refer to the story of the *miʿrāj* (Mohammed's ascension to heaven), a favourite ṣūfī symbol to express the mystic finding during the advancement from one stage to another on the ṣūfī path. This is again an instance of Shāh Walī Allāh's dependence on Ibn ʿArabī since the latter similarly stocks the spheres with a prophet into whose mouth he puts a part of his mystical system (*Cf.* A .E. Affifi, *The Mystical Philosophy of Muhyid Din Ibnul Arabi*, 110).

[25] Having attained the level of *sharḥ al-ṣadr* (expansion of the breast) a believer no longer cares for property, leadership, delicious food, fine clothes, women, personal revenge (*Tafh.* I, 39).

[26] No explicit grounds for his choice of Idrīs as representative of this second *dāʾira* are advanced by the Delhi divine. It may be surmised that in his statement: *Sharḥ al-ṣadr* is actually a 'being broken' of the *nasama* in its essence by the impact of *jadhb* ('attraction' to God)" (*Tafh.* II, 64), he has in mind Idrīs' being raised to heaven.

[27] "The gist of it", so Shāh Walī Allāh sets forth, "is the 'becoming broken' of the essence of the *nafs nāṭiqa* (when it has a bent toward the allurements of this world)" (*Tafh.* II, 65). Noah is the *imām* of this region, inasmuch as he is the prototype of the fighters of moral depravities.

[28] *Cf.* also *Tafh* II, 161: "One of the particulars of the *dawra* of *ḥikma* is the tasting of pure eternity. It constitutes intuitive knowledge (*ʿilm ḥuḍūrī*) concerning the divine Names and Essence".

[29] Then God looks in the mirror of man's soul.

conceives love for him, and makes the name of the chosen one known to other angels, whereupon they too conceive love for him" (Mu. *al-Birr wa*ʾ*l-ṣila* 157). Here we are on the ground of Jesus[30]. The last *dāʾira* is that of *kamāl* (full maturity). This is the field of Mohammed (*Tafh.* II, 70). "One of the characteristics of the *qurb al-kamāl* is that God takes care of His servant either openly or in secret. Consequently, his manner of acting proceeds in accordance with divine wisdom, consciously or unconsciously ... Another characteristic is that the means of communication the angels use for him are the same as applied by Mary (*cf. Qurʾān* XIX, 29): intimations instead of actual speech" (*Tafh.* II, 123). Having himself arrived at this point, Shāh Walī Allāh enjoyed the following rapturous experience: "It was as if my garments were taken off, so that I became naked. Thereupon the Messenger of God appeared and came to my left side. I was clothed with a divine garb. Then I cried: 'Ḥaqq, Ḥaqq, Ḥaqq' ('O God, o God, o God') ... And a steady heavy rain of divine effluxes descended upon me from above, from the left and from the right. No tongue can describe this. Praise be to God!" (*Tafh.* II, 70 f.).

In view of the teachings prophets have to propagate, the Delhi divine remarks: "You should realize that prophethood has to comply with the *fiṭra* (people's natural disposition) ... Every nation and every climatic region (*iqlīm*)[31] has its own *fiṭra* upon which its affairs are based. Thus it is part of the *fiṭra* of Hindus to find the slaughter of animals repugnant and to believe in the eternity of the universe. It is of the nature of the children of Shem among the Arabs and of the Persians to permit the slaughter of animals and to believe in the createdness of the universe. Consequently, a prophet sets out to see what kind of creeds and customs people maintain, and he sanctions and adopts what suits the refinement of souls, rejecting what injures them ... Hence it is certainly not a matter of surprise that the modes of action of prophets differ in accordance with the different material they have to deal with". (*Tafh.* I, 68). Another characteristic of their instruction is "the habit of prophets not to engage subjects that are beyond the mental range of the people ... On that account they do not require people to acquaint themselves with their Lord through manifestations and visions, or by means of logical demonstrations and reasoned arguments ..., inasmuch as this is only possible if people practise austerities or frequent the society of scholars for a long period ... Equally, it is not their habit to discuss matters which are not relevant to the refinement of souls and the rule of the community as, for instance,

---

[30] Shāh Walī Allāh designates him as "an angel walking on earth" (*Taʾwīl* 76).

[31] According to Muslim geography, based on Ptolemy, the earth was divided into seven *iqlīms*.

the explanation of natural phenomena ... For that very reason God diverted the attention of the people from the question they had brought before the Prophet concerning the cause of the wane and increase of the moon. Instead He gave an exposition of the advantages of calendar months saying: 'They (the new moons) are appointed times for the people, and for pilgrimage' (*Qurʾān* II, 189)'' (*H.B.* I, 86).

Besides having to exercise restraint in consideration of the limited mental range of the average believers, the Prophet appears equally cautious in mystical affairs. He confines himself to exposing only the first two of the seven stages (*dawāʾir*) of the journey a mystic might accomplish. People could become confused if the remaining lofty ones were also explained. Moreover, the actual mission prophets had to execute was limited to leading mankind from the darkness of their bio-physical nature to the light of the stages of *īmān* and *sharḥ al-ṣadr*. Then they are fit to enter Paradise (*Tafh.* II, 138 f.).

Curiously enough, it is not merely mankind that profits from the appearance of prophets. God Himself can make excellent use of them for His own ends, since He badly needs these people as a substratum for the revelation of His Names and Attributes. Hence the *ʿayn thābita* of a prophet may typify one of the manifold aspects of the Divine Essence. Adam, for instance, appears to be a living symbol of the Divine Name *al-murīd* (the Purposer), that is to say He Who is busy with creating, as this prophet was very intent on procreation and cultivation of the land. Idrīs is the earthly manifestation of the Name *al-subbūḥ* (the Transcendental), a qualification still higher in rank than the Name *al-quddūs* (the Holy) which is represented by Noah. The difference between the two is the same as that found between the meanings of *ʿadam* (non-presence in the world) and *salb al-wujūd* (deprivation of existence). On that account his people did not perish as did the people of Noah. For the same reason Idrīs acquired proximity to God through the higher worlds and Noah through the lower worlds[32]. Abraham is an exemplification (*timthāl*) of the Divine Epithet *al-ḥayy al-qayyūm* (the Living and Self-subsisting). He acquired this perfection 'in a rudimentary form' (*ijmāl*), while the Lord of the Messengers obtained it 'in an unfolded fashion' (*tafṣīl*)[33]. This is why Mohammed's institutionalized religion (*milla*) is called ''the *milla* of your father Abraham'' (*Qurʾān* XXII, 78) (*Khizāna* 5).

---

[32] Here the influence of Ibn ʿArabī is obvious. Yet it should be noted that in the *Fuṣūṣ al-ḥikam* Noah turns out to be an exponent of Divine *subbūḥ* and Idrīs of Divine *quddūs*. In other words, Shāh Walī Allāh takes the liberty of making variations in Ibn ʿArabī's themes if he deems this necessary to the exposition of his own points of view.

[33] Abraham's acting as the prototype and model for Mohammed is not only the Qurʾānic way of presenting the matter but also—as is well known—the view held by Muslim orthodoxy. In this connection, it may be interesting to note that, notwith-

One major issue of the prophetic mission is intercession: "The *shafāʿa*", so Shāh Walī Allāh explains, "is actually a full manifestation of a fascinating Epithet of God, namely *al-ḥayy al-qayyūm* (the Living, Self-subsisting) of which Mohammed has become the earthly representation. The object of this Attribute is to obliterate the evil deeds written down in the Scrolls. Every prophet is entitled to intercede according to the nature of his perfection (*subūgh*) and proximity to God. The nearer people are to the prophets the greater the chance is of their intercession being granted. On that account it was prescribed by the *sharīʿa* that benedictions and blessings be pronounced on them[34] (*Khizāna* 9). "Our prophet realized that the main aim of his mission was to act as an intercessor for the believers and to serve as a medium for very special mercy on the Day of Judgment. Therefore he has retained the most significant petititon ... for that Day"[35]. (*H.B.* II, 75). Then, according to Shāh Walī Allāh[36], the intercession of both, Mohammed and Jesus, will prove to be of equal importance: "At the investiture of Jesus there will be a most illustrious intercession for his followers, and at the investiture of our Prophet there will be an equal one for his people. Both of them are jets d'eau of the same turbulent river and both of them are musical sounds of the same sonorous flute" (*Tafh.* I, 118).

---

standing this, in the opinion of the Delhi scholar it is Moses, and not Abraham, who bears the closest likeness to the Seal of prophets: "in consideration of the abundance of all sort of abilities, of the prophets Moses most resembles our Messenger" (*Khizāna* 5). "Among the prophets ... Moses and Mohammed alone have reached the highest level in the art of legislation, have perfectly commanded the injunctions of the *sharīʿa*, and have comprehend all aspects of divine instruction" (*B.B.* 175).

[34] This relates to a saying of Mohammed, recorded in Tirmidhī, *Manāqib* 1: "When you hear the *muʾadhdhin* repeat what he says; then invoke a blessing on me, for everyone who invokes one blessing on me will receive ten blessings from God. Then asks God to give me the *wasīla* (position of a go-between), which is a rank in Paradise fitting for only one of God's servants, and I hope that I may be the one. If anyone asks that I be given the *wasīla*, he will be assured of my intercession".

[35] This bears on a statement of Mohammed, mentioned in Bu. *Daʿawāt* 1: "Every prophet received the right to one petition for the intercession of his community on the Day of Resurrection".

[36] Equally the view of Fakhr al-Dīn al-Rāzī (d. 1209). See his *Mafātīḥ al-ghayb*, Cairo 1278, I, 354.

# CHAPTER NINE

## PEOPLE OF EMINENCE

### A. *Ḥakīm* (Wise Man)

In the class immediately below the prophets are *ḥakīms*[1] who serve as a connecting link (*barzakh*)[2] between saints and prophets. They function, so to speak, as the potential intellect[3] for prophecy, which represents the *intellectus in actu* (*al-ʿaql biʾl-fiʿl*) (*Khizāna* 7). "They are experts in moral science and in knowledge pertaining to the second stage of man's socio-economic development" (*B.B.* 172). Hence they possess a refined practical knowledge in the fields of ethics, domestic economy and politics (*Izāla* II, 2). *Ḥakīms* are favoured with the possibility of gaining a very close proximity to God by means of the so-called *qurb al-wujūd*[4]. They are characterized by an extraordinary sublimation of the mind (*samāḥa al-nafs*) (*Tafh.* II, 66), being submitted to the rule of the *ʿayn thābita* which is purely good; i.e. in a way the *ʿayn thābita* is a representation (*timthāl*) of good (*Khizāna* 6). The *ʿayn thābita* is actually the origin of the *ḥakīm*'s knowing God, so that when he watches his *ʿayn thābita*, his eye penetrates to God. As a result he acquires *ḥikma*, *ʿiṣma* and *wajāha* (*Khizāna* 4)[5].

---

[1] In a state of frenzy they may even become like prophets, though without receiving *waḥys* (*Tafh.* II, 23).

[2] The prophet as an *ummī* (whose mind is a *tabula rasa* free from preconceived ideas) receives instructions (*aḥkām*) directly from God. The *ḥakīm* gains the *aḥkām* indirectly, i.e. by way of his *ʿayn thābita*. The *walī* also acquires them indirectly, not through his *ʿayn thābita* which is of a transcendental level, but through his inmost being (*sirr*) which is bound to his empirical existence (*Khizāna* 4).

[3] It is the human intellect in its dormant form; by the *ʿaql faʿʿāl* (active intellect) it can be roused from its state of latency. Accordingly, this potential intellect is transformed into an *ʿaql biʾl-fiʿl*. In Shāh Walī Allāh's thought the function of the *ʿaql faʿʿāl* is performed by the divine Name al-Raḥmān.

[4] I.e. during an overflow of God's pure being (*wujūd*) the *ḥakīm* becomes connected with the divine Name which is the root of archetypal individuality (*ʿayn thābita*) (*Khizāna* 4). As a result of this, he "becomes what since eternity he is destined to be, inasmuch as his *ʿayn thābita* worships God, getting near to Him and keeping aloof from evil and vile deeds" (*Tafh.* II, 66).

[5] Three salient features of a believer are;

1. *ʿIffa* (abstinence from what is unlawful). The correlative attribute of a *ḥakīm* is *ʿiṣma*.
2. *Tafarrus* (being endowed with acumen), i.e. the God-given capacity to deduce knowledge from Qurʾānic verses quickly as well as to corroborate intuitively the reality of the Self-existent, the mission of the prophets and the truth of the Resurrection. The correlative attribute of a *ḥakīm* is *ḥikma*.
3. *Sakīna* (assurance), i.e. the firm predisposition that incites man to obey the injunctions of the Law. The correlative attibute of a *ḥakīm* is *wajāha* (*Tafh.* II, 112).

*Ḥikma* (wisdom) is the science by which the true nature of existing things[6] can be perceived (*Tafh.* II, 24). It is revealed in its earthly dimension by clairvoyance (*firāsa*), vigilance and quickness of understanding. The principle lying at the root of *ʿiṣma* (immunity from sin) is that he who seeks God by *qurb al-wujūd*, cannot reflect anything evil in his character or doings. Its mark is *ʿiffa*, i.e. abstinence from trivial and exciting pleasures. *Wajāha* (i.e. being held higher than other people in the eyes of God) is, in essence, a being gifted with the capacity to divest oneself of one's earthy (*majāzī*) shape so that the rational soul can assume its original form. Its characteristics are dignity, assurance and authority (*Khizāna* 7).

It is necessary that a *ḥakīm* be self-possessed (*wasīʿ al-ṣadr*), i.e. attaches but little value to a particular mood or exhiliration, and refrains from the cultivation of fine arts such as music and poetry[7], by which somebody may be wholly taken up (*Khizāna* 7 and 4). Further, a *ḥakīm* shares in the prophetic knowledge of the 'tablets' (= specimens of the 'Guarded Tablet' on which the decrees of God with reference to mankind) are recorded (*Khizāna* 3).

A *ḥakīm* differs from a prophet in at least three respects:

1. He does not approach the Truly Good One by means of the *qurb al-farāʾiḍ*, but by means of the *qurb al-wujūd* (*Khizāna* 8).
2. A prophet is led by *waḥy*, a *ḥakīm* relies on his *dhawq* (*Tafh.* II, 121).
3. Because the prophet has to concentrate on the revelatory processes as such, he has hardly any time left for the elaboration of the information received by revelation, such as the substantiation of ethical rules and so on. This now is a task reserved for his heir[8], the *ḥakīm*, in his capacity as materialized intellect (*Khizāna* 8). Is it surprising that Shāh Walī Allāh, being called through divine visions to act as a reformer, considered himself a typical representative of the *ḥakīm*-family?[9]. Speaking of himself he tells us: "Eleven ages after the *hidjra* there was a man, gifted with inner light (*zakī*), who began to apply himself to the *qurb al-wujūd*. Thus he became an *imām* (leader) of the pious and an *ʿiṣām* (loop-shaped handle) of the *ḥakīms*, and he prayed

---

[6] A *ḥakīm*, therefore, knows that all that exists must have a direct cause (*ʿilla*); there can be no breach in the laws of nature (*Khizāna* 4).

[7] In another work, however, we are told that "by means of poems a *ḥakīm* can encourage people to do good and frighten them if they do not" (*B.B.* 172).

[8] To the other heirs of prophets Shāh Walī Allāh reckons the *mujaddids* (renewers) and *waṣīs* (trustees). It is the duty of the latter to discuss the hidden significance of the injunctions of the *sharīʿa*, to rouse a desire for Paradise and to frighten with Hell-fire (*Tafh.* I, 78).

[9] Once during his meditation near the tomb of the Prophet he received the titles of *zakī* and *ḥakīm* (*Intibāh* I, 8).

to God that He might make him a seal of the pure *ḥakīms*'' (*Khizāna* 4).

B. *Walī* (Protégé of God)

The task of the *walīs* is the establishment and propagation of the esoteric aspects of religion, of which spiritual purity (*iḥsān*) forms the nucleus. Characteristic of the *walīs* are miracles[10] wrought by means of the God-given talents of inner revelation (*kashf*) and thought-reading (*ishrāf*), theurgy (*taṣarruf*) and answer to prayer (*H.* I). They are inferior in rank to the *ḥakīm*. Unlike the latter the *walīs* cannot give effective guidance to the community as a whole, because they are not in possession of both theoretical and practical knowledge, a combination essential to leadership. They are either of the type *homo theoreticus* as, for instance, Ibn ʿArabī, or of the type *homo practicus* like the founders of ṣūfī orders, but never both types in one (*Khizāna* 7).

A *walī* is inferior to a prophet if only because the prophet's range of effectiveness and utility is much wider than that of the *walī*;[11] many more people experience the wholesome influence of prophets (*Kalimāt-i ṭayyibāt* 164 ff.). The Delhi divine bases a second argument in favour of the superiority of prophethood over saintliness on the assumption that the prophets are nearer to God than the saints (*Tafh.* II, 151 and 20).

Other distinctions observable between prophets and *walīs* are:

a) The prophets know God as the Necessary Cause (so that they have an insight into God's predestination and planning) and Purpose (because of which they are acquainted with God's will, commands and prohibitions). They are wholly merged into His will. The *walīs* know God only as the Necessary Cause and they are completely absorbed in this divine aspect.
b) The prophets obtain a knowledge of the statutes of the *sharīʿa* at the moment they are formulated, whereas the divine institutes given to *walīs* already received their fixed form long ago.
c) It is proper for prophets to marry, since their standing places them under obligation to have a social and a family life: for *walīs* it is more suitable to remain celibate, as they are dyed with the dye of sanctity and sublimity (*Khizāna* 7). The structure of their ʿ*iṣma*, therefore, is

[10] But, according to Shāh Walī Allāh, the *walīs* lose their miraculous power when they die and attain a perfection more universal than their earthly one (*Tafh.* II, 75).

[11] Cf. also *B.B.* 170: "All the divine states a *walī* experiences will unavoidably lead to the purification of his own soul, but there will not be anything that will also be conducive to the perfection and enlightenment of other people".

different from that of the prophets[12]. Because of their ascetic attitude towards life they are by nature men of *taqwā* (godliness), continence, and insensitive to sexual attractions. It does not make any difference to them whether they are confronted by a charming lady or a wall. Prophets, however, do know sexual passions. Consequently, *ʿiṣma* has to be spread over them as a protecting garment (*Tafh.* I, 260 f.). An illustration of this is the case of Joseph, in whom a flame of love for the wife of Potiphar leapt up. Then a *burhān* (manifestation of truth) was sent by God to protect him (*Taʾwīl* 34 f.). It is interesting to note that Shāh Walī Allāh holds the prophetic *ʿiṣma* to be of a more sublime nature than that of *walīs*. He seems to feel more sympathy for really human people than for 'unnatural' renouncers of the world.

d) Both prophets and *walīs* are ordered to show the right way and to give guidance, but the command the prophets receive refers to universal purposes, whereas the guidance of *walīs* pertains to individual cases and particular situations (*Tafh.* II, 212).

e) Revelations to a prophet are of an ethereal nature, whereas revelations to a *walī* are constituted of an earthly structure. Unlike what happens a *walī*, the inner revelation of a prophet is realized by a tunnel which opens into the Reality of God. So the prophet is a beloved of God upon whom the inner revelation is poured out. Since the *walī* is a man with a strong mind and of an intense purity, the inner revelation is reflected by him. Should a prophet be incapable of reflecting the revelation, he must rely on prayer (*duʿāʾ*). A *walī* has *himma* (spiritual power) at his disposal instead. Succour can be sought from divine Attributes and Names, both by *duʿāʾ* and by *himma* (*Tafh.* II, 46).

f) a *walī* possesses a special aptitude for *qurb al-nawāfil* (attaining proximity to God by supererogative works), a prophet for *qurb al-farāʾiḍ* (attaining proximity to God by discharging the duties prescribed by God) (*Khizāna* 5). The Prophet explains *qurb al-nawāfil* by referring to the *ḥadīth qudsī* in which God declares: "My servant continues to draw nearer to Me by supererogatory works until I love him; and when I love him, I become the ear with which he hears ...", and he extols the *qurb al-farāʾiḍ* by referring to the statement of God: "My servant draws nearer to Me by means of nothing dearer to Me than that which I have established as a duty for him" (Bu. *Riqāq* 38)

---

[12] A heterodox view, since Sunnīs hold *ʿiṣma* to be the exclusive privilege of prophets. According to Shāh Walī Allāh, the concept *ʿiṣma* implies that besides prophets other people may also be disposed by nature to truthfulness, continence, self-restraint (*waraʿ*) and performing good deeds (*Tafh.* II, 21).

(*Tafh*. II, 129). Through a *qurb al-nawāfil* man is enabled to see himself in the mirror of God, so that he is coloured with the colour of the mirror, i.e. the majesty of the Self-existent. Effects of this *qurb* are pride, glory and (a claim to) lordship (*rubūbiyya*). In the event of a *qurb al-farāʾiḍ*, however, man is put in a dependent position: he cannot know the very Essence of God of his own accord and has to bide the moment that God will manifest Himself in his *ʿayn thābita*. Characteristics of this *qurb* are feelings of impotence, humble submission and a waiting attitude (*Khizāna* 4).

g) A *walī* is the recipient of *ilhām* (inspiration), a prophet of *waḥy* (revelation). The difference between *ilhām* and *waḥy* is that in statements produced by an *ilhām*, in contrast to what is revealed by a *waḥy*, heresies might be included. *Waḥy*, however, is all truth without any trace of falsehood (*Khizāna* 2) and provides sure knowledge (*Saṭ*. 17). It is *ilhām* if somebody's disposition is prepared for God's teaching in a special way; if the Universal Divine Planning prepares the emanation without such a preparation, it is *waḥy*. All that God conveys through *waḥy* forms part of the works of obedience, and all that with which He inspires *walīs* pertains to ways of obtaining access to God (*Tafh*. II, 28).

h) When on his journey to God a mystic leaves the first stage of *walī*-hood[13], two possibilities are open to him: either to follow the way of the inheritors of prophethood, or to take the path of full-fledged *walī*-hood. In the first instance, he is fascinated by the *tajallī aʿẓam*, by means of which he rises to the *dhāt baḥt* (Pure Essence); in the second case, his spiritual eye is fixed on the *nafs kulliyya*, and from there he ascends towards the *dhāt baḥt* (*A.Q.* 122 ff.).

Various types of *walī* can be distinguished according to their psychic disposition; these are those:

a) whose *nasamas* are more prominent than their *nufūs nāṭiqa*; and through their *nasamas* they go off into trance (*jadhb*). Representatives of this category are Najm al-Dīn al-Kubrā (d. 1220), founder of the Kubrawī order, and Khwāja al-Dīn ʿUbayd Allāh Aḥrār (d. 1490), a well-known Naqshbandī of Central Asia;

b) whose *nufūs nāṭiqa* are more prominent than their *nasamas*; through their *nufūs nāṭiqa* they are thrown into trance. Characteristic of them is that they are more amply endowed with spiritual knowledge (*ʿilm*)

---

[13] At this stage the heart of a mystic experiences expansion (*basṭ*) free from any contradiction (*qabḍ*), elective affinity (*ulfa*) without disturbance, and ecstacy (*wajd*) without losing consciousness. His intellect becomes acute and receives superior knowledge of the Unseen through clairvoyance, illumination, voices from heaven, and the like. And his soul (*nafs*) gains tranquillity (*H.* XIX).

than with exhiliration (*ḥāl*)[14]. To them is to be reckoned the celebrated ṣūfī al-Junayd (d. 910);

c) of whom the *ʿayn thābita* preponderates. To this class of saints belongs Ibn ʿArabī[15], the great mystic philosopher (d. 1240) (*Tafh.* II, 131).

Another classification of *walīs* can be made, if the source of their impulses (*dāʿiyya*) is taken into consideration. Then two levels can be distinguished:

a) a higher level. Here an inner urge is evoked by an inspiration from God when He wishes to promote human welfare. At that time the *walī*, being of a prophetic status, is equipped with laws (*nāmūs*) by the intermediary of the *mala aʿlā*;

b) a lower level. This refers to *walīs* who receive stimuli from the *mala sāfil*. Their main function is to become a refuge and a point of union for the people. They obtain the robe of honour relating to *quṭb*-hood (spiritual leadership) (*Fuyūḍ*, 43th Vision).

### C. *Caliph*

Shāh Walī Allāh characterizes him as follows: "characteristic to the caliph is that he is of all men acquainted best with running an empire, waging a holy war and administrating the *sharīʿa*" (*B.B.* 174). "he sees that justice is carried out on earth and injustice is removed from it as far as possible. This can be done because the light of God envelops him and he receives inspirations furthering the establishment of the third stage of socio-economic development ... When people join him, a fire of love for them is lighted in his heart. No resort has to be made to political or military force (*B.B.* 172 f.). Three categories of caliphs can be distinguished: 1. the *khāṣṣ*; 2. the *ʿāmm* (ordinary type) and 3. the *jābir* (despotic ones).

The four 'rightly guided' caliphs typify the first class of the illustrious representants of the caliphate. They were among the direct heirs of Mohammed and had to fulfil a very special mission. When the Prophet died, some of the activities pertaining to his prophethood were not yet accomplished. The two main unfinished tasks were:

a) compilation of the Qurʾān from texts written on straight palm leaves and thin whitish stones;

---

[14] *Cf.* also *Khizāna* 7, which explains that *walīs* marked by *ʿilm* use their discretion and are not averse to concerning themselves with the means of livelihood, whereas *walīs* characterized by *ḥāl* are constantly engrossed in submitting their earthly existence to the laws of eternity; their only goal is *tawakkul* (total abandonment to God's hands, leaving one's needs directly to God).

[15] His range of spiritual knowledge was wider than that of any other *walī*. He established the foundation for esoteric prophethood and abolished legislative prophethood (which remained in existence) after (the death of) the Seal of Prophets (*Tafh.* II, 33 f.).

b) phrasing rules (*aḥkām*) given by the Prophet which had not yet been divulged to the people (*Izāla* I, 262). "Consequently, the divine Will had directed that their completion was to be brought about by the agency of some individuals from his community ... An allusion to this is found in God's Word, stating: 'God has promised those of you who believe and do righteous deeds that He will surely make you successors' (*Qurʾān* XXIV, 55)[16], and in His Word: 'like the seed that has put forth its sprouts' (*Qurʾān* XLVIII, 29). Similarly, Moses appointed Joshua caliph and it is told how divine promises[17] were fulfilled by the latter" (*Izāla* II, 3). In elucidation of this point, the author makes use of the simile: "the caliph of a prophet is like a flute in the mouth of a flute-player" (*Tafh.* I, 243), and says: "Just as the production of a high tone and the fine quality of a melody by the flute-player who raises the flute to his mouth, are credited to the player (and not to the flute), so the work done by the caliphs as successors to the Prophet, who was called back by God before his mission was completed, is in fact credited to the Prophet; the caliphs themselves are considered as mere organs of the Prophet" (*Izāla* I, 9f). Hence "The period of the caliphate (of the 'rightly guided' caliphs) constitutes the remnant of the prophetic era. (The only difference between the two epochs is that) in the days when Mohammed was still alive, the Prophet gave lucid verbal explanations, whereas in the days of the caliphs he sat still and made signals with his hand or head (as he was wont to do when appearing to his followers in dreams; *cf. Tafh.* II, 248)" (*Izāla* I, 25).

Further, the Delhi divine draws a distinction between a political (*ẓāhirī*) and a spiritual (*bāṭinī*) caliphate. Political caliphate aims at domination and sovereignty for the sake of the maintenance of religion (*dīn*). The duty of holders of a spiritual caliphate is to give instruction in the *sharīʿa*, Qurʾān and *sunna*, to enjoin what is known to be good and censure what is evil, and to explain how spiritual perfection can be attained (*Fuyūḍ*, 36th Vision). We are confronted with an illustrious (*khāṣṣ*) caliph when the capacities of a political and spiritual caliphate are united in one person (*Izāla* I, 260).

"The fruits of perfect intellectual power in a prophet include *waḥy* (revelation), and the fruits of the same capacity in a caliph include the

---

[16] Shāh Walī Allāh declares that in this respect he altogether disagrees with the later Ashʿarites who claim that no clear *naṣṣ* (text of the Qurʾān or traditions used as an authority in an argument) can be adduced for the caliphate, and that it can only be founded on *ijtihād* (individual reasoning) (*Izāla* I, 14).

[17] Islam's victory over Jews, Christians and Zoroastrians is to be reckoned among the divine promises realized by the first three caliphs. It is announced in *Qurʾān* IX, 33: "that He may make the religion of truth victorious over every other religion" (*Izāla* I, 14).

status of a *muḥaddath*[18], of a *ṣiddīq*[19] and reliable mind-reading (*firāsa*). The fruits of perfect practical power in a prophet include immunity from errors (*ʿiṣma*) and finding the right way, and to the fruits of the same capacity in a caliph belong integrity, continence and being kept (*maḥfūẓ*) from sin ... The excelling disposition of a prophet, if both powers are united in him, results in miracles and extraordinary experiences as, for instance, the *miʿrāj* (ascension)—and to a caliph of a similar disposition belong excellent habits (*maqāmāt*), lofty experiences (*aḥwāl*), miracles (*karāmāt*), answer to prayer and the effect of his sermons upon men'' (*Izāla*. I, 263 f.).

Embarking upon the intricate question whether the era of the illustrious caliphate ends with ʿUthmān or also includes the tumultuous reign of ʿAlī, Shāh Walī Allāh begins with the citation of Mohammed's statement, related by his Companion Abū Bakra al-Thaqafī: ''After me there will be a caliphate of thirty years''. ''The actual presupposition of this tradition'', he continues, ''is that an orderly illustrious caliphate bears two characteristics:

1. the presence of an illustrious caliph;
2. the enforcement of his authority, to which full recognition is accorded by the whole Muslim community. Between these two characteristics some discrepancy may arise. Divine wisdom requires that there should be a gradual transition between two opposite conditions (i.e. that the illustrious caliphate would not suddenly turn into a despotic sultanate). Hence, at first one characteristic got lost, to wit the unity of the Muslims and a proper order of the empire. ʿAlī himself possessed the qualifications of an illustrious caliph, and he exercised the office of caliph by right. Only ... his authority was not established throughout the empire'' (*Izāla* I, 142).

As for the order of merit with regard to the four 'rightly guided' caliphs, Shāh Walī Allāh accepts the view of the great majority of Muslims: ''the most eminent personality of the *umma* is Abū Bakr, then comes ʿUmar, followed by ʿUthmān and ʿAlī'' (*Khizāna* 10 and *Tafh*. I, 148). The main criterion to determine their order of merit is the amount of utility each of them had for the *umma*. Just as the superiority of a prophet over a saint is founded on the fact that the former has more ways

[18] A *muḥaddath* possesses a proper understanding of the prophetic saying (*Izāla* II, 3).

[19] ''A *ṣiddīq* is ... as kindred to a prophet as sulphur is to fire'' (*H.B.* II, 93). He perceives the very root of things by merely hearing the words of the prophet. Consequently, acknowledging the truth of the prophet unreservedly and without any desire for a confirming miracle, is a requisite of this status. The very prototype of a *ṣiddīq* is Abū Bakr who used to hear the sough of Gabriel when a revelation descended upon the Prophet (*Izāla* II, 3 and *H.B.* II, 93). Because of this special spiritual affinity to Mohammed, Abū Bakr is to be regarded as the most eminent caliph and even superior to ʿUmar.

of serving the community than the latter, and more individuals are benefited by a prophet than by a saint, so the superiority of Abū Bakr and ʿUmar over ʿAlī rests *inter alia* on their giving wider currency to the revealed Law and achieving a greater multiplicity of military victories for the sake of Islam (*Kalimāt-i ṭayyibāt* 166).

Shāh Walī Allāh typifies their personal relation to the Prophet as follows: Abū Bakr followed the example of the Messenger of God in the cycle (*dawra*) of the *qurb al-kamāl*. This attitude is characterized by the concentration of one's being upon God (*tawajjuh*)[20] and is comparable to *yād-dāsht* as practised by saints. ʿUmar followed the example of the Prophet in gaining proximity to God by the fulfilment of the prescribed religious duties[21], while ʿUthmān imitated the Prophet by achieving *qurb al-wujūd*, being enabled to do this by a pure nature (*fiṭra*). ʿAlī also became firmly rooted in the *qurb al-wujūd*. He obtained wisdom in legal matters and gained ascent to the World of Sovereignty (*malakūt*). So he was charged with expounding the Law (*sharʿ*) and religion (*dīn*) revealed to the Prophet (*Tafh.* I, 39 f. and II, 73), and "he has deflected the fire of prophethood, of which the flames shot up, in the opposite direction so that its flames vanished into *buṭūn* (levels of esoteric meanings)[22] (*Tafh.* I, 76).

In his definition of what is to be understood by 'ordinary caliphate' Shāh Walī Allāh enumerates most of the principal constituents of the 'illustrious caliphate': "it is general leadership in lieu of the Prophet, directing its attention to the enforcement of religion by means of a revival of

---

[20] *Cf.* J. S. Trimingham, *The Sufi Orders in Islam*, Oxford 1971, 213 f.: "*tawajjuh* involves the worshipper in so readying the mirror of his heart in unclouded purity that his Beloved is reflected in it".

[21] In the eyes of Shāh Walī Allāh ʿUmar was a kind of super *imām*, considering the *fiqh* of the *imāms* of the four schools to be only a commentary on what was already established by the *ijtihād* of this caliph (*Izāla* II, 85). In contradistinction to ʿAlī, ʿUmar seems to have a keener feeling for the confessional import of religion than for its spiritual aspects, as the author infers from comments he made during the *ḥajj*. Once ʿUmar declared while he kissed the Black Stone: "I know very well that you are but a stone that neither helps nor hurts. If I had not seen the Prophet kiss you, I would certainly never kiss you" (Mu., *Ḥajj* 248). Thereupon ʿAlī observed: "there is a benefit in kissing it". Shāh Walī Allāh explains this anecdote as follows: The difference of opinion has to do with the different functions ʿUmar and ʿAlī had to perform. ʿUmar was responsible for keeping religious practice (*sharʿ*) free from curruption (*taḥrīf*). So his remarks were made in refutation of idolators. The special task with which ʿAlī was entrusted was to uncover hidden symbolism. Accordingly, he perceived that an imperishable shape (*hayʾa*) had been effused upon that stone, since it was said originally to have descended from Paradise (*Tafh.* II, 171 f.).

[22] To give one example: "The saying: 'There is no god besides Allāh' has many *buṭūn*. First, the repulse of plain idolatry; secondly, the repulse of secret idolatry; thirdly, the removal of impediments which bar the way to obtaining knowledge of God" (*H.B.* II, 72).

the religious disciplines, by means of undertaking the Holy War and matters connected with it (such as the training of armies, fixing the salaries, assignment of spoils to its participants), by means of taking charge of the judicature, and so on'' (*Izāla* I, 2). Yet, there is one basic distinction between the two caliphates which has far-reaching consequences. Instead of being appointed by the designation (*naṣṣ*) of the Prophet, an ordinary caliph is elected by the people, with the unpleasant risk is that a caliph is selected with all kinds of human fallibilities; he may even lapse into tyranny. One of the most probable weaknesses of an ordinary caliph is that he might be satisfied with having founded his knowledge and sense of justice on his private opinion (*raʾy*) only (*Izāla* I, 10). In the course of times the two main corrupting elements in the process of the caliphate's deterioration appeared to be:

1. the increase of property which excited the spirit of greed;
2. the growing preference to follow solely one's own discretion, without any desire to consult other people. The Delhi scholar calls the first abuse 'the *fitna* (temptation) of property (*māl*)', the second 'the *fitna* of reprehensible inclinations (*hawā*)' (*Izāla* I, 144).

Although the Umayyads could not always exercise a stable rule and their caliphs, without any exception, did not come up to the standard of their position, they nevertheless proved to be better qualified as rulers than the Abbasids whose methods were marked by despotism and arrogance. The latter modelled their conduct upon the customs of Persian kings and Byzantine emperors (*H.B.* II, 212). The condition of the caliphate worsened still more during the reign of the Turkish (*ʿajamiyyān*) monarchs who succeeded the Arabs. Their government turned out to be similar to that of the Zoroastrians, the only difference being that they performed the *ṣalāt* and professed the *shahāda*-formulae with their tongues (*Izāla* I, 157).

Although in his capacity of serving as a model to the Muslim community a caliph has, in principle, to comply with the most rigid standards, this does not mean that, if he happens not to possess all the qualities needed for a proper execution of office, one should immediately raise opposition to him. For the deposition of a caliph most likely involves strife and affliction of which the disadvantages might be greater than the benefits to be hoped for. However, as soon as he is guilty of *kufr* (infidelity) by rejecting one of the basic institutions (*ḍarūriyyāt*) of religion, it is not only allowed but it is even imperative to fight him (*H.B.* II, 150).

D. *Muḥaddath* (somebody who is inspired with true visions)[23]

In the view of Shāh Walī Allāh, *muḥaddath* is an epitheton that can be applied to a prophet, an intimate companion of Mohammed, and a particularly privileged believer. As for the first category, we are referred to Jonah: "Jonah was originally a *muḥaddath*—and not a *mukallam* (spoken to by God through *waḥys*)—prophet. Isaiah sent him to the people of Nineveh. At that time he was not yet independent of his lower self (*nafs*), but God wanted to clothe him with the garb of rectitude, so that he would belong to the righteous messengers (*Qur'ān* LXVIII, 50). During the resistance of his *umma* (*sc.* the Ninevites), the desire rose in him to pray for their perdition ... However, their repentance was accepted (by God). Consequently, he was in great confusion ... When he recognized that his orientation (*tafhīm*) was wrong, he was afflicted with (all) sorts of trials, till in the end ... he was dressed with the garb of rectitude and being no longer dependent on his lower self (*sc.* his personal sympathies and antipathies) was sent to his people" (*Tafh.* II, 119). From that time he recieved *waḥys* (*Tafh.* II, 123).

ʿUmar is, as we know from the traditions[24], the very prototype of a *muḥaddath*. "When somebody in the *umma*", so we read in one of Shāh Walī Allāh's arguments, "in his very nature resembles the prophets to a similar extent as an intelligent student resembles a practised teacher, he is a *muḥaddath* if the resemblance refers to intellectual capacities[25]. He is a man whose mind dashes towards the mines of knowledge in the World of Sovereignty (*malakūt*) as fast as it can, in order to derive from It all kinds of knowledge God has prepared to serve as a *sharīʿa* for the Prophet and as a means to the reform of mankind. An allusion to this is made in the tradition[26] which relates that the Prophet saw in a dream how—after having quenched his thirst—he gave the milk[27] (left over in the goblet) to ʿUmar" (*H.B.* II, 93).

[23] In the definition of the Delhi divine: "A *muḥaddath* can be inspired in two ways: sometimes he receives suggestions from the universal soul and impulses of the full-fledged ego (*anāniyya-i kubrā*) percolate upon him. At other times he receives suggestions from the *rūḥ al-quds* and impulses of the *mala aʿlā* descend into him by a system analoguous to that of the mesaraic veins". Consequently, he impersonates the felicitous integration of two life-styles, that of full-fledged saint-hood and of the inheritors of prophethood (*A.Q.* 37).

[24] Bu. *Anbiyā'* 54; Mu. *Faḍā'il al-ṣaḥāba* 23: The Messenger of God said: "Among the nations before your time there were *muḥaddath* people, and if there is one among my people he is ʿUmar".

[25] *Cf.* also *Izāla* II, 3: "Such a *muḥaddath* is gifted with true clairvoyance (*firāsat-i ṣādiqa*) and his reason is strengthened by the *ḥaẓīra al-quds* ... He is a companion (*ṭufaylī*) of the Prophet ... To the inseparable attributes of *muḥaddath*-hood belong (the fact) that the revelation (granted to the Prophet: *waḥy*) comes down repeatedly in accordance with his findings (*ijtihād*) and things happen as he has imagined beforehand".

[26] See Bu. *Faḍā'il aṣḥāb al-nabī* 6; Mu. *Faḍā'il al-ṣaḥaba* 15.

[27] Symbol of knowledge!

The third group of people who can be qualified as *muḥaddath* are believers[28] endowed with the gift of *tafhīm*[29] (*Tafh.* II, 121). Their excellences (*maqāmāt*), comprising *ʿiṣma*, wisdom, power of prayer (*daʿwa*), missionary zeal, fighting against evil, and professing the right articles of belief, are comparable to those of prophets[30]. The Messenger of God once said: "The vision of a believer is a forty-sixth part of prophethood" (Bu. *Taʿbīr al-ruʾyā* 4) (*Khizāna* 5).

E. *Fard* (singular man)

Among ṣūfīs *fard* denotes a rank of high eminence. Only three hundred persons, being the total number of the participants in the battle of Badr[31], would be entitled to it. In the expositions of Shāh Walī Allāh, however, *fards* are not primarily qualified as 'exceptionally gifted mystics'. According to the Delhi scholar, their most conspicuous characteristic is their ability to establish particular connections with cosmic elements and entities.

People in general, he tells us, appear to possess—in spite of their common share in humanity—remarkably distinctive properties owing to the predominance of a very special feature in their nature. Thus we find persons in whom the 'plant-form' is predominant. Hence they are known for their exceptional bio-physical powers. Other people are endowed with a predominantly animal form so that their outstanding traits are sensuality, violent motion, passion, libidiousness, and gluttony. People in whom the human form prevails are blessed with virtues like courage, magnanimity, wisdom, and eloquence. Persons gifted with a predominatingly 'personal' (*shakhṣī*) form are marked by extraordinary mystic experiences, while God sends illuminations (*tajalliyyāt*) in the *aʿyān thābita* of those in whom the *ʿayn*-form predominates.

Yet, *fards* do not belong to any of the categories mentioned. Their pecularity rests on something else. They are distinguished by either: a) a predominating 'water[32] form' because of which they resemble a

---

[28] The Delhi divine avows that he himself aspires to belong to the *muḥaddathūn* (*A.Q.* 37).

[29] Defined by H. Corbin as follows: "une inspiration (*ilhām*) dont Dieu est à la fois le sujet, l'objet et la fin, ou la source, l'organe et le but" (*Histoire de la philosophie islamique*, Paris 1964, 24). Ismāʿīl Shahīd thinks it proper to qualify *tafhīm* as *waḥy bāṭin* (interior revelation) (*ʿAbaqāt* 199).

[30] Because of the common endowment with *tafhīm* and the same tasks assigned to it, the epithet *mufahham* (see p. 88) is in the terminology of Shāh Walī Allāh apparently a synonym of *muḥaddath*.

[31] J. S. Trimingham, *Islam in the Sudan*, London 1965, 131.

[32] Held to be the most fundamental element in the Universe. Up till the present day, there are Arabs who distinguish types of human being according to the one or the other predominating element (See H. Granqvist, *Birth and Childhood among the Arabs*, Helsingfors, 1947, 173).

talented physicist (*ḥakīm ṭabīʿī*) who strives to uncover the basic elements of existing things; or

b) a predominating *ʿamāʾ* (primordial matter)-form *ʿamāʾ*, i.e. the substance which emerges first from the Raḥmūt, Realm of Mercy. Such a man bears a close likeness to a mathematician (*ḥakīm riyāḍī*); or

c) a predominating Raḥmūt-form. This is the highest class of *fard* who is able to penetrate into the source of things[33]. He is most akin to a theosopher (*ḥakīm ilāhī*).

In short it is typical of a *fard* that without any tool he knows the things as they are in their very essence, for the knowledge he possesses dripped directly from the Raḥmūt, *ʿamāʾ* or water (*Tafh.* II, 195 f.).

When knowledge like this seeps down, a kind of light is manifested in his soul, although hardly any effect is observed by the world outside (*Tafh.* I, 230). In human society *fards* remain unnoticed. Still God grants them knowledge and theophanies (*tajalliyyāt*) with which He does not make other people acquainted (*Tafh.* I, 190). To this end *raqīqas* (fine links) standing in an opposite correlation to the sun, moon, planets and other cosmic forces are deposited in them. Each of these *raqīqas* has a peculiar quality and activity. Thus, for instance, literary talents are developed through the *raqīqa* which is in communication with Mercury. A sense of the beauty with which God has endowed things is acquired through the *raqīqa* correlated with Venus, etc. Consequently, when a *fard* notices something that might be beneficial to him or to somebody else, one of his *raqīqas* expands towards the cosmic force that may serve the purpose. If, for instance, he wants to inform people of an occurrence in the near future, the *raqīqa* which has a connection with the moon expands (*Fuyūḍ*, 45th Vision).

One of the exclusive properties of a *fard* is that during his earthly lifetime he can take off his earthly form. Then he is in a condition to pass from the land of the living into the realm of the dead (*barzakh*), the world of Resurrection, Paradise and *ḥaẓīra al-quds*. After that he reaches God and beholds His face. When later on he dies everybody's death, he will pass through phases he already knows from past experience. Another of his characteristics is that on the approach of death he longs for a solitude and wants to keep away from blemish. The duration of his life lies between fifty and sixty years (*Tafh.* II, 196 f.).

After his death a *fard* is again enabled to produce miraculous effects. For, when he enters the world of the grave, a yearning for the Universal

[33] The eye of a *fard* even penetrates into the very essence of the *nafs kulliyya*: at that moment the door of *aḥadiyya* (absolute Oneness, the ultimate metaphysical stage) is opened to him (*Tafh.* I, 64).

Nature (*ṭabīʿa ʿāmma*) arises in him, in consequence of which he becomes at time a means for the Universal Divine Planning (*tadbīr kullī*). Accordingly, somewhere on earth blessings are manifested (*Fuyūḍ*, 45th Vision).

F. *Mujaddid* (renewer)

In connection with the prophetic saying: "On the eve of every century, God will send to my community a man who will renew its *dīn* (religion)" (*Sunan Abī Dāʾūd* II, 518), Shāh Walī Allāh states: "Every prophet is definitely in need of a *mujaddid* to purify his religion from undue assumptions of sectarians. Hence the latter is somebody whom God grants a share of knowledge concerning Qurʾān and Ḥadīth so that he is able to explain the secret tenets of the institutionalized religion (*milla*). Next, he will be clothed with the garb of *sakīna* (inner surity). Consequently, he becomes occupied with determining what is to be considered forbidden, imperative, reprehensible, desirable,and permitted, and with pruning the *sharīʿa* from spurious traditions and deductions by analogy. Equally, he guards against an over-rigid observance of the Law (*ifrāṭ*) as well as against any neglect of it (*tafrīṭ*). Then, God will make people anxious to acquire knowledge from him" (*Tafh.* I, 29, 40 and II, 133).

Shāh Walī Allāh discerns an interrelation between the offices of a *mujaddid* and a *waṣī* (executor to the Prophet). Both of them are heirs of Mohammed. One of the tasks of a *mujaddid* is to discuss legislative matters (*fiqh*) in the light of the sublime *sunna* without the application of a reasoning by analogy (*qiyās*), while a *waṣī* has the duty to discuss the hidden significance of the injunctions of the *sharīʿa*. Similarly, the methods used by them both have to be adapted to the different conditions. If eloquence is highly valued by a people, the elucidations should be offered in a very eloquent manner; if the method of demonstration (*burhān*) appears much in favour with a people, the explanations should excel in sound reasoning (*Tafh.* I, 78 and 82). If one wishes to fix the date of the appearance of a *mujaddid* one should, so the Delhi scholar argues, take a space of time of roughly—and not exactly—a hundred years; and one should count from the death of the Messenger of God (*Tafh.* I, 40). "The view that one has to count from the date of the *hijra* ... is unfounded' (*Tafh.* II, 114). In this way Shāh Walī Allāh tries to corroborate his claim of being himself appointed as a *mujaddid* of the 12th century, since the year of his birth is 1114 A.H. A hardly covert allusion to his divine election is made in the following passage: "We want to entrust you with important information, to wit that God has predestined grace for these days. He wants to pour forth important kinds of knowledge in our time

... Thus, at the very moment the lights of prophets and saints were united in the *ḥaẓīra al-quds* ..., it has the necessary result that the Universal Soul descended into a soul endowed with inner light (*zakī*) who ... would reform the world as a whole" (*Tafh.* I, 100)[34]. All veils of mystery are raised on p. 40 of *Tafh.* I, where we are told that at a certain stage of his spiritual journey God clothed him with the robe of *mujaddid*-hood: "consequently, I became acquainted with the methods to reconcile conflicting opinions; and I was notified that we have to do with 'distortion' (*taḥrīf*) if people exercise personal opinion (*raʾy*) in the *sharīʿa* as such, but that it is a blessing when a cadi gives judgment according to his own discretion (*raʾy*)".

## G. *ʿUlamāʾ*

In Shāh Walī Allāh's 21st Vision, recorded in the *Fuyūḍ al-Ḥaramayn*, we read: "I asked the Prophet's permission to refute criticism leveled against some ṣūfīs by *ʿulamāʾ* of Mecca and Medina, but I did not obtain it. I found that the *ʿulamāʾ*, who act according to their principles, and somehow occupy themselves with the refinement of hearts[35] and the spread of true knowledge and faith are closer to Him, more respected and beloved by Him than the ṣūfīs, although the latter are people who practise *fanāʾ* and *baqāʾ*, go into trances (*jadhb*) and ... may reach lofty stages (*maqāmāt*) such as the gate of unity (*tawḥīd*).

The explanation of this (divine preference) is in substance as follows; in this connection we have to consider two paths (leading to Eternal Life):

1. the path which has been conveyed to mankind by the Prophet. It is supplied with various means (*wasāʾiṭ*); by means of ritual acts of devotion the limbs are put into a correct state, while psychic faculties are sublimated by means of *dhikr*, purification (of the heart) and love of God and the Prophet; people are set right by the distribution of true knowledge, by enjoining what is known to be good and censuring what is evil and by advocating the public interest ...
2. the path which establishes a direct link between God and His worshipper, in such a way that, wherever he may have been born, he will find it; and with whatever he may be blessed, he will be blessed with it. It is without any medium. For him who travels on it, the only concern is to be conscious of the reality of his ego and, in consequence

---

[34] Also by means of visions (*mushāhadāt*), Shāh Walī Allāh is assured of his privileged position of being enabled to act as a *mujaddid* (*cf. Tafh.* I, 29 f.).

[35] *Cf.* also *Tafh.* II, 250, where mention is made of another vision with a similar trend: "I saw that *ʿulamāʾ* who study traditions and apply themselves to the refinement of the perceptible *laṭīfas* are more beloved by the Prophet than many ṣūfīs who want to outstrip them by engaging in the refinement of the concealed *laṭīfas*".

of this, to become conscious of the Divine (*al-ḥaqq*). On the way there are experiences like *fanāʾ*, *baqāʾ*, *jadhb* and *tawḥīd*.

As for the second path: we are of the opinion that the Prophet had no high regard for it and did not like it very much, for he himself advised for the following of the first path''.

Though in this way Shāh Walī Allāh was corrected in his predilection for fellow-ṣūfīs and was told by the Prophet that God does have a preference for *ʿulamāʾ*, he still deemed fit to regard the latter with a critical eye. One should guard oneself against associates of those who—instead of confining themselves to the study of the Qurʾān and prophetic *sunna*—concern themselves with Greek lore, etymology, grammar and rhetoric[36] (*Tafh.* I, 214). They are, actually, *ʿulamāʾ* longing for the splendour of the present life; it has nothing to do with faith (*Tafh.* I, 37).

## H. *Philosophers*

More than once Shāh Walī Allāh raises his warning voice against the Greek philosophers who influenced and shaped Muslim thought to a considerable extent: ''beware of caring for people who call themselves *falāsifa*. God has made them to go astray, in spite of their knowledge, and ensnared them in their intellectualism, so that they cannot find a way to escape from it. If you want to go to the heart of things and determine hidden meanings (*sirr*), their knowledge will be of no use to you. True knowledge is gained from the spring of the *sharīʿa* together with pious deeds and seeking proximity to God'' (*Khizāna* 10). Similarly, contemporary philosophers are deviating from the right path: ''although the metaphysicians (*maʿqūliyyān*) of our time may comprehend abstruse points, they are really far from the divine grace (*fayḍ*) ... With respect to them one can state that by applying themselves to novel sciences they remain excluded from the legacy of prophets''[37] (*Qurrat* 161). These people are afflicted with ''all sorts of doubt and confusion, making the Day of Resurrection 'a thing forgotten and out of sight' (*Qurʾān* XIX, 22)''

[36] Or historical investigation (*Tafh.* I, 37). Just as theologians under the ʿAbbāsids (see I. Goldziher, *Muslim Studies*, II, 192) Shāh Walī Allāh considered this a useless profane entertainment. In consonance with Awrangzeb's orthodox principles, ''official historiography stopped'' during his rule (A. Schimmel, *Islam in the Indian Subcontinent*, Leiden 1980, 102).

[37] Exceeding the bounds of prophetical lore, however, is an aberration of which Shāh Walī Allāh himself cannot always steer clear. In this respect, the way in which he apologizes for having discussed two possibilities of the origin (*ḥudūth*) of the world is significant: ''do not protest too loudly (against the argument we just made). Leading Sunnites also treated difficult subjects which were never broached either by the Companions or by the Followers. Still they remained good Sunnites. Similarly, with our *dhawq* we enter on intricate questions which these leaders have never taken up or even summarily indicated, as those questions were not yet of topical interest'' (*Khizāna* 2).

(*F.K.* 40). "They are worse than dogs, for a dog does not sniff at an old bone. These worthless people sniff and lick at bones that are two thousand years old. The cause of their erring is that our intellect (*ʿaql*) (on which solely they rely) is deficient ... It badly needs the additional help of the *dhawq* (intuitive appreciation). The *ʿaql* is merely an apparatus of analysis and abstraction; the *dhawq* perceives the unity behind the multiplicity" (*A.Q.* 142 ff.).

Another heresy is their assumption of a hierarchy of separate and independent intelligences[38], each lower one emanating from a higher one. Their postulate of the existence of ten *ʿuqūl*, being a kind of creative and regulating powers that govern the universe, cannot be right because "the stage of the (divine) Mind (*ʿaql*) (in which God at first ordered the existence of the universe) is prior to the universe in its present shape (*nafs kulliyya*). The *ʿaql*-stage is the level of *thubūt* (transcendental determination) and the *nafs kulliyya* represents the level of *wujūd* (actualization)[39] (*Tafh.* I, 192). Another fallacy of the philosophers is to maintain that the divine Will is identical to the divine Essence. In this way, they infer that an uncreated attribute can take created forms (which is an obvious incoherence). This error can be avoided by postulating the existence of an intermediary, to wit the *tajallī aʿẓam* which implies that the divine Essence is in the possession of an *irāda mutajaddida* (i.e. a Will causing continuous processes of renovation in the universe) (*Saṭ.* 11).

When holding that carrying out or refraining from an act merely rests with a higher *maṣlaḥa* (consideration of expediency) the philosophers's view of the human will, so our author claims, turns out to be too narrow: "they observe only a part, whereas various other aspects remain hidden from them. They are veiled from witnessing this zone (in the World of Divine Omnipotence, namely the *ḥaẓīra al-quds* where consensus of the *mala aʿlā* concerning the doing or omitting of acts are achieved. Those consensus are based, among other things, on a valuation of deeds performed by men on earth) ... A clear argument against them is that when, for instance, one of us stretches out his hand for a pen, he is doing that

[38] These *ʿuqūl* are deemed to be the originators of the movement of the nine spheres around the earth. They bring God's management of the universe into operation. The main objection Shāh Walī Allāh has to the *ʿuqūl* of the *falāsifa* is the assumption that they are independent substances that act on the universe. It is al-Raḥmān who is the actor, and the *ʿuqūl* are to be regarded as aspects (*iʿtibārāt*) and modes (*jihāt*) of the Ultimate Reality. When they rise to the world of the divine Essence (*lāhūt*), they vanish into It; and when they descend to what is close to multiplicity, you find them actualized as Names (*Tafh.* I, 168).

[39] "Substance (*jawhar*) and accident (*ʿaraḍ*) are both subsumed in the *nafs kulliyya* ... The philosophers have not established the reality of this common factor between substance and accident and fail to take the *nafs kulliyya* into account as the highest genus" (*A.Q.* 148 and 152).

intentionally and deliberately ..., although (in principle) everything happens according to a higher *maṣlaḥa* ... Two things are equally true:

a) a human will (*ikhtiyār*) is subject to a cause; it cannot go against its cause; ...
b) a human will is at liberty to enjoy in considering the possibilities open to it without being concerned about 'what goes beyond that' " (*H.B.* I, 67 f.).

I. *Mutakallimūn* (scholars in the field of speculative theology)

Shāh Walī Allāh's opinion on the *mutakallimūn* appears to be nearly as unfavourable as in the case of the philosophers: "the heresies suggested by the *mutakallimūn* are without any foundation and should not be adopted from them" (*Khizāna* 10). Instead of being content with simply noting the 'final' manifestations and operations of the divine Attributes as they are observed in the phenomenal world, the *mutakallimūn* also try to ascertain their fundamental aspects[40] by speaking in metaphors (*B.B.* 103).

In particular, the Muᶜtazilites are denounced. They are qualified as 'heretics' (*H.B.* I, 135) and 'aftergrowths' (*nawābit*) (like weeds on cultivated land), "for ultimately this group holds many doctrines which would be unacceptible to the first generation of the Muslim community" (*Kalimāt-i ṭayyibāt* 174 and *Qurrat* 314); this is contrary to the teachings (*madhhab*) of al-Ashᶜarī which "resemble those of the Companions of the Prophet" (*Khizāna* 10). True, al-Ashᶜarī himself belongs to the *mutakallimūn*, but among the orthodox he enjoys a much better reputation than the Muᶜtazilites, and the Delhi divine strives hard to defend him. He often establishes a surprising agreement between his own theories and those of al-Ashᶜarī: is not what the latter says about the 'capacity is with the act'[41] exactly the same as what Shāh Walī Allāh himself has demonstrated when arguing that "the contingencies (*mumkināt*) rely on God to the same extent as light relies on the sun?" (*Khizāna* 10). And indeed, if the Delhi scholar endorses al-Ashᶜarī's tenet of the *kalām nafsī* (inner speech inhering in God's Essence of which the revealed Qurʾān is an expression) (*Khizāna* 10), he contradicts the Muᶜtazilites who reject this theory[42]. And if al-Ashᶜarī formulates a dogma[43] rather awkwardly, it is

[40] I.e. viewed from their base-side (*mabādiʾ*) as they subsist in the Essence of God.

[41] I.e. that he for whom God does not create a capacity (*istiṭāᶜa*) cannot acquire a thing, whereas the Muᶜtazilites hold that the capacity is before the act and is power (*qudra*) over the act and over its opposite and does not make the act necessary.

[42] Further, contrary to the Muᶜtazilites, he affirms that prayers for the dead and alms given on their behalf are effective (*H.B.* II, 32), holds that God forgives a believer even if he died without repenting his grave sins (*Ḥusn al-ᶜaqīda* 13) and that saints can work miracles (*Khizāna* 7).

[43] As, for instance, when stating that the finger, right hand and face are Attributes of God (*Khizāna* 10).

said to be due to his being an *ummī*. (i.e. an unsophisticated man). Yet, the matter is not as simple as Shāh Walī Allāh wants us to believe. Thus, for instance, problems already arise as soon as he has to deal with the thorny question of how to determine the criteria for good and bad: "When al-Ashᶜarī says', so we read, "that the goodness and badness (of human deeds) is fixed by the *sharīᶜa*, he means that this is in accordance with actual practice". So far, it seems, Shāh Walī Allāh agrees with al-Ashᶜarī's point of view, but then he continues: "Conclusive as to what is good or bad is, to my mind, the fact that from the beginning of times something has been good or bad and that human reason can make this clear and prove it, and that when the *sharīᶜa* came down, good and bad could be verified for a second time" (*Khizāna* 10). Here al-Ashᶜarī's opinion is complemented by the Muᶜtazilite standpoint![44]

Shāh Walī Allāh's professed Ashᶜarite stand, however, becomes the more disputable at the moment we discover in his writings at least as many views agreeing with the Muᶜtazilites as with the Ashᶜarites. Instances of conformity with Muᶜtazilite teachings are:

a) Once, in a discussion of the *visio beatifica* (the question whether God will be seen by the eyes of the faithful in Paradise), he explicitly declares that the Muᶜtazilite conception of it is right (*Tafh.* I, 145). Such open concessions to the Muᶜtazilite viewpoint are very rare however. In general, it apparently seems to him more opportune to qualify the Muᶜtazilites as dangerous heretics, and to bracket them with Shiᶜites (*Izāla* I, 46 f.) or with philosophers[45] (*Khizāna* 9).
b) When Shāh Walī Allāh states that only God and those firmly rooted in knowledge (*al-rāsikhūn fiʾl-ᶜilm*) can explain matters which are ambiguous (*mutashābih*) (*H.B.* I, 110), it means that like the Muᶜtazilites in *Qurʾān* III, 7 he places the pause (*waqf*) after *ᶜilm*, and not after Allāh, and, accordingly, reads: "None knows the interpretation of what is *mutashābih* save only God and those firmly rooted in knowledge"[46].
c) In his *Ḥujjat al-nubuwwa*, 145f., the Muᶜtazilite al-Jāḥiẓ (d. 869) observes "la principale caractéristique du peuple arabe était le bien-dire; le miracle de Muhammed fut donc le Coran inimitable" (tr. by

---

[44] The position of the Muᶜtazilites in this question G. C. Anawati and L. Gardet define as follows: "C'est à la raison à reconnaître le caractère de convenance ou de disconvenance de l'acte, et l'acte est intrinséquement tel, antérieurement même à la Loi" (*Dieu et la destinée de l'homme*, Paris 1967, 81).

[45] *Cf.* also *Taʾwīl* 82: "The occupation with allegorical interpretations has been introduced (in Islam) by the Muᶜtazilites who had secretly adopted this science from the philosophers.

[46] *Cf.* I. Goldziher, *Die Richtungen der Islamischen Koranauslegung*, Leiden 1920, 129: "Jene *mutashābihāt* zu deuten sei demnach die Aufgabe der muᶜtazilitische Exegese".

Ch. Pellat in *Stud. Isl.* XXXI, 1970, 228). Our author uses exactly the same argument: "People in the time of our Prophet were busy with poetry and rhetorics. They owed their renown to them ... Accordingly, God sent down the miracle of the Qurʾān ... Thus He proved to be the supreme authority in the dispute by checkmating them on their own ground" (*Tafh.* I, 82).

d) The Delhi divine follows in the track of the Muʿtazilite Abuʾl-Hudhayl (d. 840/1), when he holds that God's Attributes are identical with Himself (*Tafh.* II, 18; *Maktūb* 29), and not an addition (*zāʾida*) to the divine Essence.

e) The emphasis Shāh Walī Allāh lays on man's being placed in the state of accountability (*taklīf*). The unjust, mentioned in *Qurʾān* XXXIII, 72 (the famous passage stating that man accepted the 'trust' which heavens, earth and mountains refused to carry), is he who does not practise justice though he is capable of doing so. Unlike an angel who is perfect *in esse*, man is perfect *in posse* (*H.B.* I, 19 f.).

f) The superiority of angels over prophets (*Khizāna* 3) as is the opinion of the majority of the Muʿtazilites (see A. J. Wensinck, *The Muslim Creed*, London 1965, 201).

g) The reluctance to apply *naskh* to Qurʾān verses is in agreement with the Muʿtazilite way of thinking, as for them *naskh* may introduce a "principe de mutabilité dans le Vouloir divin" (L. Gardet, *Dieu et la destinée de l'homme*, Paris 1967, 217).

CHAPTER TEN

# QURʾĀN

*The Genesis of the Qurʾān.* "You should know that when in pristine ages the *tajallī aʿẓam* became distinct on the plane of Ultimate Reality, a perfection (*kamāl*) of the *tajallī aʿẓam* appeared there like the appearance of light on the body of the sun. That perfection was the guidance (*tadbīr*) of the human souls by revelatory knowledge to be transmitted by perfect souls ... After that, because of the reflection of the *tajallī aʿẓam* which became distinct in the *ḥajar al-baht* of the *mala aʿlā*, this perfection took another shape. Five kinds of knowledge were fixed: the remembrance of the boons and Day of the Lord and of the requital at the Resurrection; polemics against disbelievers; fixation of the rules for worship; economics and polity. After that, when the Prophet was sent (into the world), those kinds of knowledge were clothed in the garments of Arabic, and the original style of *sūras* and Qurʾān verses were fixed in the mind of the Prophet by unseen help which arose from the heart of the *ḥaẓīra al-quds*[1] ... And for their communication the Prophet became an instrument of God ... Thus the Qurʾān is uncreated (*qadīm*) by its origin, but originated in time by coming down and (being revealed in) Arabic[2] ... It came down through the intermediary of an angel, is recited by the tongues of men, is written down on copies of the Qurʾān[3] ... and has been articulated through words amidst the *mala aʿlā* and in the *ʿālam al-mithāl*" (*Kalimāt-i ṭayyibāt*, 166 f.).

In *Khizāna* 6, Shāh Walī Allāh distinguishes three levels of evolution of the Qurʾān in its created condition:

---

[1] I.e. the ideas (*maʿānī*) flowed down from the Unseen World (*Tafh.* I, 185), while from time to time articulate speech descended into his rational faculties through the agency of the *mala aʿlā (Saṭ.* 19). In other words, the wording of the Qurʾān is no accomplishment of Mohammed. It is therefore a misunderstanding on the part of Sir Sayyid Aḥmad Khān when he concludes in the fourth principle of his *Taḥrīr fī uṣūl al-tafsīr* that, according to Shāh Walī Allāh, at the genesis of the Qurʾān there was only a pouring down of ideas, whereas the words which were the medium of expressing these ideas were the Prophet's (*Maqālāt-i Sir Sayyid* (ed. by Muḥ. Ismāʿīl Pānipatī), Lahore 1961, vol. II, p. 228).

[2] *Cf. Fuyūḍ*, 38th Vision: "The Qurʾān came down in the language of the Quraysh".

[3] This resembles the view of the creed formulated in the Ḥanafī-Māturīdī text *Fiqh Akbar II* (A. J. Wensinck, *The Muslim Creed*, London 1965, 189).
In *Saṭ.* 23 our author points out that a work like Saʿdī's Gulistān and the Qurʾān have many features in common: both of them are written on leaves of paper, are recited by tongues of men, are preserved in their hearts and are the creation of a writer, or speaker (*i.e.* God) respectively. The Qurʾān has the extra quality that it is *qadīm* (primeval), "for a form of it was already in store in the eternal Providence before the existence of the world".

1. The Qurʾān reached the stage of becoming created at the moment when through the *ism mutajaddid* (Name with renewing force), which the Delhi divine equates with the Holy Spirit, the Word of God entered Mohammed's heart. This happened in the period previous to his prophecy.
2. It is only at the time of his factual prophethood that the divine words, present in the *ʿālam al-khayāl* (world of imaginative thought) as mental speech (*kalām nafsī*)[4], appeared in the *ʿālam al-talaffuẓ* (world of articulation) and were put into "intelligible, forceful speech and literary style".
3. At this time the Qurʾān was assimilated by Mohammed's *mudrika* (faculty of comprehension). This happened for the sake of the development of the *sharīʿa*.

Nevertheless, the superior literary form of the Holy Book was not an end in itself; indeed, it had an immediate relevance to the historical setting of prophetic activities: "People in the time of our Prophet were busy with poetry and rhetorics. They owed their renown to them ... Accordingly, God sent down the miracle of the Qurʾān ... Thus He proved to be the supreme authority in the dispute by checkmating them on their own ground"[5]. (*Tafh.* I, 82).

Not only as regards the form but also with respect to the content, Shāh Walī Allāh discovers a noteworthy adaptability of the Qurʾān to the era of its revelation. "Know, that in our opinion adequate knowledge is that which meets the requirements of the age, and that the Qurʾān ... has come down in accordance with the conditions of the moment; i.e. in accordance with 'the fulness of time' (*dawrat al-kamāl*) it has brought down practical wisdom, admonition, knowledge of good works, God and the hereafter, instruction concerning *dhikr*, *duʿās* and the stages (*maqāmāt*) of people striving after perfection" (*Tafh.* II, 166). "You should be aware", so the Delhi scholar argues in another writing, "that the Qurʾān was sent down for the correction of Arabs as well as non-Arabs, for townspeople as well as inhabitants of the desert. Hence divine wisdom required that ... what was said about God's Attributes and Names ... should be understandable without a training in metaphysics and scholastics ... (and that for God) some perfect human qualities, which

---

[4] *Cf. H.B.* I, 23: Knowledge prefigured in the Absolute Mystery (*ghayb al-ghayb*) is termed by the Ashʿarites *al-kalām al-nafsī*.

[5] *Cf.* also *Saṭ.* 21: "(God knew that) if people are dedicated to rhetorics, the Word (of God) will not prove effective among them as long as it is not of extraordinary eloquence; and that surely the Qurʾān had to come down in a style which would be neither poetry nor prose, neither common parlance (*muḥāwara*) nor written language (*risāla*) so that it would be the most stimulating for them".

were generally known and of which people were proud, should be chosen instead of Attributes with too subtle a meaning'' (*F.K.* 12 f.)[6].

When discussing the 'collection' of the Qurʾān, Shāh Walī Allāh makes a comparison between the disorderly state of the Holy Book on the death of the Prophet and the short poems and *qaṣīdas* taken down in note-books, which a poet leaves in the hands of his friends at his death. These literary compositions are in danger of becoming lost if the leaves (of these note-books) land in water or fire, ''just as a flock of birds is already widely dispersed by a soft gust of wind''. When 'rightly guided' disciples of the dead poet set out to collect those literary products in order to arrange them properly and prepare them for distribution throughout the world, then those who afterwards profit by those poems will partake of the beneficial work of these disciples. Similarly, the rightly guided caliphs set out to 'collect' the Qurʾān (*Izāla* II, 5).

*Qurʾānic Teaching.* For the elucidation of the teachings imparted by the Qurʾān, the Delhi scholar introduces a division of his own into five kinds[7] of information. In the Holy Book one finds:

1. the regulations required for religious practice, mundane affairs, household and political economy;
2. polemics with four groups of erring people: the Jews, Christians, polytheists, and *munāfiqūn* (lukewarm followers);
3. 'remembrance of the benefits of God'[8] by explaining how heaven and earth were created, and by pointing out that, thanks to divine instruction, man can acquire the necessities of life;
4. remembrance of the 'Day of the Lord' (*ayyām Allāh*)[9], i.e. the lessons of history;

---

[6] Still in this matter too one should guard against exaggeration. Thus there are people who deduce from *Qurʾān* XVIII, 85 (''They will question you about the Spirit (*rūḥ*). Say: The Spirit belongs to the providence (*amr*) of my Lord; of knowledge, only a little is given to you'') that nobody in the blessed *umma* had been acquainted with the reality of the Spirit. This conclusion is mistaken, as appears explicitly from the reading of al-Aʿmash, found in the codex of Ibn Masʿūd, stating: ''Of knowledge, only a little is given to them''. ''It follows'', so Shāh Walī Allāh argues, ''that the persons addressed (in this passage) were Jews (and not Muslims)'' (*H.B.* I, 18).

[7] Elsewhere seven Qurʾānic sciences instead of five, are summed up: in *Khizāna* 6, the knowledge consisting of remembering the benefits of God is replaced by a) theology and b) natural sciences (*takwīniyyāt*), and the instruction to be derived from the stories of prophets is added as a seventh branch of Qurʾānic teaching.

[8] In all likelihood this expression is taken from Sūra VII, 67.

[9] Also a Qurʾānic phrase; see Sūra XIV, 5. In illustration of such lessons, ''God chose histories which were already well-known, ... and not curious and strange tales from Iran, nor Persian or Indian allegoric stories ... The divine Wisdom behind it is that the attention of common people, when they hear stories of rare events, is drawn to curious details ... and not to the essence of those stories'' (*F.K.* 44 f.).

5. remembrance of death and what happens after it at the Resurrection, the Day of Reckoning, etc.[10].

After this stock-taking of Qurʾānic learning, Shāh Walī Allāh continues: "The exposition of those *ʿulūm* is rendered in the style of writing used by the Arabs of early times, and not by those of later days! Hence, the legislative and terse verses of skilled authors are not deemed necessary, nor are the rules for provisos observed, as is done by scholars versed in the science of *fiqh* principles. In the polemical verses it is thought essential to refer to generally known data and to deliver profitable sermons; but in them no rational arguments are produced, as is done by logicians, and no attempt is made at a close coherence between successive subject-matters, as is the rule with literary men in later times" (*F.K.* 11 f.). On the contrary, the Delhi divine points out some ninety pages further on, a complete disregard of any systematization is characteristic of the Qurʾān; sometimes even a dislocation of verses has taken place. Thus, for instance, in Sūra II the coming down of verse 144 ("We see you often turn your face to heaven; now We shall turn you to a direction that shall satisfy you") must have preceded that of verse 142 ("The fools among the people will say: What has turned them from the direction which they used?") (*F.K.* 106).

Instead of offering a coherent line of thought when expounding sundry aspects of its message the Qurʾān prefers to give instruction through repetition, and the five categories of learning mentioned above are dealt with over and over again for the sake of *istiḥḍār*, i.e. a vivid evocation of its designs before the mind of the people addressed. In that manner the ideas to be conveyed "come so clearly to the imagination of the one spoken to that he tastes their subtle shades, and they eventually overpower his heart and mind ..., as happens with a poem which, after having understood its meaning at a first reading, we recite every now and then in order to taste its delicacy each time afresh. It is on account of this delight that we like to repeat it" (*F.K.* 130).

*Qurʾānic Style and Language.* However, if we wish to give some characterization of its mode of expression, the Qurʾān "should be compared to a collection of edicts which rulers issue to their subjects from time to time, as the situation demands ... Precisely in the same way the King of kings sent down *sūra* after *sūra* upon His Messenger for the guidance of His servants according to the requirements of the moment

[10] The third category of Qurʾānic lore was a 'support' (*ʿumda*) by which Abraham in particular was sustained, while the fourth one was an insight with which notably Moses was favoured. But knowledge of this fifth branch of Qurʾānic learning was reserved for Mohammed (*H.B.* I, 55). This last remark is indeed very true, since the Old Testament is almost silent on eschatological issues.

... Since there is a most remarkable resemblance between the style of the *sūras* and that of royal edicts[11], the pattern of an edict is chosen for the exordium and final part of the *sūras*. Thus, some edicts begin with the praise of God, others with an explanation of the motive for its being issued, and others again with the name of the sender and the person addressed. There are also short letters missive and extensive royal orders without a heading ... Exactly in the same manner God allows one *sūra* to begin with celebrating the praise of God, another with an explanation of the motive for its being written, as for instance ...; "A *sūra* which We have sent down and in which We have set down the obligatory statutes" (*Qurʾān* XXIV, 1), and again another with the name of the sender and the addressed, as for instance: "The revelation of the Book is from God ... We have sent down to you the Book" (*Qurʾān*, XXXIX, 1 f.). And there are also *sūras* of the category of short letters missive and orders without a heading as for instance: "When the hypocrites come to you" (*Qurʾān* LXIII, 1) (*F.K.* 112-5).

When referring to instances of Qurʾānic 'liberties' flouting all grammatical rules[12], the Delhi divine recommends ignoring the linguistic laws set up by Sībawayhi and al-Farrāʾ and relating the language of the Qurʾān to the idiom of the ancient Arabs, who were not averse to syntactic licence (*F.K.* 157). Similarly, in the matter of Qurʾān prosody the standards of Arabs poets are not strictly observed. The latter take the *ʿarūḍ*, by which correct meters are distinguished from faulty ones, as a measure of the lines of a poem and apply to them the rules of *qāfiya*[13] which fix the final consonant and vowel. "But the Qurʾān verses", so our author argues, "are based on a meter and *qāfiya* which are not fixed in all details, on account of which they lead to a more natural manner of expression". In view of the different and varying literary tastes found among peoples like, for instance, the Indians, Greeks, and Arabs, this testifies to very wise divine management. And "when God wished to speak in the same language as man, created from a handful of earth, He turned His mind towards that flexible and elegant form of style, and not towards figures of speech appreciated by one people but not by another, ... neither towards norms which may change with time" (*F.K.* 118 ff.).

---

[11] *Cf.* also *Tafh.* II, 123: "The manner of expression (*uslūb*) of the *sūras*, however, resembles partly the style of letters missive (*risāla*), partly that of a *qaṣīda* (poem with a characteristic tripartite structure)". The three parts into which a *sūra* can be divided, are: a) the exordium (*maṭlaʿ*), b) the 'padding' (*ḥashw*) and c) the conclusion (*maqṭaʿ*) (*Khizāna* 6).

[12] A long list of linguistic imperfections of the Qurʾān is contained in the *Neue Beiträge zur semitischen Sprachwissenschaft*, 1-30, by Th. Nöldeke.

[13] The last part of a line on which the rhyme of a poem rests.

*Taʾwīl* (exploration of basic ideas in Qurʾānic tales) and *Tafsīr* (exegesis of the Qurʾān). "On the first discipline", so we are told by the Delhi scholar, "I wrote an essay, entitled *Taʾwīl al-aḥādīth. Taʾwīl* here means that the predispositions of a prophet and his people as well as the regulations which God deems expedient for a given epoch, form the base of prophetic stories" (*F.K.* 163 f.). The Qurʾānic account of Moses and the enchanters is an example which shows how predispositions of people in a prophetic milieu might be taken into consideration by divine interference. The expediency of providential rule in the situation at the Pharaoh's court is evident if one realizes that the sorcerers were attacked and overpowered by their own weapons (*Taʾwīl* 46). An illustration of the adaptation of divine action to the predisposition of a prophetic individual is that in the valley of Ṭuwā God spoke to Moses in a fire; this was in consonance with the Moses' fiery nature (*Taʾwīl* 45).

In the opinion of Shāh Walī Allāh, the basic starting-point for a correct *tafsīr* is "to let the Qurʾān narratives speak for themselves and leave out one's own views" (*F.K.* 147)[14]. Teachers are advised by him to see that their disciples first study the Qurʾān without a commentary or translation (*Tafh.* II, 245). Should somebody strive after true faith, he should read the Qurʾān "as it clarifies itself" (*Tafh.* I, 37). An application of the principle that the Holy Book is understood best if it be its own commentator is the following: according to an explanation of the Companion ʿIyāḍ b. Ḥimār in Sūra XV, 9 the 'protection' of the Qurʾān means 'keeping it undamaged'. Against this interpretation the Delhi scholar sets his opinion that a proper understanding of the verse can only be obtained if it is combined with Sūra LXXV, 16-9. Or, to put it in other words, the 'protection' referred to in Sūra XV, 9 is the 'exegesis' of the Qurʾān, as it is explained in Sūra LXXV, 16-9. In that passage, according to Shāh Walī Allāh, 'collecting' refers to 'the collection of the Qurʾān into a book' (*sc.* at the time of Abū Bakr and ʿUmar), the 'recitation' to 'the divine concern to provide reciters of the Qurʾān in the *umma* of the Prophet', and 'upon Us devolves the making clear of it' by 'supplying in every epoch people capable[15] of elucidating it' (*Izāla* I, 50 f.).

---

[14] It appears for instance that common mystics become the prey of great confusion (*ishtibāh*) if they fail to distinguish clearly between notions derived from the Qurʾān in a subjective manner (*iʿtibār*) and the objective meaning of the text (*A.Q.* 97).

[15] Requisites for a proper interpretation of the Qurʾān are knowledge of the language in which it is revealed, acquaintance with that which has been handed down from the Prophet, his Companions, and representatives of the second Muslim generation about the explanation of unfamiliar expressions (*gharīb*) in the Qurʾān, of the occasions of revelation (*asbāb al-nuzūl*) and of the abrogating and abrogated (*nāsikh wa mansūkh*) verses in the Qurʾān (*H.B.* I, 172).

A correct appraisal of the self-explanatory nature of the Qurʾān texts affords the exegete not only a useful independence of commentaries stemming from the Companions, but it is also helpful in view of the urge often felt by Muslim scholars to adduce information from Jewish or Christian traditions in elucidation of succinct references in the Qurʾān to Biblical events. It turns out that in these cases the Qurʾān often proves itself able to supply material to fill the gaps. Thus, for instance, the condensed report of Jesus in Sūra XIX, 21 ("And We will make him a sign to mankind, and a mercy from Us") can easily be provided with some more detail by what is recorded in Sūra III, 43 ("And I have been sent as an apostle to the people of Israel, saying: Now have I come to you with a sign from your Lord") (*F.K.* 147 f.).

Shāh Walī Allāh disapproves of reading more into the Qurʾān than is intended: "the allusions (*ishārāt*) and subtle indications (*iʿtibārāt*) which ṣūfīs[16] discover in the Qurʾān do not actually belong to the discipline of *tafsīr*" (*F.K.* 158). The ultimate end to be pursued by Qurʾān exegesis is to gain an assent (*taṣdīq*) to the message of the Qurʾān. Therefore, "one should refrain from adding words of one's own" (*F.K.* 146).

With a similar carefulness in regard to the proper sense of the Qurʾān texts Shāh Walī Allāh warns against overrating the explanatory value of the so-called *asbāb al-nuzūl*, occurrences in the days of Mohammed which are said to have occasioned the revelation of certain Qurʾān passages. In this field one should proceed with caution: "Scholars of *ḥadīth*[17] append to Qurʾān verses many things which are actually not *asbāb al-nuzūl* but arguments of Companions that they advanced (in support of a private view) when they had controversies on (the correct interpretation of) a particular Qurʾān verse". Yet in two respects *asbāb al-nuzūl* might be useful:

1. The understanding of certain passages would be difficult indeed if one did not have them at one's disposal. An instance of this is the story told to account for the strange phrase ("no blame") used in Sūra II, 158 in connection with the custom of traversing the distance

[16] Likewise Shāh Walī Allāh disapproves of the endeavours of Muʿtazilites to read an allegorical meaning into Qurʾānic anthropomorphizations and eschatological images. One ought to rest satisfied with the literal meanings of the terms used (*Taʾwīl* 82). When, however, in a later writing he sets forth that the balance, which will be set up for the Day of Resurrection (*Qurʾān* XXI, 47), stands for the divine attribute of the faculty of discrimination by which good and bad actions are discerned (*Khizāna* 9), he himself, in fact, appears not averse to the interpretative methods of the Muʿtazilites.

[17] But the *asbāb al-nuzūl* mentioned by historians as Ibn Isḥāq (d. 767), al-Wāqidī (d. 822/3), and al-Kalbī (d. 763) are according to Shāh Walī Allāh, of an even more inferior quality. They are generally believed to be unreliable (*F.K.* 78) by the scholars of tradition (*muḥaddithūn*) also.

between Ṣafā and Marwa seven times during the *ᶜumra*. Once ᶜĀ᾽isha was asked: 'If running between Ṣafā and Marwa is obligatory, what is the sense of "No blame" (attached to it)?' She replied: "There were people who avoided it (because they thought doing it was a sin). Therefore it is said: 'No blame".

2. Sometimes the *asbāb al-nuzūl* can be of help in the illustration of universal truths, implied but hidden in the Qur᾽ān verse "which came down like this". These *asbāb al-nuzūl* apparently wanted to leave undecided whether the tale reported actually happened. Their very intention, however, was then to bring to light the proper purport of the Qur᾽ān passage by means of an illustrative story from the time of the Prophet (*F.K.* 69 ff. and 76 f.).

When discussing the *mutashābihāt* (the 'ambiguous' Qur᾽ān verses)[18] as opposed to the *muḥkamāt* (the 'perspicuous' verses), Shāh Walī Allāh is two-tongued. Putting himself on a par with the average believer, he scorns the efforts of the *mutakallimūn* in explaining the *mutashābihāt* dealing with anthropomorphisms or eschatological subjects, and declares: "My course is that of Mālik (b. Anas) (d. 795/6), of (Sufyān) al-Thawrī (d. 778), or Ibn al-Mubārak (d. 797) and the other ancients, and that is to take the *mutashābihāt* at their face value without engaging in hermeneutic ingenuities" (*F.K.* 156)[19].

In his capacity as a gnostic, however, the Delhi divine claims that for him the *mutashābihāt* have become perspicuous because of his having been a witness of the *ḥaẓīra al-quds* and having become conversant with its processes. This possibility, however, is not given to him who has not been a witness of this celestial abode; and he must trust these matters to God[20] (*Fuyūḍ*, 25th Vision).

*Taḥrīf*. The charge of falsifying the texts of the Holy Scripture (or their meaning) (*taḥrīf*) is in Islam usually directed against the *ahl al-kitāb* or

---

[18] Treating of the Attributes of God, matters concerning the hereafter or obscure details in prophetic tales (*Ta᾽wīl* 104).

[19] Knowledge of the *mutashābihāt* should be left to God, for it concerns issues of too speculative a nature, about which unanimity can never be gained in the *umma* (*B.B.* 204; *H.B.* I, 173). "(Proper) knowledge can only be derived from the unambiguous verses of the Qur᾽ān" (*Tafh.* I, 214).

[20] From *H.B.* I, 110, where the Delhi divine maintains that only the Prophet and those firmly rooted in knowledge (*al-rāsikhūn fi᾽l-ᶜilm*) can solve matters which are *mutashābih*, we can deduce that he, like the Muᶜtazilites, in *Qur᾽ān* III, 7 does not put the *waqf* (pause) after Allāh but after *ᶜilm*. Thus he reads: "None knows the interpretation of the *mutashābihāt* save only God and those firmly rooted in knowledge". "A distinctive trait of theirs", so he explains elsewhere, "is that their knowledge seems to have descended from God directly into their very hearts, and seems to emerge as fire struck with a flint" (*B.B.* 158). They are in possession of *ᶜilm ladunī* (knowledge imparted directly from God) (*Ḥusn al-ᶜaqīda*, Delhi n.d., 27 f.).

against the Shiʿites (by Sunnites) and Sunnites (by Shiʿites). In the first case it pertains to words of the Bible, in the second to the readings of the Qurʾān. Here again Shāh Walī Allāh shows his originality by taking Jews, Christians and Muslims *conjointly* to task for tampering with their Holy Books. Instead of merely accusing those who are outside the pale of his own community, his criticism is levelled at co-religionists as well: "*Taḥrīf* is spread in all sorts of groups. Among the ṣūfīs teachings are divulged—and this applies especially to views pertaining to the doctrine of *tawḥīd*—which cannot be brought into line with the Book and the *sunna* ... As for the *fiqh* of the scholars of *fiqh*, you often do not know what made them settle things as they did ... And where is the end if I start to mention the errors of the philosophers, poets, the rich and common people who worship idols and make the tombs of saints places of worship and festivities?" (*Tafh*. II, 135).

"To the causes of *taḥrīf* belong:

a) Indifference (*tahāwun*). The essence of this is that the generation following the disciples (of a prophet) neglects the *ṣalāt*, indulges its lusts, and does not care for the spread of the acts and articles of faith ... Subsequently, another generation tainted with still more indifference follows it, so that nearly all religious knowledge falls into oblivion ... On that account the religious communities of Noah and Abraham perished ...

b) Excessive scrupulousness (*taʿammuq*).
The essence of this is that when one of the *umma* learns of a command or prohibition of the Expounder of the *sharīʿa* (*sc*. Mohammed) ..., he extends the regulation to a somewhat comparable case ... Thus, when the Expounder of the *sharīʿa* prescribed fasting to check the passions and forbade sexual intercourse for a period, people thought that ... one was forbidden to kiss one's wife ... Then the Messenger of God disclosed the wrongness of this conclusion and explained that it was (an instance of) *taḥrīf*[21].

c) Aggravating (*tashaddud*).
The essence of this is that rigorous forms of worship, not imposed by the Expounder of the *sharīʿa*, are chosen such as ... the observation of celibacy (*tabattul*)[22] ... This is a disease of Jewish and Christian recluses.

d) Advancing a discretionary opinion contrary to strict analogy for reasons of public convenience (*istiḥsān*). The essence of this is that

---

[21] See Mu. *Ṣiyām* 62: "ʿĀʾisha related how the Messenger of God kissed one of his wives while he was fasting, and then she smiled".

[22] Thus the well-known case of ʿUthmān b. Maẓʿūn who expressed the desire to live in celibacy. This idea was rejected by the Prophet (Bu. *Nikāḥ* 8).

when somebody discovers that for every rule given by the Expounder of the *sharīʿa*, a rationale and an appropriate application is provided and that legislation is founded on this base, he seizes an opportunity to avail himself of such an underlying idea of legislation in order to introduce regulations which he thinks expedient for the people. Thus, for instance, when the Jews discovered that the Expounder of the Torah had ordained heavy punishments as a prevention of crimes and recognized that (the penalty of) stoning to death (in case of adultery)[23] gave rise to dissension and squabbling and caused a lot of trouble, they regarded the blackening of the face with coal combined with flogging a suitable substitute for stoning. Accordingly, the Prophet explained that this is *taḥrīf* (*cf.* Mu. *Ḥudūd* 15) ...

e) The following of an (unauthentic) *ijmāʿ* (consensus). The essence of this is that when among religious authorities, there are people of united opinion to whom common men accord their confidence, assuming that they are mostly or generally in the right, people believe this unanimity to be decisive evidence for the validity of a law, although it is not based on the Book and *sunna*. This kind of unanimity is unlike the *ijmāʿ*, on which the *umma* is agreed ... and which rests on the Book and *sunna* ... The Word of God says (in respect to this unauthentic *ijmāʿ*): "And when they are told, 'Follow what God has sent down', they answer, 'No; but we will follow the usages which we found with our fathers'" (*Qur'ān* II, 170). The only argument the Jews have for their denial of the prophethood of Jesus and Mohammed are the inquiries their fathers (*salaf*) made into the life stories of the two[24] ... The Christians possess many laws which are at variance with the Torah and the New Testament. The only ground they have for it is the *ijmāʿ* of their fathers.

f) Reliance on the teaching (*taqlīd*) of somebody who is not 'preserved' (by God from what is not right) (*maʿṣūm*), i.e. who is not a prophet whose preservation is established. The essence of this is that when one of the *ʿulamā'* has used discretionary reasoning (*ijtihād*) in a legal matter, his followers believe that he is surely, or at least most probably, in the right. In this way they can even act in contrary to a sound tradition. This kind of *taqlīd*, however, is not the same as the *taqlīd*, on which the *umma* is agreed ... (and which implies that the

---

[23] See Deuteronomy XXII, 21.

[24] *Cf.* also *F.K.* 32: "Well then, if you want to see in these days an example of Jewish scholars, look at the deceptive *ʿulamā'* whose ends are wordly, who have become accustomed to imitate the *salaf* and turn away from the texts of the Qur'ān and *sunna* ... and rely on ... absurd exegeses".

man of *ijtihād* who is relied on) has carefully examined what the Prophet has stated on that very issue ...

g) Mixing of two religions so that in the end the one cannot be distinguished from the other. This can happen when somebody who previously professed another religion enters the Muslim community, but still feels attracted to what was close to his heart before. Consequently, he tries to introduce such matters into the Muslim community ... Such matters which have crept into our religion include: teachings of the Israelites, admonishments of preachers of the 'heathen darkness', philosophy of the Greeks, imprecations of the Babylonians, histories of the Persians, astrology, geomancy and 'defensive apologetics' (*kalām*)'' (*H.B.* I, 120 ff.).

h) ''Instead of assigning to a word its obvious meaning, to choose a meaning you yourself think proper. The Prophet has already alluded to this, saying: 'Presently people will be found who will name wine by another name and fornication by another name. And they will assert that this is not what God has forbidden in His Book. So there is no objection to it for you'' (Ibn Mādja, *Ashriba* 8). Have you not met people who assert that an intoxicating liquor prepared from honey and the like is not wine at all, and then declare it lawful?'' (*B.B.* 127).

*Naskh*. On the delicate subject of *naskh*, i.e. the repeal of a former heavenly decree substantiated into a Qurʾān verse by a newly revealed message, the Delhi scholar has a lot to say. To begin with: there are various occasions for an abrogation of regulations, including the following:

a) developments in the personality and status of a prophet. In the matter of *jihād*[25], for instance, Mohammed attained a rank higher than the previous one.

b) changes in the spiritual state of a prophet. An example of this is given in the tale of Abraham and the sacrifice of his son. For, when Abraham had come very near to the Holy One, he understood that the universal aspect of sacrifice would have its concrete expression in the sacrifice of his son who was the best qualified for it. Therefore, the divine Name which manifested itself in his very essence (*ʿayn*) ordered him to make this sacrifice. But as soon as he recovered from the immersion into his very essence, he confined himself to the substitutive sacrifice of an animal.

---

[25] An allusion to Mohammed's well-known saying: ''We have returned from the inferior type of *jihād* to the superior one (i.e. the inner struggle against one's evil inclinations)''.

c) a situation requiring new statutes because of rites that have become obsolete, as was the case, for example, with transmutations in the ways of *zakāt*. At first, it consisted of an *ʿatīra* (ewe[26] offered as a sacrifice to a pagan divinity during the month of Rajab); next, the appointing of a special time (for a sacrifice) was repealed, and after that only the *dhabḥ* (victim destined for immolation) remained in force. Finally, the institute of *niṣāb* (minimum amount of property liable to payment of the *zakāt*) was introduced (*Khizāna* 8).

In an excursus on the purport to be derived from *Qurʾān* II, 106 ("For whatsoever *āya* We repeal or cause to forget, We bring a better or the like"), Shāh Walī Allāh argues that two sorts of *naskh* can be distinguished:

1. Pertaining to the *ijtihād* of the Prophet. As we readily understand, Mohammed himself made a regular study of the implications to be inferred from the ordinances sent down from above. But then it might happen that God completed or corrected the results of His Messenger's research. An instance of completion is the revelation of the passage concerning the *qibla* which had to be changed (see *Qurʾān* II, 144). A divine correction of prophetic *ijtihād* can be reconstructed from an abrogation of a prescription mentioned in a *ḥadīth*, *viz.* with respect to the prohibition of drinking *nabīdh* (a kind of drink made of dates) from any vessel but a leathern bottle as this would lead to fermentation (*cf.* Bu. *Ashriba* 8).
2. Pertaining to the requirements of the moment. In the course of time certain laws may lose their relevance on account of which they are revised or repealed. Thus, for example, at the time when the Prophet emigrated to Medina the fellow emigrants could no longer count on assistance from their blood relations. For relief they depended wholly on brotherhood. Consequently, the Qurʾān came down with the institute of hereditary right based on brotherhood. But when Islam got a stronger hold and kinsfolk of the emigrants joined them, hereditary right was founded on consanguinity[27].

When towards the end of this excursus Shāh Walī Allāh arrrives at the question which meaning is finally to be attached to the words "the better" or "the like" in *Qurʾān* II, 106, he first concludes that through the establishment of Islam in the Medinian period Mohammed became the caliph of the nation. Accordingly, he proposes taking "the better" as a reference to "prophethood enhanced by caliphate"; on the other hand,

---

[26] As being the means of purification. See *Qurʾān* XXIII, 4: "And who are acting for (God's) purification (*zakāt*) (of them)".

[27] Mention of this case of *naskh* can be found in al-Bayḍāwī's commentary at *Qurʾān* VIII, 72.

"the like" would merely imply that "laws change with the situation" (*H.B.* I, 123 f.).

In another work, i.e. *al-Fawz al-kabīr*, Shāh Walī Allāh starts with the observation that the concept early Muslims held of the *naskh*-principle differs to a great extent from the views of later generations. "The Companions and Succeeders took *naskh* in a literal (*lughawī*) sense, i.e. of 'removal' (*izāla*), and not in the (more restricted) technical (*muṣṭaliḥ*) sense of the scholars of the theoretical bases of Islamic law (*uṣūliyyūn*). According to the latter *naskh* merely denotes 'removal of a provision' in an earlier Qur᾽ān verse by a later Qur᾽ān verse. The occasion for it could be: either the circumstance that in time it was no longer obligatory upon a certain provision to act, or the situation that the discovery of a certain meaning in one Qur᾽ān verse suddenly threw new light on the purport of another Qur᾽ān verse, on account of which its former interpretation was abolished, or the fact that at a given moment the incidental character of a certain stipulation in a Qur᾽ān verse is recognized so that a general application of it is no longer desirable" (*F.K.* 56 and 151).

But if *naskh* is understood in the more extended sense attached to it by representatives of the first Muslim generations, it can be applicable to instances such as the 'removal' of astrology and geomancy, or the abrogation of certain religious customs dating from the time of heathendom such as the clipping of an ewe's ear to consecrate it or setting a she-camel at liberty to pasture freely, after having brought forth females (*Khizāna* 10). "So with the Companions and Succeeders, reason had a wide domain to wander in for the application of *naskh*; and as a result of that one came to the pretty total of 500 repealed Qur᾽ān verses!" (*F.K.* 57 and 151).

After this exposition of the two chief currents in the history of Islamic *naskh*-practice, Shāh Walī Allāh prefers for the viewpoint of the later generations over that of the early Muslims in this case[28], simply because it results in a considerably lower number of repealed verses. And in imitation of Abū Bakr b. ᶜAbdallāh b. al-ᶜArabī (1076-1148)[29], Jalāl al-Dīn al-Suyūṭī (1445-1505) reduced their number to a score.

Yet Shāh Walī Allāh himself, by nature a master in reconciling conflicting opinions and issues, deems even twenty too great a number. If the procedure of *tawjīh* be adopted, a further reduction is possible. In origin, *tawjīh* (i.e. providing a *wajh*, an alternative decision) designates

[28] An interesting exception, for as a rule Shāh Walī Allāh, being an admirer of Ibn Taymiyya, exhorts to follow in the footsteps of the first Muslims and to keep away from the practice of the ᶜ*ulamā*᾽ of later ages.

[29] Interpretor of the Qur᾽ān and author of *Qānūn al-ta᾽wīl fi᾽l-tafsīr* and *Aḥkām al-Qur᾽ān*, not to be confounded with the mystic philosopher Ibn ᶜArabī (d. 1240)!

a method, applied in *fiqh*, for deriving rules from decisions of the founder of a *madhhab*. But the Delhi divine makes it a new art, by which contradictions between indications or between the 'rational' and the 'traditional' can be suspended and divergent issues can be made congruous (*F.K.* 153).

To give one of the applications of this kind of *tawjīh* by which he manages to prove the redundancy of *naskh*: "There is no need", so it is affirmed, "to regard *Qurʾān* III, 102 ("Fear God with the fear that He deserves") to be abrogated by *Qurʾān* LXIV, 16 ("Fear God, then, as much as you can"), because the former verse relates to *shirk*, *kufr* and other matters of faith, whereas the latter bears upon religious practice, for instance if somebody cannot perform *wuḍūʿ* with water, he may do it with sand" (*F.K.* 61 f.). By thus searching out the *wajh* (contextual motive) implied in the verses which are still supposed by al-Suyūṭī to be *nāsikh* and *mansūkh*, Shāh Walī Allāh succeeds in abating the total number of *naskh*-cases to five only[30].

Further, among the kinds of privileged learning concerning the Qurʾān Shāh Walī Allāh also reckons:

a) his translation of the Qurʾān into Persian, called *Fatḥ al-Raḥmān*[31] (*F.K.* 164). In the preface he says that first of all his translation is meant for the sons of craftsmen and soldiers. As soon as they have attained the age of discretion they should make use of it, lest they are misled by the discourses of heretics or become confused by the idle talk of philosophers and Hindus;

b) the knowledge of Qurʾānic *khawāṣṣ* (salutary virtues). On this charismatic gift Shāh Walī Allāh comments: "Formerly, people used to speak of two categories of Qurʾānic *khawāṣṣ*: 1) *duʿāʾ*[32] and the like; 2) black magic (*siḥr*) and the like—God forbid!—. But for me a door (for a direct outpouring of divine knowledge) had been opened beyond that traditional lore. All at once the most beautiful divine Names, the most sublime Qurʾān verses and benedictory *duʿāʾ*s were put into my lap as a personal gift". Here an institutionalizing of magic practices using of the Qurʾān is obviously denounced.

---

[30] Namely, *Qurʾān* II, 180 cancelled by IV, 12; II, 240 by II, 234; VIII, 65 by VIII, 66; XXXIII, 52 by XXXIII, 50 and LVIII, 12 by LVIII, 13.

[31] Shāh Walī Allāh was not the first Indian who provided a Persian version of the Qurʾān. Before him this had already been done by Makhdūm Nūḥ of Hālā (Sind) (d. 1590) This translation has been edited by Ghulām Muṣṭafā al-Qāsimī and published by the Sindhi Adabi Board, Hydarabad (Sind) in 1401/1980-1.

[32] Invocations to which miraculous effects of an apotropaic nature are ascribed. They are also termed *ḥizb* ('group' of liturgical formulae) and in that case often bear the names of great mystics, like ʿAbd al-Qādir al-Jīlānī, al-Shādhilī.

And the argument continues: "The selection or composition of Qur'ān verses, divine Names and *duʿā'*s (to be used in an emergency) is subject to criteria for which no rule can be fixed" (i.e. it is all a question of a charisma to be accorded by the unseen world) (*F.K.* 164 f.).

It should be noted that although Shāh Walī Allāh rejects black magic[33] and an uncharismatic use of *khawāṣṣ* in the passage quoted, he does not generally condemn magic as such. Elsewhere, for instance, he gives the advice: "Let somebody visited by disease seek healing with the aid of perfect charms (*ruqan*) on which Qur'ān verses and Names of God are written" (*B.B.* 59). For Mohammed himself urged the people to do so, "in order to keep them from invoking the help of idols, as they were used to in pre-Islamic times" (*H.B.* II, 34). With great respect reference is made to al-Shādhilī (d. 1258) and al-Būnī (d. 1125) who are said "to have substituted fumigations (for the purpose of a spell or an exorcism) and recitation of divine Names and appropriate Qur'ān verses for prognostication by stars (*tanjīm*) and such-like" (*Tafh.* I, 89).

Yet, in the course of time there seems to have been some development in Shāh Walī Allāh's views of magic. This can be gathered from a comparison of notions concerning the *ḥurūf muqaṭṭaʿāt* ("disconnected letters") as they are set forth in one of his early writings, and in later works. In *Hawāmiʿ*, a commentary of the famous *ḥizb al-baḥr* of al-Shādhilī, the Delhi devine points to the effectiveness of magic proper with respect to those enigmatic letters with which 29 *sūras* begin. "If an evil-doer appears and his terror and power get the upper hand, one should pronounce *kāf*, *hā'*, *ʿayn* and *ṣād* (letters at the beginning of *sūra* XIX) and at every letter one should close a finger of one's right hand; then one should say: "Our protection". Next, one should pronounce *ḥā'*, *mīn*, *ʿayn*, *sīn* and *qāf* (at the beginning of *sūra* XLII) and at every letter one should close a finger of one's left hand; then one should say: "Our guardianship" (*Haw.* p. 52).

In later works we also find expositions of the *ḥurūf muqaṭṭaʿāt*, but without any magic context. Then it is stated that they represent names of *sūras* summarizing their contents, and the effort is concentrated on tracing the symbolic sense the letters contain. "Thus, *alif*, *lām*, *mīm* (at the beginning of *sūra* II) indicate that the unspecified world of divine mystery (*ghayb*) becomes specified in the soiled empirical world".

This becomes understandable, so we are taught, if we realize that the *alif*, which points at the *ghayb* of the transcendental world, is used in Arabic for questions about matters we wish to be informed of, for in-

---

[33] This is implied in the interjection: "God forbid!" For an explicit denunciation of *siḥr* as being "concealed evil" see *B.B.* 78.

stance in respect of things still to be specified. The *lām* indicates specifying; hence this letter is added when there is a question of rendering distinct. And the *mīm*, because of its uniting the lips when being pronounced, points to soiled primary matter (*hayūlā*), in which all kinds of essentials are untied and kept together and which, after leaving the world not conditioned by time and space, came into our empirical world. "Therefore, *alif*, *lām*, *mīm*, hint at the transcendental outpouring (*fayḍ mujarrad*) which, entering into the world where things are particularized and bound by space, becomes specified in items compatible with the (prevalent) customs and ideas of the people, and sets out to remove the hardness of hearts by admonition and to fight evil thought and bad customs by defining good and evil" (*F.K.* 168 ff., *Khizāna* 10).

CHAPTER ELEVEN

# ḤADĪTH

*The Importance of the Traditions*. The *ḥadīths* form the foundation of knowledge[1] and provide the material for the following sciences: theology (*ilāhiyyāt*), ethics (*ʿilm al-akhlāq*), cosmology (*ʿilm al-takwīn*), angelology, jurisprudence (*ʿilm al-aḥkām*), eschatology (*ʿilm al-maʿād*), knowledge of prophetic tales, the science of spiritual perfection (*iḥsān*), of actions of moral elevation which bring man into contact with God (*raqāʾiq*), and the exegesis of the Qurʾān (*Khizāna* 6; *Qurrat* 312; *Sharḥ al-tarājim* 1). Consequently, the science of Tradition is the mainstay and principal part of sciences which offer established truths (*H.B.* I, 2). The traditions, therefore, ought to determine the line of conduct to be adopted (*Khizāna* 10). So the 'raising of hands' at the beginning of the three forms of magnification (i.e. of bowing, coming back to the erect position and prostrating) of the *ṣalāt* is incumbent, since the traditions in support of it outnumber those opposed to (*H.B.* II, 10). Equally, private investigation should submit to views found in the traditional literature. "If the theses I framed in respect of astrology and divination", so our author declares, "turn out to be at variance with what is recorded in the *sunna*, then of course the opinion of the latter will prevail" (*H.B.* II, 195).
"The orally transmitted Tradition (*riwāya*) is actually the only means to preserve religion to the end of time: and there is no recovery if it is affected by corruption" (*H.B.* I, 171). Hence, provisions derived from the *sharīʿa* (*tafrīʿāt*) are to be tested by the *sunna*; if they do not agree with it they are to be rejected. According to Shāh Walī Allāh, a *faqīh* (expert of jurisprudence) is only reliable when he is a traditionist as well, as is the case, for example, with the Shāfiʿī *faqīh* al-Bayhaqī and the Ḥanafī *faqīh* al-Ṭaḥāwī (*Tafh.* I, 28).

*Valuation of the Collections of ḥadīth*. Shāh Walī Allāh classifies the various collections of *ḥadith* under the following categories, according to the authority to be assigned to them:

1. To the highest level belong the collections in which the two virtues typical of traditions (i.e. that of soundness and repute) have attained a perfect form. They are considered *mutawātir*, i.e. handed down by

[1] "No nobler task can one set oneself than to try to become a *muḥaddith* (scholar versed in the *ḥadīth*) or at least a hanger-on (*ṭufaylī*) of a *muḥaddith*" (*Fuyūḍ*, 24th Vision). *Muḥadddiths* are more favourite with Mohammed than ṣūfīs, though the latter may surpass the former in the refinement of spiritual qualities (*al-Durr al-thamīn fiʾl-mubashshirāt al-nabī al-amīn*, 11th tradition).

so many transmitters that they cannot be reasonably expected to agree on a falsehood. The only three collections that can be reckoned to this supreme class are the *Muwaṭṭaʾ* of Mālik b. Anas, and the *Ṣaḥīḥ* of al-Bukhārī and Muslim[2]. The Delhi scholar wholeheartedly endorses the view ascribed to al-Shāfiʿī, that after the Book of God there is no book as sound as the *Muwaṭṭaʾ*: If you want to have an idea of its worth then you must compare the *Muwaṭṭaʾ* with works like the *Kitāb al-Āthār* of Muḥammad al-Shaybānī (d. 805) and the *Amālī* of Abū Yūsuf (d. 798) (both famous Ḥanafī jurisprudents); you will recognize that between them lies the distance between the East and the West (*H.B.* I, 134). It is, in fact, "the apparatus (*ʿudda*) and foundation of the school of Mālik, a support and capital of the school of al-Shāfiʿī and Aḥmad (b. Hanbal), and a lamp and lantern of the school of Abū Ḥanīfa[3]. You should also realize that collections of the *muṣannaf* type such as the *Ṣahīḥ* of Muslim, the *Sunan* of Abū Dāʾūd and al-Nasāʾī, and what in the *Ṣaḥīḥ* of al-Bukhārī and the *Jāmiʿ* of al-Tirmidhī is connected with the *fiqh* are but so many extracts and appendices of the *Muwaṭṭaʾ* itself, in as far as these works supply additional *isnāds* for the traditions stated in the *Muwaṭṭaʾ*, be they *mursal* (a tradition in which a Successor quotes the Prophet directly), *marfūʿ* (record of a word or deed of Mohammed reported by a Companion) or *mawqūf* (with an *isnād* going back to the Companions, but stopping short of the Prophet)" (*Musawwā* I, 5). It is only by means of the *Muwaṭṭaʾ*, that the door of *ijtihād* can be kept open (*Muṣaffā* 12).

2. The second category reaches the rank of the *mustafīḍ* (widely spread) traditions which are of an acknowledged or supposed soundness. Works like the *Sunan* of Abū Dāʾūd, the *Jāmiʿ* of al-Tirmidhī and the *Mujtabā* of al-Nasāʾī belong to it, and the *Musnad* of Aḥmad (b. Ḥanbal) is counted as approaching this category closely[4] (*H.B.* I, 133 f.).
3. Thirdly we have *musnads*, *jāmiʿs* and *muṣannafs* which were composed before, in, or after Bukhārī and Muslim's lifetime. They contain traditions which are sound, weak, *maʿrūf* ('recognized': weak, yet known because confirmed by another weak tradition), *gharīb* ('unusual', i.e. resting on the authority of only one Companion), *shādhdh* ('anomalous', i.e. a tradition from a single authority which

---

[2] Shāh Walī Allāh points out that the Mālikite scholar ʿIyāḍ b. Mūsā (d. 1149) also puts these three works together in his *Mashāriq al-anwār ʿalā ṣiḥāḥ al-āthār* (*H.B.* I, 134).

[3] In short, "The *Muwaṭṭaʾ* is the most reliable, famous, classic and complete of all works on *fiqh*" (*Musawwā* I, 4).

[4] No mention is made of the *Sunan* of Ibn Māja, i.e. the collection among the six canonical works about which "doubts were maintained longest" (I. Goldziher, *Muslim Studies*, London 1971, II, 240).

differs from what others report), *munkar* ('objectionable', i.e. of weak authority contradicted by a weaker one) or *maqlūb* ('transposed', i.e. known to have come from a person other than the *soi-disant* reporter). Among scholars these do not enjoy such a good reputation, though they are not to be rejected outright. To them belong the *Musnads* of al-Ṭayālisī (d. 818), of ʿAbd b. Ḥamīd and Abū ʿAlī (al-Bazzāz, d. 1034) and the *Muṣannaf* of ʿAbd al-Razzāq (d. 826) and Abū Bakr b. Abī Shayba (d. 849). The very aim of the compilers was to collect whatever seemed secure but without applying any correction (*H.B.* I, 134 f.).

4. The fourth category comprises collections composed in later times. Here one finds *inter alia* products of prattling preachers and people of erroneous opinions as well as stories from Israelite sources. The most trustworthy traditions in this category are the weak and equivocal (*muḥtamal*) ones (*H.B.* I, 135). Evaluating these four categories, Shāh Walī Allāh states: "The *muḥaddiths* only place confidence in (traditions of) the first and second category ... For consultation in matters of faith and morality one should not touch (traditions of) the third category, unless one belongs to the able critics[5] who are acquainted with the names of the transmitters and the defects (in the *isnāds*) of the traditions ... As for the (traditions of) the fourth category ... sectarians such as the Rāfiḍites, Muʿtazilites etc. can easily draw evidential examples for their doctrines from them; but in the disputes of the scholars of *ḥadīth* they cannot be adduced as references" (*H.B.* I, 135).

*Deduction of the legal import carried by the Traditions.* Mohammed himself warned the people to exercise caution in according the status of law to directives of the Prophet. So two categories of statements carrying unequal authority are to be distinguished in the traditions:

1. concerning things pertaining to the prophetic mission such as for instance information about the Hereafter, regulation of the canonical rites, and the like. In this instance the line to be taken is formulated in *Qurʾān* LIX, 7: "Adopt whatever command the Messenger gives you; and refrain from whatever he forbids you";
2. concerning things not connected with the prophetic mission such as for instance pronouncements on medical questions or methods of inserting grafts. On the subject of such concerns the Prophet declared:

---

[5] As, for instance, Shāh Walī Allāh himself who in his autobiography relates: "I was granted the power of discerning between the basic teaching of religion as has been handed down by the Prophet, and what has crept in and been tampered with" (*al-Juzʾ al-laṭīf* 28). So he holds himself justified to quote a tradition "whose assignment to the Prophet is not verfiable according to the principles of the *muḥaddiths*" (*Tafh.* I, 179).

"I am only a human being; whenever I give you a command in religious matters, you should obey it, but whenever I give you a direction based upon my personal opinion, then keep in mind that I am only a human being" (Mu. *Faḍāʾil* 140) (*H.B.* I, 128).

Thus the advice offered by the Prophet. The *umma* on its part, however, so the Delhi scholar continues a few pages further on, deduced conclusions from the *ḥadīths* in the following ways:

1. by sticking to the literal meaning (*ẓāhir*) of the texts;
2. by drawing inferences via personal discretion. Leading representatives of this second method were ʿUmar, ʿAlī, Ibn Masʿūd and Ibn ʿAbbās.

Both practices have their specific deficiencies and need each other to fill in the gaps. Possible dangerous consequences of the first method are:

a) that a general bearing is attached to a rule which was merely meant for a special, restricted situation;

b) that an incidental advice which is brought out strongly in order to stimulate to utmost exertion, is taken to imply an absolute command or prohibition.

Weak points characteristic of the second method are:

a) the chance that a statement from another Companion later discloses that the individual reasoning (*ijtihād*) had been mistaken. Thus, for instance, Ibn Masʿūd and ʿUmar were both of the opinion that *tayammum* (performing the ritual ablution with sand instead of water) does not purify a man who is sexually defiled. Then, however, ʿAmmār b. Yāsir records the event in which the Prophet had told him that his rolling in the dust was a sufficient purification in the present conditions (Mu. *Ḥayḍ* 110-3);

b) that often the inference of a social device by common consent of the leaders of the Companions turns out to be in conflict with the principles of the *sharīʿa*.

In view of this state of affairs, so Shāh Walī Allāh concludes, it is necessary for him who nowadays deals with *fiqh* to be versed in both ways of understanding a *ḥadīth* and to be able to connect the two (*H.B.* I, 131 f.).

A problem, with which every *faqīh* will inevitably be confronted, is the apparent contradictions between various traditions. When tackling this vexed question, Shāh Walī Allāh begins by setting up two preliminary principles:

1. one should proceed from the premise that the inconsistency discovered is not real, but only produced by our mind and wrong understanding;
2. unless contradictions are too obvious to negate, one ought to adopt the line of conduct prescribed in any tradition.

When, however, in our eyes two traditions seem to conflict—one stating that the Prophet acted in this way and another reporting that he acted in that way—and concern customs and not matters of worship, they are actually not opposing one another; one of them mentions something that is recommendable (*mustaḥabb*) and the other something that is permitted (*jāʿiz*) ... In keeping with this criterion one ought to settle questions whether one has to raise the hands (during the *ṣalāt*) to the ears or merely to the shoulders ... Or there may be a hidden accountable condition because of which at a given point of time one course of action is obligatory, and at another moment the other course of action is prescribed; or a mode of procedure is obligatory at one time, whereas at another moment there is a dispensation from this obligation. Hence it is requisite to search for the effective causes (*ʿilal*) ... and if the effective causes appear to be different, one ought to act accordingly. To give an example: Once a young man asked (the Prophet) whether he was allowed to kiss (his wife) during the fast. The answer was in the negative. It was, however, conceded to an old man. From the context we can gather that it was refused in the first instance because of its being harmful to the soul; but with the old man the case was otherwise ... If, however, it is impossible to reconcile (two contradicting traditions) or to explain them by each other, and when nothing is known of a repeal (*naskh*) of one of them[6], then they turn out to be (undeniably) opposing one another[7]. (In this case one must make a choice between the two). That tradition is preferable (*rājiḥ*) which is based on more transmitters, or authorized by a transmitter who is a *faqīh*, ... or whose the text is more convincing and without ambiguity, or whose the rule and effective cause are more in conformity with the injunctions of the *sharīʿa*'' (*H.B.* I, 138 f.).

A study of *ḥadīths* also proves that a lot of disagreement existed among the Companions and Successors themselves about the legal import deducible from acts and statements of the Prophet. Shāh Walī Allāh, however, is in no way abashed by this condition of things: ''I declare that at a given moment God inspired me with a method (*mīzān*) to find out the causes of all juristic differences arisen among the members of the religious community of Mohammed ... In consequence of this, a treatise useful for this purpose has come into being which I have called 'Fair Elucidation of the Causes of Disagreement'' (*Inṣāf* 2 f.). In the exposition that follows we read: ''You should realize that the Messenger of God has not composed legal works in his blessed age and did not discuss laws at

[6] Owing to the fact that its effective cause had become invalid, or the Prophet had become convinced of its repeal through a clear revelation or his own *ijtihād*.

[7] Instances given by Shāh Walī Allāh himself are the traditions treating the questions whether a *wuḍūʾ* is required or not after touching one's privy member; or whether a marriage is permissible for a pilgrim in the state of *iḥrām* or not. In such cases one should act with caution! (*H.B.* I, 173).

that time as *faqīhs* have done (later) ... The line usually taken in the entourage of the Messenger of God was like this: When (for instance) he performed the *wuḍūʾ* in the presence of the Companions, they simply imitated him and did not receive any additional explanation of a special basic element (*rukn*) or rule (*adab*) ... They rarely put questions ... During his lifetime they interrogated him about only thirteen matters which are all recorded in the Qurʾān ... From the context they used to infer the purport of a thing, whether it was a permitted or a desirable act, or an abolished rule, and so on. With such indications and indicia they could manage ... Then (after the death of Mohammed) they dispersed over various regions, and in the place they settled they were the people whose example was imitated. On many occasions they were asked for a formal legal opinion. Each of them gave a decisive answer according to what he had retained in his memory or had deduced (from the behaviour of the Prophet). When that Companion had retained nothing in his memory (about a certain matter) and had no deduction available, he tried to find his own solutions to legal problems'' (*Inṣāf* 3 f.).

``Thereupon various legal differences arose among them owing to the following causes;

a) one Companion had heard a judgment on a certain affair or a *fatwā* (legal opinion), but another Companion had not. So the latter tried to find his own solution ... An instance of this is what the Imām Mālik relates about Abū Hurayra (in *Muwaṭṭa* II, 89), namely that to his (i.e. Abū Hurayra's) way of thinking (*madhhab*) the fast will not be valid for him who starts a day (in Ramadan) in the state of major ritual impurity. (He held this view) until some wives of the Prophet (i.e. ʿĀʾisha and Umm Salama) told him that he was wrong (and that the Prophet did fast even if in the morning he were in a state of grave pollution). Consequently, Abū Hurayra changed his opinion ...

b) (differences in evaluation) Companions had observed a certain activity of the Prophet. Then one made the conclusion that it was to be valued as a righteous deed (*qurba*), while another Companion considered it merely an ethically indifferent action (*ibāḥa*) ...

c) Disagreement on account of receiving a different impression (*wahm*). When, for instance, people saw the Messenger of God performing the pilgrimage, some of them imagined that he did this as a *mutamattiʿ*[8], others that he did so as a *qārin*[9], and again others that he did this as a *mufrad*[10] ...

---

[8] I.e. as somebody who performs the *ʿumra* (lesser pilgrimage) first, then enjoys the freedom of a normal life, not assuming the state of ritual consecration again until the last minutes of the *ḥajj* (greater pilgrimage).

[9] I.e. as somebody who combines the *ʿumra* and the *ḥajj* without a break.

[10] I.e. as somebody who performs the *ḥajj* alone.

d) Disagreement because of inadvertence and forgetfulness. An example of this is what is related by tradition about Ibn ʿUmar who had asserted: 'The Messenger of God (once) performed the *ʿumra* in the month Rajab'. When ʿĀʾisha learnt this, she stated that Ibn ʿUmar was under a misapprehension (Bu. *ʿUmra* 3).

e) Disagreement owing to a hasty conclusion. An instance of this is the statement handed down from Ibn ʿUmar that the dead will be punished for the lamentation of the family. Thereupon ʿĀʾisha remonstrated that he had not caught the true purport of the words of the Messenger of God (spoken when the bier of a Jewess passed before him and the members of her family were bewailing her): 'She will be punished in the grave for this reason'. From these words Ibn ʿUmar had understood that the punishment was imposed for the lamentation[11] (Mu. *Janāʾiz* 25) ...

f) Disagreement in respect of the effective cause of a rule. An example of this is (the rule concerning) standing up on seeing a bier. One says: it is done out of respect for the angels—then it applies to every dead person, a believer as well as a disbeliever—; another says: it is done out of respect for death—then again it applies to every dead person—; but someone else mentions: a bier carrying a Jew was brought past the Messenger of God. Then he stood up, because he did not like having it higher than his head—then it applies only to a disbeliever (Mu. *Janāʾiz* 78).

g) Disagreement because of a (different) reconciliation of two contrarieties. An instance of this is that the Messenger of God granted permission to contract temporary marriages in the Year of Khabar (i.e. A.H. 7) and then forbade it. Later in the Year of Awṭās (i.e. after the battle of Ḥunayn in A.H. 8) he again permitted it and then forbade it. Ibn ʿAbbās states: "The allowance was on account of a state of emergency. Yet the institution continued to exist. The majority (of the Companions), however, declare that the allowance was a (temporary) concession which was repealed by the prohibition" (*Inṣāf* 8 f., 11-14).

h) "Disagreement due to (different) ranks of eminence. One Companion was a rightly guided solitary, another a caliph, again another a *faqīh*, and again another a super-*faqīh*"[12] (*Khizāna* 10).

---

[11] *Cf.* the note of Abdul Hamīd Siddīqī in his translation of the *Ṣaḥīḥ Muslim* (Lahore 1973), vol. II, p. 442: "no dead person is directly responsible for the lamentation of his family over him. If he were to be punished for it, it would be due to his own negligence in instructing his near and dear ones not to do so".

[12] *Cf.* also *Tafh.* I, 213 which states that the Companions differed because of their different pattern of life. Among them there were soldiers, artisans and merchants who had to work for a living and 'were journeying in the land' (*Qurʾān* IV, 101), as well as devotees and ascetics who had made themselves free from occupation.

In short, the Companions of the Prophet held different views (*madhāhib*); and similarly the Successors took from them whatever each of them thought proper for his own use ... Then everyone of the Successors entertained his own opinions and every region had its own appointed *imām* as, for instance, ... al-Ḥasan al-Baṣrī in Baṣra and Ṭāʾūs b. Kaysān in Yemen'' (*Inṣāf* 15 f.).

*Disclosure of underlying ideas* (*asrār*) *in the texts of ḥadīth*. As we have seen[13], part of Shāh Walī Allāh's vocation was to expose *asrār* contained in traditions. Thus the prophetic saying: 'He who beats the cheeks, tears the front of the garments, and cries out as people did in pre-Islamic times, does not belong to us' (Bu. *Janāʾiz* 36 and 39) appears to cover three aspects, i.e.:

a) a psychological ground: by excessive mourning grief is the more intensified; someone afflicted by bereavement is like a sick man whose illness should be cured and whose pain should not be doubled;
b) a religious feature; immoderate lamentation may indicate unwillingness to resign to the divine decree;
c) a moral aspect: making a public show of one's sorrow was a bad custom dating from pre-islamic times, so it should be discontinued (*H.B.* II, 38).

A spiritual interpretation is given of the tradition stating: 'The souls of martyrs (having ascended to Paradise) abide in the crops of green birds which are perched on lanterns hanging from the Throne' (Mu. *Imāra* 121). Here the Delhi divine elucidates: ''They are birds, because they summarily reflect properties peculiar to angels in the same way as birds summarily reflect properties peculiar to animals upon the earth. They are green because this is a colour which is delightful to see'' (*H.B.* II, 172 f.).

In his exegesis of traditions Shāh Walī Allāh also knows how to display commonsense. With reference to the prophetic statement: 'When one of you yawns during the *ṣalāt* he must restrain it as much as possible, for the devil enters through his mouth' (Mu. *Zuhd* 59), he says: ''(I declare) the meaning of this is that yawning may occasion the entering of flies and the like which disturb the concentration of one's mind and create a diversion'' (*H.B.* II, 13). In explanation of Mohammed's argument that one ought to clean the nose three times if one performs ablution 'for the devil spends the night in the innermost part of one's nose' (Mu. *Ṭahāra* 23), he says: ''(I declare:) It means that a clogged nose may cause dullness and nightmares'' (*H.B.* I, 175).

---

[13] See p. 18.

## CHAPTER TWELVE

# THE SHARĪ'A

*Birth of the sharī'a*. As soon as the point was reached in the process of creation that man's external form and properties had become manifest, special provisions were made for him: "When the Crucial Moment, which in Scripture (*shar'*) is called 'the Blessed Night wherein all things are disposed in wisdom' (*Qur'ān* XLIV, 3 f.) had come, a concentration of spiritual entities, consisting of laws for mankind, was effectuated in the World of Sovereignty" (*H.B.* I, 25). God's legislative activity (*tashrī'*) is in fact the complement of His destination of things in the universe (*taqdīr*) (*Saṭ*. 15). Accordingly, legislation sees to it that man's angelic and bestial potentialities function properly and remain in a state of equilibrium so that bliss will ultimately become his share in the hereafter. With this end in view, divine Providence prepared[1] two kinds of directives:

1. measures designed for situations, actions and ethical qualities which are not conditioned by time and place. Consequently, the *irtifāqāt* (devices to tide over social and economic difficulties) were instituted, and the principles of good and evil were established, by which men are inspired in the same fashion as nature inspires bees and sparrows;
2. rules adapted to changes of time and place. For that purpose various *sharī'as* were revealed in the course of history (*Tafh*. I, 239; *Qurrat* 327; *Saṭ*. 24 f.). The varieties of *sharī'as* are comparable with rain-water that comes down from heaven. When reaching the earth it is immediately affected by regional conditions on the spot. Hence, ponds in the first and the second *iqlīm* (climate) contain different kinds of water (*Tafh*. II, 23). The fixation of the times for the *ṣalāt* furnishes an example of how provisions of the *sharī'a* are adapted to natural conditions. Regions with a moderate climate are kept in mind, in which day and night are of the same length and where the customary division of time is by one fourth of a day, i.e. a period of three hours (*H.B.* I, 188). Equally, the customs prevalent in an area are considered: in the Islamic regulations regarding ritual food, account has been taken of what the ancient Arabs did or did not like to eat (*Khizāna* 8).

In consequence of the principle that a *sharī'a* ought to fit in with existing local practices and religious observances, the prophets, as bearers

[1] I.e. "in the space lying between the *ḥajar al-bahts* of the *mala a'lā* and the *tajallī a'zam*, the forms of the *sharī'as* were prefigurated (*Qurrat* 328).

of a *sharīʿa*, had to sort out what might still be usable material for the refinement of souls (*Tafh.* I, 68). Abraham started by refuting astrology when he saw that the people to whom he was sent used the Kaʿba as a temple of the sun, moon, and other heavenly bodies, but the building itself he left intact, and the rituals he made obligatory were more or less the same as the ways of worship to which people were accustomed in the days of paganism (*Tafh.* I, 67). Similarly, the pre-Islamic usage of the *walīma* (marriage-feast) was allowed to continue because of the many beneficial contingencies it contained. Some correction had to be made in it, however. Thus the Prophet forbade the use of this institute as a means of emulation in dignity, resulting in a total dissipation of property (*H.B.* II, 130). On the other hand, pre-Islamic Arabs could also suffer from excessive scrupulosity. For instance, they thought it forbidden to carry on trade during the *ḥajj*-period, as it would affect the pious intentions of a pilgrim. In *Qurʾān* II, 198 ("No grievance can be held against you, if you seek bounty from your Lord during the pilgrimage"), this misconception of theirs was rectified (*H.B.* II, 56). If a custom had to be abolished, the divine management furnished compensations so that people might not become confused. Thus the Arabs of pre-Islamic days used to throw arrows if they needed to find out proper times and means for a journey, a marriage and so on. Since it was pure gambling, the Prophet had to repeal this custom. However, as a substitute Mohammed established the institution of *istikhāra*, i.e. the prayer performed with the hope of receiving divine advice and enlightenment through which people are instructed how to manage their affairs (*H.B.* II, 19). In other words, according to the Delhi divine in His revelatory activities Allāh proves to be a prudent educator who adopts the rites and rules of obligatory worship to the surroundings and situation of the various tribes and regions.

*The need of a universal sharīʿa.* "You should realize that due to dissimilar states of affairs and distinct considerations of expediency, the legislations of prophets differed ... Thus, for example, God did not permit the Jews to take spoils (*cf.* Joshuah, ch. VI), but He allowed us to do so (*cf. Qurʾān* VIII, 70: "Enjoy what you have taken as booty, such as is lawful and good"), having regard to our weak (economic) position" (*H.B.* I, 89). However, a plurality of religious communities (*milal*) may also give rise to bigotry and squabbles. In this connection Shāh Walī Allāh refers to critical observations made by Burzoe in the Introduction of his Pahlavi translation of the fables of Bidpai, known under the name of *Kalīla and Dimna*[2]. Such a situation calls for a leader who would unite these quar-

[2] See *Burzôes Einleitung zu dem Buche Kalīla wa Dimna*, übers. und erläutert von Th. Nöldeke (Schriften der Wissenschaftlichen Gesellschaft in Strassburg 12. Heft) Strassburg 1912, 15.

relsome communities into one *milla* and would supply a model *sharīʿa*, suitable for inhabitants of regions with a moderate climate, for Arabs as well as non-Arabs. At the same time "he should take into consideration the knowledge and the standard of civilization of his own people and should give them more importance than those of other nations. Then he must induce all men to follow that model *sharīʿa*, for the whole benefit of a standard legislation would be lost if it were left to every nation separately or to the leaders of every age to produce their private *sharīʿas*. Nor is it feasible to take into account the characteristics of every people and to make a separate *sharīʿa* for each of them, since it would be impossible to encompass all the differences of habits, countries, and former religions ... Consequently, when framing religious, civil, and social laws, the best and easiest way for this *imām* (leader) is to reckon only with the customs of the people to whom he was sent. The laws enacted should not be so rigid as to prove a hardship for those who come after[3], but so that on the whole they might abide by them. The first believers will be drawn to the acceptance of that *sharīʿa* out of inner conviction and because of its correspondence with their customs, while later generations will be attracted by the exemplary lives of leaders and caliphs of the community. Thus it will happen in a natural way to all people in every age, whether ancient or modern" (*H.B.* I, 118).

*Practicality of the sharīʿa*. The Delhi divine disagrees with the Muslim philosophers who claim that the phrasing of *sharīʿa* rules has no significance in itself and should merely serve the purpose of aiding people to understand ethical principles (*H.B.* I, 92): "The Straight Path is not a monopoly of an intellectual élite. Simple-minded people have an equal right to it" (*Fuyūḍ*, 47th Vision). Moreover, "the divine Law itself has been revealed in the language of common folk" (*H.B.* I, 94), and the Prophet usually did not explain a deeper sense than would be implied in the commands and interdictions given. On the other hand, Shāh Walī Allāh does not want to identify himself with the custodians of the *sharīʿa* who "content themselves with those forms". As in so many cases the right solution appears to be to steer a middle course: an acknowledgment of the relevance of moulds and forms for divine injunctions does not release a scholar from the duty of inquiring which ideas and spirit may lie at the root of them (*H.B.* I, 92). One of the primary aims Shāh Walī Allāh had in view with his work *Ḥujjat Allāh al-bāligha* is precisely to elucidate the various sound reasons for the obligations God has imposed upon His worshippers. Thus, for instance, considerations of expediency,

---

[3] Hence the Prophet urged the people not to inquire after all kinds of legal details so that specific aspects could be kept to a minimum and later generations might not feel troubled by rules which did no longer meet the requirements of the age (*H.B.* I, 91).

recognizable in the rule that sand, and not another means, has been prescribed for the rite of *tayammum* (purification of the body before prayer with sand, where water cannot be had), are:

a) as a rule it is available everywhere;
b) as such it is already a cleansing agent for certain objects, like a boot, a sword;
c) covering one's face with dust is an expression of humility and fits well with asking forgiveness (*H.B.* I, 180).

Equally, it bears testimony to the wisdom of the expounder of the *sharī<sup>c</sup>a* that he cancelled the obligation of a forenoon-*ṣalāt*, since peasants, traders and artisans usually follow their pursuits in the period between dawn and mid-day (*H.B.* I, 188). In explanation of the rationale behind the prohibition of *zinā* (adultery), the Delhi scholar argues: "Masculine types, like male animals, have a craving for females and brook no rival in their sexual intercourse; but unlike their fellow creatures they do not fight each other because of it ... For intuitively man feels that such internal fights would lead to a demolition of their cities ... Consequently, it is suggested that he keep to his own wife and not start a fight for the wife of his brother. This is the very basis of the interdiction of *zinā*" (*H.B.* I, 81). However, we do meet regulations in the Law of which the grounds seem adventitious. An instance of this is the arbitrarily fixed minimum amount of property (*niṣāb*) liable to payment of the *zakāt*-tax. It is not clear why this instead of another amount has been chosen (*H.B.* I, 130).

Nevertheless, nobody is at liberty to suspend obedience to a rule prescribed in a sound tradition on the ground that one cannot understand what the good of it might be. The Prophet, after all, has a better grasp of things than we have. The reason, according to Shāh Walī Allāh, why Mohammed mostly abstained from disclosing a deeper meaning implied in commands and prohibitions lies in the circumstance that in the opinion of statesmen subjects of a nation judge the practicality of laws by their visible results, lacking the competence to form a correct conception of the motives for introducing certain rules. For the same reason the rightly guided caliphs devote greater efforts to secular interests of the nation than to its spiritual life. So the saying of <sup>c</sup>Umar is handed down: "Even when I perform the *ṣalāt*, I calculate the tributes of Baḥrayn or ponder how to fit out the army" (*H.B.* I, 102 f.).

*Typical traits of the sharī<sup>c</sup>a.* In God's laws of legislation and of procreation public weal outweighs private interests. The *coitus interruptus* e.g. is considered reprehensible, though not forbidden, for it is in a person's private interest to practise it with a woman captive, whereas it is not in the interests of the general community, to which continuation of posterity is vital (*H.B.* II, 134).

Further, the *sharīᶜa* aims at the happy mean, and avoids extremes. There are, for instance, people who have a distaste for all sorts of binding up and prefer to leave their hair dishevelled, and there are people who appear entirely occupied in adorning themselves. In this matter the Prophet pursues a just middle course, when advising: "Do the opposite of what polytheists do, let the beard grow long and clip the moustache" (*H.B.* II, 191). Then, God's injunctions aim at rendering matters easy for man, and He declares: "God desires ease for you, He does not want to put you to difficulties" (*Qurʾān* II, 185). Once the Prophet said to Abū Mūsā and Muᶜādh b. Jabal, when he sent them to the Yemen: "Make things easy and do not make them difficult". This purpose is substantiated in various ways:

a) for the rituals no standard (*rukn*) or condition (*sharṭ*) should be imposed that will be hard on the people. Therefore, the Prophet stated on a certain occasion: "Would I not have thought it a burden to my community, I would have prescribed brushing the teeth for every *ṣalāt*";
b) religious duties should also include habits which make hem attractive, like the custom to keep mosques clean, the practice of perfuming oneself on Fridays, reciting the Qurʾān in a melodious way, calling people to prayer with a beautiful voice, and so on;
c) if anything burdensome had to be imposed, it was administered in doses. Correspondingly, ᶜĀʾisha relates: "At first, the ṣūras XLIX till CXIV were revealed, in which mention is made (only) of Paradise and Hell; not until people had been converted to Islam were laws enacted concerning what was forbidden and what was permitted. Had the prohibition been revealed in the beginning: "You should not drink wine", people would have said: "We will never cope with it!";
d) Mohammed avoided doing things on account of which people might become disconcerted. For that reason he has omitted some acts which by themselves were desirable. Thus he stated to ᶜĀʾisha: "Had your people not been pagans in the recent past, I would have pulled down the Kaᶜba" (Mu. *al-ḥajj*, 399) (*H.B.* I, 111 f.);
e) in order to facilitate things for men the Prophet could pronounce alternative decisions, like giving alternate[4] provisions for expiation (*kaffāra*). However, in the case of alternative precepts there is always the possibility that in God's judgment one of the two alternatives is more meritorious than the other, just as a deliberate act of virtue

[4] For instance, if somebody breaks the fast wilfully he may undertake a religious expiation by fasting on sixty consecutive days or by feeding sixty needy persons.

(*ʿazīma*) is superior to availing oneself of a dispensation (*rukhṣa*) (*ʿIqd* 29 and 24).

f) another inference from the principle of 'rendering easy', drawn by the Delhi reformer, is his rejection of *taʿammuq* (excessive scrupulosity) and *tashaddud* (aggravation) in respect of duties prescribed by the *sharīʿa*. Both attitudes, so he warns, lead to *taḥrīf* ('distortion', sc. of what is intended by the injunctions). As an example of *taʿammuq* he mentions the erroneous view of certain people that the consumption of a light meal shortly before daybreak would infringe the law of fasting, while taking a vow of celibacy is given as an instance of *tashaddud* (*H.B.* I, 120). "In avoiding excessive scrupulosity", the Delhi scholar concludes, "and by not multiplying to excess the ways of registering limits, the Prophet has observed a great expediency, viz. the consideration that these matters go back to circumstances which in broad outline are met in common convention (*ʿurf*) ... In such circumstances the Prophet has referred men to their own good sense, so that harmonious society could be built up" (*ʿIqd* 41 f., 45).

*Evaluation of the madhāhib* (*schools of religious laws*). By nature Shāh Walī Allāh did not favour the principle of *taqlīd* very much, i.e. being obliged to follow the legal decisions of a particular *madhhab*. In a passage in his autobiography he tells us that in the period between the death of his father and his journey to the Ḥijāz he felt most affinity with the jurists, found among the experts of the science of *ḥadīth* (*al-Juzʾ al-laṭīf* 27). In other words, at that time he was a *ghayr muqallid*, i.e. somebody who considered himself not bound by obedience to any of the four schools, and who was free to seek guidance in matters of religious faith and practice from the authentic traditions. His stay in Ḥaramayn brought him to another way of thinking, however. In a vision, divine guidance made it clear to him why he had a rooted dislike of *taqlīd*, and why notwithstanding he had to take heed of this institution (*Fuyūḍ*, 33rd Vision). In another vision he had the opportunity of asking the Prophet himself which *madhhab* should be given preference. He was told, however, that all *madhhabs* are of equal value: not a very remarkable verdict in itself, as it is the dominant view of Islam that a man of sound scholarship will never give preference to one *madhhab* over another[5]. This opinion is usually based on the saying of Mohammed that disagreement in religious matters is a blessing for the community. For the Delhi reformer, discord in the *umma* of his days was rather a curse than otherwise. Accordingly, the argument used in that same vision for the equivalence of the four schools appears to be a different one. Here the Prophet indicates that,

---

[5] See I. Goldziher, *The Ẓāhirīs*, Leiden 1971, 92.

because all of them care for the fundamentals of Islamic legislation, they are all equally valid. The Prophet proved to have no interest at all in the so-called *furūᶜ*, derivates of the *sharīᶜa*; and in view of this lack of interest on the part of the Prophet the divergencies between the schools are to be taken lightly (*Fuyūḍ*, 10th Vision). It is the 46th vision that, in the end, affords Shāh Walī Allāh a mysterious insight into the truth of the *madhhabs* and their relative value. A clear distinction is made between the Ḥanafī and the other *madhhabs*. Whether the Ḥanafī or the remaining schools 'carry greater weight' depends on the criterion applied. If we judge of them from the aspect of their relative agreement with the very purport of statements made by the Messenger of God and his Companions, the other *madhhabs* are to be preferred. On the other hand, if all attention is concentrated upon the requirements of the time present, the Ḥanafī school is far preferable to the others.

A final solution is received in the 31th vision: "Thereupon a method was revealed to me showing how I could bring the Ḥanafī *fiqh* into harmony with the *sunna*; and that is by selecting from the three most authoritative Ḥanafī scholars (sc. Abū Ḥanīfa, Abū Yūsuf and al-Shaybānī) the view that fits in best with the traditions"[6].

From works written after the *Fuyūḍ al-Ḥaramayn* we can gather that the Delhi scholar became more and more fascinated by the working-method of al-Shāfiᶜī: "the *madhhab* of al-Shāfiᶜī, which gets to very root of things, is among the four most in agreement with the *sunna*. This *imām*, indeed, quickly discovers the true direct (*ᶜilal*) and remote causes (*asbāb*) (underlying the statutes of the *sharīᶜa*)" (*Khizāna* 10). In his survey of the causes of divergencies between the schools, Shāh Walī Allāh concludes that the *madhhab* of al-Shāfiᶜī appears to have at its command the most qualified lawyers capable of systematic reasoning (*mujtahid*), is best provided with Qurʾān exegetes and experts of *ḥadīth*, has the best preserved decisions of its founder, and distinguishes clearest between the verdicts of the *imām* and those of his disciples (*Inṣāf* 77f.). Maẓhar Baqā has established that in 70 out of 80 decisions of Abū Ḥanīfa, which he rejects, the Delhi divine prefers the view of al-Shāfiᶜī[7].

In the meantime, year by year the conviction grew upon him that under present conditions the right course for Muslim India was "to combine the schools of Abū Ḥanīfa and al-Shāfiᶜī into one *madhhab*. For this purpose the rules of both schools should be examined in the light of prophetic traditions recorded in compilations of traditions; whatever be founded in complete conformity with them should be retained and

---

[6] For that reason, experts of *ḥadīth* must be acquainted with knowledge of the *fiqh*, and scholars of the *fiqh* need to possess familiarity with the traditions (*Tafh.* II, 202).

[7] Maẓhar Baqā, *Uṣūl-i fiqh awr Shāh Walī Allāh* (Islamabad 1973), 40.

whatever appears to be without a basis or confirmation should be discarded'' (*Tafh.* I, 212)[8]. In a letter to his student Muḥammad Amīn al-Kashmīrī, who had asked him which *madhhab* he followed, he declared that he tried, to the best of his ability, to combine the well-known *madhhabs* (*Kalimāt-i ṭayyibāt* 161). In other words, eventually Shāh Walī Allāh knows no better than to adopt the eclectical devise of *talfīq* (''piecing together'', i.e. combining the doctrines of more than one school). The two commentaries on the *Muwaṭṭaʾ*, entitled *al-Musawwā* and *al-Muṣaffā*, which were written towards the latter part of his life, are the concrete results of this endeavour. Maẓhar Baqā has worked out that in these two works the opinion of al-Shāfiᶜī is valued the highest 133 times, while Abū Ḥanīfa, Mālik, and Aḥmad b. Ḥanbal score only 21, 19, and 5 respectively (*al-Raḥīm*, May 1965, 36).

*Ijtihād and taqlīd.* Shāh Walī Allāh is not exactly an adherent of the doctrine of the ''closure of the door of *ijtihād* (the possibility of drawing valid conclusions from the sources of systematic reasoning)'': ''the simpletons of our time'', so he complains, ''are totally averse from *ijtihād*. Like she-camels, in the nose of which a piece of wood is put to guide them, they do not know whither they are going''. *Ijtihād* is actually a *farḍ kifāya* (i.e. a collective duty, the fulfilment of which by a sufficient number of individuals excuses the other individuals from fulfilling it) for every epoch since ''every age has its own countless specific problems, and cognizance of the divine decisions with respect to them is essential'' (*Muṣaffā* I, 11). The Delhi scholar himself claims to hold the office of a *mujtahid* within the *madhhab* (*F.K.* 39 f.). The occupant of this office is qualified to exercise *ijtihād* whenever an affair comes up for which he does not find an unequivocal judgment of the founder (*imām*) of the *madhhab*; he has the right to elicit judgments in the same manner and by proceeding analogously the verdicts of the *imām* (*ᶜIqd* 17). He has acquired so much knowledge of the Qurʾān and prophetic traditions that in the case of disagreement with views of former jurists he can give preponderance to the view he thinks weightier. Though his equipment may be not as perfect as that of the so-called *mujtahid al-muṭlaq*[9], a man like him is allowed to combine *madhhabs* in an eclectic way (*talfīq*) (*H.B.* I, 157).

[8] This passage in the *Tafhīmāt* is quoted by the Pakistani divine Abuʾl-ᶜAlāʾ Mawdūdī in his monograph *Tajdīd wa iḥyāʾ-i dīn* (Lahore 1963), 107. The logical inference that Shāh Walī Allāh was apparently not averse to *talfīq* has moved the Turkish divine Hüseyn Hilmi Işik to great indignation; ''Upon reading these (lines in Mawdūdī's book), a moslem who knows his religion and sect gets infuriated. In truth, we cannot believe that shah Veliyyullah would think so ignorantly and so indecently'' (*The Religion Reformers in Islam*, Istanbul 1970, 211).

[9] *Mujtahid* of the first rank, a title of honour reserved for founders of *madhhabs* and some of their contemporaries. They possessed the right to work out all questions from the very foundation.

As is mentioned above, the Delhi divine had little liking for *taqlīd*, i.e. the assumption that the work of interpretation and expansion had been exhaustively accomplished by the great jurists of the past, and accordingly the privilege of *ijtihād* was replaced by the duty of unquestioning adoption of their legal decisions: "I swear by God that He is too lofty and too righteous to charge men with observance of the *sharīᶜa* till the Day of Resurrection, and then impose it upon them as (if) they were blind (in mind), not able to distinguish between what is true and what is baseless" (*Tafh.* I, 209).

On the other hand, Shāh Walī Allāh—as a rule set on preserving the just balance—has written a chapter in his *ᶜIqd* under the title 'Stress on adopting (the lead of) the four *madhhabs* and a serious warning against withdrawing the association with them' (*ᶜIqd* 53). And in another work he sets forth that under certain conditions a particular *madhhab* may be the only one fit to be followed strictly. Thus, e.g. in India and Transoxiania, where no Shāfiᶜite, Mālikite or Hanbalite jurists are usually available, an unlettered person is bound to conform to the rules of the Ḥanafite school, having no other choice (*Inṣāf* 70). At the same time Shāh Walī Allāh is able to formulate reasons why it might even be very expedient to rely on the statutes of only one *madhhab*. They are:

1. the agreement of the *umma* that for the knowledge of the *sharīᶜa* people need the support of the ancients;
2. the prophetic command: "Conform yourselves to the collective body (of the Muslims)";
3. since the ages which were memorable for blessedness are past, people must be withheld from trusting in evil *ᶜulamāʾ* who follow their private heretic tendencies (*ᶜIqd* 54-7).

Still, there are limits to the allegiance required. *Taqlīd* is correct only as long as the *mujtahid*, in whom one puts his trust, issues decisions that are in agreement with the *sunna*. *Taqlīd* is equally unjustifiable, if one assumes a legal scholar to be such a perfect expert that he never can fail (*ᶜIqd* 121 ff.). After all, every *ijtihād* of each *mujtahid*, even though he be a Companion of the Prophet, may be liable to error (*Izāla* I, 19)[10].

*Ijmāᶜ and qiyās.* In the mind of Shāh Walī Allāh only a very limited period of existence is to be allotted to the actual functioning of *ijmāᶜ*, i.e. the consensus of opinion among *mujtahids* on a regulation imposed by God: "on issues, which had remained unsolved in the time of the Prophet and Abū Bakr, an *ijmāᶜ* was reached during the days of ᶜUmar; whatever has been left unsettled by ᶜUmar will continue to be controver-

---

[10] *Cf.* also *Tafh.* II, 202: "Criteria for distinguishing between good and evil are a correctly explained in the Qurʾān, and what is known to be good in the *sunna*—not the *ijtihād* of the *ᶜulamāʾ*".

sial till the Day of Judgment'' (*Qurrat* 59). For it is unimaginable that in later periods all the legists dispersed over the whole Muslim world could assemble simultaneously in order to fix a *communis opinio* on legal questions. Accordingly, the Delhi scholar refuses to endorse the generally accepted interpretation of Mohammed's saying: ''My community will never agree upon an error'' as implying a confirmation of the validity of perpetual *ijmāʿ*-activities. In his opinion these words merely indicate that there will always be a group of people in the *umma* who will maintain the truth (*Izāla* I, 118; *Tafh.* II, 118): ''they are the 'proof of God' (*ḥujjat Allāh*) on earth, though they may be small in number'' (*Inṣāf* 92). ''*Ijmāʿ* does not mean'', so Shāh Walī Allāh argues in another work, ''that each individual is entitled to produce a *raʾy* (juristic speculation) by means of his own reflection which turns out to be based on an expediency of the time instead of on the sacred Law of Islam'' (*Izāla* I, 56)[11].

As for the method of *qiyās* (juristic reasoning by analogy), Shāh Walī Allāh makes a distinction between the procedure pursued by the Prophet and the more restricted possibilities the legists of the community have at their disposal: ''When God had revealed to His Prophet a statute of the *sharīʿa* and had demonstrated the wisdom and good reason of it, the latter was qualified to operate with the consideration of expediency (*maṣlaḥa*) (set out to him), and to take the *maṣlaḥa* as the effective cause (*ʿilla*) and pivot of the statute. This was the *qiyās* practised by the Prophet. The *qiyās* left to the *umma* is to find out the effective cause underlying a statute, and to take that as its pivot'' (*H.B.* I, 108). On no account should people found *qiyās* on a *maṣlaḥa* (*H.B.* I, 130).

The most essential reason why, according to Shāh Walī Allāh, the notion of *maṣlaḥa* must be kept out of the hands of Muslim jurists, is that it does not constitute the chief element of laws. By *maṣlaḥa* is to be understood information about character-building, offered by the divine Lawgiver and realizable through the acquirement of ethical qualities[12] that are beneficial in this world and the next. The principles of good and evil, which the Lawgiver laid down to this end, were not supplemented with fixed quantities (*maqādīr*), nor with specific fixed penalties (*ḥudūd*).

However, it was only before the mission of prophets that the Merciful One concerned Himself with providing *maṣlaḥas*, and along with the appearance of Messengers of God *sharīʿas*, *maqādīr*, and *ḥudūd* were introduced. *Maqādīr* are actually easily recognizable forms (*maẓānn*)[13] as

---

[11] As is the view of the Ḥanafites. See M. Bèrnand in *EI²*, III, 1025: ''*Qiyās* ... together with *ijtihād*, is for the Ḥanafī a means to arrive at *ijmāʿ*''.

[12] Like e.g. sagacity and bravery.

[13] ''the *maẓānn*'', so we read in *H.B.* I, 92, ''take the place of the principles (*uṣūl*); they are their embodiments and perceptible counterparts''.

well as definite times and places, fixed for *maṣlaḥas*. Apparently, divine wisdom thought it more relevant to provide the common folk, who do not feel happy if confronted with abstract reasonings, with concrete injunctions than to leave them with general ethical lines of conduct which they themselves would have had to work out (*H.B.* I, 129). On the other hand, the number of specific rules imposed is so great that it becomes impossible for the people to have a comprehensive survey of all the acts enjoined on them. Here the legal concept of *ʿilla* can bring relief. *ʿIlla* denotes the most proximate and effective cause of a regulation (*ḥukm*). Thus drunkenness is the *ʿilla* of the *ḥukm* that it is prohibited to drink alcohol.

For the establishment of an *ʿilla* it is necessary to take the clearest possible evidence and definition as criterions of its practicality. An instance of this is the permission to shorten the *ṣalāt* or to break the fast in case of journey or an illness. Other effective causes that could have been chosen are, for instance, such strenous trades as agriculture or smithery, but their evidence is less clear, since the divine order would be disturbed if they were regarded as an *ʿilla* to break the fast. Trades like these are means of subsistence on which people depend for their survival. Equally, heat and cold are no suitable effective causes, because it is difficult to determine which temperature ought to be taken as standard. "Consequently, only those easily ascertainable cases have been taken into account that were generally accepted (as being excusable hardships) in the early times of the *umma*, to wit a journey and an illness" (*H.B.* I, 94 f.). As it is correct to apply *qiyās* by means of an *ʿilla*, it is permitted to perform the *ṣalāt* seated, if during a voyage somebody suffers from seasickness. A concomitant *maṣlaḥa*, on the contrary, can never serve as substitute of an *ʿilla*. The person who omits one of the prescibed *ṣalāts* commits a sin, even if he is occupied at the same moment with the recitation of the *dhikr* or any pious act. He who drinks wine on account of his health is notwithstanding sinning (*H.B.* I, 130).

In short, jurists practise *raʾy* if they take a consideration of harm or expediency as effective cause of a law (*Inṣāf* 29). In fact, people fascinated by the niceties of *raʾy* are not Sunnites at all (*Khizāna* 10), for *raʾy* in connection with the *sharīʿa* leads to *taḥrīf* (*Tafh.* I, 40; II, 133). Hence the prophetic verdict: "He who inserts in our religion something that is foreign to it, is to be repulsed", also has a bearing on anybody who makes use of *istiḥsān* (advancing a discretionary opinion contrary to strict analogy for reasons of public convenience) (*H.B.* I, 169)[14].

---

[14] We need hardly say that here again Shāh Walī Allāh underlines a favourite idea of al-Shāfiʿī. "he who concerns himself in *istiḥsān*", so the latter declares indignantly," wants to be a lawyer himself" (*Inṣāf* 29).

CHAPTER THIRTEEN

# TRUE AND FALSE RELIGION

The essential text for to the establishment of what is to be qualified as 'true religion', is the Qur'ānic verse which states that pure faith stands for what is consonant with man's innate character (*fiṭra*) created in him by God (*Qur'ān* XXX, 29). The very mainstay of an upright worshipper is his *fiṭra*, for he knows that his Lord has deposited in it true knowledge and true consciousness of God (*B.B.* 99). "Anyone who denies the knowledge which God has put in man's innate character and on which the imposition of religious duties is based, is a zendik" (*Maktūb*, 9 f.). The *fiṭra* actually regards "the *dīn* (religion) which does not change with the change of epoch[1] and on which all prophets are in agreement" (*H.B.* I, 25). Thus there is a concurrence of opinion among the prophets that no copartners should be attributed to God in man's worship and seeking of aid; that He predetermines all events before He creates them; that Resurrection, Paradise and Hell are realities (i.e. not mere symbols). Equally, there is unanimity on all sorts of rituals, matrimonial affairs, matters of social justice, opposition to the enemies of God and the application of tireless zeal to missionary work. Divergency of views only exists with respect to details of rites and statutes. Thus, for instance, according to the law of Moses one should turn one's face toward the Temple of Jerusalem during the *ṣalāt*, whereas the law of our Prophet enjoins that this be done in the direction of the Kaᶜba. The law of Moses ordains all committers of illegal intercourse to be stoned to death; the *sharīᶜa* of Mohammed, however, restricts of this punishment only to an adulterous *muḥsan* (a free person who has concluded a valid marriage); for others the infliction of lashes will suffice. Differences in legislation were usually due to the divergent situations prophets were faced with. Accordingly, God made booty unlawful for the Jews[2], but declared it legally permissible to us in view of our weak economic position[3] (*H.B.* I, 86-9).

A difference in rules could also arise from considerations of expediency (*maṣāliḥ*) which had to be observed with a view to the diversity of people's

[1] In *al-Budūr al-bāzigha* Shāh Walī Allāh speaks of a universal religion (*al-milla al-jāmiᶜa*), preserved in the World of Prefiguration. From this universal religion particular religions, adapted to the conditions of the time, are continuously pouring out upon a given collective body of men. In addition, God sees to it that the forms of the particular religions are suited to the varying capacities of the individual believers (*B.B.* 185).

[2] See Joshua VI, 18 f.

[3] See *Qur'ān* VIII, 69.

dispositions. Hence the Friday was instituted as a special day for the Arabs because of their being illiterate and uneducated. For the Jews, who were enlightened enough to understand dogmatic grounds, the Sabbath was made compulsory because of the tenet that God rested on this day from His work of creation (*H.B.* I, 89).

Although man is endowed with a religious nature, he usually appears unable to acquire the means of seeking proximity to God (*iqtibārāt*) on his own. Consequently, "it became incumbent on God's grace and care for the human race to establish institutionalized religions (*milal*)" (*B.B.* 181). In the course of time, however, new actions on the part of God became imperative. People, separated from each other through differing rites and institutions of their particular religion, began to vilify each other and to make war on one another. So the truth was hidden. In such conditions there is an urgent need for a rightly guided leader (*imām rāshid*) who will deal with the dissentient religious communities "as a rightly guided sovereign goes to work with deviating princes". In fine, now the hour has struck for the arrival of a religion to abolish all other religions. Requisite to the success of such a religion which renders any other religion redundant, is the establishment of a *sharīʿa* that can supply the necessary material for a natural religion (*madhhab ṭabīʿī*) suitable for occupants of moderate climatic zones, whether Arab or non-Arab[4]. Moreover, the *imām* who introduces this religion "should take into consideration the knowledge and the standard of civilization of his own people and should give them more importance than those of other nations ... Consequently, when framing religious, civil and social laws, the best and easiest way for this *imām* is to reckon only with the customs of the people to whom he was sent" (*H.B.* I, 118). "God", so Shāh Walī Allāh sets forth in another writing, "wanted to reform the Arabs through the agency of the Prophet and the remaining parts of the earth through the agency of the Arabs. Accordingly, it was necessary that the rules of the *sharīʿa* were adapted to the customs and habits of the Arabs" (*F.K.* 48).

Should the leader have to control a community of which its members do not yet as a whole adhere to this exemplary religion, Shāh Walī Allāh deems it expedient to divide the subjects into the following three categories:

1. those who are both outwardly and inwardly obedient to the religious prescriptions (*dīn*);
2. those who willy-nilly conform to the *dīn* and do not dare to oppose it;
3. despicable infidels (*kāfirs*) whom the leader will employ for

[4] The same view is also advanced by Ibn Sīnā (see: S. H. Nasr, *An Introduction to Islamic Cosmological Doctrines*, Cambridge (Mass.), 1964, 254 f.).

harvesting, threshing grain and similar work, like beasts are employed for ploughing and carrying burdens. The leader should prevent members of other religions from performing their rites in public. In addition, infidels should not receive the same treatment as Muslims in matters as retaliation (*qiṣāṣ*), compensations in cases of homicide (*diyāt*), matrimonial affairs and participation in business of the State. Under such conditions they might be impelled to embrace Islam (*H.B.* I, 119).

By the persons of the second category are undoubtedly meant the so-called *munāfiqūn* ('hypocrites'). Shāh Walī Allāh distinguishes two main groups:

1. Those who profess the creed with their tongues but in their hearts are happy with *kufr* (infidelity). The Qurʾānic verdict: "They shall be in the lowest stage of the fire of Hell" (*Qurʾān* IV, 145) refers to them.
2. Those who are lukewarm in their Muslim faith. To them belong:
   a) the people who always adapt themselves to the customs of their environment: if they live among Muslims, they become Muslim, and if they find themselves amidst infidels, they become infidels;
   b) those whose minds are so much taken up with wordly pleasures that no scope is left for love of God and His Messenger;
   c) those who are so wrapped up in acquiring the necessaries of life that they have no time to pay attention to the hereafter;
   d) those who have misconceptions and doubts about the mission of our Prophet, although they still do not remove the yoke of Islam from their necks. Their doubts concerns such aspects as: the Prophet's appearing to be equally subjected to the laws of human existence, the fact that the establishment of the religion of Islam had come about through wars of conquest, and so on;
   e) people who, out of exclusive affection to the members of their own clan, render assistance only to them, to the detriment of other Muslims and the cause of Islam[5].

The first group of *munāfiqūn* commit the *nifāq* (dissimulation) of faith; they are fated to Hell. The people of the second group are guilty of *nifāq* of conduct or morals (*F.K.* 37 ff.).

The Delhi divine also classifies the infidels into two groups:

1. Polytheists. Their basic error is that they adhere to certain holy persons and angels whom they believe to be intermediaries of God and the very fulfillers of their needs[6].

---

[5] In another writing those who are engrossed in poetry or mathematics to such an extent that they cannot make sufficient study of the *sharīʿa* are also reckoned among the *munāfiqūn* (*A.Q.* 63).

[6] But in the opinion of Shāh Walī Allāh the polytheists do not attribute copartners to

2. Jews and Christians. The Christians make the fundamental mistake of endowing Jesus with a property not shared by anyone else, to wit his being created by God without a natural cause; i.e. by means of His love for him He was said to have created him. Similarly, ᶜUzayr (Ezra) is held by the Jews to be without equal, i.e. to be a son of God in a literal sense. This is totally wrong, it is simply a metaphor[7]. Besides, both groups deny the mission of Mohammed.

Jews and Christians, who lived before the public appearance of the Prophet, however, are to be ranged with the better-class *munāfiqūn* who do not belong to the damned but will enter Paradise after undergoing a period of punishment. This inference can be deduced from the Qurʾānic statement: "We are not to chastise (a people) until[8] We send forth a Messenger to them" (*Qurʾān* XVII, 15) (*Khizāna* 10).

*Īmān* (faith in God) is the quality characteristic of the first category of subjects mentioned above (viz. the people who are both outwardly and inwardly obedient to the *dīn*). The essence and aim of *īmān* is spiritual perfection (*iḥsān*), because of which man becomes an integrated personality: 'he who strives for spiritual perfection ... should devote himself to meditation on the World of divine Essence (*lāhūt*) ... Thus the worshipper comes to the state of seeing God from a distance ... (As a result), God's light and assurance (*sakīna*) come upon him" (*B.B.* 112 f.).

---

God in respect of the creation of, for instance, the prime elements (*jawāhir*). Equally, they leave the management of major affairs in charge of God only. Further, they believe that if God has settled a matter, nobody can prevent it (*F.K.* 16).

7 In former times, so the Delhi divine argues, the term 'son' could mean 'the beloved one', 'the favoured one' or 'the chosen one' as can also be construed from the context of the New Testament (*F.K.* 33). For the Christian doctrine of the Trinity he furnishes an interesting mystical interpretation. Just as a mystic perceives in himself a luminous point, to wit the *ḥajar al-baht*, Jesus discovered in himself three components, to wit a *nafs nāṭiqa* which has a correlation with the *nafs kulliyya*, a *rūḥ samawī* which has a correlation with the *tajallī aᶜẓam* and a *ḥajar al-baht* which has a relation with the *dhāt baḥt*. On the analogy of this, Christian divines deduced three persons: one called 'Father' representing the point of the *dhāt*, the second called 'Son' being tantamount to the *nafs kulliyya*, and a third called 'Holy Ghost', i.e. equivalent to the *tajallī aᶜẓam*. (*A.Q.* 120 f.).

8 I.e., so Shāh Walī Allāh concludes, as soon as Mohammed had divulged his religion, "it was made obligatory for all people who strive after being consistent with God's will and approval. This implies that, even on the assumption that a Jew and a Christian want to adhere to the original and true religion without adding anything to it, it is—although an entering into the religion brought by Mohammed and an acknowledgement of his prophethood would not be required for their perfection and proximity to God—nevertheless necessary for another reason. The fact is that with the introduction of the original and true religion (by the intermediary of Mohammed) in the fourth stage of socio-economic development, it was God's intent (to deem) turning away from it a deed of disobedience and opposition ... Consequently, since that moment God's approval and acclaim depend on the obedience to the religion brought by Mohammed and the frank avowal of his prophethood" (*B.B.* 199 f.).

Shāh Walī Allāh distinguishes three levels of *iḥsān*. The first one is for men busy with occupations such as crafts, soldiering, and scholarship. This form of *iḥsān* is connected with devotions like *duᶜās* (personal invocations) and *dhikrs* (in which certain fixed phrases are repeated again and again in order to induce a state of inner serenity, of spiritual concentration on God). The second level is for men who desire to walk in the path of Truth. Here the rituals to be performed include fasting, passing the night awake and recitations spoken aloud. The third level is for him who desires to acquire *fanā*ᵓ and *baqā*ᵓ. So he is guided to *yād-dāsht* (concentration on the reality of the Self-existent, completely stripped of words and imagination). By applying himself to it with perseverance he is eventually coloured with the colour of Divinity (*Tafh.* I, 86 f.).

Speaking generally, two distinct kinds of faith can be recognized:

1. Faith bearing on conditions relevant to life in this world such as the protection of life and property. Its antonym is *kufr* (infidelity). Its pillar is formal obedience. So the Prophet stated: "He who eats from ritually slaughtered animals, performs his *ṣalāt* and turns his face towards the Kaᶜba as we do, is a Muslim who has the protection (*dhimma*) of God and His Messenger. You should, therefore, not behave unfaithfully to God Who is responsible for your safety" (Bu., *Ṣalāt* 28).
2. Faith bearing on conditions relevant to the hereafter such as rescue (from Hell) and the attainment of ranks (in Paradise). Its antonym is *nifāq* (dissimulation). Its pillar is every true expression of belief, every laudable act and every virtuous habit. Only in this case do we have to do with faith in the proper sense of the word, and it is this which can increase and decrease (*B.B.* 202; *Tafh.* II, 63).

Down to the present day Indian Sunni Muslims have difficulty in considering Shiᶜites be adherents of the same faith. A *ṣalāt* of a Sunnite performed under the direction of a Shiᶜite is not valid and has to be done again. If a Sunnite has given his daughter in marriage to a Shiᶜite, he should not figure as *imām*[9].

In the days of Shāh Walī Allāh the Sunnī-Shīᶜa conflicts constituted a constant threat to the stability of the Indian Muslim society. It is, therefore, quite natural that this apostle of unity set himself the task of entering into the disputes of the two parties.

One of the most important points of controversy, as is already known, is the individual merit to be assigned to the four 'rightly guided' caliphs. Two major works of Shāh Walī Allāh deal with this. The mere fact that

---

[9] *Fatāwā-i Dār al-ᶜulūm Deoband*, Deoband 1976, vol. III, pp. 139 and 237.

both books are written in Persian, and not in Arabic, already indicates that they were chiefly intended for the particular situation at home. This is corroborated by what we read in their introductions. In the *Qurrat al-ʿaynayn bi-tafḍīl al-shaykhayn* the author begins by remarking that he wrote the work at the instance of his beloved pupil Muḥammad Amīn al-Kashmīrī in order to remove the doubts of people confounded by "the lustre (*ishrāq*) of heretical views". In the opening sentence of the *Izālat al-khafāʾ ʿan khilāfat al-khulāfāʾ* he states: "I declare that in our days the heresy of Shīʿa becomes more and more manifest ... and many people in this country are uncertain as to the legitimacy (*ithbāt*) of the caliphate of the 'rightly guided' caliphs".

The line of argument of the *Qurrat al-ʿaynayn*, finished about 1740, is that during the reign of the first two caliphs the spiritual atmosphere (*nisbat*) prevailing at the time of Mohammed continued, and expired with their death. Consequently, Abū Bakr and ʿUmar walked in the path of prophethood. The caliphate of ʿAlī inaugurated the era of saintliness and since saints are inferior to prophets, ʿAlī ranked below his predecessors. This is of course a straight refutation of the Shīʿites who unanimously regard ʿAlī as the 'most excellent' (*afḍal*) of the community after Mohammed.

Twenty years later, that is to say towards the end of his life, Shāh Walī Allāh wrote his *Izālat al-khafāʾ*. It is a more general and at the same time very exhaustive disquisition on the institution of the caliphate, but the views expounded in it hardly differ from the thoughts set out in the *Qurrat al-ʿaynayn*. Yet, the Delhi scholar has not always been so confident of his standpoint in this matter. In the *Fuyūḍ al-Ḥaramayn*, an early book dating from about 1733, he confesses that if he were to obey his inner impulse, he would surely assign a higher rank to ʿAlī, as his affection for him was still greater than for the three other rightly guided caliphs (*Fuyūḍ*, 33rd Vision). He renders the following report of a dream in which he is granted the opportunity to interview Mohammed in person: "I asked the Prophet about the actual reason why Abū Bakr and ʿUmar are to be judged more excellent than ʿAlī, although the latter be of a higher descent, more advanced in sagacity and more stouthearted than the other two, and the majority of the ṣūfīs try to trace their spiritual lineage to him". Then the Prophet made it clear to him that the superiority which stems from the completion of the prophetic mission and which is characteristic of the first two caliphs[10], is universal; such in contradistinction to sublimity connected with saintliness peculiar to ʿAlī which is 'par-

[10] It is certainly not without significance, Shāh Walī Allāh observes in the same passage, that Abū Bakr and ʿUmar are buried in the neighbourhood of the Prophet!

tial', i.e. of a lower standard (*Tafh.* I, 246, *Qurrat* 331, *Fuyūḍ*, 22nd Vision).

Besides the visions granted in al-Ḥaramayn, Shāh Walī Allāh received additional mystical experiences (*wāqiʿāt*) that supplied information about the order of merit of the four great men: "After we had contacted the *ḥaẓīra al-quds* which is the rallying-point of the spiritual concentrations (*himam*) of most excellent people, we found the perfection of the souls of Abū Bakr and ʿUmar to be different from that of ʿAlī. The rays of the souls of the two shaykhs were like those of a most glaring torch and they were intermingled with the rays of the Prophet's soul ... We established simultaneously that the light of ʿAlī's soul in its relation to the Prophet was comparable to the light of the moon that owes its origin to its facing the sun" (*Qurrat* 330 f.; *Tafh.* I, 244 f.).

It is not difficult for Shāh Walī Allāh to show that this knowledge of a spiritual origin accords with Qurʾānic teaching. The divine statement: "He will surely establish their religion for them" (*Qurʾān* XXIV, 55[11]), being "a prophecy of the reign of the first caliphs", proves that the Imāmites are amiss if they assume that an approved religion has to be continuously concealed, and that the *imāms* of the family of the Prophet (*ahl al-bayt*) should constantly practise *taqiyya* (i.e. dissimulate their religion and hide their religious rituals from their opponents). The same inference can be made from the verse: "that He may make the religion of truth victorious over every other religion" (*Qurʾān* IX, 34). In conformity with divine wisdom this promise was not yet fulfilled at the time of Mohammed. Hence caliphs have been appointed for its realization (*Izāla* I, 20).

On other occasions as well, the opinion of the Prophet is asked for the evaluation of Shīʿite tenets: "I inquired from the *rūḥ* (spirit) of the Prophet what he latter thought of the Shīʿa which prides itself on showing deep affection towards the *ahl al-bayt* and casting aspersions on the Companions. By means of spiritual speech he intimated that their creed (*madhhab*) is be without foundation and that the baselessness of their creed discloses itself in the conception of *imām*. If you investigate this, you will discover that in their line of thought an *imām* is infallible (*maʿṣūm*), to be obeyed unquestioningly; he has been appointed for (the whole of) mankind and receives esoteric revelations (*waḥy bāṭin*); in other words, that he is a prophet or something similar. In fact, the Shīʿa denies the doctrine of Mohammed's being the 'seal of the prophets'" (*Tafh.* II, 244 and 250; *Intibāh* I, 8 f.).

---

[11] Known as the *istikhlāf*-verse and usually interpreted as referring to the reign of the Umayyads or ʿAbbāsids.

Yet, on closer examination it turns out that in his appraisal of the Shīʿa Shāh Walī Allāh also prefers to keep a balance. To counterpoise the voiced disapproval of the Shīʿa as such, a sincere regard is shown for the twelve *imāms*: "I saw (during a retreat in a mosque in one of the last ten days of Ramaḍān) the spirits (*arwāḥ*) of the *imāms* originating from the *ahl al-bayt* in the *ḥaẓīra al-quds* with a most sublime face and a most beautiful shape. I understood it to be very risky to repudiate them or to be ill-disposed towards them" (*Tafh.* I, 107). "I have come to recognize that the twelve *imāms* are *quṭbs* (heads in the hierarchy of saints) of one and the same genealogical tree, and that consequent on their becoming extinct, mysticism (*taṣawwuf*) has spread about[12] (*Tafh.* II, 245).

However, Shāh Walī Allāh's view on the way 'rightly guided' caliphs had to be elected, proves curiously enough to be more in consonance with Shīʿite teachings than with Sunnite opinions: "Men", so he argues, "are by nature inclined to follow their lusts and in them Satan flows like their blood. If, therefore, a caliph were to be elected by human *raʾy* ('opinion') (i.e. by the people themselves), it may well be that an unjust caliph, who does not care for the objectives of the caliphate, is chosen ... So the institution of a perfect caliphate requires that it is occupied by a wholly reliable caliph who is appointed by designation (*naṣṣ*) and hints (*ishārāt*) of the Lawgiver (i.e. Mohammed)[13] (*Izāla* I, 10).

Again it is in conformity with Imāmite faith but at variance with Sunnite persuasion when the Delhi divine claims a caliph to be preserved (*maḥfūẓ*) from sin (*Izāla* I, 264). The emphasis he places upon *taklīf* (state of accountability) (*H.B.* I, 19-25) is surely more in line with Imāmite principles than with Sunnī views (al-Ḥillī, *al-Bāb al-hādī ʿashar*, tr. by W. M. Miller, London 1958, p. 96). It is in accord with Ismāʿīlī tenets when he states that only *waṣīʾs* (trustees) can be credited with a wholly reliable interpretation of the *sharīʿa*, for "knowledge of the *sharīʿa* from the breast of the Messenger of God falls to their share[14]". (*Tafh.* II, 135). Another concept Shāh Walī Allāh had in common with Ismāʿīlīs was his obstinate belief in progress till the end of history. Thus Ḥamīd al-Dīn Kirmānī (d.

---

[12] Two centuries later H. Corbin arrived at the same conclusion, when he establishes as a result of his research; "l'imâmologie fructifie en expérience mystique, et ... elle est la présupposition d'une telle experience" (*Histoire de la philosophie Islamique*, Paris 1964, 149).

[13] Cf. Ḥasan b. Yūsuf b. ʿAlī b. Muṭahhar al-Ḥillī, *al-Bāb al-ḥādī ashar* (a treatise on the principles of Shīʿite theology, tr. by W. M. Miller), London 1958, 68 f.: "And agreement has been reached that in appointing the *Imām* the specification (*naṣṣ*) can be made by Allāh and His Prophet ... And the Sunnites say that whenever the people (*umma*) acknowledge any person as chief ..., he becomes the Imām".

[14] Cf. H. Halm, *Kosmologie und Heilslehre der frühen Ismāʿīlīya* (Wiesbaden 1978), 21.

1021), as we learn from H. Corbin, speaks in his *Kitāb al-Riyāḍ* of the superiority of his own age over the past[15].

---

[15] See pp. 58 f. in H. Corbin's edition of Nāṣir-i Khusraw's *Jāmiᶜ al-ḥikmatayn* (Teheran 1953).

CHAPTER FOURTEEN

# RELIGIOUS RITES AND CUSTOMS

*Shaʿāʾir.* According to Shāh Walī Allāh, the term *shaʿāʾir* (visible symbols) must be taken to mean "tangible and concrete entities serving for the worship of God" (*H.B.* I, 69). They are adapted to generally accepted views, to what is obvious for everybody and to what the heart can trust implicitly (*Fuyūḍ*, 4th Vision): God's directives, as we know, are founded on that which is the most easy (*H.B.* I, 70).

"The four most important *shaʿāʾir*[1] are the Qurʾān, the Kaʿba, the Prophet and the *ṣalāt* ... Part of a respectful treatment[2] of the Qurʾān is that people listen intently when its verses are recited ..., and only touch it after having performed a ritual ablution ... Part of a respectful treatment of the Kaʿba is that people may only circumambulate it in a state of ritual purity, ... and that they should keep their face averted from it and turn their back on it when they satisfy a call of nature ... Part of a respectful treatment of the Prophet is the obligation to obey him, to invocate blessings upon him and to refrain from shouting out loud to him ... The aim of the *ṣalāt* is to arouse people to the consciousness that before God they are in the same position as a slave in front of his master" (*H.B.* I, 70).

*Ṣalāt.* In the view of Shāh Walī Allāh, excellencies to be attributed to the *ṣalāt* are "that of all ways of worship it is the one which is the most important, the best demonstrable, the most widely known and the most profitable[3]" (*H.B.* I, 168), and that "there is nothing better than the *ṣalāt* for training the soul to make nature tractable and obedient to man's reason"[4] (*H.B.* I, 73), being "a salutory antidote that counteracts the ef-

---

[1] Other institutes, included by Shāh Walī Allāh in the *shaʿāʾir* reckoned by our author to the *sharīʿaʾir* are the pilgrimage (*Fuyūḍ*, 10th Vision), crying *labbayka* (*H.B.* II, 62), drinking from the Zamzam (*H.B.* II, 64), the mosque as model of the Kaʿba (*H.B.* I, 179), the call to prayer (*H.B.* II, 145), the *dhikr* and *duʿāʾ* (*B.B.* 218), fasting (*B.B.* 215).

[2] The Qurʾān enjoins that the *shaʿāʾir* of God are to be treated most respectfully (*Qurʾān* XXII, 32), being means to gain proximity to God.

[3] One of the ends for which a *ṣalāt* can be performed is "that of relieving needs. Accordingly, the prayer for the petitioning of rain has been instituted; and a special *ṣalāt* has been introduced to remove fear of an eclipse (of celestial bodies) as well as one whereby a decision is sought with the help of divine inspiration (*istikhāra*)" (*B.B.* 211).

[4] In support of this the following psychological argument is used: "The goal of all acts of obedience (to which the *ṣalāt* also belongs) is to direct the rational soul to God and to empty it from mean things ... For (as you know) the limbs obey the *khayāl*; the *khayāl* in its turn obeys the *wahm*; and the *wahm* obeys the rational soul. Therefore God prescribed acts of obedience for the limbs in order that from there light would be transferred to the

fects of all poisons injurious to spiritual health" (*B.B.* 199); in addition, it results in expiation of sins as well as enjoying the company of beautiful damsels in the Hereafter (*Khizāna* 9); further, it belongs to the seemly attitudes (*tamāthīl*) to be assumed towards the divine Names *al-ḥayy al-qayyūm* (the Living and Self-subsisting) (*Tafh.* II, 114): "prostrating oneself in prayer is the most extreme expression of respect[5]. Consequently, the *ṣalāt* is the *miʿrāj* (ascension) of the believer and the moment at which his angelic disposition becomes liberated from the chains of his animal nature" (*H.B.* II, 11).

For the ultimate fixation of the times of prayer various aspects had to be kept in mind. In its preparatory stage the following considerations were taken into account: "since the benefit of *ṣalāt* consists in plunging into the depths of eye-witnessing (the divine world) and entering into the ranks of angels ..., there is no more opportune time for it than the four hours (of a day) in which an influx of spirituality is noticeable, angels descend, the deeds of men are presented to God and their personal invocations are answered". These auspicious hours are to be found in the early morning, at the setting of the sun, at the beginning of the night and at midnight. It is, however, apparent that the majority of people cannot be charged with the obligation of a *ṣalāt* at midnight, this being too inconvenient a time for them. Hence, only the first three periods were originally intended by God to serve for the performance of a *ṣalāt* as can be deduced from His word: "Perform the *ṣalāt* at the sinking of the sun till the beginning of the night and (observe) the recital of the early morning; surely the recital of the early morning is witnessed (by the angels)" (*Qurʾān* XVII, 78)[6]. Another point to be kept in view, so Shāh Walī Allāh continues, is that "it is neither proper to have too long an interval between two *ṣalāts*, so that the spiritual effect of the previous *ṣalāt* gets lost, nor should the interval be too short, so that people have insufficient time to make a living". Times had to be fixed which would be easily observable for high and low, for Arabs and non-Arabs. This is only feasible if a fourth part of a day, i.e. three hours, is taken as a basic unit" (*H.B.* I,

---

rational soul and concentration upon God would thus become a mental attitude of it" (*Tafh.* II, 46).

[5] Here again the Delhi divine disapproves of extravagancies. He rejects the rite for which Chishtīs enjoy celebrity, *viz.* the *ṣalāt al-maʿkūs*, the *ṣalāt* of the 'inverted', i.e. the worshipper has a rope tied to his feet and his body lowered into a well (*Q.D.* 75). "This practice is said to have been adopted from certain Sadhus known as *Urdhamukhi* who suspended themselves from the branch of a tree or a framework" (J.C. Oman, *The Mystics, Ascetics and Saints of India*, London 1903, 46).

[6] Western scholarship still needed 130 years more before arriving at the same bright inference from evidence offered by the Qurʾān, namely that at first only three times of *ṣalāt* were observed. See M. Th. Houtsma, 'Iets over den dagelijkschen Çalat der Mohammedanen' (*Theologisch Tijschrift* XXIV, 1890, 127 ff.).

187 f.). In consequence of this the number of *ṣalāts* became six in toto, to wit the morning prayer, forenoon prayer, midday prayer, afternoon prayer, prayer at sunset and an evening prayer (which follows) after a fourth part of the night or something similar. Recognizing that peasants, merchants and artisans are from dawn to midday continually engaged in their main activities, Mohammed repealed the obligatory performance of the forenoon *ṣalāt* (*B.B.* 209, *H.B.* I, 188).

Similarly, the length of time chosen for a *ṣalāt* should serve the purpose aimed at by the ritual as such: "it should be neither too short, so that its intention is not realized, nor too long, so that the performance of it is too difficult for the people given all the actions they have to go through. In total, an uneven number of *rakʿas* (bendings of the torso from an upright position, followed by two prostrations) should be made (in a day), for uneven numbers are judged to be auspicious" (*B.B.* 210). Due regard should also be paid to one's conduct; "it is obligatory to refrain from talking ... (and) it is detestable during the *ṣalāt* to copy the behaviour of animals, which is incompatible with the dignity characteristic of man, such as sprawling on the ground as predatory animals do[7], pecking as a cock does, or crouching down in the manner of camels: all of these are acts which are inconsistent with humility and decorum" (*B.B.* 210 f.). The rationale of the communal prayer on Friday, according to Shāh Walī Allāh, is that in this way the *ṣalāt*, being one of the most fundamental *shaʿāʾir* of God is publicized. Then he continues: "One day in the week is fixed for it, being a proper interval observed by all communities of the original and true religion. We, however, have preference over the other two communities (i.e. the Jews and Christians), for we shall precede them (on the Day of Resurrection) because of our day of worship[8], though we were later in establishing an institutionalized religion (*milla*)" (*B.B.* 212). Nevertheless, ritual notions of the other communities may occasionally cause some embarrassment. Muslim *faqīhs* all agree that, as a rule, no *wuḍūʾ* is necessary after having eaten food prepared by means of fire; and if a *ḥadīth* recommends it, it is said to have been repealed. Yet, in this connection camel's meat remains a moot question, since there is no statement available about a repeal of this rite after the consumption of roasted camel's meat. So there are some jurists

[7] *Cf.* the tradition reported by ʿĀʾisha in which the Prophet forbids the people to spread out their arms like a wild beast during the *ṣalāt* (Mu. *Ṣalāt* 440).

[8] Refers to a tradition reported by Abū Hurayra. In it the Messenger of God states: "We who are last shall be first on the Day of Resurrection, although others were given the Book before us and we were given it after them. It was this day (meaning Friday) which God prescribed for us. The people (i.e. those who were given the Book before us) come after us with regard to it, the Jews observing the next day and the Christians the day following that" (Mu. *Jumʿa* 20).

such as, for instance, Aḥmad b. Ḥanbal and Isḥāq b. Rāhwayh who deem it required. These advocates, as the Delhi scholar explains, are troubled by the knowledge that the Israelite prophets were unanimous in their view that camel's meat is taboo. Hence they consider *wuḍū*ʾ a soothing to people, to whom it is still a trial to eat something that had been forbidden in the Torah, and a happy device to express thankfulness to the Lord for permitting the same to Muslims (*H.B.* I, 177).

*Zakāt*. To establish the expediency of this institute, Shāh Walī Allāh says: "*Zakāt*, which is a requirement for the cultivation of magnanimity, functions like food which possesses medicinal power. By *zakāt* the urban community is put in good order[9] and God is served ... It repels social injustice, allays the wrath of God, is of value against the punishments in the grave and removes impediments towards the natural progress and development of the human individual, since it checks stinginess" (*B.B.* 214). It belongs to the seemly attitudes to be assumed towards the active Attributes of God (*iḍāfiyyāt*) (like the 'Provider', the 'Feeder') (*Khizāna* 8).

In explanation of the prophetic rule that no *zakāt* is due from a Muslim on his slave or his horse (Mu. *Zakāt* 8), Shāh Walī Allāh states: "This is because as a rule slaves are not kept for procreation; likewise in many countries people breed horses to a far lesser degree than other grazing livestock. Thus they do not belong to property which increases" (*H.B.* II, 43).

In connection with the precept that it is forbidden to pay *zakāt* to the Messenger of God and his family (Mu. *Zakāt* 161-7), representing only people's impurities (*awsākh*), Shāh Walī Allāh declares: "They are impurities because they are an atonement for people's sins ... Hence there are persons of high standing who perceive 'darkness' (*zulma*) in alms ... Mystics also sometimes discern this darkness. My father mentioned alms as reluctantly as virtuous people talk of fornication and privy parts" (*H.B.* II, 45).

*Fasting*. If during a certain space of time, which should be neither too short nor too long, people are continously occupied in remembering God, reciting the Qurʾān, fasting, giving charitable gifts and performing the *ṣalāt*, it inevitably produces a healthy reformatory effect upon their mind and body. Through fasting, one is even more motivated to leave

---

[9] *Cf.* also *H.B.* II, 39: "You should realize that the major significance of *zakāt* comprises two expedients:
a) which refers to refinement of character; ...
b) which refers to the city-state which inevitably numbers among its inhabitants weak and needy people ... Besides, a proper management of a city-state depends on revenue to provide maintenance for its securers and functionaries".

off deceit, slander, and vilification. During Ramaḍān, therefore, the devils are chained, the gates of Hell are locked, and the gates of Paradise are opened (*B.B.* 216). "Fasting belongs to the seemly attitudes to be assumed towards the privative[10] predicates of God (*salbiyyāt*), such as, for instance the Attribute *al-subbūḥ* (all-glorious)" (*Khizāna* 8). So "its essence is the endurance of physical hardship for the sake of the Worshipped One. The point is that when a man loves somebody very dearly he cares little for his personal comfort and well-being, and pays no attention to it. He desires to sacrifice his love and comfort for the sake of the Worshipped One with the knowledge that He will be pleased with it and his enduring physical hardship is seen and heard by Him" (*B.B.* 119). "Among the prophets the way of fasting differed: Noah used to fast for a long period of time ..., Jesus for a day and then broke the fast for one, two or more days, and our Prophet fasted and broke the fast according to his own fancy ... That was because fasting is an antidote and the dose of antidote is fixed in accordance with the seriousness of a disease. The hearts of the people of Noah were hardened to a great extent ... Jesus was physically weak, ... while our Prophet was well acquainted with the advantages of the fast and its break and he knew what was right or bad for himself. So he chose that which was in accordance with the exigencies of the moment. For his community he chose various kinds of fasting, such as for instance the ᶜĀshūrā-fast (which is observed on the 10th Muḥarram)—it is celebrated on the grounds that it is the day on which God let Moses triumph over the Pharaoh and his people ...—, and the ᶜArafa-fast (a voluntary fast on the 9th Dhuᵓl-Ḥijja) ... The very reason for the excellence of this fast over the ᶜĀshūrā-fast is that by it one plunges into the depths of the sea of divine mercy which comes down on that day (when the pilgrims pitch their camp for the celebration of the prescribed festival assembly) whereas the ᶜĀshūrā-fast refers to mercy granted in times long past" (*H.B.* II, 54 f.).

*Pilgrimage* (*ḥajj*). "All people have a place of pilgrimage; it may be a sanctuary or a river like the Ganges where the Hindus go on a pilgrimage, or it may be a tree, a semi-desert plain, a tomb, or a porch upon which wonderful signs appeared. Crowds gather there in order to be filled with the beneficent virtue of the venerated object. This is not so much a matter of custom or habitual practice; it is rather a universal proneness to single out an object of worship" (*B.B.* 120). "And when a vehement yearning for his Lord arises in a man ('s soul), then the *ḥajj* will be the only means to satisfy his longing" (*H.B.* I, 75 f.).

---

[10] Denoting the absence of qualities like similarity to anything created, dependence on something else, plurality, etc.

It is, however, not merely the individual believer who derives great benefit[11] from the *ḥajj*. It appears to be very useful for the Muslim community as a whole: "just as it imperative for a body politic to hold a court from time to time in order to make a distinction between the sincere and the insincere, between the obedient and the rebellious, to consolidate its fame and authority again, and to get to know how people are faring, so a religious community is in need of a *ḥajj* in order to make a distinction between the reliable believer and the hypocrite, to demonstrate that the people adhere in great force to the religion of Allāh, and to have an opportunity to meet one another" (*H.B.* I, 76). Shāh Walī Allāh recognizes in the *ḥajj* ceremonies a striking resemblance with constituents of the *ṣalāt* ritual. What is explicitly found in the *ṣalāt* is already implied in the customs of the *ḥajj*. "The *ḥajj*", so he establishes," "belongs to the seemly attitudes to be assumed towards the divine Names *al-ḥayy al-qayyūm* in an implicit manner (*min ḥayth ijmālin*)", while the *ṣalāt* belongs to the seemly attitudes to be assumed towards the same Names but expressed in all details (*min ḥayth tafṣīlin*)" (*Khizāna* 8). He gives the following exposition of this point of view: "Putting oneself in the state of ritual consecration (*iḥrām*) amounts to (confessing) *Allāhu akbar* by which, in both cases, voice is given to sincere devotion and reverence. Being simply dressed is (a manifestation of humility[12]) such as bending and prostration (in prayer). The standing (*wuqūf*) at ʿArafa is particularized by standing erect (*qiyām*) (during the *ṣalāt*), and the *saʿy* (the ceremony of running the distance between Ṣafā and Marwa seven times) and *ṭawāf* (circumambulation of the Kaʿba) are expression of self-surrender to God. Shaving[13] is (comparable with) the emitting of saliva[14]. In addition, (in respect to *ḥajj* as well as to *ṣalāt*) limits, timings and rules of conduct are fixed for a full effectuation of the spiritual meaning inherent in both of them" (*B.B.* 218).

*Jihād*[15]. From sūra al-Furqān and other Qurʾānic sūras it becomes clear, so Shāh Walī Allāh concludes, that "predominance was not acquired by the Messenger of God in consequence of the presence of an angel who certified his being a prophet, or on account of the descent of

---

[11] It is at the same time "a healthy spiritual exercise since it implies the renouncing of one's belongings and family, and (in this way) symbolizes man's passing away from this world to the next" (*B.B.* 217).

[12] Because of the uniformity of dress, it is well nigh impossible to distinguish a servant from a master.

[13] If a pilgrim puts himself in the state of ritual consecration, he has his hair and his nails cut and his armpits shaved.

[14] Rinsing one's mouth is part of the ritual ablution before prayer.

[15] *Jihād* being 'an act of pure devotion' (cf. *EI*[2] II, 539) can be considered a religious rite. The Delhi divine places *jihād* with the categories of piety (*birr*) (*H.B.* I, 76).

a heavenly Book upon him[16] while people could see it descending with their own eyes. No, the way it happened was that of worldly kings who gain the ascendancy through struggles and wars'' (*Fuyūḍ*, 4th Vision).

From the explanations given by Shāh Walī Allāh it turns out that he ascribes at least three objectives to the *jihād*:

1. to extend the boundaries of right guidance (*Khizāna* 6)! Experience shows—as was also the case with Mohammed—that when faith is propagated, people as a rule, do not appear amenable to reasonable arguments. Then it for their good that *jihād* is waged against them and they accept faith under compulsion. Their servants and children, at any rate, will keep to the faith out of their inmost conviction (*H.B.* II, 170);
2. to fight criminality. *Jihād* implies ''that God curses a wicked man who does injury to the general public (*jumhūr*) and whose extinction is more in the interests of the general community than his survival ... The sequel to this is that by the ability to pursue general welfare people become convinced that it is a matter of great importance to deliver oppressed persons from the cruelty (of criminals) and to fix penal laws for obstinate sinners ..., so that security and peace is restored to the worshippers of God'' (*H.B.* I, 76);
3. to combat idolators. In a harangue delivered to soldiers, Shāh Walī Allāh says: ''O soldiers, God sends you out for *jihād* in order to raise aloft the Word of God, to destroy idolatory (*shirk*) and its adherents. However, you have failed in performing the duty for which He has created you; you have started the training of horses and the bearing of arms for personal gains ... You have taken to drinking, shaving your beards, growing your moustaches, and to wronging innocent people'' (*Tafh.* I, 216 f.). He warned the Muslims that ''if they forsook *jihād* and co-operated with non-Muslims they would suffer severe humilations and people of other religions would subdue them'' (*H.B.* II, 173).

In his capacity as a mystic, however, Shāh Walī Allāh also knows how to attach a spiritual sense to the idea of *jihād*. When the Messenger of God returning from his military expedition to Tabūk declared: 'Now we have returned from the lesser *jihād* to the greater *jihād*', he meant—the Delhi divine explains—''the return from plurality to oneness, from the world of perceptible forms (*tamaththul*) to the world of the non-material, from the plane of explicit knowledge to the plane of absoluteness'' (*Khizāna* 6).

---

[16] See *Qur'ān* XXV, 32: ''The disbelievers say: 'Why was the Qur'ān not sent down upon him all at once?' ''.

*Dhikr* (recollection of God by the invocation of God's Names), recitation of the Qurʾān and *duʿāʾ* (personal prayer). When enumerating sundry specimens of devotion Shāh Walī Allāh first mentions *dhikr* and recitation of the Qurʾān. For the cure of false conceptions (about God), for experiencing the presence of God (*muḥāḍara*) and for the removal of hardness of heart there is no better means than the *dhikr*. He who listens to the recitation of the Qurʾān and lets it act on his soul will be coloured with the experiences of fear, hope, and awe in respect to God's majesty and will be immersed in God's grace (*H.B.* I, 76). Along with the *duʿāʾ*, they "are efficacious stimulants in strengthening faith and in acquiring spiritual perfection" (*B.B.* 218).

The subject of *duʿāʾ* inspires the Delhi divine to lengthy dissertations as he obviously thinks it a fundamental part of faith: "People of all religions and creeds agree that *duʿāʾ* is heard by God and that, as man advances in years, the relationship (with God) becomes more intensive and delightful ... There exists more than one kind of prayer and its answer. There are:

a) The prayer to which a man is impelled when, for the desired result of what is prayed for from the Merciful God, the celestial processes of causality co-operate with the terrestrial disposition[17]. This can happen owing to the fact that the *nufūs nāṭiqa* (rational souls) (of the prayers) are polished or lustrous by nature (as is the case with prophets) ... We have discerned many prayers of this type to be answered. For example, Abraham's prayer that God allow him to enter Paradise and save him from Hell, and the prayer of the beloved (Prophet) that God allow him to triumph over the unbelievers after the announcement of the Word of God: "Soon the host shall be routed, and turn their backs" (*Qurʾān* LIV, 45) ...
b) The prayer whereby the soul has adopted an ardent longing (for God) after a great affinity with the lofty Primary Causes (*mabādiʾ*) has arisen in the very core of the soul, or the soul is involved in the acquisition of perfection. So, in accordance with this pursuit, prayer prepares the accompanying circumstances and appropriate conditions, on which the generosity of the Merciful God is to be based ...
c) The prayer whereby simple and compound divine Names are recited. They are indicative of (divine) Reality and function, as it were, as a nest for It. Consequently, by invoking them divine potency is engendered which provokes in the hearts of men the desire (to do good works) and produces the object aimed at, whether the wor-

[17] A view shared by Ibn Sīnā. See L. Gardet in *EI*² II, 618: "The effective prayer of request (according to Ibn Sīnā) is a result of the co-operation of terrestrial dispositions and celestial causes".

shipper is aware of it or not ... In this way, mercy is produced in the heart of a rich man so that he spend money lavishly on him (who prayed), or sells his property to someone who is in great need of it for half the price.

d) (Prayer by way of) chants and a warding off of misfortunes[18]. The Messenger of God was sent to the Arabs when they practised magic by idols. Hence he corrected their diseased customs and for magic substituted belief in God's Unity and having recourse to His light'' (*B.B.* 137 f.; 219).

''The best moment for a *duʿāʾ* is the time when blessings are newly made ... If man wishes to take a favourable opportunity, he must apply himself with perseverance to it at daybreak or in the evening; the early morning, i.e. before one becomes busy with all kinds of occupations, may further the acquisition (of spiritual perfection), while the evening, i.e. after one has been busy with one's daily routine and after 'darkness' (of sins, etc.) has come upon the soul, may further the removal of (moral) filth'' (*B.B.* 119).

*ʿAqīqa* (sacrifice after the birth of a child). This pre-Islamic custom was not abolished by Mohammed, since he recognized various valuable points in it. To the mind of Shāh Walī Allāh the most important of them is that it can serve as a suitable counterpart to the Christian baptismal ceremony[19]. Accordingly, the *ḥanīfs* (monotheists *avant la lettre*) had at their disposal a rite which made them realize that the child was a *ḥanīf* and a follower of the religion institutionalized by Abraham and Ismael. The most widely known institute introduced by these two patriarchs is the *ḥajj* which, like the *ʿaqīqa* ritual, includes the shaving of the head as well as a sacrifice. In other words, by the imitation of these two *ḥajj* ceremonies the *ʿaqīqa* betokens the religion of Abraham. In addition, off shaving the child's hair symbolized the passage of the state of a fetus into that of a child, as the hair is actually the remainder of the embryonic stage (*H.B.* II, 144 f.).

*Care of the dead*. Shāh Walī Allāh's statements as to what is proper and improper in respect of this are not always consistent. In the *Ḥujjat Allāh al-bāligha* we read that ''prayer on behalf of the dead is prescribed by law,

---

[18] Among the ten formulas by which the *duʿāʾ* can be expressed Shāh Walī Allāh mentions the entreaty: ''God protect me from that!'' (*B.B.* 119).

[19] An interesting point of view, for in the world of Islam circumcision is more often considered as the very ceremony symbolizing the reception into the Muslim community: in Java circumcision is even straightly qualified as *njelamakéselam* ('rendering Muslim'). Shāh Walī Allāh mentions circumcision only casually, and states that in the Torah it is recorded to serve as a brand-mark which God put on Abraham and his posterity, with, a purpose similar to that which kings have in mind when they want to distinguish slaves whom they do not intend to manumit from other slaves (*H.B.* I, 182).

because the intercession of an assembly of believers on behalf of the dead to a great extent furthers the descent of divine grace upon him ... It is recommended to recite the *sūrat al-fātiḥa*, for it is the best and most comprehensive of all invocations'' (*H.B.* II, 36). In *al-Khayr al-kathīr*, a later work of his, the Delhi scholar maintains that the recitation of the first *sūra* on behalf of the deceased, seeking his aid[20] and so on, is of no use. In the same passages he urges confining the care of the dead to the following four activities:

1. displaying kindness to his near and dear, as that in a way amounts to a display of kindness to the dead one himself;
2. paying a visit to his tomb and reading the Qurʾān there; thus the bonds with the deceased are reinforced;
3. acting as his agent, and giving alms or manumitting a slave or performing the pilgrimage in his stead;
4. asking God's forgiveness on behalf of the dead so that He may have mercy on him, may raise him in rank, and may close His eyes on his sins (*Khizāna* 9).

*Visiting of shrines of holy men*. Shāh Walī Allāh interpretes the rule of conduct dictated by Mohammed: 'I forbade you to visit graves, but now you may visit them' (Muwaṭṭaʾ *Ḍahāya* 8) as follows: ''According to me, it was forbidden as it gave occasion for the worship of tombs, but as soon as Islam was firmly established and the conviction had sunk into people's minds that it was absolutely interdicted to worship anybody but God, visiting tombs was allowed. The effective cause for this permit is the useful purpose it serves: it confronts people with death so that they awake to the shortness of earthly life'' (*H.B.* II, 38). Hence, it is surely fully in line with this conclusion when we hear that once during his stay in Ḥaramayn Shāh Walī Allāh visited the shrine in al-Ṣafrāʾ[21] ascribed to Abū Ḍharr al-Ghifārī, the Companion noted for trustworthiness and ascetism. The great event which then occurred to him was that the spirit of the saint appeared to him ''like the moon on the wane in the third night'' (*Fuyūḍ*, 8th Vision).

In Shāh Walī Allāh's days, however, corruption had spread over the whole Indian subcontinent. The time of heathendom recurred. In this connection the Delhi reformer tells us of his own sad experiences, stating: ''Lately I have seen weak brothers among the Muslims who choose rab-

---

[20] But no objections seem to exist to consulting the dead on personal problems, since our author states as quite an ordinary thing that once he went to the grave of his father in order to take his advice on the line of conduct he should follow with regard to one of his students (*Tafh.* I, 10). It is, however, plain *kufr* (infidelity) to imagine that one can succesfully expect provision for one's needs from a dead person (*Khizāna* 8).

[21] A place between Mecca and Medina.

bis and monks as lords apart from God (cf. *Qurʾān* IX, 31), make their shrines places of worship, and go on a pilgrimage to their shrines, their relics and their hills like Jews and Christians used to do ... They credit those who have no claim to these prerogatives with power of intercession ... They snatch elements from the Hindu and Zoroastrian religions" (*B.B.* 125). Fierce is his condemnation: "Anyone who goes to Ajmīr[22] or to the shrine of Sālār Masʿūd (Ghāzī who lies buried in Bahrāʿich, Uttar Pradesh) in order to get an urgent desire gratified, commits a sin graver than murder or adultery" (*Tafh.* II, 45).

*Magic practices.* On this subject the Delhi scholar holds ambivalent views. In his parental home the application of magic arts was not only not unknown, but even strongly recommended. In one of his early writings a whole chapter is devoted to 'useful suggestions' (*fawāʾid*) he received from his father ʿAbd al-Raḥīm in cases, for instance, of disease: "My father also used to advise: When somebody comes to you suffering from tooth-ache, head-ache or flatulence, take a blank board, sprinkle pure sand on it, write with a nail the first three words of a series of eight comprising the letters of the Arabic alphabet on it, press the nail one time extra on the letter *alif* and recites the *sūrat al-fātiḥa* once. Let him who is in pain meanwhile keep his finger firmly on the sore spot. Then ask him whether he feels relieved. If this is the case, then leave it at that. If not, press the nail on the letter *ba* and read the *sūrat al-fātiḥa* twice. Repeat your former question. If he is recovered, then leave it at that. If not, press the nail on the letter *jim* and recite the *sūrat al-fātiḥa* three times. And so on till the last of the (ten) letters. If he is still not recovered, God may cure him" (*Q.D.* 123). In an account of the activities of his father, he mentions that at the end of his life ʿAbd al-Raḥīm donated his son two hairs of the Prophet as relics (*Anfās* 41 f.). Shāh Walī Allāh himself wrote a commentary on the famous *ḥizb al-baḥr*[23] (Incantation of the Sea) of al-Shādhilī[24] (d. 1258), called *Hawāmiʿ*. Various magic practices are explained in it. To give one example: "If somebody wishes to pass enemies without being seen and without any obstruction, he should recite: 'Now the Word has been proved true against most of them' up to 'so that they cannot see' (*Qurʾān* XXXVI, 7-9), and he should breathe on pebbles, should throw them towards the enemies, or he should blow in their direction" (*Haw.* 45). Similarly, he appears to have no objection to the ap-

[22] Renowned for the shrine of Khwāja Muʿīn al-Dīn Ḥasan Chistī.

[23] A *ḥizb* is a protective litany chanted in order to quell or subject hostile forces of men or nature.

[24] Cf. *Tafh.* I, 87: "God revealed to me the principles of Shaykh Abuʾl-Ḥasan al-Shādhilī's exorcism (*daʿwa*)".

plication of spells (*ruqan*), since "it is, in essence, a clinging to words[25] which bear an effect upon the World of Prefiguration" (*H.B.* II, 194).

Yet, on the whole, the son is obviously less credulous than the father. When one day ʿAbd al-Raḥīm reports that in the street he has met a tailor, living in their neighbourhood, a few days after his death, Shāh Walī Allāh does not seem very impressed. Such stories about a return from death, so he comments, I also find in collections of traditions and in books of ṣūfī masters. All of it comes to this, that those stories refer to somebody who was afflicted with *sakta* (a disease by which a person loses his powers of speech and motion) (*Tafh.* II, 182 f.).

It is important to note that in his disquisitions on astrology, talismans and the like Shāh Walī Allāh often displays reserve. Certainly, it is not open to doubt that occult powers are operating in the universe[26] and that they can be manipulated by man. The whole point is from which angle they are evaluated and to what extent man is at liberty to make use of them: "Divine *ḥakīms*[27] and common people all agree that stars have an influence on the world of elements. According to the former, this influence is due to specific qualities which God creates in things, such as heat in fire and cold in water ... In the view of the people, however, this influence should be characterized as *taskhīr* (magic effect) due to the effusion of the essence (*ḥaqīqa*) of stars ... And what is true about the influence of the stars is, in the opinion of *ḥakīms*, equally true of *ṭīra* (augury), *hamā* (a night-bird that frequents burial places and is believed to demand vengeance not yet taken for someone who has been killed), and *ʿadwā* (infection with mange and other contagious diseases) ... In other words, when we speak with the tongue of the revealed Law (*sharʿ*), we declare that astrology, augury, infection (and so on) ... are all issues of *shirk*. When the common men remonstrate that they (stars, birds, etc.) bear real effects, we reply: 'Does wine not bear an effect on our bodily health? Nevertheless, it is forbidden'" (*Tafh.* II, 147 f.).

---

25 Spells are to be "composed of Qurʾānic verses or divine Names, for they are Names referring to powers spread everywhere" (*B.B.* 59).

26 "Thus it cannot be denied that the powers of Venus and Mars produce effects, if they descend on earth" (*H.B.* II, 195).

27 Among whom Shāh Walī Allāh reckons himself!

CHAPTER FIFTEEN

# SOCIAL AND ECONOMIC IDEAS

According to Shāh Walī Allāh, the principle of mutual aid is fundamental to a proper social order[1]. It can be applied in various ways, in trade, craft and farming. Thus there are the institutes of *muḍāraba* (sleeping partnership, whereby one partner furnishes the capital and the other the business acumen), *mufāwaḍa* (unlimited mercantile partnership, whereby the whole property of both parties is engaged; mutual guarantee as well as procuration are presupposed), *ʿinān* (limited liability company which implies mutual procuration but no mutual responsibility), *sharīkat al-ṣanāʾiʿ* (partnership of artisans in which, for instance, two tailors or two dyers take equal shares), *sharīkat al-wujūh* (credit union, without capital, in which the partners pool the credit and share the profit), *musāqāt* (lease contract for palm gardens, in which one partner provides the land and seed and the other the oxen and labour) and *mukhābara* (contract under which one partner furnishes the land and the other the seed, oxen and labour) (*H.B.* II, 116 f.).

The requirement of mutual aid is, in the opinion of Shāh Walī Allāh, the main ground for the prohibition of *maysir* (gambling) and *ribā* (interest); "You should realize that *maysir* is unlawful gain ..., and is not in keeping with civic spirit (*tamaddun)* and mutual aid (*taʿāwun*) ... Equally, *ribā* constitutes ... unlawful gain: for, as a rule, the borrowers are people fallen into a severe state of indigence, mostly not able to pay their debt in time ... When this way of earning money takes root, it leads to the abandonment of agrarian trades and skilled crafts which are fundamental means of earning a living (in a healthy society) ... Both ways of gain (i.e. *maysir* and *ribā*) are tantamount to inebriation, as they are in flagrant contradiction with the principles God has laid down for earning a livelihood" (*H.B.* II, 106).

A valuable clue to what is *inter alia* a divinely sanctioned manner of earning one's livelihood can be derived from the prophetic saying: "he who revives dead land becomes its owner" (Bu. *Ḥarath* 15). "The idea lying at the root of these words is ... that all property belongs to God ... The whole earth is, in fact, tantamount to a mosque or a hospice assigned to travellers, on which everybody has an equal claim. Accordingly, the

[1] Not an original idea. Ibn Sīnā (see *Kitāb al-Najāt*, Cairo 1331/1913, 498) and Ibn Khaldūn (see *Muqaddima*, Paris 1858, II, 368), underlined the essentiality of co-operation for the maintenance of human society.

rule 'first come, first served' is here applicable. Possessory right implies that he who brings land under cultivation has more right to it than anyone else'' (*H.B.* II, 103).

Being aware of the great number of responsibilities with which God has entrusted human beings, Shāh Walī Allāh points out that man is superior to the other species of animal in at least three respects, to wit:

1. he is intent on general welfare (*raʾy kullī*), whereas animals are merely actuated by sensual lusts and sudden promptings;
2. he is sensitive to art and beauty (*ẓarāfa*);
3. he is able to think out devices by which he can tide over his social and economic difficulties (*irtifāqāt*) (*H.B.* I, 38).

The term *irtifāq* (finding help) was already found in one of Shāh Walī Allāh's early writings[2], but in the *Ḥujjat Allāh al-bāligha* and the *Budūr al-bāzigha* it appears to be a fundamental idea forming the basis of an interesting rudimentary sociology. To this end the very specific sense[3] of 'stage of socio-economic development' is ascribed to it. The Delhi scholar distinguishes four *irtifāqāt* required for the ultimate establishment of a society as it ought to be and is purposed in God's planning[4].

''In the first phase of socio-economic development man obtains the power of speech so that he can phrase his thoughts in a natural way, unimpeded by convention. Then the circle is enlarged by making use of tropes in his speech to coin words relating the things conceived in the mind, and by varying modulations in his voice to express various moods, until at last the languages become distinct and different ... It is also in this first phase that he becomes acquainted with edible grains suited to his physical constitution, and learns how they are to be eaten and digested ... (Further, he) finds out how to tap wells for those who live in places far from the water (of springs and rivers) ..., how to domesticate animals to use them for labour otherwise hard to perform ..., how to prepare a dwelling by screening it from heat and cold, and how to make a garment from skins of animals or from the leaves of trees ... And it is in this phase that man is led to acquire for himself a wife as uncontested property to satisfy his lusts and to reproduce his off-spring'' (*B.B.* 53 f.). Again another aspect of this stage of primitive culture[5] is ''that man takes

---

[2] To wit: *Fuyūḍ al-Ḥaramayn* (11th Vision).

[3] Not found in the dictionaries. Shāh Walī Allāh nowhere explains this self-devised technical meaning explicitly. The pursued line of thought may be: finding help from the environment (fellow men, animals, materials supplied by nature) for the fulfilment of man's collective needs to an ever increasing extent.

[4] Accordingly, the knowledge concerning man's *irtifāqāt* has been deposited in the *ṭabīʿa* (disposition) of the Throne, i.e. the source of divine planning (*Fuyūḍ*, 11th Vision).

[5] Relating to ''small societies such as inhabitants of deserts, high mountains and regions far away from temporate zones'' (*H.B.* I, 39).

to barter and co-operation in some way or another ... (Further, that out of necessity of law and order) he who appears to be the most sensible person and behaves in the bravest way, becomes the leader ... and a code of conduct is enacted to settle disputes, to check a criminal and to repulse raiders'' (*H.B.* I, 40). To sum up: ''the first phase represents a stage of development based on the level of animals. However, it excels animal life by the additional qualities of purity, communal sense, civilization, and, culture'' (*B.B.* 51). In the second stage of socio-economic development we have to do with ''communities of sedentary people and townsmen flourishing in temporate zones'' (*H.B.* I, 39). Since compared by the era of primitive civilization the complexity of life increased in this stage, the need arises for more suitable institutions and prudent measures permitting progress. Thus, Shāh Walī Allāh comes to the conclusion that now the following five kinds of wisdom become requisite:

1. the wisdom pertaining to the way of living, with reference to consistency in conduct and practical knowledge about eating, drinking, dressing, dwelling, etiquette, manner of conversation, way of travelling, etc.;
2. the wisdom of earning a livelihood, which involves the various occupation people pursue, befitting their personal capacities, and the means that help them in their crafts of fellah, capenter, smith and so on;
3. the wisdom of domestic life, which pertains to rearing children, married life, slavery, responsibilities to relatives, management and manners of companionship;
4. the wisdom of mutual dealings, which concerns purchase and sale, giving presents, tenancy, lending, debt, and mortage;
5. the wisdom of co-operation, which relates to surety, silent partnership, commercial enterprise, power of attorney and tenure (*B.B.* 50).

While through the second stage of socio-economic evolution human society develops into a city-state (*madīna*) ''consisting of small towns which have joined together and in which the inhabitants carry on trade with each other ... Due to that unifying link it is an organic whole, with each group of people and each family as the constituent parts thereof'' (*B.B.* 70). As soon as a city-state is established, mankind has reached the third stage of socio-economic development. For the maintenance of a city-state, unity is essential. The instrument of Government through which such unity is preserved and developed should be a strong and powerful personality, a leader (*imām*)[6] in the fullest sense of the word

[6] To be assisted by seven public functionaries, to wit a vizier who is responsible for the collection and distribution of taxes; a commander-in-chief; a commander of guards; a cadi; a chief *muftī* called 'shaykh al-Islām' whose duty it is to uphold religion and

(*B.B.* 71). For the progress of a city-state and in its battle against corruption, abuses, disorder and decay the following requirements are indispensable:

1. Judiciary. "When ... stinginess, envy and disregard of rights enter into social life, disagreements and disputes are bound to spring up among the people of a city-state ... Hence, there must be an acknowledged institution available to which one may have recourse for an equitable settlement of disputes".
2. The institute of an executive. "When people of perverted disposition and pernicious activities prevail over other people and begin to influence them, the city-state becomes depraved and disordered. There should, therefore, be a strong body to take deterrent and punitive measures against such people".
3. Police and military force. "People often take to violent activities such as murder, robbery or rebellion and deliberately try to disturb the peace and order in a city-state ... In order to control such violent situations and preserve the city-state from the misfortune they cause, a defence force, constituted of brave fighters, is essential".
4. Welfare and public works. "The city-state has institutes and corporate bodies which, if existent, render it a welfare state, whereas, the lack of them renders guarding it defective ... Things to be taken care of, for example, are the guarding of the frontier-accesses of a country, the construction of fortresses, walls, markets and bridges, digging beds for rivers, marrying off orphans, protection of their properties, the distribution of alms among the needy, the division of an inheritance among heirs".
5. Religious and moral instruction. "Sincere faith and true religion cannot dispense with an informant, though both of them are based on such clear proofs that sane people find the way to them by themselves. However, the numerous men of corrupt nature who follow their lusts and passions and oppose the truth, are in need of a man of wisdom, a teacher of religion and a preacher who can urge them to cultivate noble qualities, to manage the house properly, and to conduct themselves correctly towards others" (*B.B.* 71 f.).

The fourth and last phase of socio-economic development is the result of quarrels arising between the various city-states and causing heavy loss of life and livelihood. Then there is an urgent need for a very powerful

---

spiritual guidance; a versatile intellectual (*ḥakīm*) who possesses knowledge of medicine, poetry, astrology, history, arithmetic and the art of composition; and a commissioned agent (*wakīl*) who takes care of the private financial affairs of the leader (*B.B.* 84). The main distinction between the public functionaries and the private citizens consists in the fact that the latter have to be taxed in order to remunerate the former (*H.B.* I, 46).

and firm overlord or caliph. Shāh Walī Allāh compares this situation with the state of emergency which once necessitated the Israelities to ask their prophet Samuel for a king (see Samuel VIII, 19) (*H.B.* I, 47). The caliph's functiọn is naturally to see that the heads of the city-states administer justice properly and do not wage war against one another. To this end, he wields two swords: a sword of subjugation and a sword of affection (*B.B.* 87). Further, "he should", so the Delhi scholar expounds, "have clearly visible symbols of people's loyalty such as for instance, prayers for him, ... and like, for instance, the custom in our days of having dinar coins inscribed with the name of the caliph" (*H.B.* I, 48).

Great rulers in history, like Alexander the Great, somehow enforced this fourth stage, but it fell to Mohammed to realize it fully by introducing a religion which would render all other institutionalized religions unnecessary (*B.B.* 199)[7]. In this way, unity of policy and of religion is warranted for all inhabitants of the earth and human society is given its final shape.

To this end social customs may constitute a momentuous support, as well as a great impediment. They yield positive and beneficial results, if they are formed by guides of human society being in the happy possession of the seven cardinal virtues and if God renders the rest of the people disposed by nature to accept their lead, making "their minds like mirrors, in which images of other mirrors are reflected" (*B.B.* 87). If man had not an inner stimulus to follow another man he would not have adopted ethical qualities, and he would not have passed through the excellent phases of socio-economic development. The world would have regressed in its evolution, and the majority of men would not have got beyond the stage of animal life. So the best customs are those by which the ethical qualities of individuals are improved and which are conducive to the reformation of the society. They should be wide instead of narrow in their application. They should not be so rigid that the slightest disregard of a minute detail in practice may lead to unbearable public disapproval. They should pursue a middle course between extravagant luxury and an extremely austere way of life such as the customs of the civilized people of the Ḥijāz[8] in pre-Islamic times and the residents of small towns in our country (*B.B.* 87 ff.).

An additional advantage that customs may offer is that they can be of help in putting a person's faith into practice. This is particularly true of

---

[7] *Cf.* also *H.B.* II, 173: "You should recognize that the Prophet was sent to lay the foundation of a universal caliphate and to render his religion victorious over the other".

[8] Who preserved moderate standards which kept a happy balance between the austere way of life of the Bedouins and the pompous status of living of Persians and Romans of those days (*H.B.* II, 126).

people who are fully occupied with their work and lack inner stability; if there were no customs, they would not concern themselves with the message of Islām (*B.B.* 195).

However, a custom may equally well produce detrimental effects. At least, three cases of this are imaginable, to wit:

1. It may prevent the emergence of ethical qualities in man, if it does not suit the nature of a particular human individual. "Thus, if it is based on pettiness or on following a leader, it will prevent a man who is a strong personality from magnanimity and domination; and if it is based on magnanimity and domination, it will prevent the man who is evil or stricken with misfortunes from reforming his ways, since it is only appropriate for such a person if it descends to the level of submissiveness and pettiness".
2. It may cause moral decadence if a custom is in violates of good manners. This is the case with "customs permitting fornication and sodomy and those allowing women to adopt the fashion of men and men to adopt the fashion of women".
3. It may impair proximity to God, because of its being based either on going to extremes in earning a livelihood, or on plunging into pastimes like flute-playing, chess, hunting, keeping pigeons, etc. (*B.B.* 88 and *H.B.* I, 49)[9].

When implementing of his socio-economic principles, the Delhi reformer at times remonstrated with different classes of contemporary Muslim society on abuses typical of their occupations or modes of life. He accuses the rulers of the country of living in the same lavish style as the kings of Persia and Byzantium in the days of the Prophet. In consequence of this, they are "forced to levy an exhorbitant rate of taxation upon the cultivators, merchants, and the like. The latter suffer from great hardships. If they refuse to pay the taxes, the rulers join issue with them and chastise them, and if they pay, they are reduced to the level of asses and bullocks, ... and are not even allowed an hour to rest from their labours so that they find no time to pay any heed to the life to come" (*H.B.* I, 105 f.)[10]. "A state can only prosper if light tributes are

[9] Other cultural activities strongly deprecated because of kindling the passions are the pursuits of Persian and Hindu literature and of poetics (*Tafh.* II, 247). "In actual practice it appears that poetry is confounded with religious exhortation (*waʿẓ*), since both of them overpower the soul. In contradistinction of poetry, however, by religious exhortation man's original (unspoiled) disposition (*fiṭra*) ... may emerge" (*Tafh.* II, 127).

[10] In a paper entitled 'A Comparison between the Qurʾānic Views of ʿUbayd Allāh Sindhī and Shāh Walī Allāh' I have pointed out that this remarkable conclusion at the end discloses that in the eyes of Shāh Walī Allāh the fatal effects of the exploitation by the aristocracy are primarily of a *religious* nature; they are not directly connected with the economic conditions of the people. So it is indeed very questionable whether ʿUbayd Allāh Sindhī's appeal to the Delhi reformer as a witness of his own outright socialistic convictions is altogether legitimate (*Islamic Studies*, Islamabad 1977, vol. XVI[3], 183).

collected and the necessary[11] number of civil servants is taken on'' (*H.B.* I, 45).

In a fierce denunciation of the *amīrs* (government officers) we read: ''O *amīrs*, do you not fear God when you indulge in short-lived and trival pleasures and neglect to take notice of your subjects who devour one another? Is it not a fact that you drink wine in public? You cannot deny that brothels, taverns and gambling-dens are set up—still you feel no qualms of conscience—, and that in this vast Empire the *ḥadd* (fixed) punishments (for certain crimes)[12] have not been enforced for six or seven centuries. In your way the weak one is exploited, whereas the mighty is left untouched'' (*Tafh.* I, 216).

Criticism is also levelled at the unbalance in the choice of trades and professions. ''A disproportionate division of professions arises if, for instance, too many people turn to trade practices, abandoning agricultural pursuits[13], or too many choose a military profession'' (*H.B.* I, 44). ''And if a majority of the people earn their living as artificers and civil servants and a minority are cattle-keepers and farmers, there will be great economic difficulties'' (*H.B.* II, 105)[14].

Another target of Shāh Walī Allāh's attacks is the class of ṣūfī masters (*mashāʾikh*). In one of his directives (*waṣāyā*) for religious life he warns: ''You should not commit yourselves to the guidance of to-day's *mashāʾikh* and you should not take an oath of allegiance to them ...; neither should you be gulled by miracles ... Nearly all miracle-mongers nowadays pass talismans and theurgies off for miracles'' (*Tafh.* II, 240 f.). ''In God's chosen body politic'', so the Delhi divine complains, ''excessive indulgence in intemperate mystical practices by both the noble and plebeian is a disease that is difficult to cure'' (*Tafh.* II, 243). One should not make the mistake of taking the flashing thoughts of *walīs* for divine

---

[11] In the foregoing the argument has been put forward that another cause of decline in those days was ''the pressure on the public treasury because of people who make it a habit to pocket money from it for sham services, contending that they have a claim on it on account of being a soldier, a scholar, or somebody who ordinarily receives presents from kings such as an ascetic or a poet''.

[12] The *ḥadd* for a thief is the cutting off of his right hand, for fornication flogging with 100 lashes, and so on.

[13] This shows that already in those days an accelerative urbanization process offered economic problems.

[14] al-Dawānī (1427-1502/3) holds the same view: ''each class (in a good city) should be kept in its proper place'' (see *EI*², II, 174). On p. 2 of Shāh Walī Allāhʾs Persian treatise on learning (*Risāla-i dānishmandī*) al-Dawānī is mentioned as one of the links that connected al-Ashʿarī with the father (and teacher) of Shāh Walī Allāh. Therefore, it is not necessary to ascribe Shāh Walī Allāh's plea for professional immobility to the influence by Hindu class and caste distinctions as is done by S. A. A. Rizvi (*Shāh Walī Allāh and His Times*, Canberra 1980, 311).

revelation; many an error of the people to-day arises from this mistake (*Saṭ*. 17).

Harangues are also delivered to the common folk: "O company of human beings, you have put your morals to sleep. Greed has overpowered you. Satan gained mastery over you. Women are running the affairs of men, or men hold women in light estimation. You find what is forbidden delightful and what is permissible repugnant ... Gratify the carnal appetites of your women by a coitus ... and do not leave her as it were 'suspended' (i.e. like one that neither has a husband nor is divorced)". Then the Delhi educationist continues: "O company of human beings, you are attached to evil customs. On the day of ᶜĀshūrā (the tenth of the month Muḥarram in which the martyrdom of Ḥusayn is commemorated) you gather together to revel in follies. You make an observance of mourning of it. Do you not know that the course of history is determined by God and that the daily happenings proceed from the will of God (so that one should accept misfortunes with acquiescence and not give way to excessive mourning)? Yes of course, Ḥusayn was killed on this day, but there are more days in which the beloved of God have died. Then people avail themselves of this opportunity to play with their spears[15] and swords ... (On the other hand, you also institute) customs by which you make life unnecessarily difficult, such as incurring extravagant expenses for *walīmas* (repasts prepared on the occasion of a wedding), or holding divorce as prohibited, and refusing to give widows in marriage[16]" (*Tafh*. I, 217 f.). Our reformer equally condems the practice of making lavish expenditures on the occasion of mournings, and the custom of fixing an extremely high sum for the *mahr* (gift that it to be given for a bride) (*Tafh*. II, 246 f.).

---

[15] *Cf.* G. A. Herklots, *Qanoon-e-Islam*, London 1832, 180: "they also take out the *neeza* (spear) on its (i.e. of Ḥusayn's standard) peregrination ... (for Ḥusayn's head was) carried by Ayzeed's order through different cities on the point of a javelin".

[16] As sometimes occurs in Indian Muslim society under the influence of Hindu views concerning the sacrality of marriage.

# EPILOGUE

In reply to a letter from his student Makhdūm Muʿīn al-Dīn of Thatta, in which the latter presses him to write a refutation of objections raised against doctrines of Ibn Taymiyya (d. 1328), Shāh Walī Allāh first of all affirms that in his opinion Ibn Taymiyya, like Ibn ʿArabī and Aḥmad Sirhindī, is among the most faithful servants of God[1]. This high tribute paid to the famous Ḥanbalī theologian and expert of jurisprudence accords with the great influence his views must have had on the shaping of Shāh Walī Allāh's thought. There are many striking similarities between their ideas; when the Delhi divine states that according to him travels to a tomb, a shrine of a saints, or to the Mount Sinai also fall equally under the Prophet's prohibition to undertake a journey for the visit of holy places except for the three mosques: the sacred mosque (i.e. the Kaʿba), the Aqṣā mosque (in Jerusalem) and the mosque in Medina[2] (*H.B.* I, 92), he echoes the standpoint of Ibn Taymiyya who declares that "if one had vowed to journey to the tomb of Abraham or the Prophet, or to the Mount Sinai ..., one is not obliged to perform it ..., since journeys to places like these are forbidden by the Prophet"[3]. If our author claims that the very foundation of civilization is co-operation (*H.B.* II, 106), he actually repeats words of Ibn Taymiyya who says: "None of mankind can attain complete welfare, either in this world or in the next, except by association, co-operation, and mutual aid"[4]. And when Ibn Taymiyya puts forward that "the choicest men after the Prophet were Abū Bakr and ʿUmar ..., both of whom are such that the sun has never shone or set on any one, save the prophets"[5], we are immediately reminded of Shāh Walī Allāh's plea for the undeniable superiority of the first two caliphs. Similarly, his view that the one very weak point of ʿAlī was his lack of statecraft, this in line with the judgment of Ibn Taymiyya[6]. While discussing the deficiency of man's knowledge of God, the Delhi scholar maintains that though it is impossible for ordinary human comprehension to speak adequately of the divine Attributes man must still be enabled to form some notion of them (*H.B.* I,

---

[1] *Maktūbāt maʿa manāqib Abī ʿAbd Allāh Muḥ. b. Ismāʿīl al-Bukhārī wa-faḍīlat Ibn Taymiyya*, Delhi 1890, 27.

[2] Mu. *Ḥajj* 415.

[3] Ibn Taymiyya, *Majmūʿa al-risāʾil al-kubrā* (Cairo 1323/1903), II, 55.

[4] Ibn Taymiyya, *al-Ḥisba fiʾl-Islām*, Cairo 1318/1900, 3.

[5] Ibn Taymiyya, *al-Risāʾil waʾl-masāʾil* (al-Manār ed.) (Cairo 1341/1922-3), I, 51 f.

[6] *Cf.* H. Laoust, *Essai sur les doctrines sociales et politiques d'ibn Taymiyya*, Cairo 1939, 217: "Au fond, le califat de ʿAlī n'a guère été, pour Ibn Taimīya, que la règne malheureux".

63). This standpoint again agrees with what is set forth by the Ḥanbalī author, namely that though the Attributes of God are contained in the *mutashābihāt* (allegorical verses of the Qurʾān) of which God alone knows the true interpretation, man can nevertheless have some idea of them[7]. Further, Ibn Taymiyya appears to have the same disgust of philosophers as Shāh Walī Allāh: "These Aristotelian philosophers", he says, "are among the lowest people as far as their teachings and living are concerned"[8].

Self-examination proved to Shāh Walī Allāh that he was a man of moderation by nature: "in fact", he confesses, "as a rule I do not like discussions in which opposing opinions clash" (*Fuyūḍ*, 33rd Vision). The same is said about Ibn Taymiyya: "his doctrine was intended to be primarily ... a doctrine of synthesis or of conciliation"[9]. Yet in this respect there is an important difference between the two. Ibn Taymiyya's efforts at harmonization are restricted to the integration of *ʿaql* (reason) and *naql* (tradition). Speculative philosophy is not included. On the contrary, he is a fierce fighter of panentheism (*waḥdat al-wujūd*) as advocated by Ibn ʿArabī. In a separate polemic treatise, entitled *Ḥaqiqa madhhab al-ittiḥādiyyīn aw waḥdat al-wujūd* (Truth about the Teachings of the Panentheists or *waḥdat al-wujūd*), he exhibits the pernicious effects the doctrine has on the Muslim faith. The Delhi scholar, for his part, is charged with a more comprehensive task of synthesizing. He was born in an age in which the effectuation of a coherent interrelation between rational, traditional *and* esoteric (*makshūf*) was urgently needed (*Maktūb* 3). In sharp contrast to Ibn Taymiyya, Shāh Walī Allāh holds Ibn ʿArabī in great esteem, and appears to have many views[10] and features in common with the Shaykh al-akbar. Like Ibn ʿArabī[11], he claims for himself the ability to discern intuitively between the basic teachings of religion as handed down by Mohammed and that part of the traditions which has crept in and been tampered with (*al-Juzʾ al-laṭīf* 28). And when he argues that the relation of the pre-existent Mohammed to the other prophets and his heirs is similar to that between a whole and its parts (*Fuyūḍ*, 11th Vision), he repeats the teaching of his great predecessor[12]. When he mentions with approval that, according to Jāmī (d. 1492), Ibn ʿArabī filled a position higher than sainthood but below prophethood (*Tafh*. II, 33), Jāmī in fact credits him with the same dignity as Shāh Walī Allāh intends for himself as occupant of the office of *ḥakīm* (*Khizāna* 4).

[7] Ibn Taymiyya, *Majmūʿa al-risāʾil al-kubrā*, II, 29.
[8] I. Goldziher, *The Ẓāhirīs* (tf. W. Behn), Leiden 1971, 175.
[9] H. Laoust in *EI*², III, 953.
[10] See also chapter III C.
[11] See *JRAS*, 1906, p. 822.
[12] See A. E. Affifi, *The Mystical Philosophy of Muḥyid Dīn Ibnul Arabi*, Lahore n.d., 72.

Starting from the maxim: "God's express will is that we should refrain from disagreement and sectarianism" (*Tafh.* I, 206), the Delhi scholar applies the following procedures to resolve, or at least minimize, seeming discrepancies:

1. by placing teachings in their historical setting. Every age has its own exigencies and particular ways of expression. So when discussing different theories and doctrines advanced by Muslim mystics in the course of time, "one should take into account that all of them were adapted to the spirit of time" (*H.* II);
2. by pointing out that contrarieties may be due to people's looking at an object from a different angle. Thus, for instance, various levels and faculties are discernible in the concept of *rūḥ* (spirit). It can be viewed in its physio-biological aspects, can be taken as a *mithālī* reality, i.e. the shape the *rūḥ* receives in the World of Prefiguration before its arrival in the World of Bodily Forms (*nāsūt*), etc. In other words, someone is right in maintaining that *rūḥ* is a subtle element which streams in a human body like fire in charcoal, just as the person who propounds that it is set apart from material pollution: "every man has a direction in which he turns" (*Qurʾān* II, 148) (*Fuyūḍ*, 40th Vision);
3. by explaining that incongruities can be the outcome of different phraseologies. In reply to a questioner who asked Shāh Walī Allāh: 'What do you think of the disparities you come upon in statements of Ibn ʿArabī, who at one time speaks of Pharaoh's belief[13] and at another time of his unbelief?"[14], the Delhi scholar author expounds that this is a question of particular phraseologies (*alsina*). "For a human individual", he continues, "there are many realities, and every reality has its particular aspects and references. For every particular aspect there is a specific phraseology to interpret it ... At one time a ṣūfī gnostic will restrict himself to what is found in the World of Immaterial Entities, at another he will concentrate on what is met in the World of Bodily Forms ... Every time he will use a phraseology that is appropriate (for that specific reality), and then it is not necessary that the same things are stated by all these phraseologies" (*Tafh.* I, 19);
4. by preserving a balance between two extreme points of view. In judging the Companions of the Prophet, so we are told, people make two kinds of mistakes. Some assume that all of them were men of noble character and that discord was unknown to them. This opinion

---

[13] Ibn ʿArabī, *Fuṣūṣ al-ḥikam* (ed. A. E. Affifi), Beirut n.d., I, 212.
[14] *idem* I, 210

rests on pure imagination. Detailed reports exist on their internal quarrels. Others take to criticizing them and to uttering imprecations against them, as soon as their attention is drawn to such conditions. Although Shāh Walī Allāh himself is immediately willing to admit that the Companions were not exactly impeccable men, he maintains that none the less it might be better not to talk about their slips from virtue lest the *umma* should disintegrate (*Tafh.* II, 244);

5. by pleading for tolerance in respect of ritual varieties. In disputes whether or not it should be prescribed to say *amīn* loudly, instead of faintly, during the *ṣalāt* and to lift one's hands at the time of bowing, matters must not be put to extremes. For both standpoints, Shāh Walī Allāh declares there might be something to be said. Under no circumstances, however, is anybody free to cause much stir among his townsmen on account of such questions (*H.B.* II, 9 f.).

Still Shāh Walī Allāh's endeavours after moderation are never an end in themselves. This is a good thing, for people whose only aim is to pursue a just middle course can be extremely dull, if not annoying, apprehensive as they are of any deviation. His sense of balance is harmoniously coupled with a remarkable independence of thought, on account of which he produces many ideas of refreshing originality.

It is true that in order to evade unnecessary trouble with zealous heresy-hunters, he occasionally condemns Muʿtazilism, but this does not prevent him from making use of Muʿtazilite doctrines if they agree with his own convictions. When he is asked to write a refutation of Shīʿī contentions because of the political unrest they caused in eighteenth-century India, he complies with the request. Nevertheless several Shīʿī notions, as we have seen, are recognizable in his dissertations, and apparently their origin did not constitute an insuperable impediment to their possible utility. The fact that he lives in a country in which the Ḥanafite school is normative did not withhold him from applying a Shāfiʿite rule, if he considered it more fitting to a case under consideration.

So it is not surprising that in later ages orthodox people—and in particular *ʿulamāʾ* outside the Indo-Pakistan Subcontinent[15] were fairly often shocked by tenets he courageously advanced, whereas liberal thinkers, who were unafraid of views originating from the West, as e.g. Sayyid Aḥmad Khān[16] (1817-98) and Sir Muḥammad Iqbāl[17] (1876-1938),

---

[15] Still even Indian *ʿulamāʾ* sometimes appear displeased at views entertained by their venerated countryman. When asked about a judgment in the matter of a ritual detail on which Shāh Walī Allāh dissents from the Ḥanafī experts, the Deobandi divine ʿAzīz al-Raḥmān (d. 1928) straightway rejects the opinion of the Delhi scholar (*Fatāwā-ī Dār al-ʿulūm Deoband*, Deoband 1963, vol. II, 228).

[16] *Cf.* Ch. W. Troll, *Sayyid Ahmad Khan*, New Delhi 1978, 33 f.

[17] *Cf.* A. J. Halepota, 'Shāh Walyullāh and Iqbāl, the Philosophers of Modern Age', *Islamic Studies*, Islamabad, XIII (1974).

wholeheartedly acknowledge their indebtedness to their reverend compatriot.

In fine, the ultimate concern of the Delhi divine was to make an independent inquiry into the basic truths of religion (*asrār al-dīn*)[18], and for every student of his thought it is a privilege to trace the impressive achievements he attained in this lofty enterprise.

---

[18] Following in the footsteps of his famous predecessor al-Ghazālī (d. 1111), who inserts in his *Iḥyāʾ ʿulūm al-dīn* elaborate discourses on the *asrār* of cultic purity, *ṣalāt*, *zakāt*, *ḥajj*, and fasting. Both of them were eager to expose the rationale of the various institutes of Islam, thereby enabling their co-believers to assent unreservedly to its tenets and to willingly obey its commandments.

# BIBLIOGRAPHY


Abbott, F., 'The decline of the Mughul empire and Shah Waliullah', *MW*. LII (1962).

ᶜAbd al-Ḥayy al-Ḥasanī, *Nuzhat al-khawāṭir*, Part VI, Hydarābād, Deccan, 1957.

Abū Muḥammad Imām Khān Nawshahrawī, *Tarājim ᶜulamāʾ-i ḥadīth Hind*, Delhi, (1938).

Ahmad, Aziz, 'Political and religious ideas of Shāh Walī-Ullāh of Delhi', *MW*. LII (1962).

Ali, S. A., 'The Medinian letter', *Recherches d'Islamologie. Recueil d'articles offert à G. Anawati et L. Gardet*, Louvain, 1977.

Asiri, F. M., 'Shāh Walī Allāh on social evolution', *Viśva-Bharati Quarterly*, N. S. XVI (1950-1) and XXV (1960).

ᶜAtiq Fikrī, 'Shāh Walī Allāh kā naẓriya-i zamān wa makān', *Iqbal Review*, X, (1970).

Baljon, J. M. S., 'Psychology as apprehended and applied by Shāh Walī Allāh Dihlawī', *Acta Orientalia Neerlandica*, Leiden, 1971.

transl. *A Mystical Interpretation of Prophetic Tales by an Indian Muslim: Shāh Walī Allāh's taʾwīl al-aḥādīth*, Leiden 1973.

'The Ethics of Shāh Walī Allāh Dihlawī', *Akten des VII. Kongresses für Arabistik und Islamwissenschaft*, Göttingen, 1974.

'Shāh Walī Allāh's Terminology of Creation', *Actes du 8ᵐᵉ Congres de l'Union Europeenne des Arabisants et Islamisants,* Aix-en-Provence, 1976.

'A comparison between the Qurʾānic views of ᶜUbayd Allāh Sindhī and Shāh Walī Allāh', *Islamic Studies*, XVI, 3, Islamabad, 1977.

Bashīr Ahmad Ludhiānawī, *Imām Walī Allāh Dihlawī awr un-kī falsafa ᶜumrāniyyāt wa maᶜāshiyyāt*, Lahore, 1945.

Bausani, A., 'Note su Shāh Walīullāh di Delhi (1703-62)', *AION*, N.S. X (1960).

Coslovi, Fr., 'Osservazioni sul ruolo de Šāh Walīullāh Dihlawī e Šāh ᶜAbd al-ᶜAzīz nella Naqšbandiyya indiana', *AION*, N.S. XXIX (1979).

Dar, B. A., 'Wali Allah: his life and times', *Iqbal Review*, VI, 3 (1965).

Dāʾūd Rahbar, 'Shāh Walī-ullāh and Ijtihād', *MW*. XIV, 4 (1955).

Faruqi, B. A., *The Mujaddid's conception of Tawhid*, Lahore, 1940.

Fazle Mahmud, 'Philosophy of Shāh Walī Allāh', *Oriental College Magazine*, Lahore, 1957

'Shāh Walī Allāh's Hujjatullahil Balighah', *J. Arab. and Pers. Soc. Panjab Univ.*, Lahore 1960-61.

Fazlur-Rahman, 'The Thinker of Crisis, Shah Waliy-Ullah', *Pakistan Quarterly*, VI, Karachi, 1956.

Halepota, A. J., *Philosophy of Shāh Walīullāh*, Lahore n.d.

'Shāh Walīyullāh and Iqbāl, the philosophers of Modern Age', *Islamic Studies*, XIII, Islamabad 1974.

Ḥasan al-Maᶜṣūmī, M. S., 'An appreciation of Shāh Walīyullāh al-Muḥaddith ad-Dihlawī', *IC*. XXI (1947).

Hermansen, Marcia K. *Shāh Walī Allāh's Theory of Religion*, Ph.D. diss. Univ. of Chicago, 1982.

ᶜIrfān Habīb, 'The political role of Shaikh Ahmad Sirhindī and Shah Waliullah', *Indian History Congress*, I, Aligarh, 1960-1.

Ismāᶜīl Gōdharawī, *Walī Allāh*, Delhi, n.d.

Ismāᶜīl Shahīd, Muhammad, *ᶜAbaqāt*, Karachi, 1960.

Jalbani, G. N., *Teachings of Shah Waliyullah of Delhi*, Lahore 1967.

*Life of Shah Waliyullah*, Lahore 1978.

Kamali, S. A., 'The concept of human nature in Hujjat Allah al-Baligha and its relation to Shah Waliy Allah's doctrine of fiqh', *IC*. XXXVI (1962).

'Shah Waliy Ullah's doctrine of irtifaqat', *Iqbal*, XI (1963).

Khalil, ᶜAbdel Ḥamid ᶜAbdel, ᶜAdl, *God, the Universe and Man in Islamic Thought: the contribution of Shah Waliullah of Delhi*, unpubl. thesis, University of London, Oct. 1971.
Khan, Ahmad, 'A unique MS. of Fath al-rahmān by Shah Waliullah', *IC.* LV (1981)
Mahmood Ahmad Ghazi, 'State and Politics in the Philosophy of Shah Waliyullah', *Islamic Studies*, XXIII, Islamabad 1984.
Maḥmūd Aḥmad Barakātī, *Shāh Walī Allāh awr unkā khāndān*, Lahore 1976.
Malik, Hafeez, 'Shāh Walī Allāh's last testament', *MW.* LXIII (1973).
Manāẓir Aḥsan Gīlānī, *Tadhkira-i Ḥadrat Shāh Walī Allāh*, Hydarābād, Deccan, 1946.
Masᶜūd ᶜĀlim Nadwī, 'Shāh Walī Allāh awr un-kī siyāsī taḥrīk', *Maᶜārif*, Aᶜzamgarh, 1943.
Mawdūdī, Abuʾl-ᶜAlāʾ, *Tajdīd wa iḥyāʾ-i dīn*, Lahore, 1953.
Maẓhar Baqā, *Uṣūl-i fiqh awr Shāh Walī Allāh*, Islamabad, 1973.
Mīr Valīuddīn, 'Reconciliation between Ibn ᶜArabī's wahdat-i wujud and Mujaddid's wahdat-i shuhud', *IC.* XXV (1951).
Muhammad ᶜAbḍul Baqi, 'Theories of state and problems of sociology as expounded by an Indian Muslim divine of the eighteenth century', *Islamic Review*, XXXVIII (1950).
Muḥammad Ikrām, *Rūd-i Kawthar*, Lahore, 1978.
Muhammad Ismâᶜîl al-Salafî, *Ḥaraka al-inṭilâq al-fikrî wa juhûd al-Shâh Walî Allâh fiʾl-tajdîd*, Benares 1977.
Muḥammad Miyāṃ, *ᶜUlamāʾ-i Hind kā shāndār māḍī*, vol. III, Delhi 1957.
Muin-ud-Din Ahmad Khan, 'Shāh Wali-Allāh's conception of ijtihād', *Journal of the Pakistan Historical Society*, VII (1959).
Mujeeb, M., *The Indian Muslims*, London, 1967.
Nizami, K. A., 'Shah Waliullah of Delhi: his thought and contribution', *IC.* LIV (1980).
Nuᶜmānī Muḥammad Manẓūr, (ed.), *al-Furqān, Shāh Walī Allāh Nambar*, Barelī (1940).
Pendlebury, D. and Jalbani, G. N., *The Sacred Knowledge and the Higher Functions of the Mind* (transl. of *Alṭāf al-quds*), London, 1982.
Qāḍī Jāwīd, *Afkār-i Shāh Walī Allāh*, Lahore, 1977.
Raḥīm Bakhsh Dihlawī, *Ḥayāt-i Walī*, Delhi 1901.
Rizvi, S. A. A., *Shāh Walī-Allāh and his times*, Canberra 1980.
*Shāh ᶜAbd al-ᶜAzīz*, Canberra 1982.
*A history of Sufism in India*, Vol. II, New Delhi, 1983.
Saeeda Iqbal, *Islamic Rationalism in the Subcontinent*, Lahore 1984.
Saeeda Khatoon, 'Shāh Walī Allāh's Philosophy of Society—An Outline', *Hamdard Islamicus*, VII, 4 (1984).
Schimmel, A., *Islam in the Indian subcontinent*, Leiden, 1980.
Shams al-Raḥmān, *Shāh Walī Allāh ke ᶜumrānī naẓariya*, Lahore, 1968.
Shiblī Nuᶜmānī, *ᶜIlm al-kalām*. Aᶜzamgarh, 1902.
Tara Chand, *A history of the freedom movement in India*, Delhi, 1961.
Ṭufayl Aḥmad Qureshī, *Iqtiṣādī masāʾil awr un-kā ḥall Shāh Walī Allāh kī naẓar men*, Karachi, 1970.
ᶜUbayd Allāh Sindhī, *Risāla-i maḥmūdiyya*, Lahore, 1945.
*Shāh Walī Allāh awr un-kī siyāsī taḥrīk*, Lahore, 1945.
*Shāh Walī Allāh awr un-kā falsafa*, Lahore, 1949.
Zubaid Ahmad, M. G., *The Contribution of Indo-Pakistan to Arabic literature*, Lahore, 1946.

# GLOSSARY OF TECHNICAL TERMS

*ʿadāla*, rectitude, 94-5
*ʿadam*, non-being: not-yet existence, 45-46, 48, 50-51, 54
*ʿadl*, justice, 43, 94
*aflāk*, sg. *falak*, celestial spheres whirling around the earth like the whorls on a spindle, 24, 47, 49
*aḥadiyya*, absolute oneness; the One as apart from all possible relations and individualisations, 38, 128
*aḥkām*, sg. *ḥukm*, instructions, regulations; peculiarities, 29, 73, 81, 99, 122, 170
*ahl al-kitāb*, possessors of the Scripture: the Jews, Christians and Zoroastrians, 143
*aḥwāl*, sg. *ḥāl*, conditions to which a worshipper is transferred by purifying his *nafs*; ṣūfī states; ways of being; momentary traits, 10, 53-54, 71-73, 121, 123
*ʿajam*, non-Arabs, 2
*akhfāʾ*, 'most arcane' *laṭīfa* situated in the dura meter. Through it a mystic receives information from the *tajallī aʿẓam* as well as from the *nafs kulliyya*, 67-69, 74-75
*akhlāq fāḍila*, ethical virtues, seven in number: valour, proper sexual behaviour, magnanimity, consistency in conduct, mastery of language, *diyāna*, wisdom, 94
*ʿālam al-ajsām*, physical world, 80
*ʿālam al-arwāḥ*, world of immaterial entities, 21, 27, 80
*ʿālam al-jabarūt*, the World of Omnipotence, i.e. of the divine Names and Attributes. Things in this world are still in a state of superformal existence in distinction to the lower *ʿālam al-mithāl* where the objects possess subtle forms, 28, 47, 75, 81, 94
*ʿālam al-lāhūt*, the World of the Godhead, the incommunicable world of the divine Essence, 34-35, 47, 58, 75, 81, 132, 174
*ʿālam al-malakūt*, the World of Sovereignty, i.e. of the angelic beings and spiritual realities; intermediate between the *ʿālam al-jabarūt* and the *ʿālam al-ajsām*. Here the decree of God takes shape before being translated into physical manifestation, 46, 75, 104, 124, 126
*ʿālam al-mithāl*, the World of Prefiguration, in which things are shaped before they are embodied in actual existence upon the earth, in the same way as an architect draws the shape of a house on a piece of paper before he builds it in empiric reality, 21-26, 28, 35, 53, 56, 66-68, 80, 99, 136
*ʿālam al-nāsūt*, phenomenal world, world of bodily forms, 46, 52, 202
*ʿamāʾ*, 'dark mist', i.e. simple essence devoid of qualities and relations; primordial matter, 45-46, 128
*anāniyya*, I-ness, egoity. It is full-fledged (*kubrā*) if it regards the self-consciousness of the cosmos, and it is in an embryonic stage (*ṣughrā*) if it concerns the nascent self-consciousness of souls possessing volition, 29, 67, 74, 76, 81, 126
*ʿaql*, intellect. A perceptible *laṭīfa* residing in the brain. It covers the area lying between the concrete and the abstract. One of its distinguishing marks is sure knowledge in respect of matters related to traditional doctrines. It can also refer to the stage at which God becomes conscious of Himself, 33, 36, 46, 67, 70-74, 81, 89-90, 101, 109, 132, 201
*ʿaraḍ*, pl. *aʿrāḍ*, accident. It is the opposite as well as the complement of *jawhar* which is the constitutive form of it, 132
*ʿārif*, he who possesses *maʿrifa*: advanced mystic, 36, 43-44, 47, 63, 84
*arwāḥ*, souls, 66, 99, 178
*asbāb al-nuzūl*, occasions of revelation, 141-142
*aṣḥāb al-aʿrāf*, Companions of Limbo, being neither in Paradise nor in Hell, 91
*aṣḥāb al-yamīn*, Companions of the Right-hand Side (of the Throne during the Last Judgment): the ordinary believers, 90-91

*ashghāl*, sg. *shughl*, meditation techniques, 67-69, 84
*asmāʾ*, sg. *ism*, divine Names; attributes in action, i.e. powers scattered through the *ʿālam al-amr* (world of instantaneous creation) and the *ʿālam al-khalq* (world of what is created by degrees). They depart from God's Essence as *asmāʾ badiyya* and return to It as *asmāʾ ʿawdiyya*, 38-40
*asmāʾ ḥāditha*, divine powers regulating daily happenings, 26, 42
*asrār*, 'mysteries', underlying ideas, 18, 159, 204
*āthār*, workings; external products of God's Names, 32, 46, 57
*āya*, token; miracle; verse of the Qurʾān, 147
*aʿyān thābita*, immutable archetypes, i.e. the ontological models which are established in divine Consciousness and upon which the phenomenal things are produced, 13, 42, 46, 53, 57-58, 66, 104
*ʿayn thābita*, essential character of man which determines his fate, 32, 66-67, 112, 114, 116, 120-121, 127
*ʿazīma*, see *rukhṣa*, 165

*barzakh*, 'isthmus': connecting link, e.g. between two spheres of existence; interval of time (between death and Resurrection), 22, 26, 65, 97, 106, 116, 128
*baqāʾ*, 'subsistence': after having been annihilated in God (*fanāʾ*), the mystic lives through Him and in Him, 60, 81, 130-131, 175
*basṭ*, 'expansion'. This may refer to earthly processes of causality as well as to a spiritual state of the ṣūfī who experiences gladness through the widening of the heart, 28, 120
*bayʿa*, vow of allegiance of a ṣūfī novice to the initiating master by clasping his right hand, 79
*burhān*, apodictic proof; rational argumentation; manifestation (of truth), 15, 105, 119, 129

*dawāʾir*, sg. *dāʾira*, circles, spheres, regions where prophets reside, and which have to be traversed if a mystic wants to reach ecstacy, 112-114
*dhāt*, Essence of God; absolutely self-subsistent and the subject of the Attributes (*ṣifāt*), 36, 54, 57, 68, 83
*dhawq*, 'tasting': immediate experience, intuitive appreciation, 36, 67, 117, 131-132
*dhikr*, recollection of God by the rythmic recitation of formulas containing God's Names. It may uttered aloud (*jalī*) or silent (*khafī*), in which ultimately the worshipper forgets the words, and thinks only of the Named, 10, 30, 59, 68, 71, 78, 82-83, 87, 89, 94, 130, 170, 175, 180, 187
*diyāna*, scrupulosity; the capacity to properly co-ordinate man's cognitive faculties with his external behaviour, 93
*duʿāʾ*, personal prayer; invocation to which miraculous effects of an apotropaic nature are ascribed, 43-44, 119, 137, 149-150, 175, 180, 187-188

*falāsifa*, sg. *faylasūf*, Muslim philosophers who owe a lot to the legacy of Greece, 54, 131-132
*fanāʾ*, ceasing to exist individually on account of which the rational soul can be coloured with the colour of God, 3, 60, 81, 130-131, 175
*faqīh*, pl. *fuqahāʾ*, expert of jurisprudence (*fiqh*), 152, 155-158, 182
*fard*, pl. *afrād*, 'a single individual'; a saint who is not under the *quṭb*, the head of the invisible hierarchy of the saints; somebody who is able to establish particular connections with cosmic elements, 127-128
*fatwā*. In cases where the old doctrines or obsolete usages clash with the new realities of society, the solution which is in line with practical necessities is found and adopted through the means of a *fatwā*, i.e. an answer of an expert to a legal or theological question, 157
*fawāʾid*, sg. *fāʾida*, useful lessons, valuable information, 2, 190
*fiqh*, jurisprudence, 3, 8, 15, 35, 69, 129, 139, 144, 149, 153, 155, 166
*firāsa*, inductive divination, clairvoyance, 71-72, 104, 117, 126

*fitan*, sg. *fitna*, trials of faith whereby the condition of a man is evinced in respect of evil and of good, 34, 75, 125
*fiṭra*, primordial nature, 87, 95, 113, 124, 171, 197
*furūʿ*, minutiae of the Law, 16, 166

*ghusl*, major ritual ablution, 82

*ḥadd*, pl. *ḥudūd*, God's 'restrictive statutes' concerning offences of which God Himself had 'defined' the punishments in the Qurʾān, 169, 198
*ḥadīth*, adj.; having had a beginning, transient; the opposite of *qadīm*, 60
*ḥadīth*, pl. *aḥādīth*, oral tradition which can be traced to Mohammed or one of his Companions. Thus by means of anecdotes we are informed of what the Prophet held as an opinion, or did, or of his tacet approval of something said or done in his presence, 4-5, 7, 10, 12, 35, 69, 142, 152, 154-156, 165, 182
*ḥadīth qudsī*, divine saying not occurring in the Qurʾān, 67, 112, 119
*ḥaḍra*, pl. *ḥaḍarāt*, state in which God presents Himself to the heart of a mystic; stage of Being in which God descends and reveals Himself, 25, 30, 44
*ḥajar al-baht*, 'gem of stupefaction'. A center in the heart of man which functions as a telescope for the reception of light waves transmitted by divine radiations. Consequently, glaring rays of light spread from this 'gem', and stupify the mind and other faculties of the mystic, 34-35, 67, 74, 76, 82, 100, 103, 109, 136, 160, 174
*ḥajj*, pilgrimage to Mecca, 5, 78, 157, 161, 184-185, 188, 204
*ḥakīm*, wise man characterised by an extraordinary sublimation of the mind, 19, 106, 116-118, 191, 195, 201
*ḥāl* see *aḥwāl*
*ḥanīfiyya*, monotheism *avant la lettre*. Before the time that monotheism had become a well-defined doctrine and an established institution, it was *ḥanīfiyya*, i.e. the religion in accordance with the natural disposition created in men by God. So it was the faith of people like Abraham, Joseph, and the parents of Moses, 56, 188
*ḥaqīqa muḥammadiyya*, 'the Reality of Mohammed'. In this pre-creation light God deposited all potentialities that will work out till the Day of Resurrection, 33, 106
*hayʾa*, configuration; habitude, predisposition, 79, 84
*hayūlā*, primary matter. A technical term derived from the Greek ʿυλη. It is the receptacle of form, 45, 84, 151
*ḥaẓīra al-quds*, 'Holy Enclosure'. A luminous circle formed by the shining figures of the supreme angels and souls of perfect men convened to take decisions in view of devices considered to be beneficial for the inhabitants of the earth. Thus it functions as the will-power of the universe, 24-25, 30, 52-53, 66-67, 73, 81, 126, 128, 130, 132, 143, 177-178
*ḥikma*, wisdom, prudence. It may consists of practical knowledge or of intuition concerning the divine Essence and Names, 93-94, 106, 112, 116-117
*himma*, pl. *himam*, spiritual concentration; craving, 24-25, 31-32, 43, 119
*ḥiss mushtarik*, *sensus communis* which co-ordinates the percepts of the individual 'external' senses, 65, 97
*ḥurūf muqaṭṭaʿāt*, 'disconnected letters'. These mysterious letters may have served the purpose of adapting Qurʾānic sūras for inclusion in the written scripture Mohammed was preparing, 150

*ibdāʿ*, process of origination, i.e. the divine Essence's producing effects on the *nafs kulliyya* which is free from all impurities, 53-55
*iḍāfiyyāt*, Attributes of correlation which produce effects in the phenomenal world. The things of the empirical world are in essence partial realities and internal productions of the one absolute Reality, 40, 74, 183
*idrāk*, cognitive faculty: logical comprehension, 36, 97
*ʿiffa*, abstinence from what is unlawful; temperance; displaying a proper, i.e. natural sexual behaviour, 87, 92, 94, 117

*iḥāla*, mutation, transformation, 28, 30
*iḥrām*, state of temporary consecration of someone who is performing the *ḥajj* or the *ʿumra*, 156, 185
*iḥsān*, spiritual perfection which consists in adoring God "as if you were seeing Him, for if you do not see Him, He sees you", 71, 78, 107, 118, 152, 174-175
*ījād*, the giving of existence to creatures by God, location in being, 41, 58
*ijāza*, licence to transmit the material taught, 8, 11, 13
*ijmāʿ*, consensus of the Muslim community on a regulation imposed by God, 145, 168-169
*ijtihād*, independent deduction; use of individual reasoning, 13, 62, 126, 145-147, 155-156, 167-169
*ʿilla*, pl. *ʿilal*, effective, direct cause. Requisite for a proper conclusion by analogy (*qiyās*) it represents the common feature in the original and in the parallel case, 58, 156, 166, 170
*ʿilm* see *ʿulūm*
*ʿilm ḥuḍūrī*, presential knowledge, i.e. not acquired through the canals of ratiocination, 41, 68, 112
*ʿilm ḥuṣūlī*, 'acquired', i.e. discursive knowledge, 68
*ʿilm ladunī*, knowledge imparted directly by God through inner perception, 143
*imām*, head (of a community, of a school of law), leader in ritual prayer. In Shīʿite faith the *imām*, who is a descendant of ʿAlī and Mohammed's daughter Fāṭima, functions as a living representation of God. His mere existence is necessary for the subsistence of the world, and it is through the infallible *imām* that men are guided and saved, 65, 94, 112, 117, 159, 162, 166-167, 172, 175, 177-178, 194
*ʿināya*, providential ordering, 27-28, 48
*insān ilāhī*, Divine Man, i.e. the prototype of the human species, 24
*insān kāmil*, Perfect Man who has realized in himself all possibilities of being, 80
*insilākh*, 'sloughing off' (as the skin of a snake) of possible coverings in order to reveal the true self of a man's personality, 102
*irāda mutajaddida*, God's creative will that brings about the changes and continuous processes of renovation in the universe, 33, 39, 45-46, 132
*irtifāqāt*. *Irtifāq* means literally 'gaining benefit by'. Shāh Walī Allāh coined of its feminine plural a technical term denoting the ways and means people have at their disposal to raise cultural and social standards, and he qualifies the stages reached by their efforts to make a continuous progress simply as the first, second, third and fourth *irtifāq* i.e. respectively the stages of nomadic life, urbanization, the establishment of polities, and supernationalism, 10, 160, 193
*ishārāt*, esoteric allusions, 142, 178
*ʿishq*, ardent love, 83, 85
*ishrāf*, thoughtreading, 31, 87, 118
*ishrāk*, attributing associates to God, 96
*isnād*, chain of transmitters, 153
*ʿiṣma*, divine protection, immunity from sin, 106, 116-119, 123, 127
*istiʿdād(āt)*, innate receptivity, predisposition, 43, 46, 54, 64, 107
*istiḥsān*, advancing a discretionary opinion contrary to strict analogy for reasons of public convenience, 15, 144, 170
*iṣṭilāḥ*, mutual convergence, 62, 87
*istikhāra*, entrusting God with the choice between two or more possible options, 161, 180
*iʿtibārāt*, imaginary indications; aspects, 62, 67, 132, 142
*iʿtibārī*, only existing subjectively in the mind and not directly drawn from a concrete extra-mental piece of reality, 62-63

*jabarūt* see *ʿālam al-jabarūt*
*jadhb*, attraction by God, 3, 79, 83, 112, 120, 130-131
*jāhiliyya*, 'state of ignorance': the condition of the pagans in pre-Islamic times, 108
*jāmiʿ*, collection which contains all the different classes of traditions, historical, ethical, dogmatic, and legal, 153

*jawhar*, substance, prime element. It is the 'substrate' for the realisation of 'accidents' (*aʿrāḍ*) in the world, 32, 174
*jihād*, holy war against the infidels; constant struggle against one's basic instincts, 78, 92, 146, 186
*jinn*, cosmic spirits, generally believed to be part of the world of the unseen, 26, 30, 81, 106

*kāfir*, infidel, 15, 172
*kalām*, speech; speculative theology; apologetics for the sake of banishing doubts of Muslim intellectuals, 4, 8, 35, 146
*kalām nafsī*, mental speech which is an eternal quality, inhering in God's Essence. The revealed Qurʾān is an expression (*ʿibāra*) of it, 36, 44, 133, 137
*kāmil*, perfect man who is superior to other men because of the appearance of the universal soul in his self making the latter an instrument of its will, 29
*karāmāt*, charismatic deeds, 2, 88, 123
*kashf*, 'unveiling' of the world of mystery; inward revelation, 31, 63, 71, 78, 118
*khafī*, 'arcane one': concealed *laṭīfa* which is found between the eye-brows, 67-69, 74-76
*khalīfa*, successor of the prophets in general, and of Mohammed in particular; deputy of a spiritual leader, or a head of an order, 7, 90
*khalq*, creating, i.e. having a free disposal over matter so that many forms materialize. It is in fact an inferior activity which is not properly applicable to the divine Essence, 54-55
*khāṣṣ*, distinguished, illustrious, 121-122
*khawāṣṣ*, sg. *khāṣṣa*, exclusive properties; salutary virtues, 63, 149-150
*khayāl*, imagination. It is a retentive and totally passive faculty, 21-22, 25, 35, 53, 65, 103, 180
*khilʿa*, robe of honour. The bestowal of a garment of honour is a standard mark of investiture, 18
*khirqa*, patched garment, symbol of a novice's vows of obedience. The investiture with it forms part of the introduction into the order, 79
*kufr*, infidelity, 4, 125, 173, 175, 189

*lāhūt* see *ʿālam al-lāhūt*
*laṭīfa*, pl. *laṭāʾif*, subtle substance; psychic center of a subtle substance, 34, 64, 67-71, 73-77, 79, 81, 89, 130

*maʿād*, 'the Return of the souls to the bodies': the Hereafter, 97
*maʿānī*, sg. *maʿnā*, spiritual entities; concepts, ideas, 52, 57, 65, 99, 136
*madhhab*, pl. *madhāhib*, legal school; method of traversing the ṣūfī Path; doctrine; view, 18, 29, 133, 159, 165-168, 172, 177
*madrasa*, college for higher studies, 2, 5
*māhiyyāt*, sg. *māhiyya*, quiddities; realities of the possible phenomena; that what makes phenomena what they are, and not something else, 41, 57-58, 63
*majāzī*, not real: being in existence by way of a trope only; earthy, 58, 102, 117
*majdhūb*, the ṣūfī who undergoes the divine attraction (*jadhb*), the opposite of a *sālik*, 83
*majūs*, Zoroastrians, 56, 76
*mala aʿlā*, 'High Council'. These are supreme angels and the souls of departed prophets and other specifically qualified men. Just as a nervous system regulates the body of a human individual, so the *mala aʿlā* regulate the affairs of the human species and its individuals, 22, 27-30, 52, 56, 73-74, 87-88, 94, 102-103, 108-109, 121, 126, 132, 136, 160
*malakūt* see *ʿālam al-malakūt*
*mala sāfil*, 'Low Council'. These are auxiliary angels. The sole occupation they are charged with is looking out for what may filter down of orders given by the *mala aʿlā* from above, 29-30, 87, 121
*maqām(āt)*, stage on the ṣūfī Path; moral habit, 10, 60, 71-74, 123, 127, 130, 137

*maʿrifa*, true knowledge gained by direct experience of enlightenment: gnosis, 56
*maṣlaḥa*, salutary purpose; universal expediency, 23, 26, 132-133, 169-171
*mawālīd*, the three (mineral, vegetable, and animal) kingdoms of nature, 30, 46, 59
*mawjūd(āt)*, being found by means of the intellect, i.e. by argumentation and inference: conceptual being; existent, 51-52, 57, 74
*milla*, pl. *milal*, institutionalized religion; religious community, 29, 34, 56, 103, 108, 114, 129, 161-162, 172, 182
*miʿrāj*, Mohammed's midnight journey to the seven heavens in which he reached the immediate presence of God, 65, 105-106, 123, 181
*muʾadhdhin*, announcer of the hour of prayer, 115
*mubashshira*, annunciation in a vision of a joyful event, 17
*mufahham*, person who is informed by the *mala aʿlā*, 88, 94, 127
*muftī*, jurisconsult who gives an authoritative opinion (*fatwā*). He is not allowed to formulate his response as his personal advice, because the *fatwā* must have an absolutely objective character, 5, 194
*muḥaddath*, inspired person, 72, 123, 126-127
*muḥaddith*, technical specialist in traditions, 142, 152, 154
*muḥkamāt*, unambiguous verses of the Qurʾān, 143
*mujaddid*, renewer who is supposed to appear on the eve of every century, 19, 29, 117, 129-130
*mujarrad(āt)*, separate (from bodily material): incorporeal, 21, 36, 49
*muʿjiza*, evidentiary miracle, 105
*munāfiqūn*, 'hypocrites', lukewarm followers, 138, 173-174
*murāqaba*, constant awareness of God; spiritual communion with the divine Attributes, 1, 83, 85
*muṣannaf*, 'arranged': collection of traditions in which the traditions are arranged in chapters according to their subject-matter, 153
*mushāhada*, contemplation, 68, 130
*musnad*, collection of traditions organized on the basis of (usually) the last transmitter before the Prophet, 153
*mutakallimūn*, scholars in the field of speculative theology. They are intent on supplying discursive and reasoned apologia, 133, 143
*mutashābihāt*, not clearly intelligible passages in the Qurʾān, treating of the divine Attributes, matters concerning the Hereafter, obscure details in prophetic tales, 134, 143, 201
*mutawātir*, handed down by large-scale dissemination which guarantees the authenticity of a tradition having so many different chains of transmitters that forgery is regarded as inconceivable, 152

*nafas al-Raḥmān*, *nafas Raḥmānī*, 'breath of the Merciful' (= Bestower of Being). As words and letters are united in breathing, so the universe is created by God's exhaling the essences and forms of things. Hence it may also indicate a universe which is not yet given definite form: it is only being capable, and being ready, to appear in any determined form whatever, 32-33, 53-54
*nafs* (*shahwiyya*), the concupiscent soul which has its residence under the umbilicus, 29, 67-71, 73, 76, 81, 89, 95, 109, 120, 126
*nafs kulliyya*, 'Universal Soul'. It is the intermediate level the universe passes through. Necessitated by God, it is first at the level of the transcendental determination. Next, it enters the level, called *al-nafs al-kulliyya*, i.e. the stage of being (*wujūd*) that is spreading over the structural forms of the cosmos. After that, the universe descends into the realm of matter (*nāsūt*). It represents also the *rūḥ* (vital principle) of the cosmos. Finally, it is the point of departure and return for all individual human souls, 13, 21-22, 25, 52-55, 66, 74, 83, 101, 112, 120, 128, 132, 174
*nafs nāṭiqa*, pl. *nufūs nāṭiqa*, rational soul. It is the connecting link between the *ʿayn thābita* (archetypal individuality) — which is a purely holy entity — and the *nasama* (lower soul) — which belongs to the objects of this tainted world. It represents

the kernel of a person's personality, orders men's lives, and is able to have revelations of angels and visions of the *ḥaẓira al-quds*, 32, 44, 48, 65-68, 84, 97-98, 101, 103-104, 112, 120, 174, 187

*nasama*, fine pneuma. It stands for the physiological and psychic dispositions of man and universe, conveying potencies of perception, nourishment and growth, 32, 53, 64-65, 67, 97-98, 104, 112, 120

*nashʾa*, evolutionary stage; level of existence, 46, 50, 97, 106

*nāsikh wa mansūkh*, abrogating and abrogated verses of the Qurʾān, 141, 149

*naskh*, abrogation of divine laws; repeal of former heavenly decrees substantiated into a Qurʾānic verse by a newly revealed message, 94, 135, 146-149, 156

*nāsūt* see *ʿālam al-nāsūt*

*nāṭiq*, enunciator prophet bringing a revealed message. The first six ones were Adam, Noah, Abraham, Moses, Jesus, and Mohammed. Each of them was followed by a silent one (*ṣāmit*) who, being his *waṣī* (trustee), was charged with conveying an esoteric interpretation of the message of the previous *nāṭiq*, 19

*nisba*, a disposition in the rational soul which grants likeness to the angels, on account of which information is received from the *jabarūt*; spiritual atmosphere that presupposes affiliation and connectedness with God, 79, 84-5

*nūr al-quds*, 'sacred light': name of a concealed *laṭīfa* which is able to become acquainted with the disputes of the *mala aʿlā* and the decisions descending from them, 67, 74

*qabḍ*, 'contraction'. This may refer to the earthly processes of causality as well as to the feeling of fear and distress to which a ṣūfī is exposed because of the contraction of his heart, 28, 120

*qaḍāʾ*, divine decree which has ordered the arrangement of daily occurrences, 42-43

*qadar*, particular determination: applies to individual destiny of God's measurement connected with things at particular moments, 42-43

*qadīm*, uncreated, primeval, 60, 136

*qalb*, the heart, i.e. faculty of contemplative intuition and seat of religious apprehension, 33, 67-70, 74, 76, 81, 89-90, 93, 109

*qaṣīda*, poem with a characteristic tripartite structure, 11, 138, 140

*qibla*, the direction to Mecca to which the Muslim turns for his ritual prayer; focus of attention, 34, 66, 111, 147

*qiyās*, analogical reasoning, 129, 168-170

*qurb al-farāʾid*, proximity to God reached by the punctual fulfillment of religious duties, 18, 112, 117, 119-120

*qurb al-kamāl*, proximity to God reached by 'perfection', i.e. acting in accordance with divine wisdom, 113, 124

*qurb al-malakūt*, proximity to God brought by association with the world of angels, 18, 112

*qurb al-nawāfil*, proximity to God reached by supererogative works, 18, 112, 119-120

*qurb al-wujūd*, proximity attained during an overflow of God's pure Being, 18, 112, 116-117, 124

*rakʿa*, unit of prostrations, genuflexions and prayer formulas in behalf of the *ṣalāt*, 80, 82, 182

*rāsikhūn fiʾl-ʿilm*, 'persons who are firmly rooted in knowledge'. A distinctive trait of theirs is that their knowledge seems to have descended from God directly into their hearts, 89, 134, 143

*raʾy kullī*, motivation to act for the general good, 29, 66, 92-93, 193

*rūḥ*, vital spirit, intermediary between body and soul. It is also a perceptible *laṭīfa* lying two fingers under the right side of the breast, 17, 29, 36, 44, 47, 53, 64-69, 81, 84, 89, 102, 106, 109, 138, 177, 202

*rukhṣa*, a relaxation of the strict rule, the opposite of *ʿazīma*, an ordinance as interpreted strictly, 165

*sābiq*, 'preceding', i.e. one who excels in good works, 89

*ṣabr*, perseverance; voluntary resignation, 87, 95
*ṣadaqa*, charitable donation, 78, 80
*sakīna*, a Qurʾānic term apparently a rendering of the Hebrew word *shekhina*, the Cloud of Glory, manifesting the presence of the Lord and producing assurance in the soul, 85, 87, 129, 174
*ṣalāt*, liturgical prayer, 17, 24, 30, 56, 76, 78, 80, 86, 95, 125, 144, 152, 156, 159, 163-164, 170-171, 175, 180-182, 203-204
*sālik*, wayfarer on the ṣūfī Path, 54, 73, 80, 82
*samāhat al-nafs*, sublimation of the mind, 94-95, 116
*samt ṣāliḥ*, consistency in conduct, 92
*shaʿāʾir*, sg. *shiʿār*, whatever is appointed as a sign of obedience to God: visible symbols serving for the worship of God, 180, 182
*shahīd*, pl. *shuhadāʾ*, 'witness', martyr, 72, 89
*shajāʿa*, valour, fortitude, 92, 94
*shakhṣ akbar*, 'the Most Large Person', the macrocosm, 44, 52-54, 81
*shaʾn* see *shuʾūn*
*sharḥ al-ṣadr*, expansion of the breast for the favourable acceptance of the truth, 112, 114
*sharīʿa*, *sharʿ*, the sacred law of Islam, comprising the totality of Allāh's commands that regulate the life of every Muslim in relation to God and his fellow beings, 17, 19, 42, 44, 71, 76, 83, 85, 89, 93, 109, 115, 117-118, 121-122, 124, 126, 129-131-134, 137, 144-145, 152, 156, 160-166, 169, 171-173, 178, 191
*shawq*, yearning, 82
*shirk*, idolatry, 82, 186, 191
*shuʾūn*, sg. *shaʾn*, internal modes of being calling for their externalization. They represent a stage prior to the Names and can be defined as the virtual forms of the Names, 33, 41, 46, 58, 101, 109
*shuʾūnāt*, potential Attributes, 40, 74
*ṣiddīq*, zealous persevering believer who is 'as kindred to a prophet as sulphur is to fire', 72, 89, 123
*ṣifāt*, divine Attributes and notifications concerning God's transcendence, 36
*ṣifāt salbiyya*, 'privative' Attributes by which God's transcendency is accentuated, as He is denied qualities on account of which result taking a form, occupying a place, need and weakness, 40, 75, 184
*ṣifāt thubūtiyya*, 'latent' Attributes. They are the Attributes properly speaking and are from all eternity implied in God's Essence. By the existence of the universe they have become apparent, 40, 74-75
*sirr*, innermost part of the heart which has contact with the *ʿālam al-jabarūt*. It is also a perceptible *laṭīfa*, and a sublimed configuration of the *ʿaql*. Visions are a product specific of it, 67-69, 73-74, 81, 89, 109, 131
*subūgh*, full expansion. A metaphor either 1) of the cosmogony displaying the result of *subūgh*, a being overfilled with the divine Essence which, like an overflowing fountain, 'vomits' foam, or 2) of the condition of a mystic who is sedulous in adopting God's Attributes, 48, 98, 115
*ṣuḥba*, master-disciple relationship, which guarantees not only a personal control of the disciple's progress but also a constant flow of spiritual energy from the master to the novice, 79
*sulūk*, progression in the ṣūfī Path towards the divine Reality, 18, 81, 83
*sunna*, 'beaten track': refers to the practices Mohammed endorsed and the precedents he set; God's wont, 19, 30, 78, 85, 102, 122, 129, 131, 145, 152, 166, 168

*ṭabīʿa kulliyya*, 'Universal Nature' which as the matrix of the cosmos encompasses all the mouldable materials of the universe, 24-25, 46-47
*tadallī*, God's coming to the rescue when the universe or mankind have run into trouble. It results in disclosure of knowledge, right guidance and perfection of souls, 19, 47, 54-56
*tadallī ʿaẓīm* ( = *tajallī aʿẓam*), 24, 34, 46, 102

*tadbīr*, divine forethought; divinely provided order of the world, 23, 30, 37, 42-43, 49, 53-55, 73, 129, 136
*tafarrus*, discerning the intrinsic character of metaphysical truths, 87
*tafhīm*, interior revelation, 126-127
*tafsīr*, exegesis of the Qur'ān, 35, 141-142
*taḥaqquq*, verification of that which is; self-objectification; self-realization, 40-41, 44-45, 54, 59
*taḥrīf*, the falsification of a text in the Holy Scripture, or the garbling of its meaning, 107, 130, 143-145, 165, 170
*tajādhub*, state of tension, 87
*tajallī aʿẓam*, 'the Most Supreme Theophany': a summary of the realities of the Self-existent, instrumental to reveal the Will of God and to refine the human souls, 22, 25, 28, 32-35, 45, 53, 66-68, 71, 73-74, 81-82, 100, 103, 109, 120, 132, 136, 160, 174
*tajallī dhātī*, disclosure of the Ultimate Reality, neither in a mirror nor as a phenomenon, but just as It is, 31
*tajalliyyāt*, 'radiances', i.e. theophanies by which various predicaments of the Ultimate Reality are disclosed to the mystic and he can be coloured by the colour of God, 13, 31-32, 40, 42, 127-128
*takammul*, inner urge towards self-perfection, 92
*taklīf*, accountability, 93, 135, 178
*talfīq*, jurisprudential eclecticism, 167
*tanazzul(āt)*, descent; stage of self-unfolding. By the process of *tanazzulāt* Pure Being, devoid of qualities and relations, gradually becomes qualified, 57, 80
*taqarrur*, a thing's coming from potentiality to actuality; self-identification, 41, 59
*taqlīd*, legal conformism, 13, 145, 165, 167-168
*ṭarīqa*, religious brotherhood; the ṣūfī Path, 18, 79, 84-85
*taṣarruf*, control of a certain aspect of the material world, delegated by God to a *walī* or a mystical leader; the capacity to produce theurgies, 118
*tashbīh(āt)*, 'likening', i.e. the bringing of God into relation with human characteristics, anthropomorphism, 37, 96
*taskhīr*, subjugation with a view of turning to profitable account, 191
*tawajjuh*, concentration of the soul on the Ultimate Reality, 33, 79, 124
*tawakkul*, total abandonment, leaving one's needs directly to God, 71, 121
*tawḥīd*, affirming of the divine Unity; unification with God and consciousness of one's oneness with God, 59, 72, 76, 85, 130-131, 144
*ta'wīl al-aḥādīth*, explanation of significative events, 141
*tawjīh*, to search out the *wajh* (contextual motive) implied in Qur'ānic verses, 148
*tayammum*, ritual purification by means of sand and dust, 155, 163
*timthāl* (or *tamaththul*), pl. *tamāthīl*), exemplary representation; perceptible counterpart (as, for instance, the hand is in respect of man's practical power); seemly attitude, 22, 26, 33, 49, 114, 116, 181, 186

*ʿulamā'*, scholar-jurists upon whom the interpretation of the *sharīʿa* rests, 61, 69, 80, 130-131, 145, 148, 168, 203
*ʿulūm*, sg. *ʿilm*, kinds of knowledge forming the basic principles which make possible reflection and inference as well as the execution of the duties God imposes upon mankind, 139
*umma*, community, 16, 31, 78, 98, 123, 126, 138, 141, 143-145, 155, 165, 168-170, 203
*ummī*, person whose heart is not spoilt by outward intellectual achievement and learning; an unsophisticated man, 103
*ʿumra*, minor pilgrimage to Mecca, 143, 157-158
*uns*, intimacy, 73, 75, 79
*ʿuqūl*, intelligences, i.e. a kind of regulating powers governing the nine spheres around the earth. Each celestial sphere has a separate intelligence (*ʿaql*) of its own, 132
*ʿurf*, common convention. In Muslim legal theory it operates as a principle of subsidiary value, 165

*waḥdat al-shuhūd*, unity-in-experience implying that the Beloved and lover are joined together but their individuality is preserved, 13, 60-62
*waḥdat al-wujūd*, unity of Being based on the premise that 'Everything is He' instead of 'Everything is from Him'. The things existing are to Being as waves to the sea, 13, 59-62, 76, 108, 201
*wāḥidiyya*, relative unity, i.e. unity-in-plurality. It is the stage of the *aʿyān thābita*, i.e. latent realities of the things contingent (*mumkināt*), 39, 80
*wahm*, erroneous impression; power of abstraction. It is endowed with the faculty to perceive particular ideas or meanings in sensible objects, 58-59, 65, 97, 157, 180
*waḥshat*, estrangement, loneliness. A complementary to the experience of *uns*, 79
*waḥy*, prophetic inspiration, 26, 35, 44, 46, 106, 108, 117, 120, 122, 126, 177
*wajd*, ecstatic experience, 120
*walī*, protégé of God, saint; protector, 1, 60, 118-121, 198
*waṣī* see *nāṭiq*, 19, 117, 129, 178
*wasīla*, means of access; position of a go-between, 115
*waṣiyya*, pl. *waṣāyā*, testamentary disposition; directive for a disciple, 7, 12, 85, 198
*wuḍū*, the lesser ritual ablution before prayer, 149, 156-157, 182-183
*wujūd*, 'the finding by means of the intellect': existence; being. It can be qualified as *bāṭin* (internal) if one wants to allude to the hidden aspect of being, i.e. the opposite of *wujūd* that has come into phenomenal reality (*ẓāhir*, *khārijī*), 38, 41, 46, 49, 54, 56-59, 61-63, 66, 132
*wujūd munbasiṭ*, self-unfolding being which follows the stage of being still left in its absolute purity. It stabilizes the contingent realities, 52, 57-59, 62

*yād-dāsht*, concentration on the reality of God which is stripped of sounds, words, ecstatic emotions, and so on. A rule which a Naqshbandī is required to observe during the *dhikr*-exercises, 59, 85, 124, 175
*Yazdān*, Persian name of God, 34-35

*zakāt*, alms-tax. It is handed over to gain purification, 95, 147, 163, 183, 204
*ẓarāfa*, 'culture', i.e. everything appealing to soul and eye, 92-93, 193
*zuhd*, renunciation of the world, 73

# INDEX OF PROPER NAMES


ᶜAbbāsid 75, 125, 131, 177
ᶜAbd Allāh b. ᶜAbbās (d. 686-8) 12, 155, 158
ᶜAbd al-ᶜAzīz, Shāh (d. 1824) 1, 4-5, 12
ᶜAbd al-Ghānī, Shāh (d. 1812) 4
ᶜAbd b. Ḥamīd (d. 863) 154
ᶜAbd al-Ḥayy (d. 1923) 4, 7
ᶜAbd al-Raḥīm (d. 1719) 1-2, 67, 69, 190-191
ᶜAbd al-Raḥmān of Thatta 11-12
ᶜAbd al-Razzāq (d. 826) 154
Abdul Hamīd Siddīqī 158
Abraham 34, 43, 56, 108-112, 114, 139, 144, 146, 161, 187-188, 200
Abū Bakr, the caliph (d. 634) 6, 12, 72, 75, 123-124, 141, 168, 176-177, 200
Abū Bakr b. Abī Shayba see Ibn Abī Shayba
Abū Bakra al-Thaqafī (d. 671/2) 123
Abū Dāʾūd, al-Sijistānī (d. 889) 153
Abū Dharr al-Ghifārī (d. 652/3) 89, 189
Abū Ḥanīfa (d. 767) 153, 166-167
Abu 'l-Ḥasan ᶜAlī al-Kharaqānī (d. 1033) 79
Abu 'l-Hudhayl (840/1) 135
Abū Hurayra (d. 678/9) 107, 157, 182
Abū Mūsā al-Ashᶜarī (d. 662-4) 164
Abū Razīn ᶜUqaylī (d. 704) 45, 48
Abū Riḍā Muḥammad (d. 1690) 10
Abū Saᶜīd b. Abi ʾl-Khayr (d. 1049) 79
Abū Ṭāhir Muḥammad (d. 1733) 5, 8-10
Abū Yūsuf (d. 798) 153, 166
Adam 26, 67, 76, 106, 108, 111-112, 114
Ādam Banūrī (d. 1643) 85
Affifi, A. E. 33, 42, 112, 201-202
Aḥmad b. Ḥanbal (d. 855) 24, 27, 153, 167, 183
Aḥmad Khān, Sir Sayyid (d. 1898) 106, 136, 203
Aḥrār, Khwāja al-Dīn ᶜUbayd Allāh (1490) 120
ᶜĀʾisha (d. 678) 143-144, 157-158, 164, 182
Ajmer 1
al-Akhsīkatīm Ḥusām al-Dīn (1247) 4
ᶜĀlamgīr II (d. 1760) 2
Alexander the Great (d. 323 B.C.) 196
Allard, M. 40
ᶜAlī b. Abī Ṭālib, the caliph (d. 661) 1, 6, 83, 107, 123-124, 155, 176-177, 200
al-Aʾmash (d. 765) 138
Amat al-ᶜAzīz bint Shāh Walī Allāh 4
ᶜAmmār b. Yāsir (d. 657) 155
Anas b. Mālik (d. 709-11) 107
Anawati, G. C. 134
Aqṣā mosque 200
Arabs 2, 113, 125, 127, 137, 139-140, 160-162, 172, 181, 188
ᶜArafa 80, 184
Aristotelian 15, 201
al-Ashᶜarī, Abu l'-Ḥasan (d. 935/6) 40, 44, 133-134, 198
Ashᶜarite 40, 122, 137
ᶜĀshiq, Muḥammad (d. 1773) 4, 7, 12
ᶜĀshūrāʾ 80, 184, 199
Augustine (d. 430) 75
Awrangzīb (d. 1707) 2, 131
Awṭās 158
al-Azhar university 10
Azīz al-Raḥmān (d. 1928) 203

Babylonians 146
Badr 72, 127
Bahāʾ al-Dīn al-Naqshbandī (d. 1389) 85
Bahrayn 163
Baqī Biʾllāh, Khwāja (d. 1603) 5, 63
Basra 159
al-Bayḍāwī (d. 1286) 147
al-Bayhaqī (d. 1066) 152
al-Bazzāz, Abū ᶜAlī (d. 1034) 154
Bernard, M. 169
Bidpai 161
Bī Irāda bint Sayyid Ḥāmid ᶜAlī Sūnīpattī 4
Bilgrām 7
Blachère, R. 67
Browne, E. G. 20
Budhāna 4
al-Bukhārī (d. 870) 5, 10, 153
al-Būnī (d. 1125) 150
Burāq 66
Burzoe 161
Byzantium, Byzantine 125, 197

Cairo 7, 10
Cambay 17
Chishtiyya order 1, 4, 75, 85, 181
Chouémi, M. 67
Christians 75, 122, 138, 144-145, 174, 182, 190

Corbin, H. 53, 58, 127, 178-179

al-Dārimī (d. 869) 27
al-Dawānī (d. 1502/3) 198
Delhi 1-2, 14
Denizeau, C. 67
Deobandī 203
Dieterici, Fr. 48
al-Dihlawī, Sharaf al-Dīn 7

Effendī Ismāᶜīl b. ᶜAbd Allāh al-Rūmī al-Madanī 13, 60
Eliade, M. 51, 69
Eve 106

al-Farrā (d. 822) 140
Faruqi, B. A. 61
Fāṭima, daughter of Mohammed (d. 633) 107
Fāṭima bint ᶜUbayd Allāh Phalitī 4
Fazle Mahmud 1, 5
Fazlur Rahman 60, 108
Fērōshānī mosque of Delhi 2
Friedmann, Y. 61

Gabriel 27, 55, 100, 106, 112, 123
Ganges 184
Gardet, L. 51, 54, 57, 110, 134-135, 187
al-Ghazālī, Abū Ḥāmid (d. 1111) 22, 24, 64, 94, 98, 204
Goldziher, I. 17, 20, 131, 134, 153, 165, 201
Gonda, J. 69
Gospels 47
Granqvist, H. 127
Greeks 64, 140, 146

Haddad, Y. Y. 91
Ḥakīm al-Tirmidhī (d. 908) 19
Halepota, A. J. 203
Halm, H. 178
Ḥamza b. ᶜAbd al-Muṭṭalib (d. 625) 107
Ḥanbali(te) 168, 200-201
Hansi 1
al-Ḥaramayn 10, 25, 45, 50, 59-60, 165, 189
Ḥasan b. ᶜAlī (d. 669/70) 17-18
Ḥasan al-Baṣrī (d. 728) 159
Hasan Qasim Murad 19
Ḥaydar Amulī (d. after 1385) 58
Herbert, J. 69
Herklots, G. A. 199
Hermes Trismegistos 56
Ḥijāz 5, 7-11, 16-17, 165, 196
al-Ḥillī (d. 1325) 178
Hindus 15, 113, 149, 184, 190, 197-199
Holy Spirit 28, 137, 174
Houtsma, M. Th. 181
Hūd 108
Ḥudaybiyya 72
Ḥunayn 158
Ḥusayn b. ᶜAlī (d. 680) 17-18, 199

Ibn ᶜAbbās see ᶜAbd Allāh b. ᶜAbbās
Ibn Abī Shayba, Abū Bakr (d. 849) 154
Ibn al-ᶜArabī, Abū Bakr b. Abd Allāh (d. 1148) 148
Ibn ᶜArabī, Muḥyi 'l-Dīn (d. 1240) 4, 33-34, 41-42, 50, 52, 59-62, 76, 79, 94, 112, 114, 118, 121, 148, 200-202
Ibn al-Ḥājib (d. 1249) 3
Ibn Isḥāq (d. 767) 142
Ibn Khaldūn (d. 1406) 49, 102, 192
Ibn Māja (d. 886) 153
Ibn al-Mājashūn 105
Ibn Masᶜūd (d. 652/3) 138, 155
Ibn Miskawayh (d. 1030) 94
Ibn al-Mubārak (d. 797) 143
Ibn al-Nafīs (d. 1288) 4
Ibn Rāhwayh, Isḥāq (d. 853) 183
Ibn Sīnā (d. 1037) 4, 57, 94, 172, 187, 192
Ibn Taymiyya (d. 1328) 148, 200-201
Ibn ᶜUmar, ᶜAbd Allāh (d. 693) 158
Idrīs 56, 109, 112, 114
al-Ījī (d. 1355) 4
Ikhwān al-ṣafāʾ 48-49, 64
Imāmites, see Ithnā ᶜAshariyya
India(ns) 2, 140, 168
Iqbāl, Sir Muḥammad (d. 1938) 76, 203
Iran 138
Irāq 75
ᶜIrāqī (d. 1289) 4, 62
Isaiah 75, 126
Ismael 107, 188
Ismāᶜīlī 19, 51, 178
Ismāᶜīl Shahīd (d. 1831) 38, 49, 59, 127
Israelites 111, 146, 196
Isrāfīl 27
Ithnā ᶜAshariyya 1, 88, 177-178
ᶜIyāḍ b. Ḥimār 141
ᶜIyāḍ b. Mūsā (d. 1149) 153
Izutsu, T. 41-42, 50, 52, 58, 63

Jacob 110
al-Jāḥiẓ (d. 869) 134
Jalbani, G. N. 2, 10
Jāmiᶜ mosque of Delhi 2
Jānjānān, Maẓhar (d. 1782) 7
Java 88
Jerusalem 171, 200

Jesus 23, 28, 47, 62, 77, 108-109, 113, 115, 142, 145, 174, 184
Jews 122, 138, 144-145, 158, 161, 171-172, 174, 182, 190
al-Jīlānī, ᶜAbd al-Qādir (d. 1166) 16, 84-85, 149
Johns, A. H. 5
Jonah 108, 126
Joseph 110, 112, 119
Joshuah 122
al-Junayd, Abu 'l-Qāsim (d. 910) 79, 121
Jupiter 47
al-Jurjānī (d. 1413) 4

Kaᶜba 56, 161, 164, 171, 175, 180, 185, 200
al-Kalbī (d. 763) 142
al-Kashmīrī, Khwāja Muḥammad Amīn (d. 1773/4) 7, 85, 167, 176
al-Kātibī (d. 1276) 4
al-Kawtharī, Muḥammad Zāhid (d. 1952) 105
Khabar 158
Khalīl ᶜAbdel Ḥamid ᶜAbdel ᶜAdl 13
al-Khayālī (d. 1456) 4
al-Khiḍr 9
Khwurd, Khwāja (b. 1601) 5
Kirmānī, Ḥamīd al-Dīn (d. 1021) 178
Kubrāwiyya order 6, 120
al-Kūrānī, Ibrahīm (d. 1690) 5

Landau, R. 36
Landolt, H. 61
Laoust, H. 200-201
Luther, M. (d. 1546) 75

al-Maḥbūbī, Burhān al-Dīn Maḥmūd (13th century) 3
Makhdūm Muᶜīn al-Dīn of Thatta (d. 1748) 200
Makhdūm Nūḥ of Hālā (d. 1590) 149
al-Makkī, Abū Ṭālib (d. 996) 6
Mālik b. Anas (d. 795/6) 5, 12, 31, 143, 153, 157, 167
Mālikite 5, 12, 105, 153, 168
al-Marghīnānī (d. 1196) 3
Mars 191
Marwa 143, 185
Mary, the Virgin 100, 113
al-Mashmūdī, Yaḥyā (d. 848) 5
Maᶜsūm b. Aḥmad Sirhindī (d. 1688) 85
Māturīdī 136
Mawdūdī, Abu 'l-Aᶜlā (d. 1979) 167
Maẓhar Baqā 7, 166-167
Mecca 5-6, 9, 12, 18, 69, 107, 130, 189
Medina, Medinian 5-6, 8-9, 107, 130, 147, 189, 200
Mercury 128
Michon, J. L. 32
Mihrawli 1
Mīkāʾīl 27
Miller, W. M. 178
Mīr al-Jurjānī (d. 1413) 12
Mohammed, the Prophet and Messenger of God (d. 632) 3, 5-6, 9, 11, 16-19, 22, 24-25, 27, 31, 35-36, 39, 48, 55-56, 65-66, 72, 75-76, 79, 86, 88-91, 97, 102-110, 112-115, 117, 121-127, 129-131, 136-139, 141, 143-147, 152, 154-159, 161-166, 168-169, 171-178, 180, 182-184, 186, 188-190, 196, 200-201
Morewedge, P. 57
Moses 25, 31, 62, 75, 108-112, 115, 122, 139, 141, 171, 184
Muᶜādh b. Jabal 164
al-Muᶜammir, Abū ᶜAbd Allāh 9
Muḥammad Amīn see al-Kashmīrī
Muḥammad Fāʾiq b. Muḥammad ᶜĀshiq 4
Muḥammad Ikrām 15
Muḥāsibī, Ḥārith (d. 857) 79
Muᶜīn al-Dīn Chishtī (d. 1236) 1, 190
Mulk Ḥasan ᶜAlī 68
Mullā Ṣadrā (d. 1641) 58
Mūsā al-Kāẓim (d. 1294) 1
Muslim, the traditionist (d. 875) 10, 153, 158
Muᶜtazilite 40, 90, 100, 133-135, 142-143, 154, 203
Muẓaffarnagar (U.P.) 1

Najm al-Dīn al-Kubrā (d. 1220) 120
Naqshbandiyya order 4, 75, 81, 83, 85, 120
al-Nasafī (d. 1142) 4
al-Nasāʾī (d. 915) 153
Neo-Platonism 94
New Testament 145, 174
Nicholson, R. A. 22, 38, 71
Nizami, K. A. 15
Noah 31, 43, 108, 112, 114, 144, 184
Nöldeke, Th. 140, 161
non-Arabs 137, 162, 172, 181
Nūr Allāh b. Muᶜīn al-Dīn 9

Onan, J. C. 181

Pānipatī, Muḥammad Ismāᶜīl 136
Pānipatī, al-Qāḍī Thanā Allāh (d. 1810) 7
Pellat, Ch. 135

Peripatetics 48
Persia(ns) 113, 125, 146, 196-197
Phalit 1
Phalitī, Muḥammad 1
Phalitī, ʿUbayd Allāh 4
Pharaoh 184, 202
Pisces 47
Plato 19
Potiphar 119
Prophet, the see Mohammed
Ptolemy 19, 113

al-Qādir, Shāh (d. 1813) 4
Qādiriyya order 4, 84
Qalaʿī, Tāj al-Dīn (1734) 5
al-Qāsimī, Ghulām Muṣṭafā 10, 25, 53, 149
al-Qūnawī, Ṣadr al-Dīn (d. 1263) 4, 62, 80
Quṭb al-Dīn al-Bakhtiyār al-Kākī (d. 1236) 1

Rafīʿ al-Dīn, Shāh (d. 1818) 4
Rāfiḍites 154
al-Rāzī, Fakhr al-Dīn (d. 1209) 115
Ritter, H. 71
Rizvi, S. A. A. 2, 4, 198
Rohtak 1
Romans 196

Sadhus 181
Saʿdī (d. 1291) 136
Ṣadr al-Sharīʿa al-Thānī (d. 1346) 3
Ṣafā 143, 185
al-Ṣafrā 189
Ṣāliḥ 104, 108
Samuel 196
al-Sarrāj, Abū Naṣr (d. 988) 71
Saturn 47
Schimmel, A. 34, 88, 103, 131
al-Shādhilī, Abu 'l-Ḥasan (1258) 6, 11, 149-150, 190
Shādhiliyya order 6
al-Shāfiʿī (d. 820) 153, 166-167, 170
Shāfiʿite 5, 12, 15, 152, 168, 203
al-Shaʿrānī, ʿAbd al-Wahhāb (d. 973) 20, 50
Sharif, M. M. 58
Shaṭṭāriyya order 6
al-Shaybānī (d. 805) 153, 166
Shaykh Muḥammad b. Shāh Walī Allāh (1793/4) 4
Sheba, queen of 21
Shem 114
Shīʿa, Shīʿite(s) 8, 12, 76, 134, 144, 175-178, 203

Shuʿayb 62
Sībawayhi (d. 793) 140
Sinai 31, 200
Sindhī, Muḥammad Fāḍil (1732) 4, 12
Sindhī, ʿUbayd Allāh (d. 1944) 4, 69, 197
al-Sirhindī, Aḥmad (d. 1624) 5, 8, 60-63, 67-68, 200
Siyālkōtī, Muḥammad Afḍal (d. 1733) 4
Smith, J. I. 91
Sufyān al-Thawrī (d. 778) 143
Suhrawardī order 6, 85
al-Suhrawardī, Shihāb al-Dīn Abū Ḥafs (d. 1234) 4
al-Suhrawardī, Shihāb al-Dīn Yaḥyā (d. 1191) 63
al-Sulamī, ʿIzz al-Dīn (d. 1262) 18
Sūnīpattī, Sayyid Ḥāmid ʿAlī 4
Ṣūrat 5, 17
al-Suyūṭī, Jalāl al-Dīn (d. 1505) 148

Tabūk 186
al-Taftāzānī (d. 1389) 4
al-Ṭaḥāwī (d. 933) 152
al-Taḥtānī, Quṭb al-Dīn Muḥammad al-Rāzī (d. 1364) 4
Tantrism 69
Ṭāʾūs b. Kaysān (d. 720) 159
Ṭayālisī (d. 818) 154
Thamūdites 104
Thot 56
al-Tirmidhī (d. 888/9) 153
Torah 107, 145, 188
Transoxiania 168
Trimingham, J. S. 10, 84, 124, 127
Tritton, A. S. 40
Troll, Ch. W. 203
Turks 2, 75, 125
Ṭuwā 25, 141
Twelver Shīʿa see Ithnā ʿAshariyya

Ullmann, M. 64
ʿUmar b. al-Khaṭṭāb, the caliph (d. 644) 1, 6, 12, 72, 75, 123-124, 126, 141, 155, 163, 168, 176-177, 200
Umayyads 125, 177
Umm Salama 157
al-Urmawī (d. 1283) 4
Uthmān b. ʿAffān, the caliph (d. 656) 75, 123-124
Uthmān b. Maẓʿūn (d. 626/7) 144
Uways al-Qaranī 18
ʿUzayr (Ezra) 174

Venus 44-45, 128, 191
Voll, J. 5

Wafd Allāh, Muḥammad 5
Walker, P. E. 51
al-Wāqidī (d. 822/3) 142
Watt, W. M. 17
Wensinck, A. J. 135-136
Wickens, G. M. 29

Yahya, O. 58

Yemen 159, 164
Yoga 69

Zābid (Yemen) 7
al-Zābidī, Sayyid Murtaḍā (d. 1791) 7
Zachariah 62
Zamzam 180
Zoroastrian(s) 122, 125, 190
Zubaid Ahmad, M. G. 8